The Specter of the Archive

The Specter of the Archive

POLITICAL PRACTICE AND
THE INFORMATION STATE
IN EARLY MODERN BRITAIN

Nicholas Popper

The University of Chicago Press CHICAGO AND LONDON

The University of Chicago Press, Chicago 60637
The University of Chicago Press, Ltd., London
© 2024 by The University of Chicago
All rights reserved. No part of this book may be used or reproduced in any manner whatsoever without written permission, except in the case of brief quotations in critical articles and reviews. For more information, contact the University of Chicago Press, 1427 E. 60th St., Chicago, IL 60637.
Published 2024
Printed in the United States of America

33 31 30 29 28 27 26 25 24   1 2 3 4 5

ISBN-13: 978-0-226-82595-3 (cloth)
ISBN-13: 978-0-226-82597-7 (paper)
ISBN-13: 978-0-226-82596-0 (e-book)
DOI: https://doi.org/10.7208/chicago/9780226825960.001.0001

Library of Congress Cataloging-in-Publication Data

Names: Popper, Nicholas, 1977– author.
Title: The specter of the archive : political practice and the information state in early modern Britain / Nicholas Popper.
Other titles: Political practice and the information state in early modern Britain
Description: Chicago : The University of Chicago Press, 2024. | Includes bibliographical references and index.
Identifiers: LCCN 2023017161 | ISBN 9780226825953 (cloth) | ISBN 9780226825977 (paperback) | ISBN 9780226825960 (ebook)
Subjects: LCSH: Tower of London Record Office. | Great Britain. State Paper Office. | Public records—Great Britain—Management—History—17th century. | Government paperwork—Great Britain—Management—History—17th century. | Archives—Great Britain—History—17th century.
Classification: LCC JN329.P75 P67 2024 | DDC 352.3/87094109032—dc23/eng/20230421
LC record available at https://lccn.loc.gov/2023017161

♾ This paper meets the requirements of ANSI/NISO Z39.48-1992 (Permanence of Paper).

Contents

List of Illustrations vii
Acknowledgments ix

Introduction *1*

1: Archivization *20*

2: Pump and Circulation *53*

3: Institutions Reimagined *91*

4: Shared Practice and Rival Visions of the State *122*

5: Information Warfare *154*

6: Centralization and Orchestration *187*

Epilogue: The World of the Archive *227*

List of Abbreviations 241
List of Manuscripts and Manuscript Collections Cited 243
Notes 247
Bibliography 299
Index 331

Illustrations

FIG. 1   Mary I's "Book of Offices"   *11*

FIG. 2   Scriptorium "Book of Offices"   *14*

FIG. 3   William Bowyer's "Repertorium"   *28*

FIG. 4   William Bowyer's "Heroica Eulogia"   *31*

FIG. 5   William Lambarde's "Pandect"   *34*

FIG. 6   Drawing of Exchequer Archive   *68*

FIG. 7   Arthur Agarde's King's Bench and Common Pleas Notes   *71*

FIG. 8   Arthur Agarde's Parliamentary Pleadings Notes   *72*

FIG. 9   Arthur Agarde's Chart of Treaties   *77*

FIG. 10   Working Copy of Arthur Agarde's Register of Treaties   *78*

FIG. 11   Thomas Wilson's State Paper Office Description   *113*

FIG. 12   Frontispiece to William Ryley's "Iura et Privilegia Clero Anglicano Adiudicata"   *148*

FIG. 13 William Laud's Annotations on William
Prynne's Edition of Laud's Diary *162*

FIG. 14 Joseph Williamson Notebook *192*

FIG. 15 John Tucker's State Paper Office Catalog *206*

FIG. 16 Joseph Williamson Notes on
His "Book of Collections" *207*

FIG. 17 Drawing of State Paper
Office Front Room *210*

FIG. 18 Drawing of State Paper Office Drawing
of State Paper Office Interior Room *211*

FIG. 19 Joseph Williamson Notebook *213*

FIG. 20 Tower of London Record Office *236*

Acknowledgments

This book has evolved significantly since I first conceptualized it in 2008, mostly in response to the extraordinary and interrelated political and technological developments of the intervening period. What I once imagined as a historical study illuminating the fraught humanistic origins of the information state became an investigation into the dynamics that brought forth modern media societies, one that also integrated reflections on—among other themes—the role of archival practices of inclusion and exclusion in producing knowledge; the possibilities and perils of expertise, technocracy, and surveillance; the malleability of invented traditions as social and political weapons; and the self-fulfilling constraints and powers of political realities constructed through feedback loops and echo chambers. The final manuscript is far different—and somehow even less sanguine—from what I initially imagined, but for that I believe it better captures both the distinctive dynamics of early modern Britain and the dimensions of early modern Europe reverberating throughout the contemporary world.

The project's transformation would have been impossible without the community of scholars I have been fortunate enough to find. A proper acknowledgments section would be its own chapter, so I must take a minimalist approach, and many whose imprints are on the book are not named here.

I cannot fail to mention some few, though. Anthony Grafton and Noah Millstone commented on the entire manuscript at different times, each with extraordinary generosity and insightfulness, and I hope the final version meets their approval. The press readers were gracious in their support and targeted in their criticism, which I deeply appreciated. Ann Blair, Bill Bulman, Caylin Carbonell, David Edwards, Phillip Emanuel, Randy Head, Amanda Herbert, Norm Jones, Brendan Kane, Elizabeth McCahill, Brandon Munda, Naomi Pullin, Corey Tazzara, Kathryn Woods, Kirsty Wright, and Elizabeth Yale all read extracts for various venues and provided invaluable feedback. Conversations with Noah, Corey, and Bill were essential to my methodological and theoretical framing. Amanda Herbert provided crucial feedback at vital moments. Kat Lecky saw many elements of the manuscript at many stages and always saw possibilities that I had not.

The final manuscript has also been indelibly shaped by responses to presentations at the University of St. Andrews, Leiden University, the Huntington Library, the College of William & Mary, the Folger Shakespeare Library, Johns Hopkins University, Warwick University, the Royal Irish Academy, Harvard University, and Princeton University, and at meetings of the North American Conference on British Studies, the Mid-Atlantic Conference on British Studies, the Northeast Conference on British Studies, and the History of Science Society. I am grateful for the feedback and enthusiasm I encountered from these audiences.

My research was made possible by funding that arrived at critical moments. I was on the verge of abandoning the project for lack of opportunity to write when a residential fellowship from the Folger Shakespeare Library provided the chance to do so—I owe massive thanks to my community during my time there. Subsequent support from the National Endowment for the Humanities enabled me to turn my hyperemetic slough of raw evidence and half-cooked ideas into an actual book. Support from the Huntington Library, the Omohundro Institute of Early American History and Culture, and William & Mary was essential.

Among other things, this book is a study of the collaborative effort required to preserve materials and circulate texts, and I am deeply aware of my dependence on the labor of the staffs at the institutions whose archival practices I have benefited from—archivists are what passes for heroes of the piece. I have corresponded with many at institutions that I have not visited, but I should thank those at places where I did spend significant time—the National Archives at Kew; the British Library; the Folger Shakespeare Library; the Huntington Library; the Bodleian Library; the Inner Temple Library; the College of Arms; Gonville and Caius College, University of Cambridge; Lambeth Palace Library; the Beinecke Library; the Parliamentary Archive; and the Rockefeller Library in Colonial Williamsburg. I also thank the State Papers Online project, which made this book possible.

At the University of Chicago Press, Mary Al-Sayed made the process far more fun than it should have been; Fabiola Enríquez Flores ushered me along gracefully and efficiently; Dylan Montanari and Stephen Twilley expertly guided the book through to completion; freelance copy editor Lori Meek Schuldt refined the manuscript beautifully and Ben Shaw delivered a sleek, polished index. I am also grateful to Lily Chadwick for performing essential work on my behalf brilliantly during the lethal end stages of the book.

Colleagues at William & Mary and at the Omohundro Institute—among others Karin Amundsen, Tuska Benes, Julia Gaffield, Lu Ann Homza, Cathy Kelly, Kathy Levitan, Dan Livesay, Paul Mapp, John Marquez, Celeste McNamara, Brianna Nofil, Josh Piker, Fabrício Prado, John Riofrio, Brett Rushforth, Elena Schneider, Trent Vinson, Molly Warsh, and Karin Wulf—have for many years now offered encouragement and stimulation. Alex Bick, Daniela Bleichmar, Marisa Fuentes, Randy Head, Sara Johnson, Lauren Kassell, Peter Lake, Peter Mancall, Simon Schaffer, Bill Sherman, Asheesh Siddique, Brent Sirota, David Chan Smith, Jacob Soll, and Vanessa Wilkie have played a bigger role in this book than they likely know.

Last, none of this could have been done without the support and understanding of my family, in all its forms and branches. The research and writing of this book have crossed over many stages of all our lives, and I look upon your encouragement, patience, support, enthusiasm, and so much more with overwhelming love, gratitude, and appreciation.

Introduction

The Space of the Archive

The Tower of London Record Office was a bustling place in the early 1670s. The records it housed—predominantly Chancery documents produced prior to the reign of Henry VIII—drew a stream of visitors: landowners seeking to establish property title, representatives of corporations examining their original charters, appointees to Crown offices researching their duties, antiquaries excavating arcana of the medieval past, members of Parliament (MPs) seeking ballast for their positions, and others. For a ten-shilling fee, a clerk would consult the archive's registers and pull desired materials. Some visitors requested copies, whose cost depended on the amount of paper required. For a price, the Record Office offered access to the material evidence embodying England's past.[1]

Keeper of the Tower Records Algernon May viewed the appointment as a sinecure, so managing the swirl of people, parchment, paper, and pens fell to Senior Clerk William Ryley Jr., who had inherited the position after nearly two decades of apprenticeship to his father upon the latter's death in 1667. Ryley's job was demanding. Visitors' inquiries were often obscure, requiring him to scour inconsistent catalogs for cryptic references to the musty rolls heaped burdensomely in Caesar's Chapel in the White Tower. Some were impossible to fulfill. And the archive's activity created its own challenges, removing items from their allotted spaces and exposing them to defacement.

Maintaining order and functionality outstripped Ryley's individual capacities. Accordingly he employed soldiers for projects of sorting or carting, while carpenters from the Crown's Office of the Works built and repaired the bookshelves, boxes, or cases storing the records. But Ryley's main collaborators in these years were junior clerks Samuel Wiseman, Ralph Jennings, and William Thompson. This group was knit tightly by the conditions of their work and their intermingling of tasks. For example, they maintained accounts as a group, recording the frequent advances on salary that each took and tracking the stream of small disbursements that kept the office stocked with paper, pen, ink, parchment, sand, tape, thread, needles, pins, locks, keys, clasps, and waters "to refresh the blind and imperfect records."[2]

Much of the clerks' activity was directed by the regulations which hung in the Tower, to which they swore an oath. These obligated them to make sure that the records were not "imbezled, falsified, corrupted, razed, blotted, torne, or defaced," instructed them to refile materials directly after consultation, and decreed that they immediately repair unstitched or torn records. The regulations also prescribed quarterly audits of the holdings and dictated that "vacant time" in the office be devoted to "making more exact Kalendars & Tables to the Records for the publike goode and in reduceing the loose Records in the Office & White Tower Chappel that are useful into order & bundles."[3]

The same somber orientation extended to the integrity of the collection. The regulations dictated that no record should be removed from the office except "by the speciall order of the Kings Majestie or the Lorde Chancellor of England or Master of the Rolles or his Majesties Judges Barons of his Eschequer or his learned counsell at lawe or some other great officer of state for his Majesties service."[4] Even these elite counselors were expected to borrow materials only briefly, and an entry book was prescribed to record when items were taken and returned. The regulations also dictated that all searches be registered in an account book and none performed in private, and that the clerks adhere to a rigid schedule of fees, with payments deposited in a lockbox immediately upon receipt. They were thus responsible for policing and mediating contact between roll and subject, record and reader. They preserved and oversaw; they also opened access and disseminated.

The office was more than a workplace. It paid for the clerks' lodging and was where they took meals, and after Jennings fell ill and died, it paid for his funeral services and assumed his debts. When in late 1674, Thompson—in his fourth year of apprenticeship, for which he received £20 annually—betrayed Ryley's trust by forging a document "for a considerable reward," Ryley recorded that the episode "hath broken my heart."[5]

Aside from Ryley and the clerks, the people most constantly present in the office were the women who cleaned and performed essential tasks of upkeep. These women struggled to stave off the archive's traditional enemies of vermin, water, and fire, while making sure that the space was temperate and clean. This last point was a particular challenge. Dust leached off the parchment skins on which most original records were recorded, and it joined the soot rising from warming fires and the moisture seeping through the stone walls to create a thick, corrosive grime that disfigured the records lying on shelves. The rules accordingly commanded "that the roomes in the office shall be kept cleane & swept once or more every weeke and the writtes & records therein preserved from cobwebbs, dust, filth, & putrefaction."[6]

In the early 1670s, the woman most frequently referred to in the office's ledger as performing these tasks was a "Goody Walsh," "Mother Walsh," or "Mrs Walsh." Her employment was secure, as she took repeated advances on quarterly payments toward her annual salary of £2 and was reimbursed for her own expenditures, as when she purchased a broom for four pence. Walsh may have also been "the woman" anonymously referred to throughout the account book taking advances on a comparable salary; either she or this other woman or women regularly received bonuses for special cleaning and repayment for purchases of supplies such as brooms, baskets, and mops. Such items helped keep spaces cleared for clerks to access and pull requested materials, stave off the sedimentation of dust and filth that imperiled the durability of records, and prevent the detritus of rolls, biscuits, and sugar ordered for the clerks' sustenance from attracting rodents whose appetites might—as was often the case in other archives—lead them to feed on the records. Walsh or the other women were also likely the intended users of such items as "a hand brush to brush the records," suggesting that their responsibilities included cleaning the rolls themselves.[7] Women's labor was part of the collaborative activity of preserving Britain's material past from ruin.

These women were essential to the life of the archive, and Goody Walsh performed other caretaking services; for example, in January 1671 she was paid a shilling "for Washing Mr Jenyngs cloathes"; and the following month she received three shillings "for her attendance on him while he was sicke."[8] The lives and work of the Tower clerks were made possible by women's labor and caretaking—Jennings's nurse received eight shillings after his death, and his remaining rent was paid to his landlady Mrs. Carter. Their services thus joined carting, couriering, searching, filing, and transcribing to allow the Tower to function as the inscribed memory of the realm, making available the public testimonies of past political and legal acts for England's statesmen, antiquaries, property owners, and historians.[9]

* * *

The role of Goody Walsh and other women, of course, was never acknowledged in the texts produced from such consultations. This invisibility paralleled how women were marginalized in the records she and the clerks maintained.[10] These records emanated from the spheres of law and politics, which used gender, wealth, landownership, age, and more as grounds for exclusion, and while women might exercise power through informal means, the voluminous paperwork produced by medieval and early modern governments typically solemnified concluded business but occluded such negotiations of power.[11] To be sure, women did appear in the grants and deeds listed in the rolls. But these guises reflect their exclusion from authority; they typically were named not as legal actors but in roles defined by their relations to men and as subject to subordinating institutions and laws such as the doctrine of coverture.

The world of inscription thus mediated political business and legal proceedings by contemporary hierarchies and therefore obscured women's participation; records themselves were forms of exclusion.[12] It is therefore deeply paradoxical that the survival of the records depended on the invisible labor of Goody Walsh and others discernible only because of the unlikely survival of ledgers maintained by barely more visible junior clerks. Indeed, when I refer to the work of individual archivists, statesmen, and administrators throughout this book, their names often function as corporate identities subsuming a constellation of uncredited labors and practices performed by unknowable men and women.

The archive thus communicated the past to the present. But it did not project the past seamlessly, for the creation, maintenance, and reproduction of its records depended on processes, labor, and people those same records concealed. And as this book will argue, those very acts of recording, preserving, organizing, disseminating, and manipulating testimonies of the past shaped the political visions formulated in early modern English archives even more than the sources themselves. The archive was a central site of early modern knowledge production, comparable to the museum, library, and laboratory.[13]

The records' ability to stimulate and participate in knowledge formation, moreover, depended on their movement beyond the confines of the Tower. Their circulation was paradigmatic for an emergent media society laced with texts, which served both as ligatures binding subjects to each other and their government and as the foundations for knowledge and political practice. Intensifying dependence on the recording and collection of political writings, I argue throughout this book, constitutes a cause rather than a symptom of momentous changes in political and intellectual spheres. I use the term *inscription* to encapsulate the acts of recording, transcribing, abridging, summarizing, printing, and more by which such texts were composed and through which they circulated.[14] The regime of inscription, I maintain, recalibrated government as an information state, transformed perceptions of the past, stimulated the reimagination of long-standing institutions, restructured public politics, and shaped the infrastructure essential to the British Empire. This book aims to recover the material technologies, social mediations, and epistemic practices that catalyzed these transformations, and thus to illuminate the early modern reconstruction of British knowledge systems and political life.

The Medium of Transformation

Social and material structures determined not only how the records were preserved but how surrogates of them—in the form of transcriptions, excerpts, and abridgments—extended beyond the Tower. Paper was the primary technology facilitating the circulation of the materials under the clerks' oversight, as many searches resulted in copies of extracts being made on paper. The ease of recording, exchange, and replication afforded by paper loosened the transcribed words from their contexts and enabled their transmission into others; once freed from the Tower, the extracts could enter a kinetic world of unregulated circulation. This dynamic was not unique to the Tower records, for enhanced access to paper in sixteenth-century Britain enabled the proliferation of all kinds of inscription, and paper increasingly came to mediate political and epistemological life.

Writing had been central to English governance, as Michael Clanchy has shown, since the thirteenth century.[15] Though most communication was conducted orally, authority was often conveyed by writ, patent, warrant, charter, or other documents that certified completed business. Similarly, the tangle of courts and offices in Crown and municipal governance produced a panoply of records, registers, and rolls designed to safeguard administrative memory.[16] These instruments were typically parchment, a far more durable but also more expensive and labor-intensive material than paper. Such records tended to be produced in a single or duplicate copy and registered on official rolls, but whether these belonged to the office or the officers was often unclear, and there was no central location where registers or duplicates were deposited, though most Chancery records ultimately made their way to the Tower of London and the Exchequer records to Westminster. This situation hampered the surety with which documents could be expected to adjudicate disputes. Documents were unquestionably a significant element of medieval English governance, but writing was not the primary mode of communication, and uneven preservation and access destabilized the authority of even formal records.

The emergence of paper as a fundamental instrument in the practice of politics in the sixteenth century transformed the environment for political practice. This change has not been sufficiently appreciated by historians, though many related developments—the explosion of print, propagation of commonplace books, expansion of letter writing, and proliferation of government forms—similarly depended on the increasing availability of this inexpensive, light, durable, easily inscribed material.[17] Although white paper intended for writing was present in England as early as the thirteenth century, its availability expanded dramatically starting in the late sixteenth century. This increase in white paper use came after other European polities experienced a comparable boom, and it occurred despite the absence of the English white paper industry; indeed, up until the 1670s, nearly all writing paper in Britain was imported from France or the Low Countries.

The evidence for the exponential growth in the volume of paper in this society is more cumulative than definitive. The most thorough scholars of the English paper industry have identified only a few detailed customs records before 1620, but these indicate a rapid ascent. Paper began to displace parchment as the primary writing surface in the late fifteenth century, likely helped by the arrival of print.[18] By the 1560s roughly twenty thousand reams of white paper—which could be directed toward either print or manuscript—were imported annually; the one year of records in the 1580s saw forty thousand reams; by 1620 imports reached eighty thousand reams, and the numbers continued to rise.[19] This trend can be corroborated impressionistically; as most early modern British historians would attest, the volume of materials available increases rapidly from the 1560s. Moreover, the amount of paper imported and used for manuscript writing accelerated faster than for print—the "explosion of print" should be seen as a facet of an explosion in the realm of inscription more broadly.

Though many official records and documents continued to be recorded on parchment, governance was the primary driver of the initial paper boom. A few English counselors in previous generations—most notably Thomas Cromwell—maintained extensive collections, but Elizabethan counselors collectively used paper to massively expand the volume of information streaming across their desks, hoping to discern signal within the incoming noise. Communications that once had been transmitted orally by courtier were more frequently conducted by letter; drafts and memoranda charting elements of the process of political decision-making were preserved; and journals and minutes of meetings were recorded and stored. At the same time, paperwork increasingly appeared throughout the realm in shapes such as parish registers and censuses of the poor as well as in formwork such as recognizances and indentures.[20]

It is impossible to quantify the scale of expansion precisely. Comparing the volumes of surviving manuscripts assumes that survival rates are static over time, but they likely vary for contingent reasons. For example, sizable collections might be destroyed at once by vermin, fire, or warfare; subsequent generations might neglect inherited materials, choose to keep them in private hands invisible to historians, or not know of their existence moldering in the corner of ancestral attics. It is possible that Elizabethans operated in an environment just as text-saturated as their predecessors but that their more consistent practices of preservation ensured higher rates of survival for their materials, thus creating the illusion of larger production. More likely, the attention to preservation stemmed from a political practice that equally encouraged inscription and preservation as modes of capturing ephemeral moments, and both should be seen as forms of archivization—of designing systems aimed to enhance the orderly preservation and potential accessibility of selected texts.

Comparing the surviving evidence from Henry VIII's reign with that from Elizabeth's, however, is particularly illuminating, bearing in mind that he ruled for thirty-six years and she for forty-five. There are various indications of the scale of inscription under Henry VIII. The *Letters and Papers of the Reign of Henry VIII* (*L&P*)—compiled in the nineteenth century from records concerning both domestic and foreign business surviving in the National Archives, the British Library, and numerous other archives—consists of roughly 20,000 modern pages, containing at most around 6,000 documents. Although this collection does not include every item produced during Henry's rule, it is very thorough and includes many materials produced not by secretaries and outside government.

There is no equivalent of the *L&P* for later reigns. The closest analog for Elizabeth's might be the *Calendar of State Papers Domestic*, also produced in the nineteenth century, but this only includes papers produced in domestic governance and consists of brief descriptions of documents rather than sizable abridgments. Yet these brief snippets alone occupy 4,600 pages. Counting the number of documents elaborated in its pages is tricky, but it crosses 6,000 documents—the maximum number of documents in the *L&P*—in the mid-1570s, roughly fifteen years into her reign, even while drawing on a considerably narrower pool than the *L&P*.

Comparing papers produced by secretariats suggests an even greater transformation. The State Papers series in the National Archives contains slightly over 325 volumes in total of Henrician materials, compiled by archivists in the early nineteenth century.[21] In comparison, Elizabeth's State Papers Domestic series alone amounts to 297 volumes. While the volumes vary in length, these and the Henrician volumes were compiled at the same time according to the same principles, and neither group is systematically longer than the other. The difference between specific sets of papers is also revealing. Henry VIII's Scottish materials fall into 9 volumes, and his Irish require 16; Elizabeth's fill 137 for Scotland and 222 for Ireland. There is no Henrician equivalent to the 148 volumes remaining in Elizabeth's State Papers Foreign series for her reign up to 1577, after which the series were distinguished by locale, so that there are, for example, 48 additional volumes in the State Papers Foreign, France, series for the rest of her reign. And these numbers for Elizabeth's reign do not include archival collections such as the Cecil Papers series at Hatfield House, which contains thousands of documents produced by and for Lord Treasurer William Cecil, Baron Burghley, and his son Robert Cecil. Factoring all this together, it appears that the volume of materials produced by Elizabeth's secretariats was astronomically larger than Henry's, a minimum ratio of 20:1 and likely much higher. And production did not stabilize after this initial boom but continued to accelerate in the seventeenth century.

* * *

The emerging dependence of political practice on paper from the 1560s onward reflected a conjunction of circumstances whose impact was most concentrated within upper and midlevel government officials. A series of political crises escalated the urgency of counsel and political communication; intellectual currents nudged political aspirants toward a humanist attentiveness to the empirical and particular; and a sociological terrain developed of intensified competition for preferment. Contemporaries used inscriptions on paper to advise, discuss, record, persuade, petition, and impress, and as expanded demand deepened paper's penetration of social, intellectual, and political life, counselors relied increasingly on practices designed to capitalize on its availability.

Paper was essential to the webs of correspondence that undergirded the power of such Elizabethan statesmen as Burghley and Principal Secretary Francis Walsingham. These figures accumulated intelligence through their networks. But they also used their correspondents and informers to transmit messages, exact professions of loyalty, and broadcast statements supporting their preferred counsels.[22] And they encouraged their correspondents and clients to rely on paper for this political work, spurring, for example, the rise of parish registers and the proliferation of formwork such as recognizances.[23] Petitioning—sometimes though by no means always stimulated by such counselors—also appears to have increasingly taken a written form in this period.[24] Elite preference for paper animated its increasing use to mediate between levels of government and between government and polity.

Coordinating communication was only one use of paper such individuals devised to confront the spiraling crises confronting the Elizabethan regime. Many of them had trained for statecraft by historical study, which was perceived as the most valuable training for statesmen and which in the 1560s became characterized by the conviction that mastering what early modern scholars in other contexts would call "particulars" enabled skilled observers to discern the subtleties of causation in earthly events.[25] In the context of political expertise, "particulars" often took the shape of news, correspondence, records, and other texts containing empirical information.[26] But particulars could also be more ephemeral, and the studies of statesmen overflowed with journals, drafts, memoranda, lists, and other jottings of a sort unlikely to have been produced or preserved during an earlier period. Access to paper, in conjunction with the emphases enshrined in the education of statesmen, augmented the likelihood of recording interactions and ideas that previously would have escaped inscription or been written on ephemeral technologies such as wax tablets.[27] The increase of paper thus encouraged a surge in writing, as the scraps speckling early modern archives testify, that verged on graphomania.

But the overflowing archives of these statesmen did not spill out beyond their studies solely because of their own correspondence and notes. Perhaps the most significant transformation of political practice made possible by the prevalence of paper was not the inscription of new materials but the copying of preexisting ones.[28] In this instance, the pathology was less graphomania than a "collectomania" comparable to the hording practices better known among early modern naturalists.[29] The very survival of so many copies from this period testifies to the fervency with which statesmen visited or dispatched clients to visit studies and libraries to gather their own copies of letters, records, and policy proposals. Similarly, their collections often included notes drawn at second or third hand from documents stored in the Tower of London, Westminster Abbey, the Exchequer, or other state archives; their studies constituted translations of these spaces.

The result of these enterprises was that those participating in governance accumulated previously unimaginable archives, sometimes numbering hundreds of volumes containing thousands of letters, lists, drafts, notes, and copies of official records such as patent rolls, close rolls, treaties, and warrants. Such iterative copying emanated political materials throughout distinct sites, and individuals from broadening social and geographical positions relied on scribal workshops and personal connections to augment their holdings of evidence of political business.

This proliferation of paper transformed political dynamics. It extended and strengthened webs of communication across geographical and social distance. By enabling the inscribed remembrance of fleeting moments, it made fragmentary shards of the past more retrievable, perpetuating them and solidifying them in prosthetic memory.[30] It revivified records of England's distant past, enhancing their force and immediacy, while also allowing the replication of records and experiences across discrete communities throughout the realm. And this transformation in the mechanisms available for producing political knowledge stimulated a shift in political action and epistemology.[31]

Political Knowledge in the Regime of Inscription

In May 1610, one Abraham Wallis surprised Sir Christopher Hilliard at a house in Holborn by presenting to him a manuscript volume entitled, "A survaye or Booke of Offices aswell of his Majesty's Courts of Recorde as of his Majesty's most noble household. The Counsels of the North, or Wales, & the Marches. The Admiralty, the Mint, the Armory, Officers at Armes, the Townes of War, Castles, Bulwarks, & Fortresses, the Islands, with his Majesty's Houses, Parks, Forests, & Chases, collected in Anno 1610."[32] Hilliard was an MP and a member of the Council of the North; about Wallis, nothing else is known. But Wallis's goals were clear, for he appended to this collection an introductory letter stating that

> I have made Choyse of you from many others (upon the generall good report that is most deservedely geven of you) to present unto yor favorable good acceptance this Booke being A Collection of the Offices of England in generall. Though My self am a stranger unto your worshipp yet (havinge taken paines in collecting the same, being a work fytt for your private use and entertainment) yet worthy disposition and kind prospect, gives me hope that you will not dislike my good will, But rather give encouragement towardes good exercizes.

Wallis hoped that Hilliard would see benefit in owning this survey and reward him accordingly. This desire was not unreasonable, for his gift offered something inaccessible to all but a few early modern Britons: a synoptic view of the regime that governed them, a bird's-eye perspective on the state previously available only to those surveying it from its most elite offices.

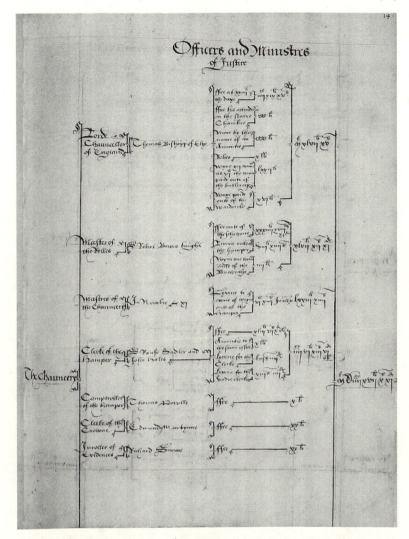

FIGURE 1. "Officers and Ministers of Justice," from Queen Mary's "Book of Offices," 1553. Society of Antiquaries MS 125, f. 14r. © The Society of Antiquaries of London. By permission.

Wallis's claim that he had taken particular pains to collect the document, however, was exaggerated. His manuscript was of a specific genre invented upon Mary Tudor's accession to the throne as Queen Mary I in 1553 as a kind of mini–Domesday Book of England's Crown government. This volume named all the offices, officeholders, and fees in Mary's grasp, down to the queen's bagpiper and wheelwrights.[33] Its production resulted from an unprecedented audit of rolls containing records of patents and grants as well as correspondence with the overseers of castles, parks, and other Crown possessions. Perhaps because of the labor entailed, such an effort was not repeated in subsequent years. But new versions of the text were created and updated beginning in the late 1570s, growing in numbers after James VI and I's ascension to the English throne in 1603 and through the late 1610s.

Early in this period, these were prized texts; the copy from the 1580s that likely belonged to William Fleetwood, Recorder of London, noted that it was "particular mete for the vewe of her Majestie and of her heignes most honorable previe counsellers and to be kept from all others excepting souche as be verie discrete and dutiful subiectes."[34] But such confidentiality was not maintained, and by King James's reign, hundreds of these texts circulated bearing variations on Wallis's title or, frequently, "A general collection of all the offices of England with their fees and allowance in the King's Gift," often scribbled only half legibly.[35]

These "Book of Offices" differed markedly from humanist descriptions of English government such as those written by Thomas Smith and William Harrison. Each was a skeletal list, devoid of descriptions of duties, constitutional theorizing, history, or genealogy, and was a "collection" in the sense that their initial production entailed not bundling discrete works but summarizing information collected from distinct sources. Their sections were divided into offices such as the Exchequer, Chancery, and Admiralty, but also by customs ports, castles, forests, parks, and other Crown possessions as well as household offices such as the kitchen and wardrobe—all the offices and occupations subject directly to the monarch. Rows under each heading listed specific positions, which were followed by spaces for names to be entered and their annual salaries. At the end of each section was a place for the sums of the unit, with another at the end of the volume for the grand total.

There was little standardization beyond this template, however. Whereas units on the central Crown offices and household were never omitted, those on the forests, customs, or castles sometimes were. And this core was frequently supplemented by additional lists, most commonly of the nobility or of England's and Wales's bishoprics (in order of precedence) with their livings and tenths, and occasionally lists of the number of men and horses available for muster in the counties or numbers of fugitives. The sequence of the components also varied from copy to copy. Rather than set texts, these manuscripts were thus hybrid concatenations of discrete reference lists that could be joined or disaggregated by their creators.

Owners of these resources occasionally updated their books when offices changed hands, added names to blank areas, or supplemented the list of nobility with new creations. Few, however, capitalized thoroughly on the template. Some copies populate around half the spaces for names, but more often these columns were blank or only listed a few names. Perhaps more surprisingly, the fees paid to the offices were occasionally omitted, and frequently sums were not entered. Moreover, these totals were often inaccurate, as it seems that the fees owed to specific offices might be updated without adjusting the total at the end of the relevant section; the numbers seem to have been conventionalized rather than calculated.[36]

Providing a precise and thorough summary of the civil list or of Crown finance, however, was not the purpose of these manuscripts. Their main value instead lay in mediating knowledge of the state by elaborating the regime as a set of offices. Suitably, prominent statesmen owned these texts, including Robert Cecil; Lord Treasurer Thomas Sackville, Baron Buckhurst; Lord Chancellor Sir Thomas Egerton (who may have owned up to three); Sir Julius Caesar (who had at least three); Thomas Wentworth, the Earl of Strafford; Secretary of State Dudley Carleton, Viscount Dorchester (whose copy was probably transmitted to the subsequent Secretary of State, Francis Windebank); Chief Justice of the King's Bench John Dodderidge; and Lord President of Munster Edward Legge.[37] For these counselors, these lists likely served as crib sheets for understanding the government in which they participated. For example, Buckhurst received his as a gift "To our verie good Lord the Lord Buckhurst Lord highe Treasurer of England" in 1600, shortly after his appointment to that post. The phrasing of the dedication suggests it was a gift from the queen to familiarize him with the full scope of offices under her remit. These books thus helped administration by imposing illusory fixity on the moving object of the state.

The manuscripts served other instrumental purposes. Even for those who had already achieved relatively high office, they provided a menu of positions to pursue. Wallis's gift likely held this purpose, supplying to Hilliard both an object for reflection and targets for advancement. Similarly, George Montgomery, Dean of Norwich, explained to John Willoughby in 1603 that he used his to identify openings and determine whether the fees due to them would be worth the initial investment to purchase the office.[38] Because they elaborated the enormous roster of clerks, recorders, messengers, and other unspectacular offices required in governance, moreover, aspirants to lower offices would likely have sought these texts too. For example, the writing master Peter Bales entered at the end of his copy a rueful poem: "When in your hande yow houlde / All offices alone / Twere marvell if yow should not get / Mongst manye thowsande

[14] INTRODUCTION

one," followed by, plaintively in Latin, "si non tibi saltem amicis" (if not for you, at least for your friends).[39] These manuscripts supplied job listings by way of a synoptic view of government.

Bales's production draws attention to another distinctive social dimension of these texts: since scribal expertise was his distinctive skill, the very quality of handwriting constituted part of the appeal of his copies. Many of these texts produced during James's reign were written not by the same hand but in the same handwriting, perhaps in a single scriptorium. That this orthography should be seen as a distinctive feature is reinforced by the series of "Books of Offices" produced by the obscure scribe John Peers in the 1630s, all written in deliberate imitation of that earlier handwriting from twenty years prior.[40] And in fact, Peers's versions described the government of this earlier time—on the front of his "A book of offices . . . collected in anno 1607," he inscribed "John Peers his book written this 11th of July 1636."[41] During this period

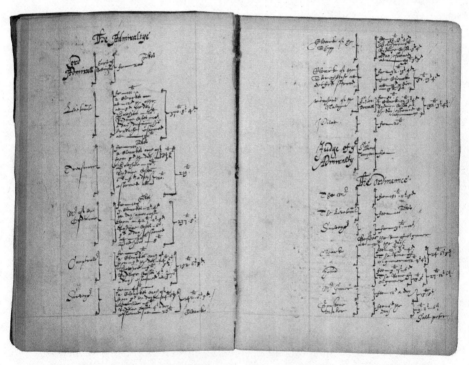

FIGURE 2. "The Admiralty," from "Book of Offices," 1607. Many spaces for names remain blank; other copies similarly excluded fees or other elements from the underlying "Books of Offices" template. Beinecke Rare Book and Manuscript Library, Yale University, Osborn MS B7, f. 12v–13r.

he also copied at least two 1608 and two 1611 versions. Peers's production of these out-of-date texts was unlikely to have been for instrumental or administrative ends; more likely, reproducing their handwriting as well as their contents exhibited his scribal abilities.[42]

"Books of Offices" would thus have served as ideal manuscript samples for the ambitious scribe. Though these "Books" originated as a functional document, as they circulated they became an instrument to demonstrate scribal skills that also hinted at access and suggested a grasp of the contours of the state. Because possession of this manuscript might accordingly be taken as an index of a desirable constellation of expertise, credit, and knowledge, those looking to enter the regime continued to write and circulate new copies from ever-more-liminal positions. And through repeated iterations of this process, the social value of this manuscript and technological ease of reproduction multiplied this description of the regime throughout the realm.[43] The trajectory of "Books of Offices" thus exemplifies how inscription practices emanated throughout Britain, bearing with them new political perspectives.[44]

The "Book of Offices" had a surprising midcentury coda. In 1647, the devout Parliamentarian captain Lazarus Haward oversaw the printing of an Elizabethan "Book of Offices." In his dedicatory epistle to "The Lords and Commons of Parliament," he explained:

> Imboldned by divers friends to Publish this which I have kept secret for many yeeres together; but now at last reflecting upon the overture of things in these distracted times, [I] am imboldened under your Honours favour to conceive the publishing of such a subject may conduce to the profitting of the Common-wealth ... long time, and the face of war having ruined, distracted and desolated many of those Ancient particular establishments ... which by your great wisedomes, and pious care is now like to be re-established in all the particulars, as cannot in the first place but conduce to the good of the republike, and secondly to the good of all those who are or may be interessed herein; this then cannot hinder, but rather give light to so honourable a worke.[45]

Haward presented the volume as more obscure than it likely had been. But the import of the work had shifted dramatically. Previously it had derived value as an instrumental administrative tool, list of potential places for preferment, or demonstration of qualities exhibiting the employability and knowledge of its bearer. In these cases, the document itself was fundamentally descriptive. But as Parliament confronted the tatters of the kingdom, Haward saw it as an instrument for reviving the ruined state. The text, no less significantly, was republished upon the Restoration of Charles II to the throne in 1660. No longer descriptive, it instead became normative.

The World Paper Made

The example of the "Book of Offices" illustrates how the spreading technology of paper and practices of inscription forged new of ways of conceptualizing England's political life and techniques of constructing social and political ties. It thus distills this book's argument that the emergence of generating, collecting, and circulating inscriptions as dominant methods of establishing knowledge and authority drove a structural transformation of political practice and knowledge formation.

Historians' inattention to the proliferation of textual evidence in the sixteenth century reflects a broader tendency to understate the importance of material conditions through which political action and thought were performed and a preference for discursive sources over the occasional, fragmentary, and frequently inscrutable papers that suffuse every early modern archive. In this book, by contrast, I begin my examination of early modern politics with those scraps of evidence and trace how such inscriptions produced in the process of governance were mobilized in the re-creation of political knowledge. Coming to terms with this restructuring demands reconsidering the fundamental organizing frameworks of early modern history: moving from political thought and ideology to political practice and the history of knowledge, most broadly, but also from a perspective that opposes manuscript and print to one that recognizes a generalized surge in inscription; from attentiveness not only to writing but also to preservation and circulation; from a focus on a few "great men" to the functionaries responsible for so much of the labor of governance; and from a bias for letter writing and discursive argument to the churn of fragmentary scraps and papers typically overlooked despite their ubiquity within archives.[46]

Without proper boundaries, such a study could lead down a rabbit warren of endless conjectures associating sloppy lists of statutes with little-known owners. Accordingly, though I have integrated discussion of other archives, this book focuses on two of early modern England's primary political archives: the Tower of London Record Office and the State Paper Office, an office for secretarial papers founded in 1578 by Queen Elizabeth I that is the ancestor of the National Archives. My selection of these two runs against the tendency of recent studies of British archives that, in contrast to Continental studies, have explored municipal or personal archives over relatively brief chronologies. The Tower and the State Paper Office, like all archives, had local characters, but their significance and longevity have allowed me to examine the dissemination of their materials over an extended stretch of time, while distinctions in their holdings have enabled insights into patterns of using older and newer records.[47]

As this suggests, rather than viewing archives as static repositories best understood through their systems of organization and classification, I integrate examinations of these aspects into a broader emphasis on circulation and knowledge production.[48] Approaching archives in this way not only illuminates their role in the remaking of knowledge and expertise but also reveals the porous boundary between institutions of government and the public sphere, and that these phenomena shared communication dynamics. Two key insights emerge from this recognition: first, that early modern Britain's information world was a thick web of overlapping networks, and that it is misleading to draw a rigid distinction between public and private; and second, that the mobilization of both archival and new inscriptions was essential to the linking of state and locality, as well as to how administrative offices conducted their own work. This latter point is especially significant for illuminating the process of state formation in the sixteenth and seventeenth centuries, which historians have tended to portray as a means of securing collaboration between central and local governments or as a consequence of fiscal-military imperatives.[49] By contrast, my account characterizes these two developments as effects of an emergent political practice which, through its participants' emphasis on producing, collecting, and controlling inscriptions to make knowledge and pursue authority, generated an organ of governance that was in its very construction an information state.

While I discuss significant events throughout the book, I do not mean to reduce them solely to the forces investigated here; I hope instead to show that the practices of this new regime had causal, if contingent, force. Similarly, though the book is organized chronologically, this arrangement is not intended to signal a linear progression; rather, each chapter highlights a distinct aspect of the emergent regime of inscription. The first five chapters trace, respectively, inscription and archivization, circulation, reimagining of institutions and the past, forging and fragmenting of epistemic communities, and information conflict. The order of these chapters also exposes structural tensions and ironies that emerged over time: increased attention to storing texts also facilitated their circulation; accelerated circulation stimulated the production of new texts claiming to supplant the authority of their sources; these new texts aimed to foster consensus but instead provoked division; such conditions intensified the use of inscriptions as tools of conflict rather than unity. The sixth chapter examines the integration of the discrete methods outlined in previous chapters within a holistic political practice that fully internalized the regime of inscription, emphasizing the possession of asymmetrical information resources as the foundation of expertise, precipitating a never-ending cycle of circulation within and beyond political institutions, and solidifying England's government as an information state. The epilogue explores some of the consequences of this transformation, in particular its shaping of Britain's imperial project. It also foregrounds a prominent theme lacing previous chapters by exploring the limitations on knowledge obtained through this new organ—in particular how it introduced its own distortions and blind spots, which have redounded to historians using the inscriptions provoked by this regime to make sense of the past.

Finally, I make no claim that England's experience was the same as that of other early modern polities. England adopted the regime of inscription belatedly, and not until the late seventeenth century was there a sustained effort to stimulate domestic production of the paper so essential to its critical political practices. By this time, regular correspondence had characterized Italian diplomacy for more than two centuries; the Spanish Empire renowned for its copious paperwork was decades into decline; a suite of complex archival apparatuses had matured across the cities and towns of the Holy Roman Empire, Swiss Federation, and beyond; and French statesmen had fused paper technologies into sophisticated tools of absolutism. Britain's experience proceeded according to its own tempo and was shaped by local contingencies.

But ultimately, the transformations described in this book resemble those that struck other early modern European polities more than they differ, as they were entangled aspects of a political and media transformation driven by dynamics of communication and preservation enabled by technologies of inscription. As paper proliferated across these societies, its availability and replicability improved access to inherited texts, and networks and communities emerged to produce responsive, kinetic systems of communication about their present. As a result, the scale of collection and accessibility of information increased dramatically. Aspirational statesmen and projectors seeking advancement or wealth combined and correlated inscriptions to rethink the past, present, and future; they also sought to control processes of cataloging and circulation. As the volume of texts surged into overload, the shared practice of knowledge formation multiplied perspectives, for the seeming infinity of sources enabled contradictory interpretations of ostensibly authoritative evidence, undermining consensus and encouraging innovative, competing, and sometimes incompatible visions of the state. Within this divided terrain, conflict was increasingly articulated through measures to disrupt and control the generation, circulation, and interpretation of information. Accordingly, power also derived from possessing these expertises, and the integration, centralization, and routinization of information systems proved effective grounds for claims to exercise authority and build knowledge. Integration also enabled those overseeing networks to thicken communication, concentrate attention at different scales, and accelerate the pace of recombination. In consequence they recalibrated governments as organs for coordinated political knowledge and action. But those within such networks found themselves incapable of seeing outside them, their perspectives and perceptions dominated by—and their knowledge limited to—the media worlds they had constructed. The result was a society in which a realm of inscriptions less reflected political life than jaggedly reconstituted it.

* * *

Tracing this early modern transformation reveals how the media-saturated world we inhabit coalesced. At the same time, it should offer a mirror to our present at the onset of another media revolution as we struggle to face, simultaneously, the destabilization of vital pathways to knowledge and the legacies of their distortions. That contemporary media technologies, for all their promise and possibility, have flooded our experience with blight, falsehood, and chimera suggests the necessity of contemplating our own archives of the past and present, and of designing such technologies to responsibly mobilize that legacy to benefit the society they are rapidly changing. Confronting an analogous disruption to the media of knowledge production that shook the early modern world reveals the enormous urgency and perennial power of questions concerning how and what we archive and how and what we learn from it as we, immutably, reenvision humanity's future by preserving and re-learning its past.

1

Archivization

At the death of Lord Treasurer William Cecil, Baron Burghley, in 1598, his son Principal Secretary Robert Cecil dispatched Levinus Munck to Whitehall to catalog the books remaining in his father's offices. Books and manuscripts had been significant tools in Burghley's political arsenal throughout his political career, as he used practices learned at Cambridge first to navigate mid-Tudor instability and then while serving Elizabeth I for virtually her entire reign.[1]

As his printed books suggest, Burghley was one of many early modern European counselors who anchored their authority in their humanistic education in rhetoric, moral philosophy, history, philology, and other arts intended to instill virtue, rather than in pedigree or in courtly or military exploits.[2] He had French and English editions of Phillipe de Commines's *Memoires*, a rhetorical compendium compiled by Domenico Nani Mirabelli, and editions of Seneca's collected works and Tacitus's *Histories*. Humanism also shaped Burghley's Protestantism, as revealed by such theological works as an English-language Bible and Peter Martyr Vermigli's *Loci Communes*. He also owned works that reflected the humanist desire for practical knowledge such as Abraham Ortelius's atlas *Theatrum Orbis Terrarum* "in collours," William Camden's *Britannia*, and John Norden's *Description of Hertfordshire*. Finally, the office held such items as a printed "Book of Statutes" to acquaint Burghley with the law of the realm. His printed books thus covered theology, rhetoric, politics, law, geography, and history.

Burghley was not solely dependent on products of the printing press. The twenty-three titles he had in print were set alongside twenty-eight "written books"—manuscript collections likely constructed by either Burghley or his secretaries. Some of these resembled his printed books; for example, one contained "Common Places, of my own collection." But many were bespoke collections of papers assembled by Burghley's secretariat. Some compiled documents, such as his "Booke of Treaties with forraign Princes," while others may have been lists of names or the responsibilities of certain offices, such as the "Book of Parliament Men," or a "Booke of Justices of the Peace." Similarly, he had a "Large Book of Musters in England 1591" and "Collections of Ordynance, and valuation of Moneys." Some abridged individual instruments of statecraft, such as the "Sommary of the Treaty of Peace between her Majesty and the King of Spayne anno [15]88," while others were likely used as formularies or patterns for correspondence, such as his "Booke of Latin Letters," and the "Style and Tytles of Princes." Nine—the largest group—bore titles such as "Booke of Low Contries and Germany" or "Collection of Scottish Matters," which likely compiled instructions to ambassadors, correspondence, treaties, and other materials. And Burghley's collection pointed him toward other places where he might retrieve similar information, for one of the books was a "Callendar" of the collections of the deceased Principal Secretary, Burghley's longtime colleague Francis Walsingham.[3]

These volumes indicate that collections of paperwork were essential to Burghley's political practice. On occasion, he himself ventured to the Tower of London and other repositories to copy materials.[4] But likely because the labor was often tedious and difficult, he more frequently sent a factotum such as Clerk of the Privy Council Robert Beale, whose copies Burghley sometimes annexed for himself and sometimes recopied.

Burghley kept only a small portion of his manuscripts at Whitehall; the majority were likely at his residence at Theobald's. The teeming paper under his purview reflects his willingness to absorb into his archive virtually any scrap of paper or moldering treatise that might benefit the health of the regime.[5] Although previous statesmen such as Cardinal Thomas Wolsey and Thomas Cromwell had amassed large collections of texts, English statesmen as a whole had never before been so devoted to creating, maintaining, and mobilizing inscriptions.

Burghley's role was essential, both for his practice and for his encouragement to others; for example, Beale, who also supplied papers to his brother-in-law Walsingham, also amassed an impressive collection.[6] The communal emphasis on such practices resulted in their normalization and the risk of marginalization for those who neglected them in favor of more traditional courtly activities such as hunting and hawking. The transformation of the resources used by the Elizabethan regime was thus driven by a collaborative adherence to methods that posed paper technologies and inscription as the foundations of political practice.

Elizabethan statesmen began to accumulate collections of textual holdings that outstripped all but the rarest of their predecessors from the 1560s, led at least in part by the example of the Archbishop of Canterbury Matthew Parker, whose efforts to establish the proper shape of the

English church rooted his authority in his ability to navigate the fractured terrain of England's evidentiary past. Parker adapted his techniques from the famous Croatian theologian Matthias Flacius Illyricus, who had overseen the composition of the massive ecclesiastical history known as the Magdeburg Centuries by synthesizing reports yielded by providing instructions to a large correspondence network concerning how to take notes on a range of sources. Though Parker resisted Flacius's efforts to integrate him into the Centuriators' network, he, too, saw ecclesiastical history as the key to the Reformation, and he followed Flacius's example by deputizing clients to unearth evidence of Rome's gradual usurpation of authority over the Church of England.[7] Under his patronage, William Lambarde, Lawrence Nowell, and others scoured the peripheries of the kingdom, sifting through unkempt cartularies in abandoned monasteries, disused collections of letters preserved by private subjects, half-legible chronicles squirreled away during the Dissolution of the Monasteries, and derelict charters, writs, and patents composed in unfamiliar scripts and little-known languages. Parker's sponsorship advanced their careers, while their labors fueled his own and underlay the ecclesiastical vision he promulgated through the Elizabethan Church Settlement.

Burghley, Walsingham, and others applied Parker's methods to civil statecraft. Like Parker, they collaborated to reconstruct the historical institutions and practices of governance glimpsed through dispersed and obscure written evidence. And much as understanding the historical church addressed urgent problems, they treated past texts as resources for contemporary political action. Written materials became not only testimonies to earlier events but also grist for policy proposals and tools for pressuring one's adversaries.

Parker had encountered England's ecclesiastical records thrust into a state of wild disorder and decentralization by the Dissolution of the Monasteries.[8] The attention of Burghley and others similarly confronted the neglect and disorganization of England's political records. Parker had sought to redress this by copying obscure materials for his archiepiscopal archive, correcting or supplementing them where necessary and printing those he considered most important; Burghley and others added other strategies to this repertoire. One method was to assert oversight of institutional archives; for example, Burghley orchestrated Thomas Norton's appointment as Remembrancer of London in 1571, which placed a reliable client in control of the city's archive, while simultaneously facilitating William Fleetwood's appointment as Recorder, enabling access to its ongoing textual production.[9] Even when unable to corral institutions, inscription-minded counselors labored to improve the conditions under which textual records were kept, for the success of the regime of inscription rested not only on writing more but also on ensuring access to past and contemporary texts. Elizabeth's regime was rife with the practice of archivization: organizing chaotic assemblages of written materials not merely to store texts but to facilitate their consultation and use.

As Burghley's books make clear, moreover, writing down events or information could also serve as a form of archivization. His collections of musters and similar volumes compiled documents that froze ephemeral moments for later consultation, and Elizabethan statesmen's preference for deriving political knowledge from written materials led them to record their own activities, preserve the paperwork produced in governance, and encourage clients to document their own observations, readings, and conversations for transmission into their patrons' studies. Experience was archived through inscription and collection.

Elizabeth's political sphere, in short, was awash in inscriptions far beyond formal humanist spurs to virtue. And when her counselors sought to understand the world, they fused heterogeneous bodies of texts into a tissue of knowledge. The power of inscriptions, however, did not arise organically but had to be developed and secured. In what follows, I show the dynamics of how these processes took hold and reshaped political practice and knowledge production.[10]

Restoring the Tower

The history of the records preserved in the Tower of London exemplifies how a dilapidated administrative collection was converted into a usable instrument of knowledge.[11] This reconfiguration was driven by local exigencies, but its systematization enabled the ease of transcribing its contents, which in turn allowed its materials to be correlated and integrated with other evidence. As those aspiring to power manipulated inscriptions culled from this archive, they transformed how statesmen and scholars formed knowledge of the past for their present.

The Tower's mountain of records testified to the bureaucratic output of medieval England. From the thirteenth century onward, textual instruments had been essential to the governance of England, as records were produced by institutions and offices to certify public authority and adjudicate disputes.[12] The flourishing production had led the Chancery, Exchequer, and common-law courts, including King's Bench and Common Pleas, to use the Tower as an off-site storage facility. Over the fourteenth and fifteenth centuries, the Chancery became its primary depositor, as most Crown offices instead annexed overflow space near their offices or in Westminster, while other offices created during this period never carted their older materials off-site. The administrators who oversaw the production of such material rarely prioritized preservation or order of past records. The result was that, at Elizabeth's ascension, the Tower of London was one disorderly repository among many throughout the realm.

Those seeking specific materials in the Tower records at Elizabeth's ascension would have faced an exasperating labor, as was true for the Palace at Westminster and the Chapter House at Westminster Abbey, which together held most Exchequer records. There were no clerks designated to maintain these archives, so searches were performed by officials for whom it was only one minor task. Calendars for these collections had rarely been produced, so searchers would need to remember where they had seen items before if they were not familiar with the array of unsystematic methods previously used to identify records. At best, these methods had included bundling documents, attaching a tag bearing a distinguishing mark on them via string, and then storing them in bags or boxes. But symbols were not uniform across or even within offices, and the bags or boxes were not typically reserved for one category. The result was a profusion of records but few ways to identify them.

Moreover, few people in the early sixteenth century would have consulted the Tower records, the bodies of material stored in the Westminster repositories, or the Rolls Chapel—where more recent Chancery records were kept—when seeking evidence concerning England's past. The dominant reason for consultation would have been to resolve questions concerning land ownership or the rights, privileges, and duties conveyed in patents, charters, or wills. But since the Tower rolls mostly registered the output of such textual instruments, the originals (if they survived) were likely held elsewhere, and consultation of the records generally was required only when the originals were lost or challenged. Nor were the rolls consulted by those investigating England's history, who tended to depend on medieval chronicles for transcriptions of official state documents. And the disorganization of the rolls discouraged recourse to them; notably, the peripatetic Henrician antiquaries John Bale and John Leland spent little time in London's archives. Other groups whose expertise required familiarity with the past similarly ignored these records; for example, heralds prior to Elizabeth's ascension relied on oral interviews or exegesis of coats of arms rather than patent rolls or other instruments when trying to deduce genealogies. The Tower records, in short, were derelict.

Elizabeth's reign, however, saw a dramatic expansion in the consultation of Tower records. Though the remaining papers of Parker evince little exploration of these documents, by the 1590s Robert Cotton, John Selden, and Edward Coke had begun to amass large collections from them, while lesser-known antiquarians, lawyers, and statesmen also more frequently accessed the Tower. The history of the Tower records supplies a perspective on the intensifying mediation of politics and history through inscription distinct from that afforded by focusing on such prominent individuals as Parker or William Camden, for it highlights the complex of Crown governance, land ownership, diplomacy, systems of patronage, and, above all, the methods of its Keepers to illuminate the trajectory of Britain's archivization.

* * *

The initial rejuvenation of the Tower records was predominantly the achievement of Keeper of the Tower Records William Bowyer. How Bowyer came to oversee the records is unknown, but he was at the nexus of Parker's and Burghley's circles. He was educated at the Westminster School under the mastership of Alexander Nowell—Lawrence Nowell's cousin and the future Dean of St. Paul's—and entered Gray's Inn in 1553. While both of these experiences may have introduced him to potential patrons, the connection with Nowell, in particular, may also have suggested new and creative possibilities for the keepership when he obtained it, for Bowyer's overall practice reflects a broader urge to convert the Tower into a usable archive.[13]

Bowyer began to assert custody over the Tower records around 1560 through the intercession of Thomas Parry, Comptroller of the Household. When Parry's death later that year left Bowyer vulnerable, he sought both to control access to the records and make advantageous use of them. The first element emerged most clearly in a dispute with Chamberlain of the Exchequer Henry, Baron Stafford, the only legitimate son of Edward Stafford, 3rd Duke of Buckingham. In his own estate management, Buckingham had evinced close attention to documents, but his records had been taken to the Tower upon his execution in 1521.[14] When Queen Mary restored Stafford by appointing him to the Exchequer, he used the access provided by this position to scour Exchequer and Tower records for evidence that would help him regain his father's property.[15]

Bowyer resented Stafford's presumption of access to the records and took extraordinary efforts to prevent it. It was standard to protect valuable rooms with multiple locks, each requiring a unique key belonging to a specific office, so that their doors could not be opened unless representatives from each office were in attendance, and Burghley and Lord Treasurer William Paulet, Marquis of Winchester, had ordered this arrangement for the Tower. But in January 1563, Stafford wrote to Burghley complaining that Bowyer had violated it. As he explained, Bowyer had asked Stafford to send a deputy to the Tower to help his servant open the door. Bowyer's servant met the deputy there and the two retrieved, suspiciously, merely one roll. Then, on the way out, "Bowyers servante would not suffer my locke to be hanged on the dore, but very evell entreated my deputies servantes and strocke him one the heade wythe a Locke, that the blode rane about his fface, and thruste him downe the staires sayinge that I had nothinge to do there."[16] Ever since this braining, Bowyer's lock had hung on the door alone.

Stafford's objections to this arrangement focused on archival integrity and order. Records were bound to hemorrhage, he asserted, "under the keaping of one mans key." Even though the Exchequer's Receipt was kept under three keys, he noted, "yet ther is lacking in that treasurye above a thousand boke which I am able duely to prove"; when the Tower records had been exclusively in the Master of the Rolls's care, so many ancient rolls had been taken that "till you come to King Johns dayes, ye have no rolles presente but fragmente and peece."[17] Stafford insisted, accordingly, that "a perfecte inventorye should be made of those books that there do the remayne," and reported that he had begun this process, making "repertories" of the rolls which "afore my travaill there was non other then knowen." But under Bowyer's custody, he lamented, "nowe they be so unplaced, that no man can tell allmost where to find them."[18]

Stafford died three months later, and any resolution to his complaint is unknown. But Bowyer does not seem to have suffered in Burghley's and Winchester's estimations. Instead, he adopted Stafford's vision of an orderly archive while widening the remit of records he sought to control and envisioning an expansion of the Tower's possibilities. In March 1567, he appealed for Burghley to have William Cordell, Master of the Rolls, deliver Chancery records to the Tower. He perceived that Burghley shared with Parry the "desire of seeing and knowing the Acts and records in the Tower, in order that you might serve her majesty with better knowledge," and he anticipated that Burghley would be enticed to agree if he recognized that Bowyer could facilitate the use of Tower records toward this end.[19]

Such better knowledge first entailed establishing order and accessibility, and Bowyer reported that, motivated by Burghley's encouragement, since Parry's death he had "consumed all his study and labore in compiling registers."[20] This effort included spending a year compiling a "Brief Compendium or Repertorium" of all the charters from the reign of King John to Edward IV.[21] Similarly, he had "transcribed in great volumes all things which seemed necessary or useful to whether to the Queen or her subiects" from the parliament rolls, patent rolls, and the foreign rolls.[22] He hoped such labors would convince Burghley to encourage the delivery of the Chancery materials, and he promised that in upcoming years he would produce desirable books, such as "A Fiscal or Fiduciary Book" elaborating all knight's fees and another demonstrating that someone had absconded with £21,000 from the Exchequer.[23]

Bowyer's strategy of promoting the Tower records' possibilities drew Winchester's and Burghley's support, and in May 1567 Elizabeth ordered Cordell to deliver Chancery records to the Tower.[24] When Cordell objected, Bowyer sent to Burghley a collection of short extracts from the rolls in the Tower supporting his claim that "the Tower as it is, and ever hathe bene a place aunciently used for the safe keepinge and layinge up of the richest and oldest Jewelles of the Realme and Crowne."[25] Bowyer thus modeled the value of the records under his care by marshaling evidence from them to describe how they should be managed.

The reference texts Bowyer had earlier produced, moreover, reflected a host of techniques for asserting order. His "Repertorium" fulfilled Stafford's desire for a "perfect inventory" (perhaps by building on Stafford's work), sorting the records by monarch, regnal year, and type — for example, the twenty-first year of Richard II's reign had produced one parliament roll, one charter roll, three patent rolls, two close rolls, one fine roll, and one Francia roll. Each year from King John to Edward IV was laid out in this way, with sums given for each year and then each reign. At the end was a list of other types of documents in the Tower.[26]

This catalog almost certainly accompanied a general reorganization of the rolls according to the same chronological arrangement.[27] This coordination would have instilled unprecedented order into the archive, for by mapping its space, the "Repertorium" became both an inventory and a finding aid. And because these holdings remained stable, Bowyer's inventory proved of enduring utility; in the early 1620s, when the newly appointed Keeper John Borough audited the records, he checked the records against a copy bequeathed by William's son and successor as Keeper of the Records, Robert Bowyer; Ralph Jennings surveyed them using a different inherited copy in 1669.[28]

Having organized the space of the archive, Bowyer produced texts that enabled more efficient consultation. In particular, the registers and transcriptions he described to Burghley — and several others he subsequently constructed — translated the archive into different material forms. Most salient was that they presented in codex — bound books — information otherwise accessible only in rolls. The effect of this material transformation was significant.[29] Rolls were unwieldy and unforgiving to work with, as their propensity to retract created difficulties when scrolling or moving between different sections. Moreover, though sometimes individual sections had topical marginal headings, these — like the contents of the

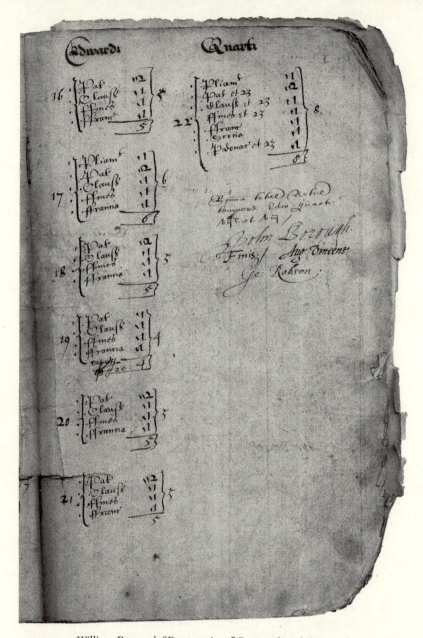

FIGURE 3. William Bowyer's "Repertorium." Bowyer listed the number of rolls for each individual year, in this image for the later years of Edward IV's reign. The later signatures, including that of John Borough, suggest that this copy was used to audit the Tower records in the 1630s. The National Archives, Kew, OBS 1/1273, np. Contains public sector information licensed under the Open Government Licence v3.0.

roll—were written in what would have been for many Elizabethans an archaic orthography. Although many Elizabethan scribes possessed the ability to work with rolls, they likely preferred codices, which enabled them to navigate the text more easily and did not require the same physical labor.

Even more than his organization of the physical space, Bowyer's codices enhanced the accessibility of the Tower records. The texts of these volumes abridged sets of rolls; for example, Bowyer transcribed summaries of grants from each patent roll, in chronological order, into two codices. These volumes could be used as brief tables of contents for the rolls or, if their extracts contained the desired information, as substitutes for the rolls themselves. To produce a volume of "extracts of Foreign Rolls," similarly, Bowyer consulted the rolls of each reign sequentially, transcribing the first words of each act into clipped entries similar to "incipits."[30] Bowyer also equipped this volume with paratextual features to ease searching both within them and in the physical archive. For one, he entered marginal notes to the locations affected by each act, allowing users to quickly scan the codex when searching for one location. Further, each entry concluded with a citation to the source roll so that those consulting them could find the complete original entry. He also limned out columns for an alphabetical index at the end. Bowyer directed these tools toward other collections as well; for example, he used this same method when distilling the Parliament rolls into a single volume.[31]

These volumes wavered between guides to the records and replacements for them; the brief entries in the codices might satisfy users or could direct them to the original source. Bowyer thus transformed the archive both by rendering it a searchable space and by translating it into bound books. Indeed, it seems likely that he, his clerks, and any other searchers consulted them first, preferring to leave the solemn, demanding rolls undisturbed on their shelves.

* * *

Bowyer developed additional tactics to demonstrate the value of his reconfigured space. In 1567, most notably, as Cordell sought to rebuff Bowyer's effort to accession Chancery records, Bowyer produced a series of texts relying on Tower records that he hoped would appeal to his patrons. These works, above all, intended to showcase his capacity to capitalize on the political power of the records in his custody.

During the discussion of the Chancery records, Winchester reported to Burghley that he had sent Robert Dudley, Earl of Leicester, a book Bowyer had made "declaring my Armes and Pedigree, which I think bee well done, and therefore I have desired my said Lord to show it to the Queen, and to my Lord, and you, that his service may be known, whereof will grow a great Reformacion among the Heraulds, that maketh their Books at Adventure and not by the Records."[32] The book Winchester referred to was a lavish genealogical volume. It began with a Latin poem dedicated to Winchester, followed by individual pages devoted to Winchester's predecessors, each limned out with immaculate coats of arms and brief biographical notes and adorned with extracts from Tower records concerning the family's lands, wealth, and titles.[33] This hybrid volume thus fused forms of authority and learning; its extravagant neoclassical verse signaled humanist expertise, but it also evoked the heraldic to exalt their nobility. Most distinctive, however, was the integration of the records of the Tower with genres of encomium and celebration.

The volume impressed Leicester, and he directed Bowyer to produce one for him. This even more spectacular "Heroica Eulogia," dated November 1567, similarly integrated humanist poetry, extravagant illustration, genealogical investigation, and copious citation from Tower records. The claims for this collection, however, exceeded the celebratory tenor of Paulet's and instead aimed to legitimize and expand Leicester's authority.

Bowyer's volume for Leicester escalated the material and technical pyrotechnics of his volume for Paulet. It was produced on parchment rather than paper. Much of it was rendered in calligraphy by the French scribe Jean de Beauchesne, and its spectacular illustrations, which rendered the coats of arms and portraits of Leicester's predecessors in expensive materials such as lapis lazuli, were doubtless created by professionals. English monarchs were similarly represented in magnificent images, with accompanying poems written as if in their voices.[34]

Moreover, its introductory epistle, while again celebrating the nobility of the volume's dedicatee, explained its underlying logic. As Bowyer explained, "I have drawn this work into three parts, as some are 'Authentic,' some 'Historic,' and others 'Poetic.' For when the chief portion of this argument is excerpted from royal Acts, it is merited to be called by law 'Authentic.' Under 'historic' I have briefly collected not only the lives and deeds of your elders, but also those of the kings by whose liberality they gained these ranks. And the 'poetical' refers to that mystery, which I express in the images and painted arms of those kings and princes, represented in verse."[35] The "Authentic," that is, referred to Tower records under his control. These records functioned less as celebratory ornaments than as instruments of legitimation.

The volume, in fact, advanced controversial claims for the earl's authority. Its central conceit was to demonstrate that earls of Leicester had

FIGURE 4. William Bowyer's 1567 "Heroica Eulogia." On the left is an extract from a charter roll; on the right, a lavish image and poem in which King Richard II is portrayed as misled by evil clerics. The Huntington Library, San Marino, California, HM 160, f. 98v-99r.

traditionally held the position of Lord Steward; accordingly, Elizabeth should confer that appointment on the present earl. But this was only the largest of many claims that Leicester should be given privileges that had belonged to previous holders of this office and to the lords of his estates. For example, Bowyer accompanied the rendering of Leicester's arms with a transcription of the grant creating him as earl. As Bowyer explained, the words of the grant, "doo importe that the Royal Majestie understode that to the estate and earledome of Leicester belonged soome farder honore preemynences service and dignitie that which by theise worrdes and creation hir Matie mean to revive in the person of my Lord nowe Earl of Leicester."[36] These powers encompassed the feudal rights that had belonged to John of Gaunt and other of Leicester's putative predecessors. Similar explications of later grants, such as Henry III's to Simon Montfort, underlay the claim that "the saide Stuardshippe was in dignitie and preemynence united to the State and Erledome of Leicester."[37] Whereas there was precedent for these types of claims—for example, the Earl of Hereford had always been the Lord Constable—Bowyer elaborated further privileges of the previous lords of Leicester's properties which, he maintained, now belonged to the earl himself.[38]

Bowyer's spectacular manuscript enlarged the use of records. They continued to function as legal evidence. But their power derived only in part from their "authentic" dimension; instead they served as spectacular precedents whose integration into an extravagant humanistic and heraldic presentation reinforced their significance. Bowyer's was a brilliant pastiche of genres, in which records played a starring role as talismans, proofs, and treasures.

Although Bowyer did not produce such a massive genealogical treatise for Burghley, at the same time that he was working on Leicester's he composed a "Book of the King Supremacy over the clergy" with Burghley as intended recipient. As Bowyer outlined, this policy paper did not "avouch any thing oderwise then warranted and duely examyned by Record," and aimed to show "how happy the Kings of this Realme have become when they refused to deale with the Papacy. And contrarily what greate happs and mishappes ensued therein and this whole Realme when they received his power."[39] Bowyer also reported that he had delivered or was working on a series of texts using "decrees and orderes" to outline the powers of the king, Privy Council, Parliament, and Star Chamber. For Burghley, then, Bowyer did not produce a genealogy but instead turned the Tower records into a repository of evidence justifying the curtailment of papal authority and illuminating the rights and duties of offices.

Despite the differences in the volumes Bowyer produced for Leicester and Burghley, both mobilized records in the Tower to serve political ends. Bowyer did not draw attention to them out of an antiquarian love of the past but as part of a campaign to enhance his authority and to accession Chancery records. His provision of treatises to Winchester, Burghley, and Leicester, that is, were transactions intended to produce affinities with these powerful patrons. And because such records were the instruments that forged these alliances, Bowyer sought to elevate their authority as well.

* * *

Though Keepers of the Tower Records after Bowyer's tenure did not innovate nearly as aggressively as he had, their work ensured the records' continued usability and authority. This future had not been clear in the time immediately after Bowyer's death as Cordell, likely mindful of the headaches Bowyer had caused, tarried in naming a successor. Ultimately, the brothers Thomas and Michael Heneage were granted joint possession of the office 1576, and though they did not transform the space, they continued the project of archivization.[40]

The Heneages' work focused on bolstering the collection of reference texts. In 1572, before they had officially gained control of the position, they likely were behind an inventory that established the number of rolls, by type, for each reign.[41] They may have also been responsible for the "Rough Coat Books" (so called because of the hair left on the leather covers)—massive indexes to the Tower records organized alphabetically by place-name, after which followed a two- or three-line entry describing the particular business and naming the source roll.[42] In 1592 they produced "A note of the names of suche bookes and kalenders as are made of the Records in the Tower," which recorded the presence of about forty alphabetically organized calendars and individual indexes or catalogs of Tower materials.[43] Though many of these were Bowyer's, some had been made in the previous two decades during their tenure.

The Heneages' catalog of catalogs would have enabled clerks to devise multiple approaches to investigating the records. Similarly, when William Lambarde assumed the office after Michael Heneage's death in 1601, he itemized twenty para-archival volumes in the Tower, though his list notably excluded Bowyer's transcriptions of the rolls, which may have migrated into Robert Cotton's possession by this point.[44] Lambarde connected the office firmly to earlier generations of collectors—he had been a member of Parker's circle, though he did not acquire preferment until Thomas Egerton's ascent in the late 1580s. And upon receiving the keepership, Lambarde set to devising new guides. Within six months, he had composed his "Pandect of the Records in the Tower," an index cataloging the rolls by "the Severall Titles, Years, Numbers of the Roll." For each type of roll, this calendar listed the years in which such rolls had been produced and then gave the total number of them at the end. This list facilitated searching within and across record classes while also illuminating the relative prevalence of certain kinds of rolls. On July 31, 1601, a copy of the "Pandect" was ordered to be kept with the records.[45]

From the 1560s onward, in sum, there was a concerted effort within Elizabeth's government to tame the maelstrom of records in the Tower. These enterprises assumed several forms. First, Bowyer physically rearranged the archive, while also producing paper instruments that mapped this spatial organization. Such inventories were related to another essential form of archivization: the production of paper codices containing transcriptions of burdensome original rolls, which in effect converted the archive into paper for those more comfortable with the latter material. Finally, inventories, catalogs, and indexes were produced to help searchers find references within the reconfigured space of the archive.

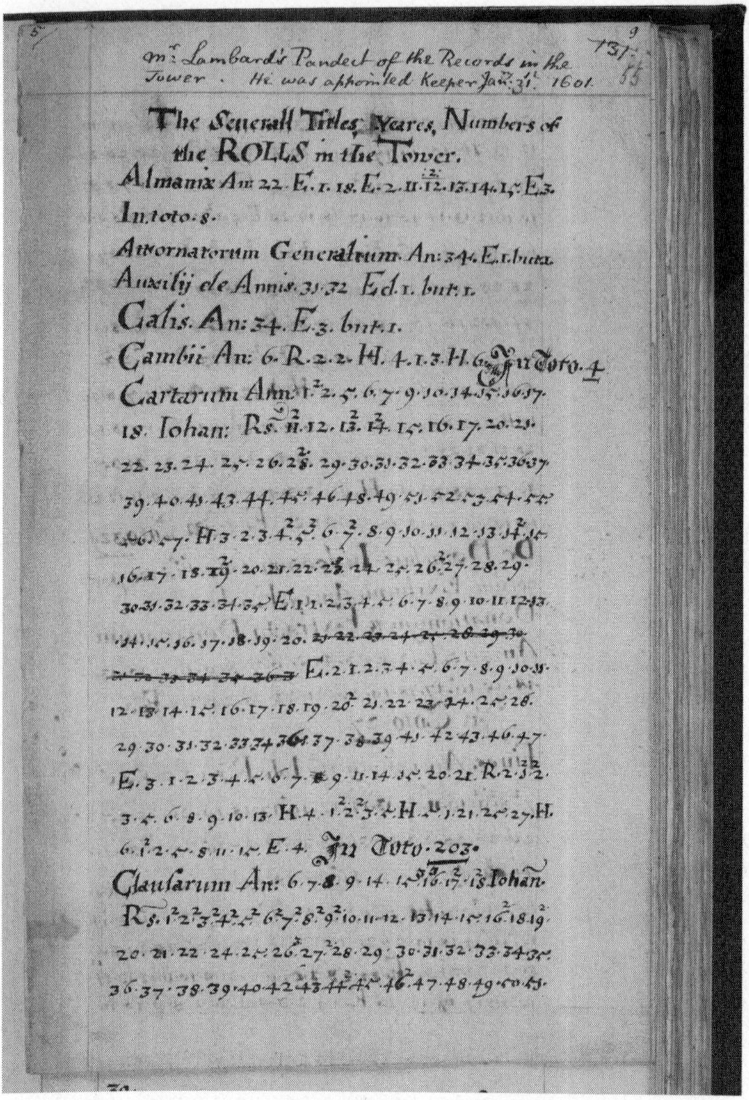

Mr. Lambard's Pandect of the Records in the Tower. He was appointed Keeper Jan. 31. 1601.

The Severall Titles, Yeares, Numbers of the ROLLS in the Tower.

Almanix An: 22. E. 1. 18. E. 2. 11. 12. 13. 14. 15. E. 3. In toto. 8.

Attornatorum Generalium. An: 34. E. 1. bun.

Auxilij de Annis. 31. 32 Ed. 1. but. 1.

Calis. An: 34. E. 3. but. 1.

Cambii An: 6. R. 2. 2. H. 4. 1. 3. H. 6. In toto. 4

FIGURE 5. William Lambarde's 1601 "Pandect." Lambarde organized this catalog by roll, alphabetically listing each type and then cataloging years in which they had been produced. For example, the first entry reveals that "Alemann" Rolls—concerning German lands—were produced in the twenty-second year of Edward I's reign, the eighteenth of Edward II's, and during the first five years of Edward III's—two in the first year and then one in each of the next four—making eight in total. BL Stowe MS 543, f. 55r. By permission of the British Library.

Cumulatively these practices transformed the Tower's clutter into a useable archive.

* * *

The enhanced accessibility of the records promoted their increased use well beyond Bowyer's texts. The earliest surviving register of consultation in the Tower extends from Easter term 1591 until Michaelmas 1596, and though mutilated, it affords some insight into its patterns of use. Above all, it reveals that the Tower was consulted far more regularly and for a wider array of legal, political, and historical ends than it had been prior to its renovation.

The primary purpose of this register was as an account book, and accordingly entries list the date, name of the searcher, and total cost of their visit, including the entrance fee, which regular visitors only paid once each term. Separate lists itemized the specific materials transcribed for some of the visitors.[46] The price of each visit varied depending on the request. Some visitors contented themselves with seeing the records and incurred no further expense. It cost eight pence to copy a sheet by oneself, while to have the clerk do it cost two shillings per sheet; exemplifications (official sealed copies on parchment) were considerably more expensive, though few visitors requested them.[47]

Traffic through the Tower fluctuated from year to year, but there were regularities. Trinity term (spring) was the busiest season, with typically more than 100 visits (including those who came repeatedly) bringing in roughly £80, and more than 140 visitors in 1595, when several voluminous requests brought the term's revenue to around £135. Hilary term (winter) typically brought in around 70 visits, which yielded between £50 and £60. Michaelmas term (autumn) varied more widely; in the plague years of 1592–93 it was particularly low—though the other terms held steady—but in 1594 it resembled Trinity and in 1595 Hilary. All told, the office could expect more than 200 visits a year, generating revenue of nearly £200, with about 90 percent of visitors requesting copies totaling roughly two thousand sheets of paper.

Since the register typically only listed the surnames of those who frequented the Tower, the majority are impossible to trace, but those who can be identified hint at rationales for using the Tower. Great magnates such as the earls of Derby, Rutland, Shrewsbury, and Northumberland or their agents were at least occasional visitors, and they often made sizable requests for copies. While these most frequently concerned deeds for their lands or the inquisitions post mortem of their ancestors, Derby made the largest request of the period when, in the late spring of 1591, he paid more than £10 for 177 sheets concerning military provisioning from the reign of Henry VI. These peers were joined by wealthy landowners such as Fulke Greville, Charles Cornwallis, and Henry Brooke, Lord Cobham, who occasionally sent messengers but more often themselves visited the Tower. The most frequent visitor was Edmund Neville de Latimer, who wrongly claimed title to Earl of Westmorland and who in these years was imprisoned in the Tower for his role in the Parry Plot. Neville de Latimer visited the record office several times a term, paying for copies of deeds, patents, and grants seeking to substantiate his claim to the earldom. Most of the unidentified visitors probably also went to the Tower seeking resources on questions of property and inheritance, as did the occasional delegations from towns—for example, "homines de Milton"—who likely came to resolve local disputes. The register thus suggests that most users of the newly accessibly records sought to use them much as Stafford had three decades earlier, and that they did so at a high volume.

The register did not record visits made by high Crown servants. But they clearly consulted the Tower records; Burghley, as noted earlier, made repeated use of the records, and he frequently sent Beale to the Tower. Such figures often used its resources distinctly from those concerned with property and title. Statesmen engaged in diplomatic negotiation were especially attuned to their importance, especially after the humiliation of John Rogers's 1577 embassy to Denmark highlighted the need for a comprehensive archive. His embassy was prompted by the Danish crown's claim that, by treaty, English merchants could not trade with Russia without Denmark's approval. He and both Heneages searched the Tower for treaties, with Rogers ultimately spending £12 on copies comprising 133 sheets but finding nothing to corroborate the Danish stance.[48] Upon arriving at the negotiations armed with this collection, however, Rogers was embarrassed by their ready presentation of three treaties, the earliest dating to the reign of Edward IV, which confirmed the prohibition. Fortunately, the Danes identified several treaties in Rogers's packet that they did not have and, rather than descend into acrimony, the parties exchanged exemplifications of misplaced treaties.[49] As this suggested, the Tower's collection and organization required improvement because they were critical to diplomatic maneuvering.

The lesson that treaties unearthed from the Tower could provide powerful leverage was learned and adapted quickly. As Elizabeth and her counselors debated how to respond to the Low Countries' rebellion against the Spanish crown in 1585, the Heneages provided notes for Vice-Chamberlain of the Household Christopher Hatton from fifteenth-century English treaties with the Low Countries. In the Heneages' interpretation, treaties from 1444, 1448, and 1495 articulated a strong justification for England's intervention on behalf of the Dutch rebels. The terms and language of these, they maintained, indicated the "King of Spayne holdeth the Low Countries not as an absolute prince or monarchy but as a vassall unto others namelie to the Empire," and could not therefore "dispose of them at his pleasure." These treaties were thus used to invert the claim that the Dutch were rebelling against their rightful prince; instead they substantiated a diplomatic account in which Spanish rule over the Low Countries was itself perverse. Moreover, the Heneages emphasized that the 1495 treaty between Henry VII and Phillip of Burgundy stated that "their heires and successors shall performe and observe all and everie the Articles of the said Treatye and shall minister iustice against them that shall do any thing to the contrary. Soe as hir Majestie and this Crowne stand not onely bound, to the king, but also the state of his Countrey."[50] This treaty, the Heneages maintained, obliged Elizabeth to intervene in the Low Countries against Spanish abuse in the name of the English and Spanish crowns themselves. Hatton in turn communicated these notes to Burghley, and they became central justifications for the war, especially through the pamphlet *Declaration of the Causes Moving the Queen of England to Give Aid to the Defence of the People Afflicted and Oppressed in the Low Countries*.[51] Less than a decade after the Danish embarrassment, the Tower records were used to establish the public grounds for intervention in the Low Countries.

The register also reveals that the renovated Tower records were frequently consulted by many associated with the short-lived Society of Antiquaries, including Arthur Agarde, Robert Cotton, Thomas Lake, Thomas Talbot, Francis Tate, and Robert Bowyer.[52] Such individuals integrated their Tower research within a broader documentary matrix including chronicles, cartularies, and other materials to produce brief tracts on the histories of the Lord Constable, duels, seals, and more.

The practices of Francis Thynne illuminate how such individuals produced histories by integrating the Tower records into a broader tissue of evidence.[53] Thynne was one of the most prolific members of the Society of Antiquaries—his discourses ranged from studies of the origins of the term "sterling" to the antiquity of shires and Inns of Court—and he also contributed to the second edition of *Holinshed's Chronicles* (1587).[54] He demonstrated impressive command of a wide array of sources, as his extant notebooks are larded with passages drawn from chronicles, cartularies, genealogies, and other medieval manuscripts that he or correspondents unearthed in abbeys, cathedrals, and churches.[55]

Thynne's expansive method underlay his 1597 volume celebrating Sir Thomas Egerton's promotion the previous year from Master of the

Rolls to Lord Chancellor, at a moment when Thynne was in search of a patron.[56] This volume resembled those that Bowyer produced for Winchester and Essex, for it integrated records and coats of arms into a customized volume designed to elicit support. But Thynne configured archival and humanist expertise differently. He began by detailing the history of lord chancellorship back to its origins, then presenting in chronological order the coats of arms of English Lord Chancellors starting with the Danish Earl Turketillus in 716. The concluding portion of the text, "The Collections of certeyn Recordes founde in the rooles of the Towre conceringe the Chauncelors and the tymes wherein they were invested with that office," transcribed charters and other formal materials produced from 1205 to 1597.[57]

References to Tower records suffused Thynne's tract—a sign of gratitude, assuring Egerton that Thynne had capitalized on the access to the records granted him. Thynne acknowledged that such documents could not illuminate the deepest history of Lord Chancellors, an office Thynne claimed originated with the ancient Hebrews, nor of England's pre–Norman Conquest chancellors.[58] As he moved forward in time, however, Thynne increasingly depended on Tower records. And as he introduced the records on which he relied, Thynne repeatedly elaborated their origins and use. For example, he explained:

> The auntientest records which I have seene mentyoninge anye such persone since the invasione of the Bastarde Williame, are certine recordes of the towre, called carte antiquae a name merelye gyven unto them, for beinge but lately founde and broughte to some order (by the carefull and paynfull diligence of that worthye gentlemanne Michael Hennage . . .) these recordes I say for that they are not for the most parte orderly sett in an especiall roole of that yere of the kinge as the charters of the succeeedinge kinges were, but are onlye certeine confused collections without distinction of the yeires.[59]

Through such passages, Thynne thus conveyed the history not only of the office but also of the records themselves, perhaps hoping to demonstrate his suitability for working among them.

From these materials, Thynne detailed the Lord Chancellor's rights and duties. For example, in outlining where past Chancellors had transacted business, he cited rolls from Edward II's reign that "your Lord shall see in manye recordes of the Towre mentyoninge the makinge of the Chauncelor, that when he had the seale delivered unto hym, he wente into Westminster Hall and (at the marbell table appointed to hym there fore) did use to seale and sytt amongest the clerkes of the Chauncery as the Chauncelors of olde tyme before were accustomed to doo."[60] This raised the question of whether the seal could be used when the Chancellor was absent, which Thynne in turn solved by recourse to other records. The records thus supported a fine-tuned image of the ancient practice and power of the Lord Chancellor, down to the accoutrements of the office.

Thynne's reliance on the Tower records to produce his histories reflects how the improved accessibility of the archive encouraged a host of uses, whether gravitating toward specific documents that might afford legal insight or political benefit, or integrating them with a broad array of materials to elicit granular histories of English institutions. But most striking is the sheer scale and diversity of use afforded by the attentions of Bowyer and subsequent keepers. By the 1590s the Tower was drawing in hundreds of visitors willing to pay enough to make its keepership a lucrative post, pumping hundreds of sheets of copies of records into the collections of noblemen, statesmen, lawyers, and scholars throughout the realm. Its materials were directed to multiple purposes: to political maneuvering as well as establishing diplomatic precedent, supplying authoritative sources for legal questions, and exploring historical questions. Far from the dilapidated storehouse Stafford and Bowyer had encountered three decades before, the Tower had become a vital space for intellectual and political work, exploited by high-level statesmen for resources to advance their political programs and by aspiring and midlevel administrators hoping to propel their careers forward.

Circles Virtuous and Vicious

While the intensifying reliance on paper drove many efforts to reorganize collections of older written materials, Elizabethan statesmen and administrators also sought to ensure that their own activities and observations were captured in inscription; the project of archivization was not limited to past records but was also a strategy directed at their present. As those seeking to advance within the regime highlighted their facility with these practices, they created a self-perpetuating cycle in which the production and management of paperwork was ever more essential to statecraft. In this context, archives became a laboratory for the production of political knowledge, one in which the archive mediated the horizons of what could be seen and known.

*　*　*

The Tower's pattern of archivization was not unique among government offices. Though the Chancery records Bowyer pursued were not delivered before his 1570 death, the Chancery itself implemented reforms shortly after.[61] While no extant evidence suggests a physical reorganization of their space comparable to that of the Tower, throughout the 1570s Lord Chancellor Nicholas Bacon—likely with Cordell's assistance—oversaw a massive program of indexing and cataloging to help navigate the Chancery's welter of paper and parchment.

Though many of the older Chancery records had been delivered to the Tower, the office reserved many of more recent vintage, and during the 1570s much effort was devoted to producing finding aids for these. For example, codex indexes of close rolls in the office were produced in the first decade of Elizabeth's reign. In these, each year was given its own alphabetical index, with multiple years in the same volume.[62] The lone note hinting when they were produced states that the index to Henry VIII's reign was completed in the tenth year of Elizabeth's reign.[63] Similar indexes to patent rolls were produced at roughly the same time.[64] In 1575, the first indexes of the Chancery decrees were produced, organized again in alphabetical order by year.[65] At roughly the same time an index to the Petty Bag Office—containing the most recent patent rolls—was completed, again according to the same structure.[66]

The material form of these finding aids represented their clearest point of overlap with Bowyer's, as the finding aids that medieval courts and chanceries occasionally produced to help work with rolls were themselves parchment rolls. For example, from the early fifteenth century, clerks had produced "Repertory Rolls" for the plea rolls. These were organized chronologically, with each entry giving the county, the names of the litigants, and the type of plea. They thus allowed a quick overview of the plea rolls but did not facilitate quick access to the original or cross-referencing. Under Elizabeth, however, the "Repertory Rolls" were inscribed as paper codices.[67] This shift heralded the broader usage of paper codex finding aids to ease in consulting material generated by the legal and political business of the realm. The vast majority were produced by unnamed clerks who reduced the materials clogging their offices into crisp, manageable volumes. Many today remain the most useful (or even only) finding aids for whole record classes in the National Archives; accordingly, they lie on the open reference shelves of the reading rooms—surely the only sixteenth-century manuscripts so easily handled in all of Britain.

The Chancery office's reforms thus organized past records while also introducing mechanisms to ensure the smooth recording, indexing, and preservation of ongoing business. Similar efforts were directed toward other offices; most strikingly, in 1578 Elizabeth chartered the State Paper Office to receive the papers of Secretaries of State.[68] While its first

Keepers struggled to accession materials because of the intransigence of secretaries and ambiguity of whether papers belonged to the office or to its holder, the formation of this archive reflected the ambition of consolidating and organizing secretarial paperwork.

Secretaries also devised instruments to order their own collections. Burghley's calendar of Walsingham's books was likely a copy of the "Table Book" that Walsingham ordered his secretariat to produce in 1585 as part of a program of outlining the locations and contents of his manuscript books.[69] He directed that papers should be divided by geographical location and that "the collectyons to be made for Ireland" should serve as a general model. In this arrangement, he first grouped together accounts of historical relations between Ireland and England, before collections of lists of "The Provinces, the Notable Ilandes, the Principall Ryvers, the Principall Noble men in eche province," and then categories such as revenue and religion.[70] The reorganization, along with the "Table Book," was likely completed by 1588.

While the "Table Book" suggests that Walsingham applied the same practices underlying many of Burghley's manuscript books, it also exhibits the range of materials that crossed the desk of Elizabethan statesmen. His Irish manuscripts are exemplary. At his residence in Barn Elms, Walsingham had seven bound books of manuscripts on Ireland, such as a "book of the Lord Deputies provinciall Journeis, Annis 1575 & 76" consisting of letters from Sir Henry Sidney, "a book of diverse orders gathered out of the counsel book of Ireland," and a book on "cesse and victualing."[71] In addition, at his study in London he had twenty-five bundles structured by political unit of business, such as a bundle of letters from the deputies and justices of Ireland between 1571 and 1585 and bundles from the Earl of Essex regarding the plantation of Ulster. At Whitehall he had nine similar bundles. Not all the documents Walsingham preserved fell neatly into his classification; his largest book was "A Book of Plots and Discourses," which, despite its title, contained items ranging from Irish reform tracts by Patrick Sherlock and Edmund Tremayne to letters from Nicholas Malby and orders for Irish governors.[72] The "Table Book" shows that Walsingham acquired and preserved an enormous volume of letters, memoranda, drafts, policy papers, financial records, journals, formal instructions, and more.

The size and range of Walsingham's collections reflects the increasing importance of paperwork to political practice. Such materials were essential to the operations of the Elizabethan regime, connecting those ensconced in the corridors of power to one another and those they sought to govern. And the proliferation of inscriptions, along with the emphasis on their collection, in turn provoked the production of tools to assert order over them, much as Bowyer's catalogs had in the Tower. Under such conditions, facility in managing paperwork and information more broadly became a practical necessity for governance and administration.

* * *

The scale of materials produced by the Elizabethan regime transformed the expertise her ministers prized, for navigating an environment brimming with paperwork required skill with such materials.[73] As a result, her secretaries devised means of inculcating desirable practices of inscription and textual management in their clients while generating new genres of texts and revaluing how they assessed various types of communication.

Shifts in how Elizabeth's secretaries approached information received from travelers abroad reveal the infiltration of archival practice into statecraft and administration. The most common materials that Elizabethan statesmen received from abroad were letters bearing news and spy reports, which flowed across their desks in huge quantities.[74] Increasingly from the 1570s, however, counselors' instructions to well-born clients requested methodical descriptions of foreign lands generated by precise instructions. Many travelers produced both these and newsletters, but synoptic overviews elaborating structural features of the polities they studied were understood to signal greater fitness for advancement.

In these instructions, patrons supplied travelers with detailed prescriptions for recording their observations, requesting exact lists of empirical features of the places they visited.[75] These accounts benefited their recipients by communicating their correspondents' experience. But their production also reflected skilled management of information; compiling them required the traveler not just to acquire and transmit news, but to compare, correlate, and organize information drawn from news reports, spies, observation, conversations, travel narratives, and histories. Their synopses reflected sophisticated practices of information management.

The first extant set of instructions from counselors in this vein dates from 1571, when Burghley penned a list to guide the journey through France of the young Edward Manners, 3rd Earl of Rutland. Burghley began by insisting that Manners maintain a record of his journey: "It is good that you make a booke of paper, wherin you may dayly or at the lest wekely insert, all thyngs occurrant to you in any place wher you shall come wor[th]y observation and memory."[76] Burghley did not leave these "thyngs occurrant" to Manners's discretion, instead directing Manners to record a precise list of features, such as fortifications, provincial noblemen, and the jurisdictions of courts. Above all, Manners was to note the personalities of the French royal family and court and the health of the royal coffers. Burghley thus prepared Manners to serve as a conduit for military and political information while augmenting the young nobleman's experience. Manners would remain Burghley's correspondent and, like many others who had implemented such prescriptions, he subsequently constructed his own networks to solicit reports from travelers abroad.[77]

Burghley equipped well-born travelers with similar guides throughout his career. In the early 1580s, he exacted a similar method of observation from his son Robert Cecil during the latter's travels to France that was more focused on France's commercial strength.[78] Other counselors provided similar directives. Philip Sidney's two letters to his brother Robert in 1579 during the latter's Continental tour demanded the production of similar notes.[79] Walsingham instructed a nephew preparing to travel to France to consider military matters, scrutinize the personalities of the counselors and marshals, and discern the allegiances of the gentry, insisting that "in all these aforesaid and what else soever may serve for your profit, you must observe this, to put down in writing what you have learned either by sight or conference, keeping as it were a diary of all your doings."[80]

These instructions held little in common with diplomatic instructions that directed ambassadors to speak on the monarch's behalf. Instead, they drew on models from abroad. One lay in the formal overviews, called *relazioni*, which Venetian ambassadors produced of the political, financial, military, and religious organization of the territory to which they had been posted. For three centuries, they had been charged with delivering these to the Senate upon returning home, and increasingly over the sixteenth century these missives were inscribed and circulated. For English counselors who collected them, *relazioni* provided templates for organizing information.[81] Elizabethan counselors also gradually became aware of the *artes apodemicae*, or arts of travel, that originally developed on the Continent in the 1560s among devotees of the French Calvinist Petrus Ramus.[82] Ramism was hotly debated in English universities from the late 1560s onward, and translations and original *artes* rolled off English presses beginning in the late 1570s. These works provided sprawling lists of phenomena for travelers to observe and record, while also encouraging travelers to supplement eyewitnessing by conversing with locals and reading histories.[83]

Producing a structural overview comparable to a *relazione* held distinct social value, as testified by the second of three letters of instruction traditionally described as from Essex or Francis Bacon to Roger Manners, 5th Earl of Rutland.[84] This letter enumerated dense lists of particulars to observe while traveling or reading histories. But it also carefully separated these observations' goal from standard newsletters':

> Your end must not be, like an Intelligencer, to spend all your time in fishing after the present news, humours, graces, or disgraces of the Court, which happily may change before you come home: but your Lordship's better and more constant ground will be to know the consanguinities, alliances, and estates of their princes, the proportion betwixt the nobility and magistracy, the constitution of the courts of justice, the state of their laws, as well for the making as for the execution thereof; how the sovereignty of the King infuseth itself into all acts and ordinances; how many ways they lay impositions and taxations, and gather revenues to the Crown; what be the liberties and servitude of all degrees; what discipline and preparation for wars; what inventions for increase of traffic at home, for multiplying their commodities, encouraging arts or manufactures of worth of any kind; also what good establishments to prevent the necessities and discontentments of the people, to cut off suits at law and quarrels, to suppress thieves and all disorders.[85]

News was fleeting; these reports provided comprehensive overviews of unchanging aspects of the lands visited by which incoming news might be assessed.

The first such synoptic view produced for English statesmen using this method was the "State of Germany," written by Beale likely in 1569.[86] Beale had spent the previous years in Paris and attached to embassies to German lands, and his newsletters to his patron John Hales were sometimes forwarded to Burghley. This work outlined the imperial provinces, then enumerated their secular and ecclesiastical leaders, laws of succession, noblemen, free cities, legal and conciliar institutions, royal household, military capacity, finances, commodities, relationship with subjects, and religion. This text, in fact, may have supplied a model for Burghley's instructions for Manners. It also likely helped instigate Beale's rise; he was appointed Walsingham's secretary in 1570, then Clerk of the Council in 1572, and carried out other responsibilities, even serving as interim Principal Secretary during Walsingham's absences until the early 1590s. Beale's collections, which were at the disposal of Walsingham and Burghley, contain dozens of *relazioni* received from correspondents throughout Europe.[87]

As diplomatic stresses intensified in the early 1580s, many Elizabethans began to collect *relazioni*. Francis Davison, Thomas Wilson, Charles Danvers, and Henry Wotton were among Elizabethan travelers who prepared for journeys by surveying *relazioni*, used them as models for their own reports, or collected them while abroad. These years were also marked by the surge in tracts like Beale's, often entitled "description," "state," or "view," which fused travel observation, travel accounts, and histories into empirical descriptions.[88] Large numbers of these circulated in manuscript, while printed examples included John Eliot's 1592 survey of France, Thomas Danett's 1593 description of the Low Countries, William Phiston's 1595 overview of Germany, Lewis Lewkenor's 1599 work on Italy, and six translated editions of Giovanni Botero's *Relationi Universali* between 1601 and 1616.[89]

Walsingham's personal secretary Nicholas Faunt's 1592 *Discourse touchinge the Office of principall Secretarie of Estate* illuminates how the duties of those at the center of the Elizabethan regime demanded both the knowledge embodied in such texts and the skills underlying their production.[90] Faunt recommended that the Principal Secretary rely on two clerks to organize correspondence for the Principal Secretary's attention. Pushing paper was their main task. Each morning, the home clerk should begin by "orderinge the papers" into "severall Bundells" at the Principal Secretary's desk according to subject matter and importance, then return throughout the day to remove those that had been dealt with to appropriate storage. The foreign clerk's tasks amplified those assigned to the home clerk. This clerk was charged with managing communications with ambassadors, foreign ministers, other English counselors, and "secrett intelligencers both strangers and others." This last group constituted the heart of his responsibilities. The clerk should "attend unto matters of intelligence Cyfers and secrett advertisementes to keep first in good order to extract the substance of them for the present use," determining the immediate importance of any communication. He further required that these missives be further filtered for future use, recommending "to see them well digested into small bookes if they be matteriall, and have anie refference either to thinges, past, present, or that bee likely to fall out in accion, as the most of that nature are."[91] Incoming correspondence was thus mined for information to create enduring descriptions of foreign locales in volumes such as those Burghley kept in Whitehall. Most strikingly, Faunt recommended collecting "discripcions most exactly taken of other Countries as well by mappes and Cardes as by discoveringe the present state of their government their alliances dependances etc."[92] He thus identified travel syntheses as essential instruments used by elite counselors to organize and assess incoming reports.

The practices underlying synthetic travel descriptions were paradigmatic for the clerks managing the dense plumes of information that swirled through the late Elizabethan regime, for extracting observations from foreign landscapes mirrored the ability to distill foreign correspondence. Both entailed filtering a morass of information, condensing the noise of news and rumors into lucid summaries that, like Burghley's books produced by this method, served as essential resources for Elizabeth's statesmen.[93] And as a result, preparation for such positions increasingly entailed expertise in information management.

* * *

Aspiring counselors saw themselves as performing political apprenticeships by applying the *artes apodemicae*.[94] The career of Stephen Powle, the son of Thomas Powle, senior Six Clerk under Elizabeth, exemplifies how an aspirant to Crown office might leverage travel inscription into experience and advancement.[95]

Powle was educated at Oxford and the Middle Temple before departing in 1579 for the Continent in the retinue of Sir Edward Stafford. He spent the next three years in Geneva, Basel, Strasbourg, and Paris, sending observations to his father and brother as well as potential patrons including Burghley and Walsingham. Powle's letters suggest that his father had given him initial guidance demanding observations according to precise categories: in 1580, after spending nine months in Geneva, he sent his father "The description of the Cittye of Geneva," elaborating the city's geographical situation, political institutions, social structure, and religion. Powle produced letters of travel observation more regularly the following year, likely reflecting time spent with Robert Sidney, as the two traveled together after meeting in Strasbourg in 1581, and one of Powle's notebooks contains a copy of Philip Sidney's letter regarding travel.[96] That June, Powle wrote to both his father and his older brother Thomas. His letter to his father began by articulating the precepts shaping his practices: "The only means to make the time bestowed in travaile moste profitable for his Countreys good . . . and most advantageous for his owne benefitt and advancement . . . is, heedefully to observe, and marke such things as he seeth; curiously to enquire after such things hee knoweth not; and studiously to peruse the worke of such learned men, whoe have imparted their knowledge to other by describing the Estates of all Common-Wealthes, as well modern, as ancient."[97] Reading, in fact, generated the majority of Powle's material; most of his evidence derived from Niccolò Machiavelli, Jean Bodin, Leo Africanus, and Francesco Guicciardini, with little originating in informants. Similarly, in his "Descriptio of Italy," which also reflected the disciplined travel observation he likely learned through Robert Sidney, Powle reminded his brother that he had not traveled to Italy and was transmitting things heard and read rather than seen; production of these volumes entailed working with texts.[98]

Powle's subsequent activities continued to reflect the dictates of learned travel observation and inscription; for example, he amassed a collection of *relazioni* starting in September 1581.[99] And his accumulated expertise paid dividends when, the following spring, he returned to England and entered Burghley's diplomatic service. In this role he sent regular newsletters while honing synthetic travel descriptions. In 1583 he was posted to Scotland, where in July he finished a more polished "Descriptio Italiae Modernae."[100] This anatomy had its intended effect, and in 1585 Powle was sent as Burghley's envoy to the court in Heidelberg, where he remained for more than a year, providing Burghley with regular newsletters.

Having parlayed his time with Burghley in Scotland into a position of more responsibility at a major Protestant court, Powle hoped that the reward for this service would be secure employment, and upon his return home, Powle wished to be appointed Clerk of the Council.[101] He was disappointed to discover that Elizabeth had already appointed someone else, but he continued to receive encouragement from Burghley and Walsingham. In early 1587 he was posted to Venice, finally receiving an opportunity to apply his Italian expertise. While in Venice, Powle made local contacts and organized a covert trip to Rome for the spy Stephen Rodwey, which uncovered a plot to assassinate the queen. Powle compiled their reports in newsletters sent to Walsingham, Burghley, and the news distributor John Chamberlain.

Powle knew, however, that newsletters were valued less than comprehensive overviews, and in November, he sent to Burghley an anatomy of the balance of power in Italy. In this, Powle described each principality, duchy, and city, explaining how each was disposed toward Elizabeth's government. At the end, he identified two competing alliances—one consisting of the pope, emperor, and others hostile to Elizabeth, the other of more favorable polities, such as Florence, that he described as honorable and virtuous.[102] Powle thus demonstrated his ability to collect information regarding foreign governments, compare his findings with histories, and synthesize the results into a structural description.

Burghley was delighted, and he wrote Powle a letter of gratitude that articulated the idealized value of the kinds of inscriptions Powle had devoted such time to producing:

I cannot but particularly acknowledge myself very heartily gladdened with a long letter written by you to me in the latter end of November; wherein you did at great length and in a good method anatomize the whole body of Italy, describing the conditions, the sympathies and jointures of all the states and potentates in such plain and probable manner as any discourser or inward counsellor of their countries were able to do. And truly for my satisfaction therein I could not find anything lacking to be required. And though I do frequently read the advices which commonly come from Italy and do take pleasure to see the motion of the world that cannot rest; yet the substance of your letter: containing the aspects (as the astronomers say) of every particular state one to the other either by conjunction of opposition, I do the easier judge of the probability of all other common advices which do many times so vary as without a common rule (for which your long discourse doth serve me) it were hard to determine amongst the advertisement what is true and not true.[103]

Burghley's compliments articulate how Powle's synthetic treatises provided an invaluable key with which to evaluate news and to formulate and assess potential counsels.

Powle likely provided this anatomy because he wished to be called home, and less than three weeks after receipt of Burghley's letter, Walsingham directed Powle to return. Powle's expectations of stable employment could only have been increased when he learned that he had been given a grant of arms in absentia that March. But he did not receive the preference that he desired and instead discovered that Burghley was dismayed by his return. In June he wrote to Burghley, explaining that Walsingham had orchestrated his recall, providing Burghley foreign intelligence, and petitioning for the office of Clerk of the Council that he had sought several years earlier.[104] In subsequent months, Powle continued to plead for such a post or, failing that, to serve abroad, emphasizing that some of his previous correspondence likely "as yet remaine on his (Burghley's) fyles."[105]

In the short term, Powle was frustrated; Burghley provided a small sum but no opportunities for service, and so Powle and his wife relocated to Essex, where he served as a justice of the peace. But he had demonstrated qualifications for office, and he ultimately was granted his father's positions. In 1596, he gained a deputy clerkship of the Crown, working alongside his aging father; in 1601, he inherited his father's clerkships, most importantly being appointed Six Clerk, one of the most lucrative offices—without particularly arduous labor—in the realm. In 1604 he was knighted by King James I. And Powle continued to rely on the instruments he had used to advance his career; in 1604 he reread the treatise on the Italian balance of power that had so pleased Burghley and the following year ordered William Shute to recopy the 1583 description of Italy.[106]

Moreover, sometime during James's reign, Powle penned "The mappe or public survey of A kingdome" in which, following his earlier practice, he demanded observation of the structural components of any realm, supplying examples from Bodin and Machiavelli drawn from the treatise he had written to his father two decades earlier.[107]

The value of Powle's extensive travel thus hinged on the inscriptions recorded as part of it—whether of the places he visited or those he read about while abroad. While his assiduous reading, observation of foreign lands, and management of notes and information networks did not instigate ascent as quickly as he would have liked, it impressed elite counselors and strengthened his claim to succeed his father. And when ensconced at the heart of the regime, he revived the methods developed during his apprenticeship. His expectations concerning his activities in foreign lands illuminate the practices enshrined by the Elizabethan regime and show how the inscription of political information and the value attached to its management were mutually reinforcing.

* * *

The rise of archivization stimulated a transformation in political knowledge, for Elizabethan counselors increasingly interpreted their worlds through their stockpiles of texts. Collections of inscriptions became lenses projecting the horizons of the world they saw. And like any lens, their collections had the capacity to magnify, minimize, obscure, and distort.

In 1578, Beale delivered to Christopher Hatton a manuscript treatise "Touching the Plotte for Irelande."[108] Hatton had recently joined Queen Elizabeth's inner circle, having been appointed Vice-Chamberlain of the Royal Household and a Privy Counsellor. That he solicited this text from Beale was understandable from one perspective, for Beale's expertise lay precisely in the ability to accrue knowledge about distant lands.[109] But whereas many authors of treatises purporting to rectify Ireland's perceived problems had spent time there as soldiers, judges, or administrators, Beale had not, and he instead developed his tract exclusively from his archive.[110] Beale's methods reveal how the practice of knowledge formation produced by inscription was also constrained by it.

The advice Beale produced was one of many treatises circulating throughout this period addressing the problems of Irish rebellion, poverty, and Catholicism.[111] His responded to tracts produced by Irish Privy Counsellors Nicholas White, Master of the Rolls in Ireland; John Chaloner, Secretary for Ireland; and Nicholas Malby, future president of Connaught; each inveighing against the Earl of Sussex's 1568 recommendation that "coign and livery"—a set of traditional Irish tributes and exactions—be gradually rooted out rather than aggressively abolished, which was again being considered.[112] Like White, Chaloner, and Malby, Beale was confident that introducing an English system of land tenure would increase the revenues of lords profiting from coign and livery while providing security to those whose lands and lives were often wrecked by it. Increased stability would demonstrate the benefits of English law and religion to the Irish and, he continued, obedience would surely follow in the same way as it had for the Welsh.

Beale consulted these texts through Walsingham's collections, where he obtained other Irish materials, including Tremayne's and Sherlock's reform tracts from the "Book of Plots and Discourses."[113] Beale also obtained extracts of Nowell's books via the herald Robert Glover. His collection of inscriptions became the primary lens through which Beale saw Ireland. But doing so meant that the archival object of Ireland he constructed was distinct from the place itself. And the reliance on copying and collection led to the perpetuation of materials even after disappearance of the conditions they described. For example, Beale collected an anachronistic list of "English countyes paing tribut to the Wilde Irishe yerly" devoid of dating information.[114] Similarly, some of the reform treatises he collected suggested measures that had been adopted, such as the establishment of presidencies in Munster and Connaught.[115]

The possibility for disjuncture between archive and world emerges most clearly in Beale's assessment of the military capacity of Irish lords. Beale collected several lists enumerating the towns and notable families in each Irish county, sometimes indicating whether the families were favorably disposed toward the Crown, as well as several documents supplying concrete numbers for Irish troops and armed capability.[116] His fullest reckoning of Ireland's military resources came from "A description of the Power of the Irishmen in Irland"—copied from Nowell—which enumerated the martial forces that Irish lords could muster, arranged by county. Beale carefully reproduced the numbers from his source. But the copy he made modified the text in several ways. For one, he stripped away claims made in the original that some forces, as from Wexford and Kilkenny, were "so environed with Irishmen that they cannot answere the kinges deputie;" and that others, such as the forces under Desmond and the Bourkes, were "so long & so environed & hateth the kinges lawes so as they give none ayde." Where his source reported that "these Irishmen hate the kinges lawes & subiectes mortally," Beale instead narrowed this hatred pointedly by changing "these Irishmen" to "the Irish Lords," strengthening the impression that the Irish, except for certain fearful lords, desired peace.[117] And he removed the final assessment that "God provides setting continuall dissension amongst them & mortall warre."[118] These shifts cumulatively changed the document from one that revealed the relative capacity of distinct factions to one that calculated Irish military potential as a whole under a coercive leadership. This makes it all the more striking that this document dated from the 1490s; Malby's estimation of Ulster's force in 1575 was more than double the size this older document reported.[119] Beale's tool for measuring Irish might may have been precise, but it was inaccurate.

While replicating materials throughout the realm aimed to ensure expert knowledge, the proliferation of texts mediated the world; the archive constructed what those who consulted it could know. And no less significant is that what Beale produced from his investigation was another policy paper. The goal was expertise, but the dynamic by which administrators hoped to achieve it endlessly multiplied the texts required for mastery through the media sphere of politics.

Conclusion

Shortly after his meeting with the queen, William Lambarde was struck down by the foul air in the Tower archive; as a friend later reported: "I have heard him after say for he was my good friend that the unwholsome ayer of the Recordes not well agreed and the paines he tooke in that unwholsome place brought him that sickness & consumption which made an end of him & he tooke it principally through his Nose into his Head."[120]

Not all observers agreed about the records' toxicity, and the vacant keepership was hotly contested until in 1604 Robert Bowyer, son of William, was chosen, along with Henry Elsynge.[121] Robert was not as active in the Tower as his father had been, but he did take an inventory of the records upon his appointment and worked to update the reference materials. Aided by his appointment as Clerk of the Parliaments in 1609, perhaps most strikingly, he enlarged his father's transcriptions of Parliament rolls by adding evidence of Parliaments which were attested in chronicles or records but which generated no evidence remaining in the Tower.[122] Bowyer's pattern of correcting his abstracts of the Tower records by other sources resemble how Thynne wove together his English past by integrating notes from the Tower records with evidence from multiple sources, reshaping it not as a probative repository but as one thread among a tangle of sources knitting together knowledge of the past.

The initial thrust to reduce the Tower records to order derived predominantly from William Bowyer's desire to strengthen the authority of his office. But once controlled, its contents were directed toward more expansive ends. As Bowyer's presentation volumes make clear, adept manipulation and presentation of those records established symbiosis between keeper, records, and patrons. Facilitating access to appropriate users instilled both him and them with authority. And by the abstracting Tower space into more navigable codices, Bowyer facilitated its records' replication throughout the realm, a process compounded in subsequent years as counselors, antiquaries, and researchers recorded and circulated their own notes. As such figures consulted the records, they dissolved, fragmented, and reconstituted them in other contexts. The continued cataloging and indexing further eased this task and made new analyses possible, and the Tower records grew ever more present in political and historical knowledge.

The same virtues and possibility drove the archivization of experience, streaming ever more texts through the studies of Elizabethan counselors. The generation, preservation, and circulation of texts increasingly dictated political practice, as figures such as Burghley and Walsingham pushed clients to develop expertise in sorting and sifting torrents of letters, policy papers, memoranda, and more into usable assemblages of texts. As such practices shaped the tools for comprehending the unending influx of information, the work of politics became that of collating, comparing, and contrasting texts.

The reliance on inscription did not just alter the resources of political practice but, by vesting authority in written descriptions rather than the phenomenon itself, conditioned the process of knowledge formation. This impact is illuminated in microcosm not only by how Beale's preference for archival sources resulted in his flawed estimation of Ireland's military power but also by the practices within the Tower itself, where the renovated space of the archive ultimately become subordinated to written inventories of it. On several occasions, starting by 1609 and until at least 1621, Robert Bowyer borrowed calendars of Tower records from Robert Cotton, which he copied to create newer versions of outworn versions.[123] But he did not simultaneously audit the rolls or otherwise inspect the space of the Tower. Rather, the calendars had come to represent its ideal organization and, accordingly, were used to reform the archive they purportedly described. Textual descriptions were not just reference guides to physical spaces; instead, they now both mediated and superseded them.

2

Pump and Circulation

Archivization and the textualization of politics transformed political practice in early modern Britain, as those both in and out of government eagerly pursued inscriptions whose possession they believed would enhance their authority and expertise. This demand afforded opportunities to those who mediated access to texts, but it also forced them to confront chaotic collections and to determine who could rightfully consult their materials. Accordingly, they devised measures to filter textual materials while simultaneously channeling them to potential users and controlling circulation. Their labor led to an environment deluged by inscription, in which those in positions of power found themselves swamped by the very instruments with which they sought to govern. Early Stuart England was a media sphere in which political practice depended on the possession of texts but in which the flood of material generated by relentless demand threatened to overwhelm its functioning.[1]

Pressures

Robert Bowyer does not seem to have relished his role as Keeper of the Tower Records. To be sure, he had gone to some lengths to acquire it, using the intercession of Master of the Rolls Edward Bruce to outmaneuver Peter Proby and gain a share of the position alongside his nephew-in-law Henry Elsynge.[2] But Bowyer was deluged by requests for copies and pleas for access in the first years of James I's reign in England. The stream of such appeals rose as the thirst for information reshaped early Stuart political culture. English counselors and administrators had absorbed the conviction that records were invaluable tools for producing knowledge, and Bowyer was the conduit to the Tower records. His activities provide a glimpse at a dynamic in which the perceived benefits of possessing records propelled a rapid swelling in the volume of inscribed materials, which in turn demanded mechanisms to dam and channel their flow. Deeply reliant on their habits of inscription, collection, and circulation, early modern Britons devised a host of techniques to confront new difficulties they faced and seize new opportunities glimpsed in the information tsunami they had conjured into existence.[3]

Bowyer was barraged by imperious demands from those he could not deny. Sometimes these were peremptory, as when in December 1609 Chief Justice of the Common Pleas Edward Coke demanded three copies of a list of bills from Henry VI's reign with only the terse directive, "Mr Bowyer I pray let me transcribe a copy of these. Your assured, Edward Coke."[4] If lacking the niceties of conventional letter writing, Coke had at least mandated a task of reasonable scope, as opposed to Attorney General Henry Hobart's request a week prior that Bowyer "cause present serch to be made and copyes of all the records concerning [the Mendip Hills] with as much speede as you can."[5] Worse, these sorts of simultaneously hurried, precise and capacious requests might embroil Bowyer in internecine feuds. Only a few weeks before, for example, Henry Howard, Earl of Northampton, had written to Bowyer in his capacity of Lord Warden of the Cinque Ports, explaining that specific "perticulars are desired to be proved out of record or other president" establishing that officers of the Ports were required to follow the Lord Warden's command. He also wished to know "what course hath bine taken for punishment of any such as should contemptiously stand out all processe and commissions of rebellion issued out of any the Court held by this Lord Warden or his Deputyes."[6]

At least in these cases Bowyer knew where to look and what was expected of him; other requests were maddeningly imprecise and full of inflated expectations, as when Solicitor General Francis Bacon wrote to him several weeks after these episodes that "I remember I borowed once of Mr Heneage a Collection of his (a large one) made of certen Records, especiall such as concern the Kings Prerogative and grants and ordynance and other matters of like nature. Of this I doubt not but you have copyes, and therefore my request to you is that you will lend me one of them for some tyme."[7] Similarly, a month later the Archbishop of Canterbury Richard Bancroft wrote to Bowyer, "You have a booke or two of your own Collection, and of your fathers which I would be glad to see, especially that concerning church causes," assuring Bowyer that he would return them at some point.[8] On the positive side, Bancroft's request represented a rapprochement of sorts, for the prior November he had coldly insisted on Bowyer's assistance, "Saving my quarrell, that you kept not promises with me, made unto me, when wee last spake together."[9] Bowyer, it appears, struggled to meet the pressures placed on him.

One can understand Bowyer's exasperation, faced with an unrelenting stream of haughty demands and forced to entertain the army of servants sent by elite counselors and officials to acquire copies that would strengthen their political ambitions. And they were joined by a persistent flow of visitors to the Tower willing to pay to gain entry and request searches for records, typically in the hope of clarifying ambiguities concerning property, finding legal precedents, or illuminating obscured genealogies. The strains on Bowyer became even stronger when he was appointed Clerk of the Parliaments in 1609, a promotion which recognized his contributions in acquiring and circulating texts for parliamentary business while a member of Parliament (MP) but which entailed additional responsibilities.[10]

Bowyer sought to fulfill the cascade of requests. But he pushed back when possible. For example, in December 1609 he explained to MP Richard Connock, who was conducting a search on behalf of the king, that "our callenders are old and almost wholly woorne," and that he had enlisted his clerks to make new copies of them. The office was in disarray while this work proceeded, he explained, so Connock should stay his servant and send Bowyer the list of desired records, which the Keeper would attend to when possible.[11] The material infrastructure of the office made access to these instruments possible, but it also required upkeep that Bowyer could use to control the pace of distribution.

Other demands Bowyer resisted more strenuously. In October 1611, the Catholic legal writer Ferdinando Pulton received a warrant to update his previous printed book of abstracts and calendars of statute. The envisioned volume, imagined as "The Statutes at Large," would "correct the printed booke by the recorde," provide the original Latin and French, include those statutes no longer in force, and equip them with an expanded commentary.[12] Because of Pulton's advanced age, he asked that Bowyer each morning deliver to a room he had rented a Parliament roll, to be returned each evening. Pulton also requested the waiving of all fees. Bowyer objected on several grounds. Ultimately the two took their argument to Robert Cotton for arbitration. Cotton, an MP and frequent adviser on historical precedent to many in the Jacobean regime, was an avid collector of manuscripts and, like Bowyer, earlier had been a member of the short-lived Society of Antiquaries.

As Bowyer explained to Cotton, the Keeper's oath prevented him from delivering the rolls in the suggested manner. He and Elsynge, Bowyer continued, had intended to publish a similar edition, and he insisted that they could read the records more assuredly than Pulton and his unknown servants might be able to. Moreover, Bowyer cautioned, he and Elsynge uniquely understood the degree to which the extant Parliament rolls were an inexact record of Parliaments, for "iniquitie of tyme and negligence" had led to imperfect recording and preservation. This was not merely an inconvenience; publishing the rolls would reveal to subjects that some statutes had not been recorded in the way they were currently understood and that others had originated in proclamations or ordinances. Consensus concerning the law would dissipate and, worse, he warned, "Yf the secreate be opened: then the dealing of our predecessors wilbe disputed and a question perhaps arrise what the king may doe by proclamation, and how the subiect may be bounde thereby."[13] The collection imagined by Pulton would not stabilize and broaden legal knowledge, Bowyer warned, but foment disorder by undermining it.

Bowyer insisted to Cotton that access must be steadfastly controlled as he sought to deny Pulton's request for open admission to the records. He continued by arguing that the frustration of the recent 1610 parliament had resulted from his predecessors' willingness to give access to the records, which allowed MPs time to produce evidentiary obstacles to political business. Leisurely scrutiny of the records, he maintained, had led to nitpicking by precedent, confounding essential political action. Bowyer contended that he and Elsynge were better equipped than Pulton to conceal the slippages between acts that enabled such quibbling, for mediating access was their job.

Cotton did not respond to the particulars of Bowyer's argument, and he ultimately determined that Pulton should proceed. But Cotton also ruled that, given the extent of the labor it would entail from the keepers, they should split the profits equally with Pulton.[14] And safeguards were devised in response to Bowyer's concerns that the law might be published too literally; in particular, Pulton should consult "the Judges of the Realme, and to the gentlemen of the fower Innes of Court" concerning "statutes which might seem dangerous."[15] Though Pulton accepted this increased oversight, the full task proved too onerous, and he excluded superfluous material such as royal pardons and the Latin originals of private legislation, which also decreased the book's price by eleven shillings.[16] Ultimately the volume was published in 1618, with an index and digest, and buttressed with references to ordinances, proclamations, registers, and other texts beyond the rolls to address the concerns of Bowyer, who was mentioned nowhere in it.[17]

This episode illuminates many dimensions of early Stuart archival culture. There was a sizable group who sought not only illumination but also profit and political advantage in political records, and accordingly they devised schemes to capitalize on their knowledge and access. Cotton is the best known of them, but there were many who acquired copies of letters and treatises, inventoried depositories, abridged lengthy collections, and amassed their gains in new collections that could seed new copying.[18] Their practices ensured that the materials in archives did not remain inert but instead circulated throughout the realm.

While such individuals perceived records as authoritative, they also recognized that many of these records encased ambiguities that could endanger the health of the Commonwealth instead of securing it, and thus they were suspicious of excessive circulation and unstructured access. But they operated under the conviction that a regime of inscription was an essential part of their political landscape, and accordingly they pursued their own copies while devising means to control and channel circulation.

In this way, inscription promoted inscription, with networks of communication further accelerating their production—a hydraulic machine made of social connections and technologies of inscription which ultimately buried early Stuart Britain under an avalanche of text. The rest of this chapter details the practices and ambitions constituent of this infrastructure and then outlines the frightening condition of information overload faced by statesmen graced with the mixed blessing of operating within the early Stuart information sphere.

Draws

The materials that Stuart statesmen and administrators collected emerged from a range of pathways, and understanding how inscriptions proliferated throughout the realm requires closer inspection of the engines and logics of circulation. Many of the documents that circulated were inherited from medieval governance, including warrants, charters, commissions, and other instruments produced in official capacity. While statesmen increasingly copied these, they also diligently preserved drafts that lacked official force or correspondence and notes that had been part of the process of composition, and they demonstrated a stronger appetite for saving correspondence and letters as well as policy papers, histories, and more. The entrenchment of practices that stimulated the production and copying of such evidence constituted the primary feature of a replication economy transforming the structural foundations of politics.[19]

Since the mid-1980s, scholars have paid attention to the role of print in circulating ideas throughout the early modern British polity and opening access to political ideas and participation. A "print explosion," in these accounts, delivered information and arguments to audiences previously blockaded from them and disconnected from realm-wide politics, thereby honing a new political awareness. Print was thus essential to the glimmerings of a democratizing public sphere which, if never fully free from government interference, nonetheless abetted the development of political consciousness in the British population.[20]

Recent work, building off other scholarship from the 1990s, however, has revealed the continued, and increased, vitality of manuscript circulation throughout the realm long after the advent and maturation of print.[21] Scribes produced dozens of copies of manuscript newsletters that traversed the realm, where they might be read in public spaces such as inns and taverns or be perused in private and then either discarded as they became obsolete or preserved in individuals' collections. Commercial workshops like that operated by Ralph Starkey circulated manuscript treatises arguing for particular political policies, lampoons of political or religious opponents, and scurrilous invective poems, fomenting in their readers engagement with the realm of politics no less robustly than did print.[22]

While many of the texts that circulated widely in manuscript resembled those that could be found in print—such as political pamphlets and sermons—some were primarily circulated in manuscript. These included news, libels, and verse, but perhaps most strikingly, early Stuart scribes such as Starkey published and disseminated letters and speeches from late Elizabethan and early Stuart figures—especially controversial figures such as Robert Devereux, 2nd Earl of Essex, Walter Ralegh, and Francis Bacon.[23] For example, copies of Ralegh's 240 surviving letters can be found in nearly two hundred distinct volumes—many of which contain several of them—and more than 100 copies of Ralegh's 1618 scaffold speech survive. To the extent that the replication of these texts can be dated, moreover, copying seems to have initially surged in the first decade of the 1600s, expanded in the 1610s, and increased after his 1618 death through the 1620s and 1630s. The same pattern holds for Essex, whose 1601 execution speech exists in more than 160 copies, many dating from decades later. These numbers are orders of magnitude larger than the quantities of copies of surviving material from earlier controversial Tudor luminaries such as Cardinal Thomas Wolsey, Thomas Cromwell, Thomas Cranmer, and Edmund Grindal, and they seem to have been collected both by those who saw the authors as political fellow travelers and by those who reviled them as agents of sedition. The surge of circulation at this moment increased the celebrity of those who lived in it, as the proliferating medium of paper expanded their social imprint and invested them with an unprecedented potency as political symbols. And through copying of such texts, ordinary Britons—regardless of their prior political engagement or feelings toward their authors—were brought into networks of political communication. These sorts of letters thus constituted some of the first media events in early modern Britain.

Such viral documents often traveled bundled together—or at least along the same channels—and accordingly are found together in collections with a consistent selection of other items such as texts concerning the debates on monopolies, letters by James's favorite Robert Carr, and scurrilous verses lampooning the Duke of Buckingham. They were often compiled into small miscellaneous codices, frequently interspersed among personal correspondence or family accounts. Such miscellanies themselves constituted small archives.[24] And these could in turn serve as sources for replication, allowing the texts to reverberate throughout early modern Britain and beyond.

Such texts appear in the archives of the elite along with more ordinary figures, and they supply exemplary evidence for how the technology of paper and the practice of copying facilitated the inflection of a circumscribed sphere of political communication to a broader audience. One dimension of the expansion of inscription was thus the reformation of Britain as a community entangled in text, a limited public sphere in which a real, if admittedly constrained, market for political evidence encouraged attention to texts that supplied foundational material upon which readers could erect their own beliefs.

* * *

Tracing the mechanics of copying records and the rationales of their collection provides a perspective on the economy of circulation distinct from that afforded by focusing on print publication or manuscript letters and treatises. It reveals a far more naked power dynamic in which those presiding over collections of texts functioned as brokers circulating texts as instruments to entrench existing power relations. The increase of inscription had effects that manifested beyond a new seemingly unruly public sphere; it also created conditions to reinforce long-standing hierarchies by transmitting instruments of authority to audiences invested in perpetuating and deepening them.

The surviving register of Tower searches for private business covering the period from Michaelmas term 1614 to Trinity term 1617 shared the same organization as the 1590s register discussed in chapter 1, but because it is in better condition, it more precisely reveals the routine labor, output, and clientele of the office.[25] The three years covered in the register describe a total of 620 visits by more than five hundred visitors, averaging just under one visitor per day it was open. These visits followed similar tempos over all three years—in Michaelmas and Hilary terms, the office received twelve to eighteen each month; the rest of the year between twenty and thirty. As with the 1590s register, the consultations initiated by high officials described at the beginning of this chapter were omitted, but if Bowyer's few surviving letters are any indication, these added another significant layer of labor. There was thus a steady stream of work.

These visitors placed consistent demands on the keepers and clerks. More than 60 percent of those who visited the Tower generated copies in one form or other, and their costs ranged from a single shilling to over £5. The fees in the register and those in the audit of records copied do not align perfectly, but the more thorough audit suggests that just over three hundred visitors in this period paid for roughly 6,750 pages of copies (slightly more than 20 pages per request); this list also omits roughly seventy visitors who also paid unknown amounts for copies. One might conjecture that on this account, the office generated almost 3,000 sheets a year, which would have been a significant increase over the numbers in the 1590s register. It also appears that the records drew in slightly more people in this time than in the earlier period, but that while a smaller percentage of them made copies, those who did on average requested larger collections. Overall, the fees recorded for seeking records, copying, and notarizing records during these three years was likely close to £650. Splitting over £200 a year between the cokeepers and clerks—not including what they received from Crown servants—would not have made it a wildly lucrative post, such as a Six Clerkship, but the money was on par with the Crown's midranking clerical positions.

The vast majority of paying visitors to the Tower records in these years again sought records concerning property and title. While it remains difficult to identify most individuals named in the account book, many appear to have been lawyers representing gentry clients. The impression that they were motivated by questions or suits concerning property rights is reinforced by the types of documents they sought; the majority of requested copies of patent rolls, from which they drew evidence of how individuals had gained title to land, reports of property sales, perambulations of forests, and more. Other common searches were for inquisitions postmortem and escheat rolls.

Further evidence for this property-based use of the Tower lies in the fact those recognizable figures on this list typically obtained copies concerning their estates rather than their offices. The Tower was used by a large number of Jacobean elites, including prominent statesmen such as Thomas Lake, Lord Treasurer Thomas Howard, future Lord Treasurer

James Ley, and Charles Howard, Earl of Effingham; clerics such as Edward Topsell and Bishop Francis Godwin; and Judge of the King's Bench George Crooke. Some dispatched agents, but many appeared in person. Their purposes for consultation, however, were nearly uniform, for the transcriptions they requested were keyed to property in counties where they were landowners. For Godwin this is particularly striking, as at the time he was revising and translating his Catalogue of the Bishops of London, serving as the bishop of Llandaff, and angling for promotion to the see of Hereford—all of which might have benefited from searches in the Tower. Yet his research exclusively concerned surveys, patents, and inquisitions in his home county of Buckinghamshire.[26]

The same can be said for the most lucrative customer of the Tower in this period: Thomas Wentworth, future Earl of Strafford. Wentworth had returned from a Continental tour in 1613, and after representing Yorkshire in the Addled Parliament the next year, he stayed in London and began to frequent the Tower to replicate records concerning estates in his home county. The following year he was made custos rotulorum for the West Riding of Yorkshire—many custodes rotulorum made use of the Tower records in these years—marking the beginning of the precocious twenty-two-year-old's public life. There were others who visited the Tower more than Wentworth—he paid the ten-shilling fee three times during the time frame covered by the register—but the clerks retrieved and delivered materials for him in eight of the twelve terms, for costs totaling almost £17.[27] For this, they sent him more than four hundred pages of transcriptions of inquisitions, licenses, surveys, pardons, patents, and more, virtually all concerning properties in York. That he was allowed to pay in arrears and that they sent him large packets suggests that, by dint of his status and credibility, over two years the clerks retrieved materials for him when time and opportunity allowed.

Wentworth's usage highlights one function of the Tower, which entailed using records to convert the past into a pattern for structuring the present. This practice enabled serious challenges to customary usages distinct from formal inscribed regulation, tightening the grip of those who could use access to its records to enhance their own power. Strikingly, Wentworth's reform efforts twenty years later in Ireland were predicated on using written records describing arrangements that had fall into abeyance to reorganize property and title.[28]

The ability of the records to facilitate encroachments on custom while ostensibly reinforcing historical precedent was maximized by the Examiner in the Court of Chancery Otho Nicholson.[29] Around 1600 Nicholson was given a patent to examine assarts—lands within royal forests that subjects had long cleared and cultivated in common—and in 1604, he was appointed commissioner for the sale of these lands. This role tasked him with scrutinizing medieval perambulations of forests, conducting visitations to determine where their boundaries had been violated, and determining what fines or rents were owed to the king. Bowyer proved an invaluable aid; for example, in late March 1609 he sent Nicholson eighteen items drawn from various roles in the reigns of Edward I, Edward II, Edward III, and Henry III on 96 sheets. Three weeks later he copied eighteen more items onto 113 sheets, and then two weeks after that another thirty-five items on 191 sheets. This help was not inexpensive, and though Nicholson at least once in 1607 was able to get the Exchequer to pay £17 to Bowyer directly, he explained two years later in a petition to the House of Lords that he "hath expended great summes of money in searching out Records advise of learned Counsell in surveying of the assarte in examyning of witnesses," to the total of over £28.[30]

The occasion for Nicholson's petition also highlights the social function of the circulation of the records. Equipped with these records, Nicholson ventured into the forests and surveyed the lands themselves. This process exposed swathes which had been cleared and used for tillage, and he then took depositions concerning the antiquity of these customary acts. But Nicholson's work proceeded upon the assumption that medieval records in the Tower held more authority than custom or common law. Around 1609, those whom Nicholson identified as illegally farming Crown lands complained to Parliament that many of them had received assurances from commissioners under Elizabeth that their activities were legal, citing "Equitie and Lawe Usage custome." Nicholson responded that without official patents granting them freehold—whether from the Crown, commissioners for the sale of royal lands, or justices of the forest—they lacked legal title and thus must pay, further introducing a system of "compositions" that legalized this farming of royal demesne at high rental prices. This action enraged the assarters. And worse, as they maintained in a livid petition to the House of Lords, Nicholson had inhibited discussion of these issues in front of the Crown, Privy Council, or Lords, and reneged on a promise to allow the issue to be adjudicated in Parliament even when the House of Commons reserved time for it. These actions, the petitioners maintained, "he hath so sowed well knowing the weakness of his case."[31] But despite their pleas, the commission continued until 1616.

Nicholson, in short, animated the inscriptions found in the Tower as prescriptive legal instruments, synthesizing them into an archival map of property ownership that constituted a social organization legally superior to custom. And he used the divergence between records and lived experience as a means to extract fines from individuals whose authority to farm the relevant lands had been justified by oral right and usage. While infuriating those who believed that custom protected their ancient privileges in farming royal forests, it was highly profitable. Though each individual assarter paid only a small amount, in 1609 Nicholson reported that the scheme had brought in more than £26,000, from which he took one-fifth and reimbursed expenses, resulting in a take-home sum in excess of £10,000, while more than £15,000 was directed to the royal coffers.[32] By the time the commission was terminated in 1616, it had brought in an additional £10,000.[33]

The keepers' role requires attention, too, for Bowyer and Elsynge effectively worked on commission and were collaborators with Nicholson. That they did not angle to drum up more business of this sort might have reflected more their saturation than any absence of entrepreneurial spirit. But their underlying ethos revolved around the profitability of circulating records. The entreaties of Stuart statesmen and administrators and the visits of London lawyers should be viewed in this way as well: as mutually beneficial exchanges designed to enrich the keepers and empower the recipients of these documents.

The aftermath of Peter Proby's unsuccessful bid for the keepership of the Tower records—of which he had been the deputy under William Lambarde—further lays bare the incentives built into the system of circulation.[34] After Bowyer was preferred to Proby, Sir Julius Caesar wrote to Proby suggesting that he could be appointed to a decent position if he could supply precedents—from the copies of Tower records Proby had compiled working under Lambarde—that would allow Caesar to increase his income or the authority of his offices. Proby miserably reported that though in his collection, "there is nothing that shews other particuler profyts or comand of the places your Honor now hathe," he promised to "send or bring his book of rolls before the next term."[35] In this case, no less than in Nicholson's, the possibilities of the records as instruments of authority and enrichment promoted venality.

Figures such as Bowyer and Wentworth thus mutually supported each other, as one party paid the other to substantiate a past that bolstered their own authority. The records were enlisted to mediate the past and the present, but they were valued because of the affinities they could create between the clerks who had custody of them and wealthy landowners and officeholders. The archive was not just a repository but a brokerage of instruments for the extension of authority, and the replication of paper throughout the realm testified to and reinforced existing hierarchies. While the paying customers to the Tower mostly consulted its records for questions of property, the inquiries Bowyer fielded suggested that Jacobean officeholders similarly exploited his materials to maximize the

[64] CHAPTER 2

purview and profitability of their positions. Pursuit of political, legal, and economic advantage was thus the primary form of suction pulling transcriptions and copies of records from their storehouses onto loose papers and into the manuscript miscellanies of early Stuart Britain.

Pumps

Sir Julius Caesar's envisioned transaction with Peter Proby illuminates another aspect of the forces propelling materials such as the Tower records throughout the realm. Caesar did not license Proby to scour the Tower for materials but rather asked Proby to search his notebooks—to treat his personal collection as an archive for the further replication of Tower materials. As this request suggests, each collection and text could be used to produce others. The copying or transcription of Tower records seeded unique archives such as Proby's or Wentworth's, and these, too, could germinate collections for users far from the original location. Each copy might inaugurate a new stemma of transmission, tributaries unpredictably winding records across the realm.

By James's reign, replication of Tower records no longer depended on the Record Office itself, for accelerating transcription created an information ecosystem in which Bowyer's account book incompletely captured the circulation of records originating in the Tower. Most significantly, Robert Cotton's collections were studded with volumes transcribing Tower records, and his library was likely at least an equally important engine for the circulation of records as the Tower itself.[36] This also suggests how Elizabethan practices of inscription unmoored the Tower's imprint from its physical space, for once copied, material in the Tower could emanate far and wide without the Keeper's awareness.

At some point—possibly during the period between Lambarde's 1601 death and the appointment of Bowyer and Elsynge in 1604—Cotton either took or copied calendars from the Tower along with many transcripts and abstracts of Tower records. Such items then entered Cotton's own system of exchange, and those who transcribed materials while in his library often created their own copies of such volumes. For example, he delivered calendars of Tower materials to prominent early Stuart figures including Henry Montagu, Earl of Manchester; Lord Keeper Thomas Coventry; Edward Coke, who was Attorney General at the time; and future Keeper of the Tower Records John Selden.[37]

Cotton also circulated Tower notes; for example in 1611, he recorded that James Ley—at the time Attorney of the Court of Wards—borrowed "All my Tower Notts in lose shetts" from the reign of John to the end of Edward IV, along with "10 Originall records of Ireland in parchment" and the controversial fourteenth-century *Modus tenendi parliamentum*."[38] As this suggests, transcriptions of Tower records—as well as calendars and notes from other repositories such as the Exchequer—were frequently included within the packages of texts he delivered to those in his massive network, which included nobles and high officeholders such as Bacon, Coke, Caesar, and Thomas Howard, Earl of Arundel; clerics such as Bancroft, Godwin, Ussher, and future Archbishop of Canterbury William Laud; historians and antiquaries such as William Camden, John Selden, Ben Jonson, John Speed, and Augustine Vincent; and officials characterized by archival expertise such as Thomas Wilson, Cotton's cousin John Borough, and Deputy Chamberlain of the Exchequer Arthur Agarde.[39] Though at least some of these figures also visited the Tower itself, they likely accessed his library as a surrogate for it. That Cotton's archive could function as a proxy is further reinforced by Selden's experience; though he was appointed Keeper of the Tower Records in 1643, his research into its records appears to have relied on Cotton's collections, and there is little evidence that he visited the Tower itself.[40]

Cotton's archive offered several advantages and few disadvantages compared with going to the Tower. While the Cotton collection could not produce exemplifications, the Tower account book suggest that these were little in demand during this period. On the other hand, Cotton's lending policies did not require the expense demanded by the Tower, and those he trusted also borrowed his books for lengthy periods. Knowing Cotton thus allowed access to a more convenient Tower of London. Of course, it was not possible to gain access to Cotton's collections for a fee the way that one could to the Tower; his list of borrowers likely all came with attestations of their credibility. The result was that though his network of correspondents might have been more eclectic—less dense with lawyers concerned with property disputes and with greater representation of those predominantly driven by antiquarian concerns—it could also be construed as more exclusive.

There were other advantages to Cotton's collection. His copies of records were a subset of a broader library containing chronicles, treaties, letters, treatises, discourses, cartularies, psalters, printed texts, histories, and other materials. Indeed, along with the calendars described above, Bowyer borrowed other volumes, including a copy of Ralegh's "Dialog about Parliament," the Red Book of the Exchequer, a collection of evidence on Lincolnshire lands, the Lollard tract *The Lanthorne of Light* in Old English, and a register of Deeds from Westminster that Cotton had received from Agarde.[41] Ralegh's "Prerogative of Parliaments" was one of the best-known sources to circulate in manuscript in such large quantities during this period (more than thirty copies survive). Its inclusion among materials sent to Bowyer suggests that although Cotton more frequently circulated Tower notes and antiquarian texts, he also disseminated recent policy papers, letters, and pamphlets of the sort churning through scribal news networks.[42] For example he lent to Arundel "A meditation of the state of England during the raigne of Queen Elizabeth by the lord Burghley," provided the recusants William Howard and Basil Brooke with "A letter of the Kyngs to Sir Thomas Parry about answering the Popes Nuntio," sent Elizabethan letters to Camden, and supplied "Speeches in the star chamber about my Lord of Essex" to Northampton.[43]

The morphological parallels between the networks of circulation centered on Cotton's collection and those that brought Elizabethan and early Stuart speeches into provincial manuscript miscellanies suggests that the nascent public sphere was not a distinct audience operating according to different mechanisms or logic from a concurrent sphere of interelite communication. Rather, both were formed by a honeycomb of networks and information infrastructure which projected printed pamphlets, verse libel, notes of legal records, medieval chronicles, and more throughout the realm. On this view, early modern Britain might be conceived as a pulsating hive of media communities lashed together by the transmission and preservation of inscriptions, some secreting outward into the peripheral cells where they intensified political involvement, others coagulating and deepening its inner core where the realm of governance became its own media sphere.

Filters and Conduits

Like Cotton, Deputy Chamberlain of the Exchequer Arthur Agarde was a specialist in circulating textual resources.[44] He perceived the records as the buttresses of the realm, and over his long career he conducted them from obscurity to visibility for the advantage of the realm's counselors and statesmen. But his role in mobilizing arcane records required strategies distinct from Cotton's, as Agarde's career was devoted to confronting Exchequer records that were moldering, disorganized, and mystified by neglect and time. Whereas his resuscitation of these records resembled Bowyer's, Exchequer records presented a different challenge from the Tower's, as they were dispersed across multiple spaces and denser with notoriously impenetrable items such as assize court and Parliament pleadings.[45] The techniques he used to manage chaotic collections strewn across England's scattered documentary landscape exemplify the basic methods devised to help navigate the flood of texts he and his contemporaries eagerly stimulated.

Agarde's expertise resulted from his longevity in the Exchequer; he was appointed a Deputy Chamberlain around 1570 and served in this capacity until his death in 1615. Few records of his activities exist from his early years, though he likely performed standard tasks of recording income and payments, fulfilling inquiries, and certifying documents.[46] But he was not exclusively a functionary; he also had started obtaining copies of older material, and the networks abetting his practices reveal how such methods were nurtured by a wider intellectual culture that valued omnivorous collection.[47]

In the last years of Elizabeth's reign, Agarde's practices of collection seems to have been keyed to historical investigations undertaken for the Society of Antiquaries. Agarde's investigations for this group addressed an unequaled range of questions, including essays on the antiquity of shires and forests; the etymology and dimensions of England; the histories and privileges of the Heralds, of the Inns of Court, Inns of Chancery; of the Lord Constable, Steward, and Earl Marshall and Baronage of England; of the usage of trial by combat, and of the antiquity of Christianity in England; and the history of Parliament. His essays frequently cited documents squirreled away in the Exchequer as well as grants and confirmations of monastic houses that had been scattered into private hands by the Dissolution of the Monasteries. Indeed, they predominantly constitute catalogs of extracts pulled from these sources, assembled in chronological order, with little editorializing or argumentation.

Assembling such evidence required the voracious acquisition and copying of sources by Agarde and others. Such collaboration was essential when, for example, he collected extracts from "a Register of the Abbey of Osney" and other documents into notebooks between 1592 and 1614; in May 1599, for instance, Agarde and Richard Knight authenticated and transcribed a copy of an "ancient register" containing "certeyne old charters concerning Stowe & Didford, from a Register of the Abbey of Osney" in the possession of a "Mr Jeffs" in Buckinghamshire.[48]

Agarde's notes concerning Osney were likely dictated less by a specific question than the desire to consolidate fragmented sources that might prove useful to future inquiries. For example, six weeks before James's coronation as king of England, Agarde and eight other members of the Society of Antiquaries produced discourses investigating the history and authority of the Lord High Steward, likely because one would be needed for the coronation. To do so, Agarde consulted his Osney collection, invoking, for example, "a fine then levied, which I copied out of the ledger book of Osney" to confirm "the words of the Red and Black books" of the Exchequer.[49] This essay further fleshed out the history of the office using such sources as the Domesday Book, a charter from Edward the

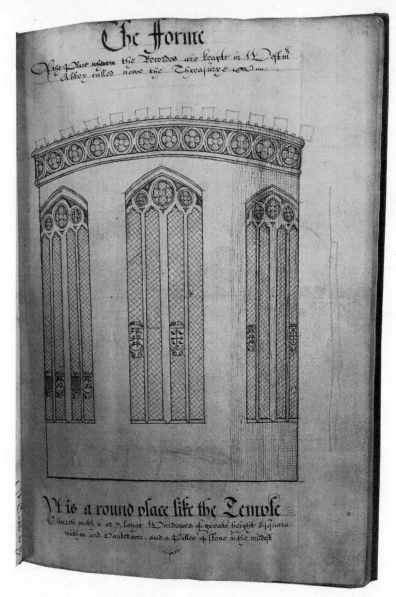

FIGURE 6. Image of the Chapter House in Westminster Abbey, which housed many Exchequer records, drawn by an unknown visitor who consulted its records between 1606 and 1611. The volume containing the image consists mostly of extracts made during such consultations, which the anonymous compiler noted had been witnessed by Deputy Chamberlain of the Exchequer Arthur Agarde. He also commended Agarde for abridging many records and making tables of them according to "sheires, yeares, & terms, a methode verie easie and ready for any mann to finde the Recorde, and his Booke, without searchinge the Recorde will shewe the substance of the Whole Recorde, which much easeth the search." The Bodleian Libraries, University of Oxford, Rawlinson MS C 704, f. iiir (image); ivr (quote).

Confessor's time, and Henry Knighton's chronicle of Leicester Abbey. As this suggests, Agarde did not accumulate sources with predesigned ends in mind but turned to them as evidence when occasion arose.

After the society's demise, Agarde largely ceased producing such essays. But he was never short for work, as in the first decade of James I's reign Robert Cecil and other counselors often relied on his archival acumen. For example, in 1600, Cecil dispatched Agarde to Arthur Throckmorton, son of the Elizabethan diplomat Nicholas, to retrieve "meete matter . . . which maye nowe serve to purpose, for the precedency between England and Spaine."[50] Indeed, producing inventories of obscure documents was one of his most valued skills. In 1610, he along with Cotton, St. Loe Knyveton, and Francis Tate received an unusual warrant from Caesar (then working under Cecil as Chancellor of the Exchequer): according to "sondry ancient records" found in the Exchequer, many documents in previous years had been delivered to the royal wardrobe, and this group was now entrusted to catalog and return these materials from this accidental archive.[51] Combing this chamber turned up 350 letters, exemplifications, commissions, treaties domestic and foreign, confirmations, patents, charters, and more from Edward I to Elizabeth I.[52] Similarly, for the Archbishop of Canterbury, Agarde calendared a hodgepodge of Henrician materials—likely once held by Thomas Cromwell—slopped within a press in the New Treasury in the New Palace.[53]

The texts Agarde produced during these investigations exhibited his patience and discipline in cataloging disorderly collections. But in addition to creating registers, he often created calendars consolidating summaries of dispersed sources into individual volumes. This task generated its own problems of order and organization. He confronted this challenge by paying careful attention to the layout of pages and creating paratexts, hoping to not only consolidate scattered and illegible records but also design his volumes to facilitate their use.

Agarde's compilation of the records of the courts of King's Bench and Common Pleas during the reign of Edward I illuminates some of the problems that arose when using notebooks to compact multiple archives. The cases abridged in this volume predated those in the law reports that had been published for over a century—most notably by Edmund Plowden and Anthony Fitzherbert—which began with cases from the reign of Edward III. Agarde engaged this project likely in the 1580s and pursued it for more than twenty years, delivering a copy of it after 1610 to the Lord Chief Justice with the intention that that "he may examine the same with the yeare booke."[54] The challenge this volume posed was considerable. The records generated at quarter sessions had been arbitrarily preserved and maintained, and they were dispersed across a bewildering variety of sites. Throughout the volume he noted how he had come into possession of the materials he abridged, for example recording that "I excerpted this from the manuscript book of Statutes of Mr [Edward] Grimston of Grays Inn in 1590. And confirmed it through a Register from Coventry 1595."[55] He also recorded searching registers in the Tower, various Westminster locations, cathedrals and churches in Essex, Ely, Norfolk, Oxford, and other repositories. These notes served both to verify the records and as memorials indicating how to reconsult them if necessary. Occasionally he made notes of searches he hoped to conduct—for example, reminding himself after transcribing a pleading from Burgh Castle to "seek the book which is called Swatham in Peterborough."[56] Inside the back cover he listed the materials he had consulted.

When he obtained new sources, Agarde sometimes entered notes from them next to related passages already in his notebooks, but more frequently he simply entered notes where he had left off writing previously—in part because he did not know how the extracts would prove useful in the future. The result of this was a dense, forbidding bricolage of text, lacking chronological, thematic, or geographical order, that required its own range of strategies for navigation. Accordingly, he used page layouts and rubrication to distinguish headings, themes, place-names, and other elements of the text.[57] He also created paratextual items such as indexes and tables of contents to enable efficient scrolling. For example, he equipped a collection of notes from a dozen assize and eyre rolls records from Henry IV to Henry V that he produced around 1606 with a calendar of the contents, an index of county and town names, and a separate thematic index with entries such as duels, magic, violence toward servants, sewers, and outlaws.[58]

The same repertoire of aids was more prominent in Agarde's collection of extracts concerning pleadings in Parliament under Edward I and II that he produced predominantly by consulting rolls in the Chapter House at Westminster Abbey.[59] In this volume, he relied heavily on orthographical modifications to distinguish basic identifying material from the entries themselves, which were written in black ink. On a typical page, he rubricated the relevant year in the left corner with the regnal year centered next to it; underneath he inscribed in larger lettering and with wider margins the title of the roll—again in red—and then its number within the full series of rolls. He also rubricated the name of relevant place-names in the external margins and themes such as "mortmain" or "foreign merchants" (*mercatores extranaei*) in the internal margin. These spatial and chromatic contrasts allowed more effective skimming.[60] And he again produced finding aids and indexes

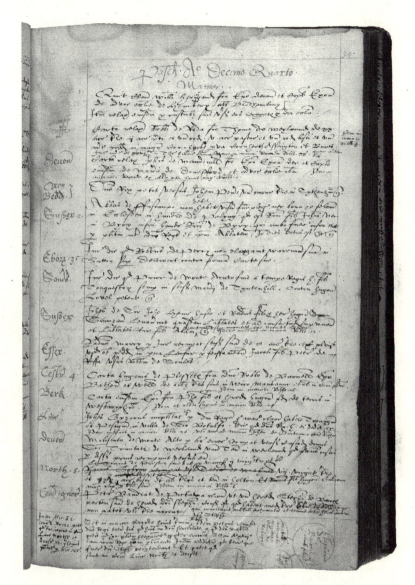

FIGURE 7. Arthur Agarde's notes on King's Bench and Common Pleas proceedings. Agarde additions, excisions, and crosswise notes at the bottom of the page show strategies for incorporating new material into his already packed text. The Huntington Library, San Marino, California, EL 34/C/4, f. 34r.

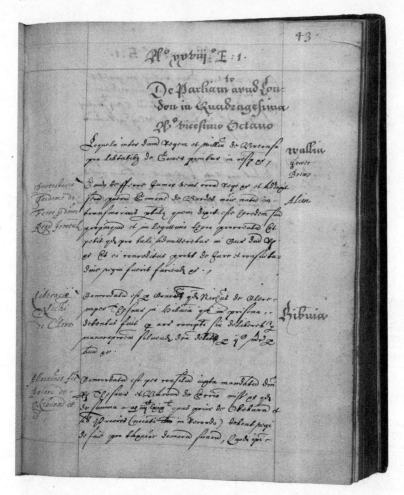

FIGURE 8. Arthur Agarde's notes on records of Parliamentary Pleadings. Agarde's use of headers, marginal notes, and rubrication were designed to give order to the barrage of notes he collected. The Huntington Library, San Marino, California, EL 35/C/36, f. 43r.

for the volume, such as an alphabetical index of town names by county keyed to page numbers.

These volumes reveal Agarde's primary practices for confronting inventories of materials drawn from multiple sources or archives: he channeled extracts from dispersed and impenetrable texts into notebooks, designed layouts such that enabled swift recognition of basic features of the passages, and introduced paratextual tools that allowed readers to move swiftly between material according to various logics. These methods turned his notebooks into centralized reservoirs of dispersed archives, which could be drawn on for those seeking to navigate England's documentary bedlam, either by using the volume's extracts or by returning to his sources.

* * *

Agarde's most ambitious project was an inventory of the records in the Exchequer archives commissioned by Robert Cecil and completed in December 1610. This volume presents in microcosm the particularities of the challenges Agarde faced, the practices he devised in response, and the envisioned audience for his products.[61]

Cecil hoped to capitalize on Agarde's grasp of the maelstrom of materials strewn throughout the Exchequer's storage spaces in Westminster. These spaces included rooms in the treasury of the Court of Receipt over the New Palace, the nearby "gatehouse treasury," the Chapter House in Westminster Abbey, and the Pyx Chamber in the Cloister of the Abbey. These had never been narrowly restricted to financial records and stored many kinds of materials; for example, the Pyx Chamber, originally intended to store sample specie that was tested to ensure that the coinage was pure, had become the de facto depository for official copies of treaties. Across the Treasury's four archival spaces, organization had been haphazard, and the materials in each lacked any underlying logic, either in their distribution across or arrangement within each space. Agarde's years of sleuthing through the bags, cabinets, and shelves strewn across these rooms gave him an unrivaled sense of their contents and the ability to quickly deliver large quantities of desired materials.[62] His searches had also turned up lost materials, such as the official copy of Thomas Cranmer's renunciation of papal authority.[63]

Agarde's 1610 collection for Cecil constituted a mammoth, thorough inventory. He fashioned this catalog into a presentation volume, prefaced with an exaltation of the value of the records and the virtuous kings who had overseen their production and care. As he gushed, "Howe Carefull and provident our former princes of this realme and such like as have had the manageing of the states under them have bene for the preservacion of records as monument of antiquities, Oracles of truth and tyme, Principles of our lawes and Customes: A whole world of woorthie witness of former Judgments, decrees, & ordinances: The best decyders of debates: and decipherers of titles, will well appeare by that which followeth in this book."[64] The records here he portrayed as unimpeachable authorities and as models of English governance.

Despite this lofty power, Agarde maintained, the records had been treated with disdain, and he had found those "which concerned the kings prerogative and decydeing of titles betwixt the Soveraigne and subiect, and between the subiect themselves," in disastrous unkemptness.[65] As he explained, "In this laborious search I found a huge and neglected chaos of most statelie records, Arcana Imperii concerninge in highest nature the kings & this Common wealth of all others: Al Treaties of Peace & Concord with forraine Nations, but lieng so confusedlie together full of foulness and mildew, corroded by rats and mice [*Squalore et rubigine plena, muribus & soricibus corrosa*], wet with wether, stuffed together nation with nation the seales broke and rent, and the worst of all, subiect by fier (which God forbid) to be utterlie ruyned, that it grieved me not a little to behold this pitifull (or as I might tearme it) dissolucion of so woorthie memorials."[66] Knowledge of the sovereign past had been shattered by contempt for its material representatives.

Agarde's preface consciously evoked the Dissolution of the Monasteries, which had wreaked confusion by dispersing manuscripts of untold importance throughout the realm. The dissolution Agarde sought to counter, however, he described not as a by-product of the Reformation but instead as a senseless consequence of preventable neglect. Accordingly, he enumerated the best ways to stave off the ordinary dangers to the records. To avoid fire, records should be kept in safe vaults where the use of candles should be limited; to minimize water damage, Exchequer officers should make sure to take a careful inspection of the spaces "after a great flutt of raine, snowe or tempest." Vermin posed a problem that attentiveness alone could not solve. As he put it, the "remeadie against Rattes, Myce, Weesells &c the best way is to put the Recordes in Boxes, Chests, and stronge presses: And surelie I find that manie goodlie Notable Records have bene spoiled with that kinde of vermyn by gnawinge yea and as evell that by pissing upon them."[67] A stable architecture for the records would also help against the last danger of "misplaceing ... an enemye to all good order and bringer in of all horror and inconvenience amongst Records," as it would make it easier for the keeper to return documents to their intended locations.[68]

The greatest danger, however, was the combination of interest and carelessness of the Crown's officers. As Agarde explained, these repositories hemorrhaged records "when one Pryvy Counsellor or moe, Iustices or anie of the Kinges learned Counsell direct a warrant to the officers to bring to them leagues bookes or other Records and then the same must be left with them. Although thofficer comme to them for them demaund them never so oft yet shall he seldome or never gett them out of their hands. As by experience I have found."[69] Those who recognized the value of these materials were the prime agents of dissolution, for they scattered records into offices where they did not belong, disrupting the integrity of holdings and impairing the collection's ability to serve the exalted purpose Agarde outlined for it. Disorder was predicated on use; the functioning archive was its own worst enemy.

Agarde's catalog worked to counteract the damage incurred by usage. Above all, it provided a detailed reckoning of the records in the four Westminster archives, and thus established where they belonged. But by simply inventorying the spaces, the catalog also narrated the chaos Agarde confronted as simply endemic to England's documentary patrimony. For example, he recorded that in the Court of Receipt, the Domesday Book was surrounded by a diverse array of records, including "a patent roll of Edward 2 tyme," "a bagg of Canvass of speciall Recordes abbreveated in a sheete of paper in the bagg," "the auncient keyes of the Threasuries of Leagues in the Cloyster of Westminster Abbey," and "sundrie bagges of the foiles of Sheriffs baylifs Tallyes, which by default of order of the Pype were nevre Joyned." These records shared neither chronological, geographical, thematic, nor bureaucratic continuity, though some were among the most used items by Exchequer officials. And his register did not impose an overarching order on these collections; instead, he described the records according to where they lay before specifying the contents of bags, boxes, drawers, and rooms. For example, following his description of the mess surrounding the Domesday Book, he noted, "there is a little room adioyning to the same Court wherein are three chests in which are records placed," and then listed their bewildering array of contents: pleas from Edward I's reign, a parchment book of extracts from the Domesday Book joined to a collection of papal bulls; bags of rolls concerning forests.[70]

Unlike William Bowyer's project, which had simultaneously inventoried and rearranged the space of the archive, Agarde aspired to enhance searchers' ability to navigate the archive as it stood. But he adopted Bowyer's approach for one component of his project—the reorganization of the many treaties scattered throughout Exchequer repositories. With the help of George Austen, Robert Cotton, and Walter Cope, Agarde noted that he had "gathered out of sondry Corners of the Threasuries diverse leagues misplaced & lieng unknowne," and then "destinguished every Country with whome our Princes and nation have had comerce and Traffique." He then "indorsed upon every treatie the chefe effect thereof, In what kings tyme, with the yeres of his raigne, the days of the month,. & the yere of the Lord." The treaties were then organized chronologically and placed into boxes or bags, labeled by treaty partner and year. As he further explained, Agarde and Austen then "conveyed these baggs & boxes into a Treasury in Thabbey of Westminster . . . and have placed them in Chests and marked the contents thereof," occupying much of the Cloister archive, where they came to rest as an orderly archive of fifteen bags and two boxes for foreign treaties. They subsequently calendared the contents of the collection while deputizing George Moore to help them list the buckram bags, boxes, and shelves containing treaties with the Scots.

The catalog Agarde produced from his audit of Exchequer archives also adopted many of his ordinary practices of inventorying. In the sections describing records strewn about the archives, he rubricated running headers that noted the types of records listed on the page. To ease consultation of the descriptions of the treaties, he arranged them first by treaty partner and then chronologically. The names of the treaty partners were rubricated as headers as well, as were temporal indications such as the regnal year and, in the margins, the year of their consecration. He also included a chart at the end providing a synopsis of the full list of treaties. Throughout the volume he left ample blank space to ease legibility and skimming.

Agarde expressed the hope that "for manie ages after There shall not need anie further paines to be taken eyther for their preservacion of their readie findeing when they shalbe called for by the Kinge of his Counsayle as in this book and the Kalender therof may plainely appeare. Which I have registered into a book of Parchment remaineing in his Majesties Treasury to be kept there needfull for the officers direction when they shalbe comaunded to produce the same."[71] The catalog, that is, was not primarily concerned with settling and fixing the contents of the archive; rather he envisioned it as an instrument abetting consultation of spaces that remained chaotic. And in this aspect, as in those of its process and design, it exemplified Agarde's practices, which strove to use manuscript codices as guides consolidating the contents of archives that had been fragmented and dispersed throughout the realm or were rendered opaque by disorganization.

The catalog fulfilled Agarde's aspirations, as in subsequent years a copy of it in the Court of Receipt offices—though not the parchment version—was used to record new accessions and borrowings from the collection.[72] In 1612, for example, treaties found in the Court of Receipt and inherited from the deceased Lord Treasurer Thomas Sackville, Earl of Dorset, were added, and later custodians would note when documents had been removed and recovered and changes to the boxes and bags' physical appearance.[73] Into the 1620s, Keeper of the State Papers Thomas Wilson and Secretaries of State George Calvert, Robert Naunton, and others recorded when they had taken and returned treaties from the Chapter House.[74]

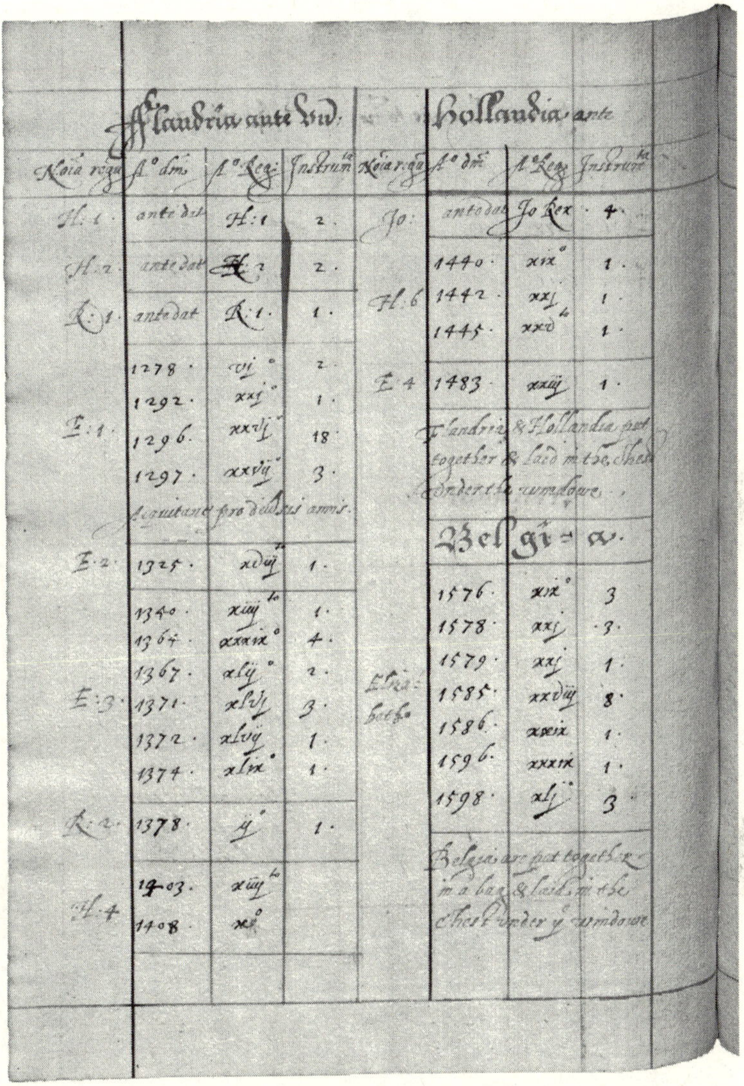

Flandria ante Vn. | Hollandia ante

Noia regum	Ao dni	Ao Reg	Instrumta
H:1	ante dat	H:1	2
H:2	ante dat	H:2	2
R:1	ante dat	R:1	1
E:1	1278	vi°	2
	1292	xxj°	1
	1296	xxvj	18
	1297	xxvij	3
Acquitanc pro diversis annis			
E:2	1325	xviij	1
E:3	1340	xiiij	1
	1364	xxxix°	4
	1367	xlij°	2
	1371	xlvj	3
	1372	xlvij	1
	1374	xlix°	1
R:2	1378	ij°	1
H:4	1403	xiiij	
	1408	ix°	

Noia regum	Ao dni	Ao Reg	Instrumta
Jo	ante dat	Jo Rex	4
H:6	1440	xix°	1
	1442	xxj	1
	1445	xxiij	1
E:4	1483	xxiij	1
Flandria & Hollandia put together & laid in the chest under the windowe			
Belgica			
Elizabeth	1576	xix°	3
	1578	xxj	3
	1579	xxj	1
	1585	xxviij	8
	1586	xxix	1
	1596	xxxix	1
	1598	xlj	3
Belgica are put together in a bag & laid in the chest under ye windowe			

FIGURE 9. Arthur Agarde's Treasury Chart, enumerating England's treaties with the Low Countries housed in the Exchequer archives. The orderly table represents a system of information management distinct from the strategies of the previous images. Hatfield House, Hertfordshire, CP 252/1, f. 80v.

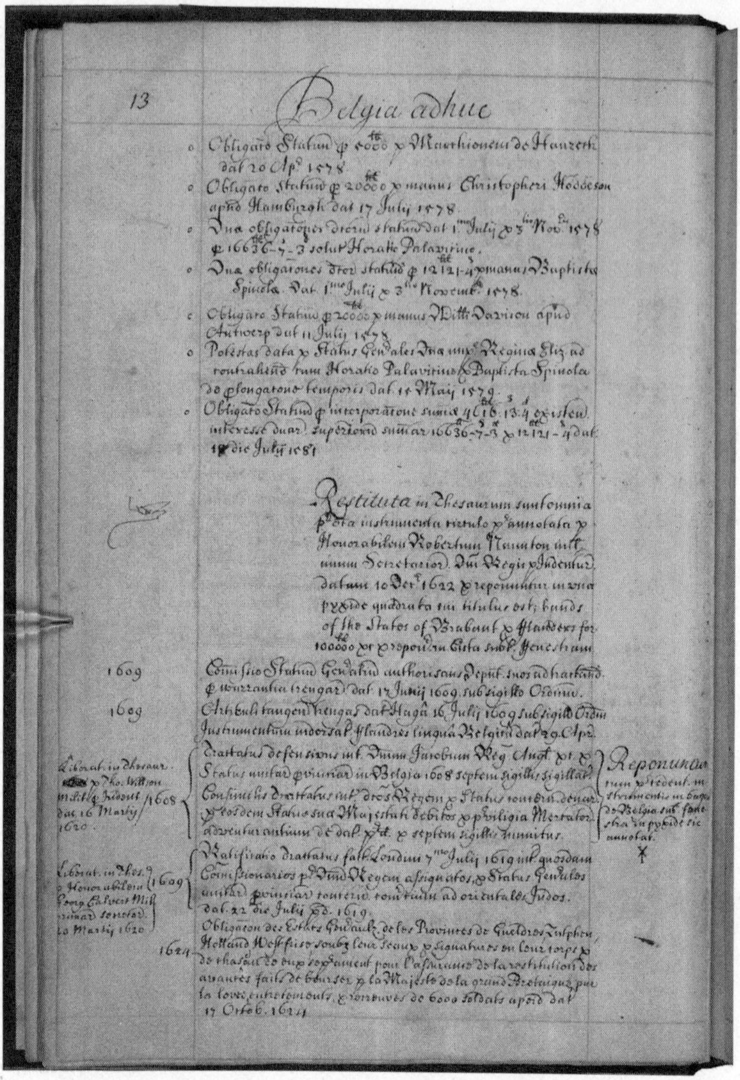
13

Belgia adhuc

FIGURE 10. The eighteenth-century antiquary Thomas Astle's copy of the working document of Arthur Agarde's register of Treaties held in the Exchequer (TNA IND 1/17126). The marginal notes indicate that Thomas Wilson had borrowed several of them—likely to substantiate his claim that the Low Countries owed the English crown £100,000—which he then lent to Secretary of State Robert Naunton, who subsequently returned them. Astle collected and copied many such manuscripts. BL Stowe MS 138, f. 9r. By permission of the British Library.

Agarde's expertise, in short, lay in imposing order on bodies of texts whose physical disarray or dispersal rendered them unmanageable. He achieved this by channeling elements of their contents into his codices, whether by transcribing passages, devising summaries, or simply noting their locations. This process in turn created its own textual mess, which he addressed through orthographical and typological features. The effect was to reduce and filter documentary chaos into legibility for the Stuart elite, who could now access important archives despite their disorganization or distance through his collections.

* * *

Contemporary copies of Agarde's catalog further testify to its perceived usefulness, for versions of it circulated among the elite of the realm beyond its initial dedicatee and the working copy. The mechanics of its circulation, furthermore, illuminate how the regime of inscription was disseminated more broadly throughout the realm, both to elite counselors who might not have direct contact with Agarde and to a wider, though still highly privileged, swath of the population.

Agarde himself was responsible for at least one copy, outfitted with a condensed version of the original dedicatory epistle, which he gave to Sir Julius Caesar.[75] Shortly after Agarde's death in 1615, furthermore, the scribe Ralph Starkey gifted a copy of a draft of the notes to Egerton.[76] Starkey did not include the catalog of foreign treaties, but—likely because he wished Egerton to support his appointment to the position opened by Agarde's death—he also included other writings by Agarde, including a description of the skills necessary for a Deputy Chamberlain of the Exchequer.[77] He also included two extracts from close rolls concerning the appointment of Exchequer clerks under Edward I and III.[78] Starkey likely calculated that fashioning himself as Agarde's natural successor would compel the aging Lord Chancellor's support.

Starkey's collection reflected a common way for Agarde's catalog to circulate, as copies of the catalog often incorporated items such as the Heneages' description of the Tower catalogs or a list of uncertain provenance from 1616 elaborating the archives of the King's and Lord Treasurer's Remembrancers.[79] Others included only the lists or only the chart of foreign treaties.[80] Much as with the "Books of Offices," that is, elements of the catalog could be disaggregated and recombined as part of wide-ranging reference packages that conveyed access and expertise.

The circulation of Agarde's catalog initially remained limited to a very narrow elite. But in 1631, the Welsh lawyer and former Solicitor General in the Welsh Marshes Thomas Powell oversaw the print publication of

Agarde's Exchequer catalog. Powell had previously authored a 1622 reference guide entitled *Direction for Search of Records Remaining*, which described records in the Chancery, Tower, and the Exchequer "out of my Collections of Twentie yeares Search of Record."[81] This was less a catalog of records than an account of the types of records that each office maintained—explaining, for instance, the difference between close rolls and patent rolls. Though Powell had dedicated the manuscript original of this volume to Attorney General Thomas Coventry, the printed version—newly equipped with dedicatory poems to James I, Prince Charles, William Noy, and James Ley—was intended for a broader audience of legal professionals. His 1631 *Repertorie of Records* was similarly intended for this sizable, if narrow, readership, but it included virtually no material that overlapped with his previous book. Instead, it collected lists, catalogs, and inventories produced over previous decades.[82] Agarde's description of the four treasuries—including the catalog of foreign treaties—was its core, but it also contained Agarde's description of the duties of the Deputy Chamberlain, Bowyer's audit of Tower rolls, the Heneages' list of finding aids in the Tower, and the 1616 inventory of the Remembrancers' records.

Agarde had demystified Westminster archives for an exclusive coterie, seemingly following the logic of Robert Bowyer's arguments against Ferdinando Pulton for the importance of controlled mediation of such materials. Powell's publication, by contrast, projected this and similar resources expected to advance professional expertise and profitability to London's legal class. The dynamics in this case resemble those of the "Books of Office," in that a textual instrument initially reserved for elite counselors was eagerly collected and circulated more broadly under the expectation that a receptive audience would discern its benefits. But in this case, rather than knowledge of the state, the textual instruments disseminated archival acuity.

Deluge and Glut

Access to archives marked one aspect of the surge of inscribed material throughout the realm. And as copies circulated—whether made from originals or other copies—each became available for recopying, often by individuals who, like Arthur Agarde, did not foresee their immediate instrumental use. Early Stuart Britain, accordingly, witnessed a surge in the collections of political materials owned by individuals of varying backgrounds. And like Agarde, such individuals devised measures such as rubrication, indexing, catchwords, and more to manage the information flows they themselves elicited, for the graphomania of the moment produced the widespread condition of information overload.

The problems of overload were especially acute for those involved in governance. The ever-growing paperwork produced through ordinary operations joined the older items that might be accessed through Agarde and Cotton to inundate offices of the Jacobean elite, creating a relentless torrent that raised constant problems of management. As the occasional inventories taken of such materials testify, the figures who sought to gain advantage from collecting inscriptions found themselves drowning under the flood of paper their practices elicited. And while these inventories also reveal the tactics they devised in response, they additionally illuminate how such methods did not resolve but instead exacerbated problems of information order.

* * *

Perhaps the most forceful testimony of this world of copious inscription can be found in the working collections of Jacobean servants and administrators. To be sure, it is difficult to pin down the specifics of such archives because catalogs of them were rare and tended to be compiled only when their holder died or fell from grace. Sufficient evidence exists, however, to develop a sense of the pace of accumulation, general organization, and overall size of some collections, and thus to illuminate the scale of the information management challenge they confronted.

In 1619, for example, at the fall of Thomas Lake—who had been Francis Walsingham's secretary and then after his patron's death occupied a variety of posts until being elevated to Secretary of State in 1616—Keeper of the State Papers Thomas Wilson cataloged his papers. These consisted predominantly of volumes with titles such as "A bundle of Letters from My Lord Sir Thomas Edmonds ioyntly about the mariage with France and some other papers about that buisiness," suggesting the persistence of the organizing principles used by Elizabethan counselors. Wilson listed 82 bundles of foreign correspondence, with each bundle limited to one location and mostly to one year, though some years demanded more (for example, the largest number, from France, consisted of four from 1614, six from 1615, and seven from 1616). Lake also had 33 bundles of copies, abstracts, extracts of treaties, commissions, and acts of attestation and 47 bundles or packets of correspondence with English interlocutors, almost entirely consisting of incoming letters rather than drafts of his own.[83] The size of these bundles varied, but in total the 150 bundles totaled roughly 15,000 sheets. Virtually all of it dated from the previous six years; Wilson had likely accessioned Lake's earlier collection when he expanded the State Paper Office at Robert Cecil's death in 1612.[84] Lake, in short, was collecting, let alone processing, a minimum of 2,500 sheets each year.

Wilson frequently recorded the number of pages in the bundles and books when he appropriated materials (though not the size of the paper). His inventories confirm that Lake's collection may have been large but was not aberrant. For example, in early 1625 Wilson received at least 68 bundles of letters totaling at least 3,250 pages from outgoing Secretary of State George Calvert, who had served since 1619. This did not include many items such as "3 written bookes concerning the business of the Bohemie, written for my Lord of Carlile 20 May 1620," nor any documents that Calvert might have reserved as private papers.[85] Amid the constant swirl of circulating paper, these figures were hoarding hundreds of documents each year.

Bundles remained the dominant mode of collection and storage, and secretaries seem to have stuffed them into their studies rather than carefully orchestrated their organization. When Wilson's successor Ambrose Randolph cataloged Dudley Carleton, Viscount Dorchester's manuscripts, he noted where the documents lay in Dorchester's "studio," giving a sense of the spatial arrangement. In a wooden chest, Dorchester had forty-seven *relazioni* and notes related to Italian matters along with twenty-one "smale pieces," almost none of which were related to Italy. Most of his material lay on disheveled presses. For example, one press had 11 miscellaneous bundles such as "One bundle of his observations, out of severall Autors" alongside two bags of letters and minutes of dispatches, thirty-seven "printed placards of the states especially touching Impositions," and 19 "bundles of letters from noblemen and other considerable persons during his employment in the low countries."[86] Other presses held 101 bundles and thirty bags of letters, eighty-six printed pamphlets and piles of loose letters, papers, discourses, and books, again exhibiting an expansive range of thematic and material diversity.[87] The studies of early Stuart administrators were unruly nests of paper—and ink, sand, wax, seals, candles, and other accessories—assembled in diverse physical formats, bound by multiple logics, and organized according to a makeshift architecture.[88]

The increasing mediation of politics by inscription enlarged the amount of information demanding management. Accordingly, under James I and Charles I, secretaries and statesmen typically collected and preserved sizable quantities of working and reference papers. The enlarged scale of collection, however, posed its own difficulties. While traditional practices continued to be used at the level of box, book, and bundle, such collections grew unusable as they expanded. Early Stuart counselors' offices were overwhelmed by paper bursting through bags and boxes and spilling off shelves, resisting order and frustrating use, as exemplified by Dorchester's shambolic study.

* * *

Sir Julius Caesar's collection of state papers, accumulated over nearly fifty years of public service, likely exceeded all those of the more transient stars in the Jacobean cosmos.[89] In the last years before his death, he drew up a catalog describing eighty-five volumes containing around 35,000 pages. In fact, this represented only a portion of his materials, as he possessed a hundred more volumes of state papers bringing the total of his archive to likely 50,000 to 70,000 pages. These volumes contained a remarkable diversity of texts obtained in the many offices Caesar occupied over the previous forty years, which included Privy Counsellor, Chancellor of the Exchequer, Master of the Rolls, Judge of the High Court of Admiralty, and Master of Requests. His archive contains scores of materials from each of these positions, but their relation to one another in his archive suggests that the accumulation of paper proved unmanageable, burying his office under a heterogeneous backfill of texts. When he did decide to organize his mountains of paper, his practices illuminate the unexpected problems introduced by the grand emphasis on inscription.

Caesar's career depended on his habitual inscription and his ability to generate and maneuver within texts. His initial spur to notice—aided by his father Cesar Adelmare's success as royal physician—had been his training as a civil lawyer, which advanced him in the Admiralty courts. But even early in his career, he searched collections for other administrators.[90] For fifty years, he engaged in acts such as circulating proclamations received from abroad and drafting Privy Council letters, royal proclamations, and petitions.[91] His signature and notes are ubiquitous in the archives of Robert Cecil, various Secretaries of State's papers, and Privy Council business, and the range of documents that passed through Caesar's hands suggest that his role in Cecil's information networks was not limited by official appointments. The longevity of some of his roles after Cecil's death—most notably, his tenure as Privy Counsellor from 1607 and Master of the Rolls from 1614 until his death in 1636—along with his constant presence on commissions and committees implanted him amid the relentless stream of papers that adjoined Stuart rule.[92] Indeed, Caesar's notes—signing warrants, taking minutes, ordering the production of documents, noting when petitions were heard, confirming receipt of papers, witnessing the fulfillment of instructions—certify the movement of documents through the corridors of Whitehall and beyond, and they exemplify how political business was galvanized and embodied through inscription. Whereas the majority of his materials originated in his official duties, furthermore, he also had many copies of documents obtained from clients and correspondents such as Cotton.[93]

Caesar was undoubtedly aware of the hazards posed by disorder. Even had he not faced it in practice, many of the policy papers he collected urged oversight of papers to keep offices functional. For example, in a tract on the Exchequer that Caesar owned, one explanation given for "evil reports" concerning that office was that "the records of the same court are soe intermyngled that one officer knowethe not in effect what imperteyneth to an other."[94] This warning may have led to Agarde's campaign to instill order in this space.

Caesar was well versed in some contemporary practices used to negotiate cumbersome quantities of information, which he also directed toward a massive library of printed books that he accumulated. For example, over the course of many decades, he updated an enormous commonplace book founded on John Foxe's *Pandectae Locorum Communium*, which he annotated extensively and, when its blank spaces were full, then interleaved extensively with sheets saturated by notes in his crabbed hand.[95] Like most at the time, his was structured with alphabetically organized thematic heads, under which he entered apposite passages from his reading. His practice reflected the intended purpose of such commonplace books, which was to compile extracts concerning categorical headers their producers deemed appropriate. These headings mediated the act of interpretation, structuring the attention and emphases of the reader. Commonplace books also encouraged correlative reading, allowing users to compare and contrast commentaries on related themes. And they also served as guides to the libraries from which they had been produced, especially when notetakers were as careful as Caesar, who frequently inscribed the page number from which he had drawn the source. Built from a practice of extraction, collection, and thematic juxtaposition, the commonplace book reduced a flurry of books into manageable digests.

Caesar devised other methods to reduce a surfeit of information to a manageable scale. He was the owner of an exceptional portable library of forty-four miniature volumes, each containing canonical ancient texts in Latin or Greek.[96] This artifact engineered a different solution to that offered by the commonplace book for those looking to compress the prudence and wisdom embedded in their sources; while the notebook culled, Caesar's traveling library shrank the physical objects of the books.

Though it would not have been feasible to direct this technology of minimization to his archive of manuscript materials, Caesar could certainly have tried to instill order in his archive through note-taking or cataloging, much as Agarde did, or impose discipline and structure on physical spaces pocked by papers, boxes, and bags strewn according to arbitrary organization. But there is no evidence aside from a brief catalog of his Italian books that Caesar produced registers, guides, inventories, or other materials until the 1630s and, as we will see, plenty to suggest that his office was an overflowing nest of paper.[97] Indeed, it is unclear how Caesar negotiated the maelstrom of papers that likely characterized his office before the 1630s, and the absence of such evidence suggests that he relied on memory and, when that failed, laborious trawling through his papers.[98]

The catalog Caesar produced in the 1630s, ironically, is the best evidence of his collection beforehand, especially when supplemented by the catalog prepared in 1757 for the public auction of his archive (which had remained relatively undisturbed since his 1636 death), and the evidence found in many of his volumes that still remain intact today.[99] These sources collectively enable a sense of Caesar's arrangement of his materials, and they suggest that he maintained an office as disorganized as Dorchester's and containing a similarly haphazard architecture, with stacks of pamphlets, papers, bundles, bags, on presses, shelves, and boxes melding irruptions of paper in a variety of material formats into arbitrary juxtapositions.

The catalog was one of two central elements in a broader project to impose order on the archive, for at the same time he produced the catalog, he also initiated a program of removing his papers from bags or bundles and binding them into codices. To be sure, Caesar had plenty of codices already in his study before he bound his papers—roughly half of his volumes were bound before the 1630s consolidation. Many of these were deliberate instruments for recording and registering Crown business; for example, he kept volumes consisting of registers of Privy Seals and Warrants under the Signet between 1609 and 1611 and then between 1611 and 1614, both of which he supplemented with lengthy indexes to the contents.[100] He had also collected volumes, using his position on the Exchequer, that tabulated Crown revenues for individual years and elaborated the finances of individual Exchequer officers.[101] Others inventoried royal lands and possessions.[102]

Caesar's collection, however, did not consist predominantly of bound books. While it contained only one roll—entitled "Orders established to be observed by all gentlemen and officers of the Prince's Householde"—his office housed tens of thousands of loose sheets.[103] And his decision to bind these sheets appears intended specifically to address the flightiness of individual papers by implanting them in a stable material form; indeed, the catalog he produced at this time did not include volumes that were already bound.

The binding program did bring together some loose but connected papers into volumes that resembled the prebound ones; for example, he created individual volumes devoted to letters received from nobility, specific foreign locales, and French admiralty causes.[104] Such books likely bound together papers that had likely long existed as bundles. But many volumes bound on this occasion adhered to no underlying logic, instead fusing heterogeneous masses of letters, copies of charters, draft policy proposals, printed proclamations, confessional polemics, and more. And it was not merely their genres that were eclectic, but the formats as well. These miscellanies were a mishmash of paper material culture, as commissions neatly inscribed on one side of thick folio with ample space between lines and folded in half to squeeze into the book abutted cheap printed octavos, or nestled next to letters written on half sheets of cheap writing paper, or surrounded notes from statutes squeezed onto scraps razored from other sheets of paper. And although the preponderance of Caesar's collections emanated from official business, it also contained scatterings of the informal writings that bubbled through his inscription-obsessed culture, such as anagrams and poems from friends and clients.

Eclecticism crossed into disorder; one typical volume, for example, combined in roughly 550 pages a range of documents including Lambarde's *Archeion*, Privy Council Orders from Henry VI, the coronation of Richard II, a "discourse upon the commission of Bridewell," matters concerning Guernsey, a "Book of Offices" and a Spanish equivalent, reports on piracy, the patent for the Lincolnshire town of Boston, some Chancery orders, and, slotted in with this hodgepodge, Caesar's pedigree, produced by his father-in-law Michael Lok.[105] Each of these volumes thus constituted an absurdist archive fusing papers of different sizes, origins, and periods, bound in every which way, parchment rubbing up against paper, neatly ruled charts yielding to scribbled notes.[106] These gallimaufries were likely a consequence of binding papers without overarching logic other than their initial resting place, which suggests that even if the piles in Caesar's office intended some thematic organization, it was maintained carelessly. The haphazardness suggests instead that his ordinary practice had been to shuttle the unremitting flow of papers into bags, boxes, or presses and, if he needed to find them later, search and hope for the best.

While Caesar's binding project intended to enhance organization, it also ensconced archival blips and introduced others. For example, one of his volumes compiled foreign treaties, ratifications, and confirmations involving England drawn from Cecil's collections into a single codex of nearly four hundred pages.[107] To help navigate this volume, he had his clerk William Bagwell produce "A Calendar to my bookes of forren treatises with England."[108] But the calendar was bound into another volume amid a disorienting variety of other materials, including printed articles concerning Admiralty jurisdiction, acts of the office of the ordinance, Walter Cope's apology for the Earl of Essex, and a safe conduct for English merchants to travel to Russia.[109] The catalog to the collection of treaties risked disappearing, as the binding intended to control the shuffling of papers embedded it in a place potentially obscured by its randomness.

Caesar's program of binding, that is, both imposed order on the archive and introduced its own disorganization. To remedy this, Caesar devised tools to help wind his way through the forest of papers now encased in bound volumes. Each of these "finding aids" constituted statements of priorities that simultaneously facilitated consultation of some sources in his archive while hiding or distorting others.

The first measure Caesar seems to have taken after having compiled so much of his swarming archive was to number the pages of each stack intended to be bound together. Likely at this time, he composed tables of contents for these towers of paper, which he then inserted at the front of the bound book. These tables of contents, however, were incomplete. Although Caesar consistently registered important documents of state business and formal treaties, ephemera such as notes, scraps, and lists were far less likely to be recorded or might be subsumed within general categories. Later owners of these books found this tendency exasperating. For example, the eighteenth-century bookseller and antiquarian Thomas Snelling (who purchased twenty of Caesar's manuscripts) was perplexed by the table of contents in a volume predominantly concerning Mint affairs; as he explained, "This, which contains only 53 articles out of 400, is in the hand writing of Sir Julius Caesar."[110] Caesar's table in this volume reflected unusual selectivity, and he tended to register more than half the discrete items. But as Snelling observed, Caesar only included select items, and many were immediately obscured through the glare of the illumination emitted by the table of contents.

Having bound dozens of volumes, moreover, Caesar sought a better way to negotiate the thousands of pages he had crammed between covers. The bindings offered another canvas. Each codex was given a number, which he wrote on a vellum or paper slip and glued inside the front cover. These numbers were determined by the size of the volume rather than thematic order. The first sixty-four books he cataloged were folio, and the subsequent volumes took a diversity of forms: seven more folios, ten quartos, three quartos, and one duodecimo, not arranged in any order, but likely simply assigned in the sequence that the previously unmarked volumes passed across his desk. Similarly, Caesar also assigned each codex multiple thematic designations, which he recorded on their outside binding. These revealed the eclectic nature of the volumes; for example, his description on the binding of one volume revealed that its contents covered "Trade, Apparell, Starchamber, Banish. Of Jesuits, Levying of soldiers. Contrib, Palatinate, Monies, Co. Fees, Chanson, verses."[111] These labels were helpful but imprecise and indicative of the miscellany quality of the volumes.

Caesar created another instrument to distill his archive. In a single volume, he transcribed each table of contents that he had created, in the numerical order he had assigned to the texts. This volume thus centralized the registers embedded into each volume, providing the ability to survey the whole collection. But the resulting catalog exceeded 240 pages, listing thousands of individual items distributed across his eighty-five volumes, and so it, too, demanded instruments of navigation. Accordingly, Caesar devised yet another tool to penetrate this wall of information: an index to the tables of contents, which he entered in the blank pages in front of the volume. But this index again shared the nebulousness of the tools he had previously fashioned. For example, his first category consisted of "Nobility. Gentry. Honour. Baronets," and it recorded that the first two folios in his catalog "touch Nobility and Baronets."[112] Though part of the contents of these codices did concern such matters, they were not solely devoted to these categories. Moreover, the final list only referred to a few volumes, wildly underrepresenting the omnipresence of references to aristocratic concerns across his archive.

All the index entries were compromised by similar imprecision. Nonetheless, these groupings created something like thematic searchability across his collection, if without semblance of comprehensiveness. Subsequent entries covered materials related first to the Admiralty; second to treaties; third to the Privy Council, Court of Requests, and Star Chamber; fourth to the Exchequer and customs; fifth to royal lands; sixth to Crown revenue; seventh to the Chancery; and eighth to "Projects, Newe Inventions." Then came letters from Secretaries of State, recusants, and finally categories devoted to the mint and to hospitals and churches.[113] Though each of these entries contained an incomplete index to material stuffed in his miscellanies, they would have likely served as Caesar's first point of consultation, thereby shaping what he was able to see within his archive. The index, in short, did not provide a neutral guide but rather magnified some preselected themes and sources while obscuring others. Using it to navigate the unmanageable archive would have yielded results simultaneously overdetermined and semiarbitrary.

* * *

Caesar's archive exemplifies the world of governance laced with inscription. The labors of brokers such as Bowyer, Agarde, and Cotton, along with the increased output of the government, distributed huge quantities of paper throughout the realm, resulting in collections like Caesar's, whose sheer size was its most striking attribute. But Caesar did not design his physical environment to channel this flood of texts, and as a result he generated a space as disorderly as the most chaotic of the Exchequer archives. And each measure to address the disorder in his archive—whether the physical tactic of binding or the inscriptive ones of labeling, registering, or indexing—introduced its own distortions, in turn encouraging the production of yet more provisional, partial methods of facilitating order. The proliferation of copying and collections of inscriptions, that is, were intended to help resolve problems of governance and circulate mechanisms for reinforcing authority and power. Instead, they replicated the problems of information management into the studies of the Stuart elite.

Conclusion

The early Stuart political world was a complex media sphere of multiple overlapping networks.[114] These networks functioned as engines for the circulation of texts, as open spigots that drowned those most committed to inscription and preservation under a relentless stream of paper. The growing population of those who participated in this system saw texts as instruments that delivered political benefits, conferred order, and secured authority, and these shared perceptions underlay their demands to replicate the written world throughout the realm. But they were also aware of the potential dangers posed by unfettered and uncontrolled access and so did not encourage widespread openness. Instead, they sought to conscientiously filter the flow of documents in ways that would also confer personal advantage, enrichment, or expertise.

Arthur Agarde's practices indicate the tensions of mediating and translating texts along these networks. Many resources deemed valuable were dispersed, obscured, hidden, or arcane. Making them available entailed not simply the practice of copying but also methods designed to structure access, legibility, and circulation for their targeted audiences. The challenge Agarde repeatedly faced of synthesizing diffuse documents and distilling legible texts from chaotic bodies of information paralleled the challenge faced by all collectors of heterogeneous bodies of materials. And the circulation of the instruments he produced reveals at once their utility, the broader interest they elicited, and the dynamics by which the regime of inscription propagated.

A widespread appetite for inscription and communication thus accelerated and increased the circulation of inscriptions. The primary material impact for contemporaries was the production of an infinitely expandible sea of resources for authority, power, and enrichment, which inundated collectors and threatened to resist management and use. Sir Julius Caesar's archive, most strikingly, suggests how the desire to capitalize on these massively enlarged collections raised the challenge of negotiating them, and how the techniques for doing so compounded the problems of information order. Under these conditions, navigating such overwhelming bodies of papers became a predicate of political action, and the challenges of information management became embedded within—even constitutive of—political practice.

3

Institutions Reimagined

As knowledge and authority were increasingly mediated by inscription, proposals advocating sophisticated information management regimes suffused the early Stuart political environment. Most were produced by the men in lower- and middle-rung political offices responsible for an enormous volume of the work of governance in early modern Britain, in the hope that the schemes would lead to more prestigious or remunerative employment.[1] Many of these texts suggested new clerical offices to manage existing inscriptions or control new ones, while others compacted textual evidence into prescriptive constitutions for long-standing offices. The producers and disseminators of these works typically disowned self-interest and denied that they were introducing innovation, instead claiming to sustain precedent and enhance the ordinary activity of governance. But their proposals reveal that the early Stuart government was characterized by flexibility, dynamism, and novelty rather than tradition or stasis. For these functionaries, the state was a project, and the regime of inscription offered the means to reimagine it.[2]

Early modern Britain was thus a site of political invention. But, paradoxically, many of the proposed projects to manage inscription relied on interpretive techniques that reduced the long-standing underlying elasticity of the government, instead using descriptive records to fix procedural norms and establish routine and continuity. The political organ such projects thus envisioned was a durable, rationalized network of text-saturated offices over which was distributed the range of government responsibilities—the palimpsest of the modern state.[3]

Ancient Institutions Reimagined

As the foundational document of the Exchequer, the Domesday Book absorbed more of Arthur Agarde's attention than any of the other records he wrangled into legibility. While he eased its use through his standard practices of abstracting and indexing, he also compiled texts that enhanced his understanding of it through comparison, collation, and contrast. The tools he fashioned to comprehend Domesday reverberated in unexpected ways, facilitating the construction of an alternate vision of the past and, concomitantly, the reconsideration of this talisman of English governance.

Agarde relied on the Domesday Book for one of his major Exchequer responsibilities, for one method of resolving property disputes entailed determining ownership in Domesday and then tracing the transmissions of title through time.[4] As he explained, Domesday had earned its name because "in former ages in all matters of question or sute in lawe either in the kinges bench or common pleas, where one party alledged the land was other auncyent demeasne or other mens landes, or a manor, or a hamlet, and the other denyed yt, ther was a wrytt as in the Register appeareth, directed to the Lord Threasurer and Chemberlaynes to certifie out of the sayd booke what they find therof, and according to the returne of the wryt of Cerciorare, was judgment geven."[5] The book was the last judgment.

Agarde used his standard methods to develop his expertise concerning Domesday. Though he consulted and even annotated the original, he did not always work directly from it.[6] By 1598 he had created a codex abstract of Domesday, recording in a more familiar hand—and with a more spacious *mise-en-page* (page layout)—brief entries abridging the whole.[7] These abstracts contained adequate material to resolve many cases, but they could also guide him to the appropriate entry in the original. To ease scanning, he rubricated running heads on each page and county names, while marginal annotations highlighted specific towns. Agarde also constructed a separate volume—again heavily rubricated—containing an alphabetical thematic index and other reference aids.[8] These aids included transcriptions he deemed useful, such as the definition of land tenure from a book called "Le grand coustoumier de pais & Duche de Normandie," and extracts from the Ely Cathedral register—received from Robert Cotton in 1609—which Agarde claimed recorded the questions that William the Conqueror had circulated to generate the survey.[9]

Among these ancillary materials was a list of definitions of archaic words, including obsolete units of land measures: the hide, carucate, and solin. Agarde had first struggled to decode these terms when trying to survey disputed property, and in 1599 he had established their sizes in an essay on the "dimensions" of England for the Society of Antiquaries.[10] But a decade later, Agarde used them as the foundation of a short reconsideration of the purpose of Domesday. Most contemporary observers accepted the account of its production given in the Black Book of the Exchequer, which recounted that after the Norman Conquest, William recognized that only the rule of law could quell continuing rebellion. Accordingly, he had assembled a counsel, which requested that they be allowed to live under the "aunciient Saxon lawes, which weare in use in the tyme of Edward the Confessor."[11] William agreed, while introducing some Norman laws that he thought beneficial. Then, as Agarde summarized, "because he knew that all controversies aryse uppon *meum et tuum* [private property]," William ordered the survey of land ownership and tenancy that yielded the Domesday Book.[12]

Agarde brought his collected materials to recontextualize and reinterpret Domesday. Most strikingly, his efforts to decode archaic units of land measurement directed him away from the presiding interpretation of its origins. The sources he integrated into an appendix to the essay—including the chronicle from Peterborough Abbey that he had earlier made a note to seek—revealed more than the conversions of these measures to miles: they all suggested that these metrics had been used by King Ethelred to raise the Danegeld, a tribute paid to the Danes to prevent invasion. Agarde discerned a significance to this that he had overlooked in his 1599 essay. As he explained, during William's Continental wars after the Conquest, the king had found the Danegeld "to falle out some yeare more and some yeare less in soundrey townes and parte of the realme, he thought it most convenyent that a view shoulde be made what everie towne village or hamlett was bound to pay."[13] Accordingly, Agarde reasoned, William had re-surveyed the kingdom using the unit of measurement appropriate for assessing land taxes.[14] Amassing materials concerning Domesday thus allowed Agarde to discern that its building blocks befit those of an instrument of taxation rather than of managing property disputes. Domesday, he concluded, represented less the enshrinement of a legal order than the resuscitation of a royal means of revenue creation.

Agarde's reinterpretation was the unexpected outcome of a program of collecting and coordinating medieval texts. His practices were devoted toward improving the information infrastructure of the realm by restoring some of the most obscure and mistreated evidence from past centuries. But by creating new constellations of texts, he also created new possibilities for interpreting his sources. And in seeing Domesday as generated by the nexus of taxation, royal authority, and records, he reenvisaged a foundational symbol of English governance.

* * *

Agarde's reinterpretation of the Domesday Book likely reached a limited audience.[15] But from the 1590s onward, scholars, administrators, and statesmen circulated scores of texts using similar methods to analyze England's political offices and institutions. Whereas Agarde's work reconfigured Domesday from a legal to a fiscal document, most of these texts attributed fixity and stability to what had previously been a flexible institutional architecture.

English government had long been a malleable body, characterized by a few enduring but evolving institutions, surrounded by a loose agglomeration of offices, all governed by personal politics. Elizabeth and early Stuart inquiries into their histories, however, typically minimized such volatility and instead defined institutional duties and protocols by enumerating—in many cases consisting exclusively of—copious quotations from rolls, patents, charters, and registers. Such collections provided resources for reinforcing or expanding claims of an office's powers, especially those which had decayed over time. The result was a proliferation of texts establishing the shape and function of political offices, presenting England's fluid government as a stable state constituted by entrenched institutions with clear constitutional foundations.

As many historians have noted, in this period Parliament was subjected to this same logic of institutionalization.[16] But this strategy was directed toward an array of offices, and closer inspection suggests that such formalization constituted another sign of the infiltration of politics by inscription and the government's recalibration as a media sphere.[17]

Sir Julius Caesar was one of the most prolific producers and collectors of studies of offices. The arguments he constructed, much like Agarde's, illuminate how creative manipulation of records could reimagine institutions. One of Caesar's standard strategies entailed arguing for the authority of offices by finding sources to impute ancient origins to them. For example, when in 1594 he read the account in William Lambarde's *Archeion* that assigned the origins of the Admiralty Court—where Caesar was senior judge—to the reign of Edward III, Caesar pushed its origins back, noting that "Mr Lambard though verie learned otherwise was mistaken in his opinion of the Lord Admirals beginning, for it appeareth by a record of a patent in the Tower of London" that Henry III had appointed a Lord Admiral. Even more, he matter-of-factly stated, there was a reference to a "*Archigubernus classis brittanorum*" in the first century CE in Justinian's digest of Roman law.[18] Caesar thus projected the Admiralty Court into Roman Britain.

The demonstration of antiquity was one of Caesar's main strategies in his 1597 *The Ancient State, Authoritie, and Proceedings of the Court of Requests*. Caesar had been appointed one of the Masters of Requests in this equity court in 1591. The Court of Requests was of relatively recent vintage, likely becoming independent from the Privy Council a century prior, as an ancillary court intended to resolve the suits of poor subjects swiftly. Its success in attracting business provoked attacks denying its jurisdiction from other equity courts in the 1590s, and Caesar assumed the responsibility of replying. He did so by correlating textual materials to argue that the court had long existed as an essential function of the Privy Council.

Caesar's book developed in stages. Upon his appointment in 1591, he began transcribing notes containing judgments from the Court of Requests. As he explained, "I held it a necessary worke, and a labor worthie of some thanks, to gather into one volume, the records of that court from the beginning of the Registrie, now dispersed in xvii great volumes, and to make them knowne, that in this Court (as in the Chancery, Kings Benche, Comon Please and Exchequer) acts past might be precedents of things to come."[19] By 1593 he had compiled a lengthy corpus of materials.[20] In 1596, as the court faced a barrage of criticism, Caesar decided to print some of these notes.[21]

Caesar equipped the printed text with an introductory table consisting of propositions concerning the court's authority, supplemented by references to supporting transcriptions within the volume. The first and most important proposition was that "The Court of Whitehall or Requests now so called, was, and is parcell of the Kings most Honourable Councell, and always called, and esteemed."[22] This claim embodied Caesar's foundational argument: that the Court of Requests held genuine antiquity—as well as prestige—by virtue of its association with the Privy Council.[23] Caesar substantiated the connection by claiming that the seeming origins of the court under Henry VII were illusory; as he explained, "The keeping of this court was never heretofore tied to any place certeine; but only where the Councell sate.... But now of late in 11 Henry VII for the ease of suitors, it hathe began to bee kept in the Whitehall in Westminster, and onely in the terme time."[24] The court's seeming invention, that is, merely constituted a minor reform of a perennial function of the Privy Council. The volume then detailed the court's status as a civil law court of record, entitled to judge a wide variety of cases, before elaborating its procedures.

The printed material, however, was only the kernel of a hybrid volume that Caesar gave to its dedicatee William Cecil, Baron Burghley, and in which Caesar interleaved blank pages covered with manuscript notes.[25] Many of these notes modified claims of the printed copy, as he crossed out cases that he now decided did not serve as precedents for the propositions and added others in support. The manuscript notes continued to stress its connection to the Privy Council, incorporating material from his collection to detail the antiquity of the Council itself, and explaining that its changes in name over time obscured its origins under Edward I. He also included a list of seventeen "reasons to prove that the Court of Whitehall or Requests is a member and parcell of the Kings most honorable Counsell" drawn from yearbooks, Britton, Bracton, Plowden, and "records in Whitehall."[26] These included that all early Masters of Requests had been Privy Counsellors, that its seal was that of the Privy Council, and that its judges sat in Star Chamber.[27]

Caesar thus directed widely used techniques toward the reconstitution of this Court's history: he assembled disparate sources, transcribed and abridged relevant materials, creatively used them to contextualize each other, and added paratextual materials to guide interpretation. The effect was to produce an illusory but noble past for the Court of Requests in which its seeming formation under Henry VII was a nominal change rather than a substantial innovation, and in which it shared the Privy Council's antiquity and stature.

Caesar's investigation of the office of the Lord President of the Council further illuminates how, in order to respond to desires in the present, such studies could refashion the histories of offices that had been either recently formed or intermittent. Though a Henrician creation and largely ceremonial, the Lord Presidency held great prestige, ranking fourth behind the Lord Steward, Lord Chancellor, and Lord Treasurer, and above the Keeper of the Privy Seal and Lord Chamberlain. Nonetheless, since Mary I's accession in 1553, it had remained empty, with little discussion of restoring anyone to it. This was not unusual—the position of Lord Steward had generally been left vacant since 1421, and the position of Lord Constable was similarly treated as ad hoc. In early 1618, however, Caesar began to research the office of Lord President, likely hoping to acquire it for himself or Edward Coke. He consulted Robert Bowyer and Keeper of the State Papers Thomas Wilson, who responded first but provided him with little succor. As Wilson explained, "most of my tyme (since I was with yor honor last) I have spent in perusing the Registers & Bookes that I have in my custody where any such matter as you required was lykely to bee but finde litle or nothing to the purpose." Charles Brandon had held the position, he reported, but Wilson had found no evidence of its existence since Edward VI's reign. Wilson did broach the intriguing possibility that "in former tymes our English Cronicles doe speak of divers that have had that dignity some Bishops, & some others and those of very antient tyme," gesturing toward the possibility of claiming that the office had been known by a different name, much as Caesar had extended the Court of Requests' history by submerging it within the Privy Council. But Wilson also concluded that "for the particuler power or priviledges belonging to that Place, I find nothing recorded." Accordingly, "what the

President of our English Councell can doe I am not able yet to sett downe but as I shall finde or learne more thereof."[28]

Caesar must have been cheered by Bowyer's more encouraging response. Bowyer sent him the Henrician statute which had appointed William Paulet as the second Lord President, but more significantly, he supplied evidence that the Privy Council had long operated with an internal hierarchy including a president. Extracts from Parliament rolls provided Bowyer's most compelling testimony; for example, during the reign of Edward III, it had been ordered that "The Duke of Cornewale shalbe keeper of England in the Kings absence, And the Archbishop of Canterbury and the Erle of Huntington to be chiefe Counsellors of the Realm." Similarly, during the same reign it had been decided that "reporte be made to the king of matters of councill, by some one or two of the counsell thereunto appointed and by no other." Bowyer traced comparable arrangements until Henry VI's reign.[29] Though not dignified by the title of Lord President, he suggested, one Privy Counsellor had long controlled the Privy Council's duties.

Caesar compiled a brief memorandum on the Lord Presidency several weeks later, relying heavily on Bowyer's research while including other material such as notes from his Court of Requests collection indicating that the bishop of Rochester had occupied the office under Henry VII. As he explained, "I find also that the same office & effect, but by an other name, was heretofore conferred on great personages," specifically noting the title of "Consiliaris principalis." Later, he added a reference to evidence of Lord Presidents under Henry V and Mary, and stated that from the "Commissions of Peace in the Crowne Office, Henry Earl of Arundell was Lord President of the Privy Councell" under Elizabeth.[30]

Caesar's ambitions extended beyond demonstrating the endurance of the office, and his notes drew on the records to adumbrate the position's duties. Above all, the Lord President was responsible for "reporting to the king the resolutions or opinions of the table," he maintained, citing a parliament roll from the reign of Edward III. He also ran the Privy Council meetings more generally, sat in Star Chamber, and exercised other privileges.[31] These notes provided a manual for the Lord Presidency which, in his depiction, was a vital and long-standing position.[32]

Delineating histories of offices thus allowed their advocates to assert and expand their authority. Similarly, in Caesar's Court of Requests tract, he itemized from his notes the range of causes it adjudicated, which spanned property disputes, riots, forgeries, dilapidations, broken contracts, theft, unpaid debts, and more, each with multiple references to cases abridged in his text. The image of the court produced by this compilation was one whose vast jurisdiction extended beyond temporal to ecclesiastical and maritime matters; the eclectic nature of the cases it had heard now justified wide dominion. In Caesar's numerous other tracts examining offices as well, each instance of the office's powers discerned in the archive became grounds for permanent legitimacy, and the compiled repertoire of powers it had asserted over its entire past was flattened into a timeless constitution.[33]

It is worth noting briefly how poorly the administrative history of the kingdom was known even by those central to it and those positioned directly among its textual legacies. Indeed, Caesar's strategies suggest that institutional antiquity was maintained not by inheriting medieval traditions nor by recovering a once stable ancient constitution but by revisiting, renewing, and magnifying medieval sources. The volatile and uncertain histories of offices thus opened them to reinterpretation, through a practice that assembled substantial collections of material to reimagine the political past in the service of a desired present. Indeed, the tracts delimiting their powers should be seen as polemical statements—as instruments that used dubious past precedents to advance the powers of those that commissioned them. Each office, under this textual regime, was represented as continuous with its past forms rather than a free-form embodiment of its holder's ambitions—even as these aspirations determined how their history was interpreted.

New Offices Projected

While some aspirants to power used the realm's paperwork to revive or enhance existing offices, others seeking roles within early English governance treated the profusion of paperwork as an opportunity to introduce new positions. From later in Elizabeth's reign, the increased solicitation of paperwork by powerful counselors such as Burghley and Principal Secretary Francis Walsingham led to heightened demand for clerkships.[34] Especially under James I, projects to create new clerical positions proliferated, and disputes concerning ownership and maintenance of records abounded as individuals sought to siphon responsibilities from the offices that had traditionally exercised them, hoping to gain the fees that came with such scribal labor.[35] The result was an environment of institutional innovation.

Sir Thomas Egerton's Chancery was a robust site for such developments.[36] His own participation in inscription culture was well established, and his archive was dense with notes drawn from records.[37] In his tenures as Solicitor General, Attorney General, and Master of the Rolls before his appointment as Lord Chancellor and Lord Keeper of the Great Seal, he had often dispatched Lambarde to crown repositories to seek evidence of the history of crown institutions, and even after his appointment, Egerton also performed his own searches.[38] For example, his 1607 parliamentary speech on the legality of the *aurum reginae*—a subsidy belonging directly to a queen consort—relied heavily on research in the Exchequer and Tower records.[39]

Egerton preserved oft-discarded materials to a remarkable degree. His extant archive teems with rough copies, brief jottings, canceled notes, and slivers of paper hurriedly inscribed with inscrutable glyphs scrawled for uncertain purposes. These indicate that he directed practices of inscription at estate management to an unusual degree; like many others, he assiduously preserved legal instruments such as his deeds and will, but his collections also abound with inventories, household audits, and recipes. Most strikingly, Egerton's notes contained numerous "checkrolls," lists of the many servants laboring at his estate in Cheshire and his London lodgings.[40]

Egerton's Chancery similarly emphasized textualization, and he both developed its practices of collection and introduced the production of indexes and calendars as part of its regular practice. For example, indexes to Chancery reports and certificates—the reports made by Masters in Chancery concerning cases on which they were consulted, which were usually smaller-scale property disputes—were first made in 1606.[41] The treatment of the affidavits generated by these proceedings—which were required in cases where the defendant could not appear, or to report acts of contempt, or to support objections—is illuminating of this environment of proliferating paperwork. Around 1606, the written affidavits from all the court's cases were for the first time compiled into bound volumes in rough alphabetical order by plaintiff's last name.[42] Each was endorsed with the case name, year, and location; this endorsement was designed to give those perusing them a sense of what each contained at a glance.[43] Those seeking specific affidavits did not have to browse the volume, however, for the Chancery also began to produce indexes to such volumes. The indexes were structured alphabetically by term, with the Master who had overseen each case noted in the right margin. To help navigate such volumes, moreover, small alphabetically labeled paper slips were pasted to appropriate pages.[44]

Even this indexing did not complete the information infrastructure for such minor documents, as beginning in 1615, Richard Frampton compiled a new register in which he entered incoming affidavits in the order which they arrived.[45] Each entry simply listed the name of the person making the affidavit, its basic matters, the Master in Chancery who had heard it, and a notarization by either the deponent or the clerk who had transcribed their testimony. In late 1616—that is, at least a year after having begun to compile the register—Frampton was given letters patent as the "Register of Affidavits" in Chancery.[46]

The textual system preserved a mass of new papers, ostensibly to allow the Lord Chancellor to oversee the work of the Masters more easily and to allow the Masters to collaborate and communicate across cases. But above all, it demonstrates how inscription produced more inscription, as new textual instruments were devised to control, mobilize, and enable access to the material artifacts that increasingly poured into the office. And the creation of these instruments opened possibilities for individuals such as Frampton to stake out fee-earning positions by proposing new clerical offices.

* * *

That Frampton started to perform the functions of his offices even before he was formally appointed highlights another facet of this innovating culture of inscription. Burgeoning government inscription created a clerical bonanza, whereby entrepreneurial individuals—and patrons who wished to augment their authority by installing their clients in new positions—sought to grab a piece of the explosion in copying, enrolling, and archiving by creating jobs responsible for specific paperwork and then fighting over control of them.

Many ambitious individuals like Frampton devised projects that revolved around archival management and the use of inscriptions to channel the paper flowing from ordinary administration. Despite his reliance on antiquity as a legitimizing tool, for example, Caesar was receptive to projects for new offices of this sort, especially when they might prove profitable. In 1609, for example, he compiled a list of more than one hundred "New Projects for Gain." The majority of them relied on financial methods such as renegotiating interest rates, calling in debts, or selling "superfluous" Crown houses; others referred to industrial or commercial projects. Still others—including Examiner in the Court of Chancery Otho Nicholson's—entailed unearthing and enforcing preexisting laws, in essence monetizing conformity to the record of the past.[47]

One class of projects listed by Caesar entailed producing new instruments of inscription and offices overseeing paperwork and records such as "A Register of all burials mariages, & Christenings," and "An office for the sole makinge of pardons."[48] Similar projects coursed through the early Stuart polity, illuminating the ambitions made possible by viewing texts as points of leverage into Stuart governance. For example, in 1617, John Ferrour, John Friend, and Henry Myles received a patent establishing an office of "General Remembrancer on Matters of Record."

This office intended to resolve a predicament faced by those investigating fees attached to land they were considering purchasing; as the patent explained, "no purchaser without a multitude of severall searches in the sayd Severall Courtes, Offices, and places, and without great charge and trouble can learne or be sure or secured from or be able to knowe or finde out such Incombrances whereby lands may be charges or the due and legall discharges of the same."[49] Accordingly, the patentees were entrusted "to write, enter, digest and keepe in bookes to be made out provided in that behalf in forme of an Alphabeticall Table, Remembrance, or Repertorie by the Surnames of the parties an abstract, brief note, remembrance, coppy or entrie of all such matters of records" concerning such encumbrances.[50] To fulfill this duty, the patentees received the right to peruse various archives, and the four treasuries at Westminster and other repositories were instructed to send notes upon request. The new office thus entailed maintenance of a register that would streamline land transactions by centralizing access to records relevant to potential purchasers that were dispersed over the realm.

Similarly, in 1611, Chamberlain of the Exchequer Walter Cope and the courtier Arthur Gorges published a pamphlet describing an office entitled "The Publique Register for Generall Commerce," for which they had secured a twenty-one-year patent.[51] As they explained, the patent licensed Cope and Gorges to open "a publique Office, roome or place of resort or repaire of people for the notice of Borrowing and Lending of moneyes, and for the better knowledge of buying, selling or chancing of land, tenements or heridatements, leases or any other goods of chattels whatsoever."[52] This office was to be situated in the still-new Britain's Bourse. Strikingly, this office exclusively entailed recording and preserving; Cope and Gorges were "to keepe one or more Kalender or Kalenders, Register or Registers, for the registring of all and singular such lands, tenements, hereditaments, leases, wares, commodities, moneyes, or any other things or chattels that shall by the meere motion or goode liking of the owners themselves or their Factors for them be brought to such Office and Offices, there to be entred and registred."[53] Possession of the paperwork—which amounted to a list to facilitate identification between buyers and sellers—was constitutive of the office.

The abstraction of commercial space into a register was highlighted by Cope and Gorges's further description, in which they characterized it as "indeed but the very resemblance of a publique Market, whereunto all men may freely repaire, and resort to Trade and Traffique, without constraint or restraint, at their owne wils and pleasures."[54] The register itself thus used textual centralization to lubricate commerce: prospective buyers and sellers would be more easily identified, for "as in Markets many

Commodities are solde and met withall more easily, and better cheape in one self place, then by seeking up and downe the Countrey for them with more trouble, and at dearer rates in several places: so is it by the use and benefite of this Office."[55] This office, like that of Ferrour, Friend, and Myles's, thus consisted entirely of a register that would abstract and consolidate information to promote efficient commercial activity.

In these cases, projectors imagined and engineered paper technologies to centralize a diffuse information environment. The patentees themselves were also subordinated within an information structure in which authority was vested in the register even more than its custodians. Though neither of these projects resulted in an office that gained a foothold in the regime, Nicholson's, Frampton's, and many others did.

Early Stuart England, this suggests, was characterized by a swirl of emergent and disappearing offices. Despite the many failures, aspiring participants in governance proposed projects, received patents, and implemented offices that monopolized acts of cataloging, registering, circulating, and more. And this was less a process of administrative rationalization than, like the effort to devise constitutions for existing offices, a response to a structure of politics that encouraged individuals to devise profitable ways to control textual resources. Through this practice, they remolded the institutions and processes of governance.

The Project of the State

The career of Thomas Wilson, Keeper of the State Paper Office, illuminates in microcosm the practices, ambitions, and consequences of early modern England's text-saturated practice of government.[56] Across the many unfulfilled schemes and bizarre aspirations of his eventful career, Wilson emerges as a master of interrogation and information, the pattern of a certain kind of early modern projector, whose energy and time were dispersed among many offices that cumulatively provided unsatisfactory remuneration.[57] But the irascible Wilson exposes the mechanics of how of an early modern administrator improvising with the resources of this terrain could invent new forms and structures of politics, for his career emblematizes the contingent practices and logics of power that wove together the nascent early modern state.

* * *

Wilson's path to government took familiar shape for those whose expertise lay in information management.[58] After spending more than ten years at Cambridge studying civil law, he embarked on excursions to Italy and Germany in the 1590s, where he developed—on his own account, at least—the ability to blend seamlessly into his surroundings. During this time, he collected copious extracts of letters, newssheets, and more, while also taking notes on conversations with local interlocutors.[59] Over the course of these expeditions, he compiled an impressive network of informants whose news he transmitted to Lord Treasurer Thomas Sackville, Baron Buckhurst.[60] In early 1601 Secretary of State Robert Cecil wrote to Wilson asking to also receive these letters, and Wilson spent the subsequent two years working for Cecil to expose conspiracies by Continental Roman Catholics bent on toppling Elizabeth from her throne.[61] During this latter time Wilson also began working on manuscript entitled "The State of England, c. 1600," an unusual text produced by directing the *artes apodemicae* to his home polity, using records and other texts, including a "Book of Offices."[62]

Wilson's tract had its desired effect, and upon returning from Italy in 1603, he entered Cecil's service.[63] Cecil gave him a wide scope of responsibilities, but his primary role was as a hub for intelligence gathering. He continued to maintain a hefty news correspondence, filtering to Cecil letters he saw as supplying worthy intelligence while reserving those that conveyed "stale" or inaccurate reports.[64] He also continued to assemble texts redolent of the values that had enabled his preferment. For example, when appointed consul to Spain from 1604 to 1605, he returned with notes and transcriptions revealing Spain's strength and wealth. One volume amounted to a "Book of Offices" for Spain, collecting materials such as lists of "all the ordinarie number of men of warre, captens, and folowers that are in Spaigne, on the frontiers of fraunce, and coastes of Barbrie; and all their stipends . . . with all the townes, castels & fortresses that they have in garde," comparable information for Milan and Naples, lists of the stipends that the Spanish king, Philip II, paid to his courtiers and officers, an account of the royal revenue, a tabulation of the number of ships under Philip's control, orders for Spain's *Casa de contratación* and lists of Spanish nobility.[65] Wilson thus continued to execute the same practices of information gathering that had earned him advancement once in Cecil's secretariat.

From his return from the Continent in 1605 until Cecil's death in 1612, Wilson's main task entailed managing the violent swirl of papers that menaced his patron's office but were necessary to manage the policy of a fractious populace and profligate king.[66] His policy of preservation was unusually disciplined, as he claimed never to throw anything away. When Cecil asked in 1605 why he was so sure that there were no letters from William Lawson from the prior two years in his study, he explained, "It may be that in the late avoydance of frivolous papers they wer discarded. Sure I am that since my tyme their hath not one paper gone out of this roome, those that I find useless in my judgment I reserve notwithstanding especially the acknowledgment of obligations, protestations of devotion, proffer of service, or such lyke," though he admitted Lawson's letters might be "in packets that I have not yett serched, or cannot without making confusion."[67] Not empowered with the judgment to cull, Wilson hoarded.

Inquiries like the one that provoked this response were common, and by February 1606, Wilson had assumed the responsibility of sending requested packets from Cecil's collection to other administrators, which he diligently recorded in a journal.[68] To facilitate these tasks, Wilson filed Cecil's papers according to the standard practice of congregating related documents in bundles or bags. These were not organized according to a preexisting system of classification but rather by correspondent or in fuzzily delimited groupings such as recusants, Cambridge, merchants, goldsmiths, sewers, beer, and revels.[69] Similarly, Wilson undertook several catalogs itemizing papers in Cecil's study and made lists of Cecil's correspondents.[70]

Wilson's initial appointment as Keeper of the State Paper Office was an auxiliary to his role as Cecil's secretary, and it was little mentioned during Cecil's lifetime. During this period Wilson seems to have treated it, much as his predecessors had, as a sinecure mostly valuable for its annual £30. Since its founding in 1578, the State Paper Office had been administered haphazardly by a series of court figures who devoted little energy toward fulfilling its charter.[71] There were many reasons why the keepership elicited so little attention, foremost among them that secretarial papers, unlike Tower or Exchequer records, lacked probative authority. Another was that the office did not afford the fee-based copying that made the Tower profitable; as the oath Wilson swore demanded, "yow shall carefully & faithfully keep secret & conceale from the knowledg of others eyther by writing or relacion all such things therin contained ... except it bee to the His Lordships & others of the privy counsell, or such as his Majestie shalbe content to have them communicated therto."[72] The Keeper billed the Exchequer for copies he produced, but payment was often delayed, especially in comparison to the point-of-sale payments at the Tower. The office thus offered few opportunities to drum up fee-paying consultations and no way to guarantee compensation for them.

In the first years of his keepership, consequently, Wilson devoted little attention to the State Paper Office, which was simply a minor responsibility potentially useful for addressing the frenetic demands of Cecil's ongoing business.[73] But his trajectory was undeniably upward, for he had capitalized on his expertise in managing paperwork to acquire the position of an invaluable clerk who—with luck and patronly intercession—might follow the examples of Robert Beale and Thomas Lake to offices of escalating importance.

* * *

Cecil's trust and patronage provided Wilson with enviable security, advancement, and possibility. But Cecil's death in 1612 left Wilson adrift and forced him to renew his efforts to carve out spheres of powers and activity.[74] His desire to improve his own standing led him to venture ad hoc opportunities and projects underpinned by his expertise, ranging from the conventional to the fabulist and arcane.

Some of the more flamboyant episodes of Wilson's life hint that his value as information broker endured after Cecil's death. In 1617, for example, he recited to the king a report recently received from Richard Cocks, the East India Company factor in Japan, which stated that wars there witnessed 300,000 casualties, that the 100,000 men resident at the royal court included 100 kings, each with revenues to match James's, and that the royal palace was the site of four hundred golden idols. Wilson later reminisced how James had "(not without cause) told me that they were the loudest lyes that ever yow heard of."[75]

The following year Wilson was charged by Secretary of State Robert Naunton to watch "one Cavane . . . a tall black man with a pointed beard a la francoyse." Naunton warned that "he hath all the marks of a bold spy, and a practiced." This claim conflicted with his report that Cavane "professeth himself to be a papist, and that he hath lately bene some six moneths in Rome, and that he hath been imployed by the duke of Guise" and, even more divulgatory, that "they tell me yesternight that he cam hither in the morning expressly to take a view of his Majesty, and that he pressed boldly to the verie end of the kinges table as he satt at dinner, and went back to London in the afternoone." Wilson was instructed to tail this rather conspicuous spy, seize any papers he found at his lodgings, and interrogate Cavane for intelligence suspected as intended for the incarcerated Walter Ralegh. For three days Wilson employed three men, six horses, and a coach to follow Cavane; there is no evidence that he found him, and the whole episode may have been a charade, for on the last day he was summoned to question Ralegh himself.[76] Over the course of several weeks interrogation, he became convinced that Ralegh would not yield any useful information, and he asked to return to his position as Keeper of the State Paper Office as he had just received Secretary of

State Lake's papers (discussed earlier), which he wished "to abstract and putt in order . . . wherin I shall spend my tyme better for your Majestyes service then I can doe heer with this archimpostor."[77]

Wilson's continuing career with Ralegh further reveals that he also performed more scholarly services. After Ralegh's execution in 1618, Wilson was charged with inspecting the prisoner's Tower library, which he cataloged and recommended that James appropriate for his own library, while requesting to requisition Ralegh's manuscripts for the State Paper Office. Among the more striking materials Wilson commended to James was "a great manuscript book in parchment nere a yard square containing the discriptions of all contries in the world confyning with the seas & the states and qualities thereof, especially the territories of the king of Spaigne & the west and east indies," and "three sea cards of the west indies which hee wuld not have given for three hundred pounds."[78] James's interest, however, was most piqued by Ralegh's instruments, and he evidently demanded that Wilson make an equinoctial dial based on materials found in Ralegh's quarters, which Wilson duly delivered to James with instructions.[79] Indeed, James seems to have viewed Wilson as a scholarly factotum. Around 1619, the king asked Wilson to oversee the addition of "a chronologicall table written by your own royall hand as an Appendix to your Paraphrasis uppon the Apocalips" to a new Latin edition of James's works.[80] Wilson had recently surfaced it in Cecil's papers, and James now commissioned him to Latinize it along with Latin Secretary Thomas Reid, but the notoriously thorny thickets of chronology evidently overcame the two and the table was not included.

Wilson also designed scholarly services for James's favorite, Robert Carr. This courtship, however, proved rocky. Carr evidently had Wilson make some abstracts of treaties on his behalf, but Wilson later wrote to him, "My Lord when it pleased you erstwile to imploy me in making some abstracts of treaties I hoped that your beginning wold have been an introduccion to further use of my service but the weake performance therof I feare hath ben an impediment to the rest."[81] To demonstrate his value, Wilson now sent Carr an *ars apodemica* analysis of England, to which he appended a textual description entitled "Partitions for understanding matter of governement in generall but especially according to the constitution and laws of England."[82]

Carr had been in England for over a decade, and Wilson's offer may have been taken as condescension—justly, as Wilson shared the low opinion of Carr felt by many others.[83] Resuming his appeal for Carr's patronage, Wilson noted that "I have often observed that in divers discourses before his Majesty at table and sometymes when your Lordship was present that ther hath ben (by men otherwise grave & learned) much mistaking of tymes, when many things recorded in histories and cronicle were done and of the times when many famous persons lived, a point that breadeth much disreputation to the speaker and error in the hearer."[84] Wilson proposed to remedy the ignorance he obliquely ascribed to Carr by gathering a time line of "the most memorable things" from histories which, having put in chronological order, "I have thought them not unfitt for your Lordships service, whose lyfe will not afforde tyme for long discourses. Your lordship may herby with one glance of one ex per series temporum see in whych tyme age of the yeare any memorable thing occurred."[85] Wilson here proffered a rudimentary time line to develop Carr's inadequate learning. Similarly, he noted, "I have also added at the end therof certayne excellent sentences collected by me into heads out of divers of the best authors," to provide an elemental education in rhetoric.[86]

Such ad hoc patronage was never Wilson's goal; rather, he hoped to ascend into higher stable employment. He always saw his standing as inadequate, repeatedly avowing poverty and endlessly soliciting offices from would-be patrons. Some of his proposals seemed far-fetched or ill-advised—for example, the two occasions in which Wilson attempted to gain masterships of Cambridge colleges by writing letters commanding his appointment, which he then requested that the king sign.[87] He also twice pursued a grant of lands in Ireland.[88] The position of Latin Secretary, too, he long sought; at Reid's death in 1624, he recommended John Dickenson for the post while noting that he had been promised it before and yet passed over.[89] Nevertheless, over the next year he renewed his own pursuit of the position, sending some of Reid's papers that had come into his possession to Secretary of State Edward Conway with the advertisement that "I knowe his Majesty cannot butt thinke me the fittest man for it that have bene as my life brough up in the studdy of such business & suckt the milk of it," and requesting that "if you doe otherwise determyne of it I beseech you thinke of me for some forrayne Employment eyether in france Spayne Italy of else where that I maye doe some service ere I die."[90]

Wilson's desired offices were not limited to those already in existence, and he devised projects drawing on his expertise in information management. Around 1617, for example, Wilson proposed to James an "office of cerches in lieger books." As he explained, in the decades prior to the Dissolution of the Monasteries, English abbies and monasteries had kept "certaine leeger bookes of all theyr lands rent possessions pensions and rights belonging to their severall houses & churches," along with updates to their grants and titles.[91] While some of these ledger books had flowed into the Augmentations Office, others had fallen into private hands. Wilson recommended impaneling a commission to license an office under his oversight to recover them, where clerks would "transcribe the said bookes" before returning the originals to the owners. This, Wilson argued, would benefit the realm by directing fees to the clerks who performed the transcriptions, resolve the "darknes of mens titles" that spurred countless lawsuits, and—most important—reveal the Crown's title to lands others had been able to usurp because the "originall evidence is smothered and kept from knowledge."[92] In short, this office would centralize the texts securing royal property while simultaneously supporting social stability.

Similarly, in 1618 Wilson optimistically drafted "A Warrant for his Majesty to sign," establishing a "Register of Knighthood." As the warrant explained, "There shold be a certaine faire recorde, & register continuallie kept by some officer nere about us, of all such persons upon whome wee shall hereafter conferr the honnor of Knighthoode and also of the tymes & places when and where the said honnor shalbe bestowed."[93] As he explained, the absence of a formal record of knighthoods caused much inconvenience and strife, for "there is much variance for precedence betwixt many of your Majesty's subjects uppon whome you have conferred the honnor of knighthood, and especially betwixt theire wives, for that there is no certaine office or Regester kept of the tyme and place when & where the said honnor was bestowed upon them." Still worse, it enabled fraud: "Divers gentlemen coming to the Court in hope to obtaine that honnor, and not fynding suche meanes to effect it as they hoped for, and returning into their contries doe cause it to bee given out by some of theire servants or frends, that they are knighted, whereas indeed there is noe such matter and having pade their fees due for the same doe pass for knights in all places to the greate dishonnor of the order and preiudice to others."[94] To quell this strife, every new knight, he proposed, should be required to pay £5 for Wilson to enter them in the register he would maintain. This text, too, as Wilson imagined it, would have constituted a standardizing mechanism for state control, using inscription to police status and privilege.

In a distinct but kindred proposal, in 1621 Wilson and John Pory sought a patent to produce a royal newsletter.[95] Wilson explained that the dissemination of such newssheets would have myriad positive effects on the Crown's subjects. For one, it would "quicken their conceipts & understanding bi geving them tasts of matters elevate from the common myre worldlyness," thus making them more amenable to reasoned rule. Similarly, he asserted that it would "establish a speedy & reddy way whereby to dispose into all the veynes of the whole body of a state such matter as may best temper it, & be most agreeable to the disposition of the head or the principale members upon all occasions that shalbe offered." It would be most useful "when there shalbe any revolt or back sliding in matter of religion or obedience (which commonly growes up rumors amongst the vulgar)," for the Crown's house organ would "draw them in by the same lynes that drewe them out by spreeding amongst them such reports as may best make for that matter to which we wold have them drawne."[96] Rather than spurring an independent public sphere, Wilson envisioned this newspaper as controlling subjects' discussion by structuring it through texts infused with royal interest. Though more public facing than his other projects, it also would thus enhance royal power by using texts as instruments of centralization and standardization.[97]

With a comical lack of tact, Wilson conceded of his proposed newsletter that "much good may come to the nation generally by these meanes ... though to say the truth it is my own particular benefitt that is the greatest motive to me in this matter."[98] While his projects sought to adapt his expertise to the perceived needs of the realm, personal stability was his foremost concern. Above all, a Mastership of Requests was his preferred avenue of advancement—ambitiously but not unreasonably, as in these years Ralph Winwood, Robert Naunton, and John Coke rose from this office to Secretary of State. How Wilson substantiated his claim explicitly reveals that he believed his tenure as Keeper of the State Paper Office exhibited his suitability for promotion. In his many petitions for a mastership, he asserted that his conduct as keeper merited advancement.[99] This was, for example, at the center of the litany of reasons he supplied in a 1617 petition wherein he stressed that in the Paper Office, "I have reduced all those things (which consist of many millions of matters) out of extreame confusion, into exact order for use & service, as both the king & all his privy counsell do knowe, & built & furnished the roomes of the office as now they are." As he further complained, he had been "3 severall tymes named for the place of Mr of Requests," including by the ascendant minister, George Villiers, 1st Duke of Buckingham, but every time had been displaced by courtly machination. Now he requested this position, for "it wilbe a greate advancement to his service, for yf by the place of Mr of Requests, I shall have access to his Majesty to acquaint him with such things, which by my long experience & study in the office of the papers I have learned, & which it wilbee fitt for his Majesty to understand & know."[100]

After Cecil's death abandoned him to his own devices, in short, Wilson agitated to return to the path to high advancement by pursuing ordinary offices and projecting new ones. His strategies in both cases were underpinned by expertise in information management and rooted in his performance as Keeper of the State Papers, for it was here that he claimed to have proven most profitable, imaginative, and effective in forwarding the interests of the Stuart regime.

* * *

In fact, Wilson's reshaping of the languishing State Paper Office was the most successful of his projects, for upon Cecil's death, Wilson seized on its possibilities.[101] After 1612, Wilson aggressively sought to accession papers belonging to the office according to its charter, imposed order on the collections, raised awareness of its holdings, secured permanent rooms for it in Whitehall near the Banqueting House, and directed its resources toward broader political goals. His tenure as Keeper offers an exemplary case study in the transformation of political practice in early modern Britain.

Any cleavage between the seemingly tedious bureaucratic elements of Wilson's keepership and his life's more colorful moments is illusory, an anachronistic minimization of the unforeseen effects of the saturation of politics by inscription. Wilson's mobilization of the State Paper Office exemplifies this change, as he maneuvered to leverage his unusual access to the neglected materials of previous secretaries. He did so by identifying latent value in disused texts and then enhancing their utility and authority through their targeted circulation.

Wilson's invigoration of the office took many forms. The most straightforward was his aggressive pursuit of official papers of secretaries that the charter assigned to his office. He frequently importuned other statesmen to intervene with those derelict in depositing their papers with him—often successfully—and consequently obtained materials in far greater quantities than had his predecessors, and even when they came in, he made note of papers he thought absent.[102] Wilson also directed this sensibility to nonsecretarial collections that might enhance his office; for example, he tried to obtain the papers of Arthur Agarde, Edward Coke, and Ralph Starkey, and he made copies of records from depositories such as the Chapter House.[103]

This program appears to have persuaded James of the office's value; in 1618, James provided Wilson with a "warrant under the royall hand for recoveringe of all such things as were uniustly deteyned from thence," while assuring Wilson that he "wold make it the rarest office of that qualitie in Christendom of Europe."[104] Though the king's sincerity might be questioned, he did prove to be an ally in securing the office from apathy, plunder, and embezzlement, as Wilson repeatedly consulted him about honoring requests to borrow or copy documents from individuals whose authority or purpose seemed unclear, and James supported a stringent lending policy.[105]

Royal approval enabled Wilson to grow increasingly comfortable pressing statesmen and officials to return borrowed items, provide him with copies of their materials, or relinquish papers to him. Under his care, the office finally began to fulfill its purported function. But as the office grew, Wilson faced increasingly complex problems of organization.[106] In response, he devised a system that, for the first time, added an abstract layer of classification over the catalogs, registers, and inventories previously used to manage England's central archives.

At first, simply creating coherent bundles out of the tumult of papers seemed paramount. Accordingly, Wilson explained in a memorandum seeking compensation for costs and labor in 1613 that "I have spent 8 yeares in reducing them out of extreame confusion, and brought them into order, made regesters of all or most of particuler papers, and bound the most part up unto bookes according to theyre subjects, heads, and yeares."[107] In fact, he was organizing the office's documents chronologically by type, as he laid out in a draft headed "The Generale heads whereunto the papers are reduced by order of yeares and months." The first type was "advises & intelligences by letters," broken into subcategories of ambassadors, agents and private men; this grouping was followed by the letters of princes and then of statesmen, treaties with foreign powers, "proiects & designes," decrees and proclamations, "discourses upon matter of state," contracts and debts, warrants, negotiations, and petitions.[108] The result of compiling materials according to this genre-based scheme yielded collections with such titles as "one great book of Treaties betwixt the princes of Italy."[109]

At some point in this process, however, Wilson grew dissatisfied with the system. Instead, he gravitated toward a more taxonomic scheme, concluding that "nowe those bookes must be all broken, and the papers that were thus devyded in place, must be made up all in one according to these heades and countreys." Instead of being rooted in document type, this scheme was anchored in categorical similarities between documents. As he explained in outlining this new arrangement, "These papers are eyther concerning business domesticall or foreign. The domestique be of these and such lyke heads: matters concerning the kings revenue or matter of estat or else particuler men's businesses, revenues," and so on.[110] Like most contemporary systems of classification, this new system allotted other polities their own categories. But, more innovatively, headings for domestic matters were divided into the conceptual categories of *regalia, legalia, ecclesiastica, militaria, politica, criminalia,* and *mechanica*—an encyclopedic system facilitating the easy organization of newly incoming materials.[111] Wilson thus devised this abstract system of classification to assert a new kind of order over the documents, one which prioritized thematic continuity over chronology, inherited order, or document type.

Ultimately, Wilson did not engage in the frenzy of unbinding and rebinding he had said was necessary; instead, he arranged his preexisting books and bundles within the new taxonomy. Wilson completed this project by 1616, when he elaborated the new organization of the office in a catalog entitled "The General Heads of Things in the Office of His Majesties Papers and Records for Business of State & Council."[112] This guide did not itself contain registers of the office's holdings, but each category was keyed to shelves or drawers in the office; it thus served as a map rather than an inventory.

As this guide revealed, the categories for foreign polities were dominated by instructions, letters, and negotiations. Separate registers for the contents of some individual drawers were produced to aid in searching; for example, the office's thirty-seven Low Countries books included "A booke of letters from Mr Secretarie Wilson, Mr Secretarie Walsingham and Sir Edward Stafford out of France & the Low Countries from 1574 till 1588."[113] Wilson's domestic categories possessed a more expansive cornucopia of materials. *Regalia*, for example, which entailed "matters concerning the Crowne and Revenue," subsumed "diverse books of Majesties title to the Crowne of England his Praerogative therein," patents, commissions, warrants, seals, grants, gifts, and more, as well as account books of revenue and expenses and materials concerning the king's lands, properties, tributes, and aids."[114] *Politica* encompassed materials produced by other offices and institutions such as the Privy Council and Council of the North, while under *legalia* he filed parliamentary acts and orders, proclamations, edicts and decrees, statutes, and more. The most capacious category was *mechanica*, which, as he explained, "conteyned all matters of Marchants, Trade and Manufactures, with their severall suites and complaynts, books concerning the business of exchange, and values of money in dyvers countryes," but also included trade treaties.[115] The new arrangement thus subordinated the empirical to the classificatory to create a system easing the absorption of new materials and enabling the ready location of desired items.

Wilson's system was an innovation in English archives. Though it resembled some of the emergent encyclopedic programs of Continental thinkers, there is no evidence of his contact with such developments, and he was likely more driven by the practical imperative to sort and find materials.[116] The system, however, also served as a map of the space of the archive, facilitating searching within it. Over the 1610s, such capability

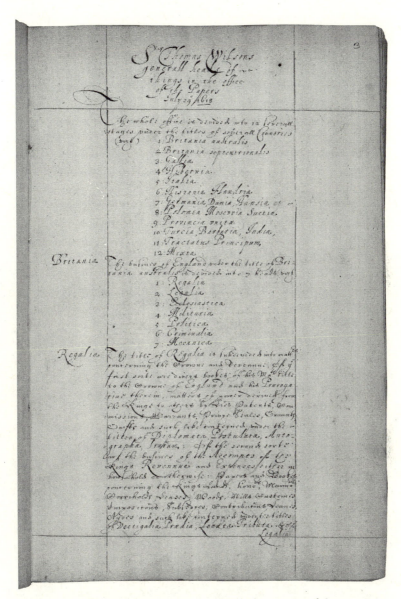

FIGURE 11. The beginning of Thomas Wilson's description of the State Paper Office's collections, which he divided into the conceptual categories of *regalia, legalia, ecclesiastica, militaria, politica, criminalia,* and *mechanica*—an encyclopedic system facilitating the easy organization of newly incoming materials. This copy was made in 1618, though the first version was completed by 1616. BL Add. MS 48008, f. 3r. By permission of the British Library.

became vital, for as he struggled to propel himself into loftier position, Wilson sought to generate increasing interest in the archive by highlighting its possibilities for enhancing counsel and diplomacy. His efforts paid off in a steady flow of requests, which he labored to satisfy in the hope that he would be rewarded for the quality of his work managing and mediating the office's paperwork. One of his foremost methods of demonstrating this expertise, ironically, was to occlude his own labor by presenting curated selections that emerged straight from his office's drawers but with minimal commentary, as if the archive was speaking on its own.

Wilson circulated a range of materials to increase the visibility of his collection. For one, he saw the catalog itself as advertising the possibilities of the office and accordingly circulated copies of it to elite statesmen. In 1616 he sent a copy to the future Duke of Buckingham, then at the outset of his meteoric ascent, suggesting that "whereby you maye make choice of such things as you will please to make use which when I shall understand from your I will make more particular collections for your service of such things as you shall chuse," and requesting that Buckingham intercede on his behalf to be appointed Master of Requests.[117] Wilson also sent copies to Edward Conway in 1623 and Sir John Coke in 1625 upon their respective appointments as Secretary of State and to Edward Barrett in 1628 when he was appointed to the Privy Council.[118]

More commonly, Wilson's circulations took the form of "transcribing, collecting & abstracting" materials for statesman and administrators.[119] Initially, he mostly copied treaties for diplomats in preparation for their negotiations—a task surely eased by his reorganization. This remained a perennial responsibility and enabled, for example, Edward Herbert to bring five copies of treaties and attestations received from Wilson on his embassy to France in 1619.[120] Wilson thus used his office to create portable archives of essential texts required by statesmen.

Over time, the material in the packets supplied by Wilson diversified, reflecting a combination of expanded inquiries and his own initiative. Between 1614 and 1616 he billed the king for twenty-five copies, virtually all of which were treaties.[121] In a report of March 1618 to James, Wilson stated that in addition to requests for treaties, the Earl of Ormond requested a confirmation of privileges, "some of the Heralds" requested information concerning the position of Lord President of the Council, and Cotton asked for a collection of signatures and subscriptions.[122] In his next surviving bill for August 1618–April 1619, thirty of the fifty items were treaties, but he also produced a "Book of Offices" and other assorted items including a collection of "certaine points out of all the letters in my custody to and from the great Turke" for Naunton.[123] Subsequent years saw an escalation in his copying and circulation. In 1625 when tabulating his copies for the late Secretary of State George Calvert, for example, he reported items on outfitting ships and levying soldiers, Dutch petitions against England merchants, notes on parliamentary subsidies, notes on Philip's courtship of Mary, a Latin discourse on holy war, letters of the kings of Denmark, and more.[124]

Although most of these deliveries fulfilled requests, Wilson regularly generated his own collections in an effort to use the archives to redress problems he perceived in early Stuart governance. In particular, he tried to use to the archives to provide relief to the king's coffers. He began agitating over an alleged debt of £100,000 owed by Flanders to the Crown in 1618, and then in 1620 cataloged and circulated supporting documents such as "an instrument obligatory of the states to the Queen for 800,000 pounds" from 1598 and three notes of bonds to the queen.[125] Despite gaining no traction, he continued to press, explaining to Lord Keeper John Williams in 1625 and then Lord Treasurer James Ley that this sum had been "borrowed by the kinge of Spaynes procurement and his Ministers of Queene Elizabeth which shee lent only to keepe them in obedience when they were first about to revolt, and for which old Phillip of Spayne in the Treaty of Brussels and Pacification of Gente did order and decree that all moneyes which the Queene had lent or should lend to them for their ayde should be duly payed."[126] Though both Williams and Ley demurred, Wilson's strategy entailed consolidating documents he had uncovered in his archive into an advertisement of a forgotten windfall.

Similarly, around 1620 Wilson began "collecting notes for a book which I am making for your Majesty of all the heds whereof most of the greate princes of Christendome do deryve their revenue into which I propose to insert what meanes the kings of England ever since the conquest have used to provide treasure when they stood in need thereof eyther by reason of warr or other extraordinary occasions."[127] Ultimately, at Ley's recommendation, the volume focused solely on elaborating the means by which English monarchs had raised money in the past.[128] The entirety consisted of brief notes from chronicles and records; for example, his first entry for Edward VI read: "He in his second yeare had an ayd of 12p the pound of goods of his natural subiects and 2s the pound of straingers given unto him by Parliament which was to continue three yeares."[129] These collections, though arranged chronologically, did not demonstrate the historical development of an office or practice but rather precedents for royal instruments of revenue extraction. In this tract, Wilson portrayed records in his archive as speaking for themselves, even if they benefited from an expert commentator.

When he collected texts regarding royal marriages at Lake's request in 1617, Wilson attributed to his materials the same objectivity.[130] But this episode also reveals how Wilson's circulation of materials might have a sharp political edge, for Wilson's selection of records masked a distinct perspective with the air of objectivity.[131]

Wilson's engagement with the question of Prince Charles's Spanish match began in April 1617, when Secretary Lake (who was in favor of the match) ordered "that certaine Treaties of Marriage between forragne Princes and Kings of this realme should be written out and made ready" for Ambassador John Digby, then preparing to head to Madrid to open formal negotiations.[132] This bundle was intended to provide groundwork for precarious diplomacy. Wilson produced it, but after having done so, as he later explained in the copy he dedicated to James, he "thought it not unfitting (as here I have done) to present unto your Majesty a Rapsodi of such things, as I have in the treasury of Majesty's papers, concerning the subiect."[133] In consequence, he compiled a manuscript tract consolidating three sets of materials, which he delivered to the king that October.[134] First was a list of royal matches that he had produced after having mined English chronicles; second was a discourse written by Burghley, "Wherein are excellently (though plainly discoursed) the reasons, pro et contra, for matching with a prince of contrary religion"; and third was a large body of "abstracts of treaties, or rather of such fragments & carcases of treaties, as I have in my custody." In his dedication, Wilson insisted that this text merely distilled and projected the collections of his archive: as he characterized it, "it is a child of my paines, rather then of my braines, and a work of my penn in transcribing, collecting, and abstracting, rather then of my judgment in devising & contriving I not daring to let any thing that is wholy myne owne undergoe the censure of your Majesty's great iudgment."[135] In dissociating the work from his judgment, he presented himself as merely the messenger of the archives, and at the end of his dedicatory letter, he renewed his request to James for a Mastership of Requests.

The message of the archives was unmistakable, however. As the inclusion of Burghley's tract hints, Wilson was highly suspicious of the Spanish match. Burghley—ironically, seeking to forestall Elizabeth's French match—had bluntly concluded that marriage to a Catholic prince could not help but threaten the Reformation in England; by reproducing Burghley's discourse, Wilson was able to articulate this perspective while disowning responsibility for it. More compelling to Wilson, however, was that reviewing past marriage treaties with the Spanish revealed that they often pursued such negotiations duplicitously, seeking political goals without intention of consummating the betrothal. Wilson explicitly elaborated his position in a letter to Lord James Hay, ambassador to France: "For doubtless Spaigne (which never makes matches but to other

& worse ends) will only seeke to Divert us from france by amusing us with great offers which in the end will prove *parturiunt montes* [a pointless labor], as your Lordship may see by some of these & diverse other treaties that have beene with them which have bene absolutly concluded of, but when they saw, their other ends were discovered, & soe not to be attained they soone brake of."[136] Even in the marriage of Mary to Philip, he was convinced, Spain's purpose had been to prevent an Anglo-French alliance. Thus the marriage treaties in his office were enlisted as evidence arguing for skepticism toward the Spanish.

Wilson could not divert royal policy, though events ultimately followed the path he had predicted. In fact, his efforts to provide counsel were rarely directed toward issues on the level of royal marriages and finances. More often he circulated collections of records and materials describing the histories, rights, and responsibilities of offices—much like Caesar's and others discussed earlier in this chapter—to individuals who had been, or expected to be, appointed to them. For example, he delivered several such collections to Buckingham. In 1623, along with copies of Elizabethan treaties with the Low Countries and his explanation for the huge debt allegedly owed by Flanders to James, he recorded that he had made for the duke "a great book in folio of all matters belonging to his office of Lord Admiral together with all abuses in all offices belonging to the navy and the meanes to reforme the same" and "another like book of all things belonging to the office of Earle Marshall when it was thought that his Lord should have had that place."[137] In the same bill he reported producing a similar study of the office of Lord Treasurer for Henry Montagu, who then held the office, and in subsequent bills he recorded having in the past produced collections regarding the royal household for the Duke of Lennox (who was the Lord Chamberlain of Scotland), "for Somerset when he was Chamberlain concerning that, for Suffolk on lord treasurer, for Northampton on admiralty," and others.[138]

Wilson proudly referred to these studies of England's offices in 1624 when responding to an insult from Secretary Calvert that "your honor told me the last daye that the office which I serve in was an office to little purpose." His defense revolved around demonstrating "the necessity of it, and the greate use that is made of it by other Councilors, and hath beene by all the Secretaryes saving yourself."[139] The testimonies he singled out that highlighted its singular worth were his tract on the Lord Treasurer for Thomas Howard, Earl of Suffolk, the collection of marriage treaties, collections on the Lord Chamberlain for Carr and Ludovic Stewart, 2nd Duke of Lennox, Buckingham's Lord Admiral and Earl Marshall tracts, and the collections compiled for Digby's embassy. Wilson, that is, viewed as most prestigious his work at fashioning miniature archives that delimited the rights, responsibilities, and possibilities of offices and embassies. Their virtues, he maintained, best enabled counselors and ambassadors to recognize the value in Wilson's transformation of the obscure repository for dead letters into an engine of circulation, as the archival replications produced by his collections gave strength to their aspirations, security to their embassies, and certainty to their offices.

Wilson continued to promote his work after James's death, sending Buckingham news and urging him to make better use of his treatise on the Lord Admiralty in early 1627, and writing to the new king, James's son Charles, to explain his office as his expenses continued to mount.[140] Not long after the new king's accession, Wilson drafted a lengthy proposal to Charles for a volume containing "a breefe abstracts of the principall points, of all leagues, and confederations, that are now betwixt your Majestie, and your neighbor Princes and states, from the beginning of his last Majesties raigne, and somewhat before, As allsoe the truest relations of forrayne Princes states that I could gett or finde in this your Majesties office of your papers and records for business of state."[141] Charles's appreciation of the volume would follow an illustrious precedent; Wilson began by noting that Augustus "ever carryed about him a booke which contayned these 3 things": first, concerning the number and quality of his soldiers; second, his expenses and revenues; and third, "what leagues and confederations he had with this friends, his neighbors, and what ther states and abilitys were, both of them, from whom he might expect help whyle they were his frends, or hurts if they became his inimyes."[142] Wilson acknowledged that others might be better equipped to supply the first two but, he argued, his keepership made him indispensable for the third.[143]

Wilson ultimately chose not to deliver this treatise to the new king. But he still wished to deliver some token, and accordingly he prepared to send Charles the abstract of the means of royal revenue that he had delivered to Ley several years prior. He saw this book as far more salient for the immediate moment, as it demonstrated "that your Majesties subiects heer have no such cause to be discontented as itt seems they are" by the controversial new means with which the new Caroline regime sought to generate income.[144] In fact, this volume revived an abandoned element of his previous collection on royal revenue; in a letter to Ley describing the book, he noted that "I had deseygned to make the preamble to this booke a discorse of what all thes princes heerin mentioned by ther meanes of raysing ther revnewe have done iustly & prudently without too great greevance of ther subiects & therein would have appeared the contrary of what they have don uniustly & unwisely and indeed to ther owne harme," for "those meanes of raysinge unnecessary unfitting or untimely impositions have ben the causes of most of the rebellions mutinyes that the commons have [had] and hereupon revolutions in states which history report."[145] Wilson recognized that the materials he had excised from his previous tract on revenue could now be marshaled to support the Crown's fiscal policy. But, as before, Wilson took care to insist that this was not a polemical inflection of his sources but a perspective embedded in the evidence itself, writing, "I have written in this book nothing of my owne but what I have stolne & enacted (as he sayd) out of your Majesties papers heer in my custodye being the relations of our late Ambassadors sent over hether out of divers countryes some in french some in Italian some in Spanish out of which I have translated and collected the principal poynts tending to the subiect of this book wherein if ther be any thing mistaken it was mistaken by them and not me."[146] Once again, Wilson presented himself as curator, not interpreter, of the invaluable papers that rested under his care.

*　*　*

Wilson sought to mediate governance through the textual legacy of which he had unique custody. His activity was structured by the desire to capture and deploy the sphere of paper to his own advantage, and his entire career was unified by a practice of information management, whether he was transmitting news, compiling a synoptic view of England, proposing newsletters, or producing historical studies of the Lord Admiralty from his archives. Especially after 1612, he was always on the lookout for unappreciated textual resources and opportunities. Wilson's reconfiguration of the State Paper Office into a site of knowledge production was his most successful project, but it depended on a landscape of inscription awash in letters, notes, scraps, and more collected in the practice of secretarial life. Under Wilson's custody, these decaying documents no longer remained inert testimonials of long-dead days but instead were given new agency as participants in the ongoing activity of governance. In his hands, the archive became a site of innovative exploration and experimentation in statecraft, where the varying past fortunes of offices were flattened and reconfigured as prescriptive, where the small set of marriage negotiations with the Spanish crown could lead to universal principles about that distrusted realm, where new modes of extracting revenue could be resuscitated from the obliviated past and given life anew. He found in the moldering papers of state a body of textual resources whose value had been neglected; through their repeated replication and widespread circulation, they could assume wide authority—and confer the same on him.

Conclusion

Thomas Wilson's and Sir Julius Caesar's quests for advancement—and those of many others—led them to direct neglected repositories of government documents toward regularizing the practices and functions of offices and coordinating the information resources with which government agents performed their duties. They thus advanced the project of building a paper empire to support English governance, for by mobilizing records of the past as the fundamental resource for knowing government, the archive coordinated the state. Despite their seeming opposition toward innovation, the same was true of the clerical projects proposed by Wilson's contemporaries and exemplified by his recalibration of the State Paper Office.

Discerning how the environment of inscription structured political practice has significant repercussions for understanding the trajectory of England's political institutions. For one, the studies of offices and practices of Wilson, Caesar, Thomas Egerton, and others suggest a nascent bureaucratization. Historical studies of bureaucracy tend to begin with Max Weber, who depicted it as a species of legal—rather than traditional or charismatic—authority, distinguished by being hierarchical, rule-bound, continuous, impersonal, and above all, rationally organized, with a "desk" (*bureau*) for each function.[147] Weber was little concerned with the processes generating this form of government, attributing it to ineluctable, abstract rationalization. Insofar as British historians have sought to depict bureaucracy as emerging in early modernity, they have tried to validate the existence of bureaucratic organization rather than detail the circumstances of its emergence. Most notably, G. R. Elton saw it as emerging from Henrician reforms to the privy chamber in 1526 and 1540; G. E. Aylmer substantiated it by delineating the professionalization of the civil service; both, like Weber, saw the unstated engine of rationalization as its cause.[148]

Neither Elton nor Aylmer attended to the role ascribed to inscription by Weber, who had noted that in bureaucracies, "Administrative acts, decisions, and rules are formulated and recorded in writing, even in cases where oral discussion is the rule or even mandatory. This applies at least to preliminary discussions and proposals, to final decisions, and to all sorts of orders and rules. The combination of written documents and a continuous organization of official functions constitutes the 'office' (*bureau*)."[149] By contrast, in recent years, historians have increasingly argued that at least some of the features Weber saw as products of rationalization instead arose from demands exerted by technologies of inscription.[150]

The examples of Richard Frampton, Wilson, Caesar, and others reinforce this latter view, but they also suggest a striking engine of change. Such functionaries formalized the desks at the heart of bureaucracy, recalibrated Crown governance as an interlocking set of historically grounded, functional institutions, and elevated the idiom of depersonalized, institutional autonomy, but they did so driven by highly personal and contingent circumstances. In this view, bureaucratization and the growth of the information state were not consequences of idealized rationalization, nor of the pressing demands of the fiscal-military state, but of projects by embattled counselors using textual resources to carve out spheres of authority.

To be sure, neither Wilson nor Caesar envisioned nor created the full-fledged bureaucracy Weber observed in the nineteenth century. But their work signals a transformed practice of conceiving government. Much as postcolonial scholars have recognized that the archive, as an organizing principle, often turned governments into echo chambers that unwittingly created social relations and political epistemologies rather than recording them, the studies of Caesar and Wilson reenvisioned government not as fluid and free-form but as a stable assemblage of offices and institutions, whose constitutions, procedures, and jurisdictions they possessed the resources to delimit. No less strikingly, in doing so, they revised the perception of government no less than Arthur Agarde had, reimagining it in the form of a state. And like him, this transformation rested on the aggressive recombination and recontextualization of textual resources. The abundance of a technology that augmented inscription and facilitated copying of past documents thus led England's government to turn a new optical device on itself, one whose distortions and refractions transformed how it saw its past and present and engineered its future.

4

Shared Practice and Rival Visions of the State

English governance transformed as individuals conjured the glimmerings of a state from a chaotic welter of inscriptions. Contemporaries shared general consensus concerning the properties of legitimate evidence, as well as a steadfast conviction that structuring England's government on the foundations of past records would realize its ideal form. Their visions of the state, however, were neither uniform nor uncontested. Not only were records often ambiguous, partial, or contradicted by others, but the shared practices meant to integrate them often exacerbated disagreements, for when participants in this world encountered opposition, they plumbed their overloaded mine of sources for others that could support their position. An ethic of combativeness compounded this instability, as diligent students of Britain's past thrashed each other mercilessly over differences of interpretation. The result was an environment calibrated to nurture division, and tensions inflamed as efforts to use inscriptions to regularize practices of governance became combats to control the form of the state. The methods that had been conceptualized as appropriate for generating consensus instead catalyzed disunity.

This chapter explores the role of this information dynamic in the breakdown of the early Stuart polity.[1] It begins by showing how this method of legitimization could support a variety of modes of constructing authority. The disastrous years of Charles I's early reign—especially the 1628 Parliament—exemplify how this combination of practices and values fueled segmentation and fracture, establishing positions that would be deepened and developed using these same tools in the decade after Charles's 1629 decision to rule without Parliament. The onset of crisis in the late 1630s—ignited in part by the Caroline regime's underestimation of alternative visions—exposed how the regime of inscription had produced a combustible environment marked by incommensurable beliefs about Britain's past and its proper state in the present.

The Noble Past

The use of past inscriptions as instruments of knowledge formation was directed toward forms of authority beyond the protobureaucratic variety discussed in the chapter 3. Perhaps most notably, written records were also used to illuminate aristocratic and honor-driven authority, as Jacobeans increasingly approached genealogical questions using the same techniques of collection, comparison, and collation that they brought to histories of offices. Such activities both reveal that such techniques could anchor multiple models of authority and how the indeterminacy of their practice engendered conflict.[2]

Agarde's successor as Deputy Chamberlain of the Exchequer Scipio Le Squyer deployed the techniques of his mentor, ultimately amassing at least seventy-eight volumes of transcriptions and abridgments from the Westminster archives among the more than two hundred manuscript volumes he collected along with nearly five hundred printed books.[3] Squyer, however, devoted far more attention than Agarde had to underwriting England's aristocratic legacy. For example, in 1607 he began compiling an armorial concerning his native Devonshire that initially took the conventional form of coats of arms accompanied by brief notes concerning each family. Over time, he inserted additional notes reflecting research in inquisitions post mortem in the Tower, deeds he had been shown by local families, and, unusually, epitaphs on gravestones in local churches. At the end Squyer inserted alphabetical indexes to families and towns, arms of trades in Devonshire, and arms belonging to towns, abbeys, or churches.[4] Though Squyer was not a herald, his methods directed techniques of the regime of inscription toward genealogical questions— realizing the reform of the heralds, as noted in chapter 1, prophesied by the Marquis of Winchester.[5]

This trajectory for genealogical inquiry is even clearer in the activities of the Derbyshire gentleman St. Loe Knyveton. The irascible Knyveton had a savage confidence in the power of records to illuminate England's aristocratic past. Though he never held formal office, he was associated with Gray's Inn and performed a wide array of inquiries in the hope of gaining secure employment. Knyveton's written works reflect expertise in archival exploration and practices of inscription. For example, when Sir Julius Caesar was granted the reversion to Master of the Rolls after Edward Bruce's 1611 death (to which Caesar would succeed in 1614), Knyveton compiled for him a collection on the office consisting of annotated extracts from the Rolls Chapel on Chancery Lane and transcriptions of Tower records.[6] Similarly, Knyveton produced substantial treatments on the Lord Constable and Lord Steward's offices for Henry Howard, Earl of Northampton.[7]

Knyveton also drew on meticulous sleuthing of Tower and Exchequer records, notes from King's Bench and assize courts, plea rolls, the Domesday Book, and more to construct lengthy collections concerning the Villiers, Frescheville, Cope, and Curzon families.[8] The most significant was a gargantuan discourse for Thomas Howard, Earl of Arundel, using evidence "collected faithfully from the royal records, archives and chests and trustworthy histories" to narrate the earldom's history since the Norman Conquest.[9] From these he outlined the case that "in the judgment of all, there is neither among nobles anyone more learned, nor among the learned anymore more noble than you."[10] The body of the volume consisted of long transcriptions from an extraordinary range of documents, beginning with "an ancient manuscript book concerning the deeds of William or Normandy," and incorporating chronicles, Domesday, registers of abbeys, charters, the Red Book of the Exchequer, pipe rolls, chartae antiquae, patent rolls, Matthew Parker's publications, and more. Interspersed among these were conjectures concerning the origins of the Howard name and other family history problems, in which Knyveton demonstrated how mastering an expansive body of records illuminated genealogical questions.

Though he was enterprising in finding sources, Knyveton procured many from Robert Cotton, including catalogs of Tower records produced by Michael and Thomas Heneage, Francis Thynne, and William Lambarde.[11] He also depended on Cotton's support as intermediary with Northampton, their mutual patron, and Cotton had likely funneled the Arundel project his way.[12] Cotton's and Knyveton's relationship, however, illuminates how individuals mobilizing their command of resources of the past wavered between collaboration and competition.

Shortly after Robert Cecil's 1612 death, Cotton wrote to Knyveton seeking to enlist him in several projects sponsored by Northampton, who was at that time the ascendant minister in King James I's regime. Cotton's immediate concern lay in reconfiguring the Exchequer to be run by a Commission—headed by Northampton—for which he requested that Knyveton produce precedents. Knyveton responded brusquely that "in discharge of my duty, though I feare farre short of your desire, I have herewith sent you a fewe notes, such as the shortness of the tyme would give me leasure to looke up, and yf I have any more to the purpose you shall have them. But I doubt yt wilbe very hard to fynd a president that the office of Threasurer was executed by a commissioner." As Knyveton continued, he believed that he merited full employment in the Exchequer rather than such ad hoc consultations: "The truth is, I speake yt vere et verecunde, that I have laboured much to enforme my selfe of the office of the Lord Threasurer of England, and the carriage of matters in the exchequer anciently, and now I would be glad by your meanes to have some such employment in some course there as might make me think that my tyme well bestowed, and not loose all my labours tyme & expenses in vaine as hitherto I have done." He had already, he reminded Cotton, given Northampton notes on the office of the Lord Marshall, the Cinque Ports, and other matters. Most acerbically, Knyveton pointed out that his work for Northampton regarding the Court of Chivalry—an occasional court of the Earl Marshall hearing suits concerning honor and status—had been performed upon expectation of future employment, which had not materialized. A speedy appointment to a suitable place would only be fitting.

Knyveton's gripe was not only with Northampton, for he was also irate that Cotton ascended while he stagnated. Knyveton confessed that he was starting to believe that Cotton was deliberately preventing his rise, threatening that "yf nothing be done to my benefite I shall blame you on whom I have most relied my self." And accordingly he made quite clear what he saw as a fitting token of gratitude: "Pardon my plainess which is I confesse my naturall fault. I doe heare that two are in hand with Mr Bowier for his office in the Tower and that they are like to through for yt. I pray you deale plainely with me what you are resolved to doe therin." As a kicker, Knyveton pressured him: "If you let yt escape your hands so, I shall think you nothing love antiquities indeed, howsoever you professe."[13] Knyveton, that is, positioned himself as the natural heir to the position of Keeper of the Tower Records. This cutting letter did not repel Cotton; though Cotton never did obtain a position for Knyveton—indeed, Knyveton overestimated Cotton's ability to command patronage—they collaborated with Agarde to search the royal wardrobe several years later, and in 1621 they were still exchanging manuscripts.[14]

This exchange illuminates the tensions of an environment in which those pursuing prestige and offices framed their expertise in manipulating records in a competitive, agonistic idiom. Knyveton's caustic side was never more on display in than in the strident notes he entered in his copy of Rouge Croix Pursuivant Augustine Vincent's 1622 *A Discoverie of Errours in the first Edition of the Catalogue of Nobility Published by Raphe Brooke, Yorke Herald*. Knyveton sided in this vitriolic debate with the contentious Brooke, who had spent almost three decades squabbling with his fellow heralds, most prominently William Camden.[15] This conflict reveals dysfunctional elements imbuing England's information culture: disagreements concerning the priority of evidence, uncertain knowledge about critical features of even the relatively recent past, and the propensity for debate to sharpen rather than resolve points of contention.[16]

Brooke perceived his colleagues as unscrupulous mercenaries easily swayed to devising questionable genealogies, and he advocated widespread reform in the College of Arms. As part of this feud, he had in 1619 published his *Catalogue of Nobility* which, much like Knyveton's family collections, used inquisitions postmortem and other sources to outline each title's creation, track its holders over time, register additional offices and titles each holder had accrued, determine when they had died, and trace their marriages and offspring. From this research, he characterized Camden's *Britannia* as insufficiently reliant on the best heraldic practices and, as a result, as conjuring an illusory past.

Like the other heralds, Vincent remained squarely in Camden's corner, and his *A Discoverie of Errours* sneeringly cataloged the mistakes he found in Brooke's text with the help of his own substantial collections.[17] But Knyveton turned an even more belligerent eye toward Vincent's response, ruthlessly assailing Vincent and his supporters in scores of annotations. For example, John Selden had contributed an admiring letter characterizing Vincent's archival investigations as—alongside Camden's *Annales* and Francis Bacon's study of Henry VII—marking a resurgence in record-based historical writing. Knyveton instead scoffed that Bacon's "The Life & Reign of King Henry 7 is in very many places written contrary the Records of this kingdom."[18] Similarly, throughout his notes Knyveton accused Vincent of introducing errors to what should have been unassailable evidence, claiming that "it is not my purpose to cavell with Records but only to shew that those are usually alledged as being in your Office not always true but may be miswritten & mistaken."[19]

Moreover, Knyveton eviscerated Vincent not just for misinterpreting evidence but for trusting dubious sources. Concerning the burial place of Gilbert de Clare, Earl of Herford, he criticized Vincent for relying exclusively on a register in Cotton's library: "Here is not true Voucher, unless you dare Conclude that every MSS in Bibliotheca Cottoniana is Sufficient Authoritie of it self which I dare Confidently deny."[20] Similarly, regarding the burial place of Lionel, 1st Duke of Clarence, Vincent's use of a "few rythmicall lines (taken out of an ancient rolle, shewing the lineall descent of the Lords of the Honour of Claire)" incurred Knyveton's merciless reproach: "You are wont to be for records now for Rithmical Old Verses & English Ballades but because they are in your custody perhaps you have entred them upon record which els any man of some Iudgement would scorne the reading of much less bragg of having them in his Custody...."

The truth is his Judgment (or want of it) is to be much pitied, his learning no witt to be admired much less envied his audacity & impudence every where to be proclaimed."[21]

Knyveton elsewhere chastised Vincent for compiling insufficient evidence, inscribing taunting notes such as "You might have vouched reverend records for yt if you had seen them."[22] Even when he agreed with Vincent, he lambasted the weakness of his proofs; for example, regarding the creations of the Duke of Norfolk, Knyveton guffawed, "Have you not Records to prove these Creations more Autentically?" and then transcribed an extract that would have strengthened Vincent's claim.[23] Throughout, his annotations refer to offices and titles held by nobles that Vincent failed to mention as well as overlooked children, wives, and exploits.

Nor, Knyveton scoffed, was Vincent's history consistent. On numerous cases when he found contradictions, Knyveton entered notes such as "Consider better with your self & read over your owne observations."[24] Sometimes he deemed these a consequence of inattention, other times of pointless disputatiousness. Where Vincent had changed the name of the second wife of Edmond Crouchback, Earl of Lancaster, from Blanche to Alianor, for example, Knyveton complained, "You say Records vowch both ways, why then do you carpe here mereley out of a Spirit of contradition to shew your own singularity. In correcting every thing you corrupt the Text for Besides those Authors you confesse are against you."[25] Introducing this error, Knyveton scornfully noted, would create subsequent ones.

Knyveton's annotations also criticized Vincent for exaggerating Brooke's errors and inflating the significance of his corrections. Over and over again, Knyveton entered notes such as "Good God how strangely here this Idle Corrector strains himself to cast an Imputation or Aspersion upon his Adversarie and in the end confesses he saith truth."[26] Similarly, he repeatedly chastised Vincent for harshly criticizing Brooke's dating of events when Vincent's corrections only moved them by several days—"A Nice & needless Reprehensions they both agreeing in the year of our Lord & in the Month."[27] The whole, he insisted, created the mere appearance of erudition, "They that indeed have true learning will never bragg of it & you would make shew of much by apprehension of fewe errours in other though your self committe grosser."[28]

Despite his complaints about the triviality of some of Vincent's corrections, however, Knyveton was similarly personal in his attacks, and he, too, was given to redating events by months, dismissively reordering the births of noble children, or archly harrumphing about Vincent's conflation of similar offices. The result was to exaggerate rivalry between distinct but largely analogous narratives drawn from similar sources.

Far from resolving thorny questions of noble genealogy, Knyveton's caustic reading reveals how past inscriptions compounded acrimonious debate.[29] And one of the most striking aspects of their argument was the degree of disagreement concerning England's medieval past, as if the murkiness associated with antiquity stretched until relatively recently, devastating the possibility of precise knowledge about titles, honor, and authority, though supplying sufficient information to fuel conviction. The exaltation of inscriptions as the fundamental evidence for answering questions less banished uncertainty than reconfigured the raw material for disputes, for the corroboration and comparison of a shared set of sources inspired competing accounts. Habitual resort to the records led quarrels to abound, proliferate, and deepen.

Fault Lines and Fractures

Both Knyveton and Vincent—like Camden and Brooke before them—likely felt that their methods should resolve questions concerning the crucial legitimating instruments of nobility and precedence. But they were confounded, as the records did not coalesce into a stable prescriptive past. Indeed, it was rare for all parties in a dispute to identify one source or narrative as definitive, as they would have preferred, as a means of conflict resolution. Rather, different passages in the same bodies of records might support contradictory logics of governance, while ambiguities demanded exegesis or interpretation by comparison with other inscriptions, and such recontextualizations often yielded incompatible understandings. Much as in the world of print, where audiences negotiated their political identities through what they purchased and how they interpreted it, early Stuart figures discovered that consulting the corpus of records multiplied competing perspectives rather than fostering concord.

In particular, debates in Parliaments—and especially the Parliament of 1628—show how early modern Britons consulted records in the hope of resolving disagreements, but instead inflamed and exacerbated division. The volume and interpretive elasticity of the sources of the English past, these debates show, rendered the epistemological ideal of certainty and the social goal of consensus elusive, perhaps impossible to achieve.

* * *

Not every recourse to the records led to division and rancor, however; reliance on records could sometimes produce consensus. For example, in 1621 the House of Commons' attempt to prosecute the Catholic Edward

Floyd for insulting Frederick V, Elector Palatine (King James's son-in-law) prompted a close consideration of the Commons' right as a court of judicature, close on the heels of recent confirmation that the House of Lords did have that right.[30] On May 1, carried by their indignation to a bloodthirsty frenzy, the Commons condemned Floyd to whipping, pillory, a massive fine, and lifetime incarceration. The decision was reached not through a formal trial but through an escalating series of imagined punishments such as John Whitson's proposal that "He wishes that after he hath halfe a dozen stripes to have hott dripping bacon dropt on him, which was called *pingaria*."[31]

As the Commons' blood boiled, various parties collected opinions about whether the lower house possessed the right to conduct a trial. The day after Whitson's suggestion, the Crown dispatched Chancellor of the Exchequer Fulke Greville to the House of Commons equipped with a paper referring to a roll from the reign of Henry IV, with the note: "In the margins it was written that the Commons be not parties to judgments."[32] A brief that Cotton produced for Lord Treasurer Edward Montagu, by contrast, supported the Commons' right. Drawing on chronicles and records, Cotton noted that the council of "great lords" under King Harold had held the right of judicature from its inception. This body's power had increased until Henry III, in order to curb it, commanded the "service of many Knights, Citizens, and Burgesses to that great Councel." To Cotton, this directive marked the introduction of the Commons to Parliament, and thereafter they often participated in the Lords' judgments, as he demonstrated with a list of precedents.[33] His account thus suggested the Commons' right of judicature was part of its origins. Similarly, during debate in the House of Commons, Edward Coke maintained the body's right to prosecute by drawing on examples indicating that the Commons possessed the features of a court of record.[34]

Lord Montagu was unswayed, however, coolly dismissing Coke by noting the absence of positive evidence: "My Lord expected to hear some president of your possessory right."[35] Being party to Lords' judgments, from Montagu's perspective, was not the same as entitlement to its own. This position won the day and, having failed to produce sufficient precedents to legitimize its judicial aspirations, the Commons ceded authority over Floyd's impeachment to the Lords.[36]

The episode prompted the Lords to impanel a Commission on Privileges to delimit its rights, which deputized Selden to accumulate precedents of the Lords' powers.[37] The resulting tract circulated in many manuscript copies—with one remaining in the House of Lords—before its printing in 1642 as *Privileges of the Baronage*. As Selden explained in his introduction, "such store is here collected as the tyme would permitt out of Parliament Rolls, and Jornalls, Patent and Close Rolles, Plea Rolls, Crowne Rolls, the proceedings of the English Courts at Westminster, the Registers of the Archbishopp of Canterburie, and of the Delegates yeere-bookes of the Common Law, statutes and other good authorities; and in such sort that frequentlie the wordes of the chiefest testimonies are transcribed, least the freedom of the Readers Judgement might be otherwise prevented by Short Collections."[38] Selden explained that though he had simply accumulated extracts, they were sufficiently copious to ensure agreement.

Selden's codification of the privileges of the Lords exemplifies the ideal that drove early Stuart counselors and advisers: that corralling and integrating evidence from unassailable records would provide the grounds of political stability by delimiting the proper boundaries of institutional authority. Those who had faith in this practice engaged in a reverberative process, re-creating the past with the participation of the records they selected while at the same time seeking to shape the present in its image.

* * *

That Selden used the records to establish parliamentary right reflected his established expertise, for despite the axiom that the England's ancient constitution was unwritten, he and Coke deployed the same inscription-based practices as those underlying contemporary texts that claimed to establish the powers of other English institutions. Coke's *Institutes*, for example, sought to establish the contours of common law by collecting, compacting, and comparing records and legal commentaries. At the same time collections of extracts of ancient—or allegedly ancient—texts such as the controversial *Modus Tenendi Parliamentum* and Clerk of the Parliaments Henry Elsynge's *Manner of Holding Parliaments* circulated as foundations for debates concerning parliamentary procedure.[39] Their work was part of a broader effort to elaborate Parliament's history and practice.

Such enterprises were not politically neutral, and—especially in the first years of Charles I's reign—Selden and Coke portrayed past records as testifying to a tradition of parliamentary oversight in which tyrannical abrogations of the proper balance had been exposed and corrected.[40] Although James's reign had provoked some exploration of these questions, the Caroline regime's aggressive fiscal policy of the late 1620s—embodied by the financial success and political outcry sparked by the 1626 Forced Loan—escalated the sense of urgency, motivating his critics to construct from the records visions of history and the state that would delegitimize Charles's innovations.[41] Much like the studies of offices, these texts claimed to capture past practice but in fact bundled evidence from discrete events into unprecedented delimitations of the powers of Crown and Parliament.

Sometime likely in these years, for example, an anonymous compiler produced a lengthy manuscript collection concerning "The King his oath, office, Aucthoritie Royall, and Prerogatyve," which brought together dozens of extracts from Tower records to produce for the monarch the equivalent of Caesar's Court of Requests tract or Knyveton's on the Master of the Rolls. The first set of extracts provided evidence concerning how "he governeth," while subsequent sections examined such topics as the structure of the Privy Council and the king's role in martial matters. Most strikingly, this collection explicitly identified actions prohibited to the king in a section entitled "The kinges Aucthourytie limited and restrayned." The first extract was a writ from Edward III's reign declaring that the execution of Roger Mortimer had been unlawful because it had happened "with out arraignement of triall by his Peeres"; shortly afterward, the judgment had been "reversed as erroniouse and iniurious to the Common Lawe & Libertie of Magna Carta."[42] Though Mortimer's actions demanded extraordinary measures, the compiler noted, the writ stipulated firm limitations on prerogative. Subsequent examples included grants of lands that had been invalidated and the rejection of patents granted without written warrant.

Most of the evidence of the restraint of royal authority came from the reign of Richard II. Crown finance was the dominant area where this compiler saw parliamentary authority as curtailing Richard's improprieties—especially his usage of parliamentary-approved funds for unapproved purposes. During his reign, for example, "the Commons petitioned in parliament that the kinge would care to keep his Expences within the compasse of his Revenue, so as the money cominge of his wardes, escheats, forfeitures &c be reserved for maintenances of the warres in defence of the Realm." Similarly, in each of the first two years of Richard's reign, Parliament had asserted that subsidies "graunted for maintenance of the warres & in defence of the Realme be not imploied to other uses, And that certeyn appointed Tresorers & Receyvors thereof be sworne and do make accompte accordinglye in the Parliament followinge." Other extracts from Parliament rolls reinforced that their vote of supply to the king was "granted for maintenance of warres & defense . . . & not mixed with the king revenues." Most notably, this reader extracted statutes from Richard II that "tenthes and fiftenes are graunted to the king by protestacion & under certen condicion to be performed or ells the same to cease & be voyde."[43] Parliament, that is, could include provisos nullifying its own grant of taxes. This compilation thus constituted a record-based history of the office of the king that outlined how parliamentary authority bounded royal taxation—clearly exposing that Charles's measures exceeded his authority.

Using past inscriptions, however, was not solely the province of those unnerved by Caroline rule. Thomas Wilson's tract on royal revenue (noted in chapter 3) cataloged extraparliamentary impositions from records in the State Paper Office, only one of many such projects—often instigated by the Crown—that responded to Charles's financial troubles by mobilizing archival expertise to discern potential revenue streams. In 1628, for example, Cotton received a royal order to accumulate materials concerning the right of kings to exact impositions without parliamentary approval. Though some close to the king were suspicious of Cotton because of his connections to critics such as Selden, he had long expertise investigating historical practices of taxation. Under James he had proposed several financial projects, many of which entailed close examination of Tower and Exchequer records; for example, around 1606 he proposed a scheme in which a reorganization of the Tower records would enable the introduction of compositions for entailed lands, and in 1609 he compiled a collection that would be printed in 1642 as *An abstract out of the records of the tower touching the kings revenue and how they have supported themselves*.[44] Cotton also collected similar proposals, such as one the Exchequer official Christopher Vernon produced in 1612 by finding records in the "chaos and thick dust" in the Westminster Abbey Cloisters, which revealed that stewards had been suppressing rents in royal lands and pocketing the difference—and that by collecting back rents, the Crown could recoup nearly £200,000.[45]

The volume Cotton produced in 1628 cataloged mechanisms found in Tower records whose revival would generate revenue for the Crown. Individual sections detailed how previous kings had raised funds under the auspices of mustering and provisioning soldiers, "attendance on the Kings person in Time of War," defending the coasts, and other military needs over which the Crown exercised authority without parliamentary oversight.[46] For example, in the tenth chapter, entitled "Defence of the State," Cotton transcribed an extract from Edward III's Scottish rolls revealing that the Crown introduced realm-wide levies to protect against rumored Scottish invasion of Cornwall and Devon.[47] Much like Caesar's tracts on offices, Wilson's and Cotton's texts seemingly projected the rents, fees, and dues described in the records as dispositive evidence of Crown right. In such collections, the records did more than articulate momentary agreements; they furnished testimony of perpetual authority.

Whether supporting or decrying Charles's fiscal program, tracts investigating the history of royal finances in the late 1620s relied on evidence drawn from a shared body of sources. But they differed concerning which extracts they portrayed as constituting prescriptive evidence of England's ideal government. Trust in records thus deepened conflicting interpretations of what the English past licensed in the present—to some dictating expansive royal latitude, to others firm parliamentary oversight. Far from forging consensus, the regime of inscription instead precipitated distinct visions of the English state.

* * *

Those responsible for compiling evidence delimiting the powers of Crown and Parliament sometimes recognized the challenges preventing records from anchoring a normative political past. In his 1628 tract, for example, Cotton—perhaps reflecting ambivalence about his assignment—demonstrated an acute awareness. At the end of the first section, he elaborated the complications of using records as prescriptive guides to political powers. First, as he explained, "many of these though entered upon Record may never be produced to effect: The Rolls of the Recept perused to see what Received levyes of men or money have been returned in pursuit of any of these intents, will cleare that doubt."[48] Archives were littered with projects that had been approved but never realized—raising the question of whether the prescribed action or its lack of execution constituted the appropriate precedent. Nor would confirming the implementation of such projects, Cotton continued, always substantiate their worthiness. As he explained, "the successe of these may be examined by search of storyes of those Times wherein they were so put in practise, & which I have most remayning with mee. The smooth and usuall cure of all deserts and maladies of state, have been by parliament except some few in Henry III & Richard II and Henry VI Times, where, such remedy proved more dangerous then the disease; malignant spirits bearing more of power then well composed tempers."[49] Collaboration with Parliament had typically proven more effective than ruling by fiat, which often created a cascade of unintended consequences.[50] Certain political actions were legal, Cotton suggested, but not advisable.

Cotton argued that the records should be seen in a historical vein and that the merit of reviving the actions they described could be determined by consulting other sources. Recourse to the archives could never furnish simple answers, he recognized, for recontextualization could generate new perspectives that complicated seemingly stable textual claims. Even in this tract establishing the legality of extraparliamentary revenue creation, Cotton modeled how to undermine any assertion that any individual piece of evidence illuminated the ideal form or practice of government, exposing the indeterminacy of contemporary practices of producing political knowledge.

*　*　*

The structure of early modern British political practice thus possessed its own mechanics of division, for recontextualizing inscriptions according to new sources produced a dizzying array of interpretations that undermined the finality of any single utterance. If Cotton diagnosed how the regime of inscription inhibited consensus, however, most contemporaries did not articulate such skepticism. Instead, many participants in the 1628 parliamentary debates that led to the Petition of Right trumpeted their own fidelity to the records while accusing their opponents of outrageous violations of norms.[51] These debates also further reveal why the practice of relying on a fecund corpus of inscriptions pushed opposing parties toward further divergence.

Throughout the 1628 debates, Coke and Selden invoked records to outline the purported excesses of Charles's actions while condemning Crown representatives' handling of written evidence. Initiating the debate concerning whether to vote supply on March 22, for example, Coke chummily referred to a Parliament roll: "The way I shall take, I am absolutely to give supply to his Majesty, yet with some caution. . . . I'll begin with a notable record, it cheers me to think of it: 25 Edward III num. 16. It is worthy to be writ in letters of gold. 'Loans against the will of the subject are against reason and the franchises of the land, and they desire restitution.'"[52] Repeatedly Coke developed his position through statements such as "I will prove out of records of Parliament in 11 kings' times that it is not lawful to compel any man to give the loan."[53] And as Secretary of State John Coke propounded the military and moral necessity of financing the king, Edward Coke dismissively responded, "Find a way to speak out of record, I will tell you my opinion."[54]

This positioning sharply contrasted with Edward Coke's and John Selden's depiction of the Crown's behavior. In early April, Selden raised an uproar over the management of records concerning the case of Sir John Heveningham, one of the knights whose suits of habeas corpus against imprisonment for refusing to pay the Forced Loan became known as the Five Knights Case.[55] The Commons had formed a committee to investigate the trial, in part provoked by suspicion of Solicitor General Richard Shelton's boasts concerning the strength of precedent for the Crown's prosecution. But when Selden reported that he "and other lawyers had met about the precedents and had searched the records and brought the copies into the House, as also of the acts of Parliament," they perceived numerous improprieties in the Crown's conduct during Heveningham's case. Most significantly, though Shelton and Attorney General Robert Heath had claimed victory, no judgment had been entered in the Coram Rege roll.[56] Pressed to provide proof of the judgment, Shelton produced an incomplete draft of what they had intended to enroll and maintained that they had not departed from ordinary practice or acted mendaciously. Selden disdainfully "much commended the ingenuity of Mr Solicitor that brought to the subcommittee the case of Sir John Heveningham in a copy of a record of judgment." Moreover, when Shelton "showed the copy . . . it was full of blanks. The beginning was confessed to be written by the clerk, the latter end by another hand, and so foisted in, and certainly intended to have been recorded and the blanks filled up."[57] Shelton's explanation that this process of enrollment was common procedure failed to placate his questioners.[58] The deposition of the court's clerk, John Keeling, only compounded their hostility, for Keeling reported that Heath had repeatedly requested that he enter the judgment on the roll using the incomplete form Shelton had just shown the committee.[59] While the Crown's lawyers insisted that they had followed conventional process—and pointed out that the judges had been unperturbed by Heath's actions—Selden argued that Heath had tried to force Keeling to circumvent legal requirements to obtain a counterfeit record of judgment against Heveningham. Heath's actions constituted, in his account, an attack on the constitutional and material foundations of the realm.

Although it is impossible to say with certainty what motivated the Crown's behavior, Mark Kishlansky has persuasively argued that there were legitimate precedents for Heath and Shelton's behavior, and that while the regime may have not hewed strictly to formal regulations, there were no violations tantamount to the forgery and deceit Selden alleged.[60] What is clear is that Selden seized on such ambiguities, constructing a demonizing narrative that accused Crown officers of brazen desecrations and outrageous abuses of the integrity of the records.

Heath's rumored perversion of legal apparatus of records prompted a retaliatory rumor directed against Selden. Two weeks later, the MP John Strangways reported that Theophilus Howard, Earl of Suffolk, had asked him, "Will you not hang Selden?" When Strangways answered, "My Lord, I know no cause for it," an astonished Suffolk replied, "By God he had razed a record, for which he was worth to be hanged."[61] Selden strenuously denied it, and the Commons formed a committee to investigate, headed by John Eliot. Three days later, the House of Commons heard a report from the committee, to which Christopher Neville had reported that "Suffolk told him that Mr Attorney had cleared the business and made the cause clear on the King's side, and told him that Mr Selden had razed a record and did deserve to be hanged, and that this House should do well to join with the Lords in a petition to the King to hang him. Said Mr Selden went about to divide the King and his people."[62] The matter seemed destined to escalate until Howard offered that he likely misheard Heath, which, while ending this controversy, redirected the growing animosity to others.

Debate and disagreement in these cases manifested as arguments over which practices embodied appropriate reverence toward paperwork and past records. The next major point of debate in the 1628 Parliament, concerning the customs tax devoted toward defense of the realm known as *tonnage and poundage*, further reveals how these debates revolved around competing claims of fidelity to England's documentary inheritance. And the Crown's course of action in particular suggests that this agonistic environment encouraged interpretive choices that exacerbated division.

Tonnage and poundage had been a source of strife since Charles I's ascent, as Parliament had become incensed by the king's limited collection of it before their approval and insistence that they assent to it as a lifelong grant without satisfactorily redressing their grievances, while he in turn grew exasperated at their truculence.[63] The Commons' "Remonstrance against Tonnage and Poundage" from June 1628 portrayed the tax as a recent innovation, claiming that only since the reign of Henry VII had it been consistently granted for life and that even this king delayed collecting it until Parliament voted approval. In response, Charles directed his advisers to consult the records and construct from them a history both minimizing the need for Parliamentary consent and asserting the tax's tradition as a lifelong grant.[64]

This request yielded at least two anonymous collections of extracts, which themselves reflected separate interpretations. One set of "Notes out of the records in the Tower concerning Tonnage and Poundage" circulated to at least three of Charles's counselors. The compiler of this memo began by summarizing from a close roll that "the first mention that I fynde upon Record of Tunnage is in the 22 yeare of Edward I." Crucially, the compiler reported, "What the consideracion or conditions of this imposition doth not appeare upon Record, but the wordes shew yt was commaunded to be taken by the King and not by graunt made in Parliament." A marginal note, however, indicated that "yet the succeeding words of the Record ... shew that yt was not paid."[65] This extract thus upheld the legality of tonnage and poundage without parliamentary consent from its inception in the late thirteenth century, with the caveat that this first levy had not been collected. A series of extracts then evinced that tonnage and poundage had always been an injunction rather than a grant, and that Henry V had been the first to receive the subsidy for life early in his reign, though this had not held for of all his successors until Edward IV. This set of notes thus provided an account in which tonnage and poundage was an ancient tax but had assumed various forms.

The second compilation drew a contrasting history, perhaps because it reflected substantial consultation of Exchequer as well as Tower records. "An abstract of the receipts and grauntes of Tonnage and Poundage collected out of the records in the Towre and in the Rolles, and out of the Accounts of the Pipe Office" began with the report that in 1371, Edward III "had graunted unto him Act of Parlament for the defence of the Kingdome and guard of the Seas 2l upon the tunne of wine and 6p in the pound for other marchandize and is soe accompted for in the Pipe during his raigne." By comparing Exchequer and Tower records, this account concluded that tonnage and poundage originated nearly a century later than alleged in the previous set of notes, though still a century before Parliament's claimed date of origin. On the other hand, this account also claimed that Parliament had granted it for life to Richard II in 1387—much earlier than in the other version. Moreover, in this collection the lifelong grant quickly became routine; as Exchequer records detailed, Henry IV had received it in his second year; Henry V in his first, and though Edward IV had waited four years after his coronation for it to be granted, "it was receaved and accounted for in the Pipe from the beginning." Under Edward VI, the terms of the subsidy were modified to include "a recitall in the nature of a prescription that Henry VII and Henry VIII and other the Kings progenitors had time out of mind for the defence of the realme and guard of the seas the subsidies of tonnage and poundage graunted unto them." Parliament's role, these notes suggested, had always been purely symbolic, and as this author concluded, "all the Kings and Queenes of the realme from Edward the III's 45 [year] of his raigne have received and continued their possession of a subsidy till the time of the graunting it by Act of Parliament and soe during theire lives. And from the time of 45 Edward III to this day is 257 years that this subsidy hath been graunted and payed without deniall or interruption."[66]

Both collections asserted Charles's right to tonnage and poundage for life with or without parliamentary approval. But they created disparate histories to do so. The first extended the tax deep into the past and emphasized its legality while recognizing early departures from the norms that Charles wished to set; the second stressed its collection, excluding its murkier early history and instead depicting its collection without parliamentary consent as customary.

When Charles adjourned Parliament in March 1629, his explanatory Declaration of Causes emphasized his devotion to the records and stressed that his actions accorded with what they allowed. After the failure of the 1628 Parliament, he recounted, he had "resolved to guide our self by the Practice of former Ages, and Examples of our most noble Predecessors; thinking those Counsels best warranted, which the Wisdom of former Ages, concurring with the present Occasions, did approve; and therefore gave Order for a diligent Search of Records." This process, he explained, had determined that "although in the Parliament holden in the first Year of the Reign of King *Edward* the Fourth, the Subsidy of Tonnage and Poundage was not granted unto that King, but was first granted unto him by Parliament in the third Year of his Reign; yet the same was accounted and answered to that King, from the first Day of his Reign." The same practice then persisted: "It having been so long and constantly continued to our Predecessors, as that in four several Acts of Parliament for the Granting thereof to King *Edward* the Sixth, Queen *Mary*, Queen *Elizabeth*, and our blessed Father, it is in express Terms mentioned, to have been had and enjoyed by the several Kings, named in those Acts, Time out of Mind, by Authority of Parliament."[67]

Both the details of Charles's chronology and the language of "time out of mind"—more frequently associated with common law than royal prerogative—reveals that the second, sharper set of extracts had been used in composing the Declaration of Causes.[68] Though the first asserted more ancient origins for the tax, Charles preferred to avoid its ambiguities and instead adopted a history univocally coordinated with his broader message.

Charles's decision reflected a strategic response to his combustible environment. Relentless debate led political figures—and publics—to generate distinct interpretations of the past and of the ideal form of British government. To strengthen arguments inevitably built on incomplete and ambiguous evidence, they proclaimed their own faithfulness to the records and condemned the purported laxity of their opponents. Even those who agreed with each other might generate different interpretations, and accounts that sheathed past ambiguities in uncompromising and aggressive argumentation offered demonstrable advantages. These were the dynamics of an information ecosystem that, even when confronting agreed-upon problems and sharing consensus concerning the best methods to resolve them, impelled toward rupture.

* * *

Whereas records and paperwork were mythologized as moderating tools to bring the government to its idealized form, the practice of creating visions of the state from them instead often fomented division. The surfeit of evidence sedimented in the written materials of England's past overwhelmed the possibility of mastery, and the practice of contextualization failed to narrow possibilities and instead fed an infinity of interpretations. In such an agonistic terrain, participants often gravitated toward arguments that bluntly reinforced their preexisting desires, regardless of mitigating complexity, as Charles did when adducing a history of tonnage and poundage. Such preferences, moreover, created a system of perverse incentives encouraging pamphleteers and politicians to deliver not just sharper arguments but attacks marked by exaggeration and outrage, masquerading as logical extensions or clarifications of preceding arguments. As such utterances increasingly characterized the political landscape, even seemingly preposterous claims about one's adversaries gained the patina of feasibility; increasingly vituperative assertions grew more plausible and perhaps even more likely through a species of dysfunctional symbiosis. Far from providing the tools of consensus, the records fueled a media environment galvanized by innovation, rancor, and conflict, whose perpetuation turned divergent perspectives into incommensurable ideologies.

The Tower Records and the Personal Rule

Though Charles I's dissolution of Parliament in 1629 and the period of Personal Rule—in which Charles ruled without Parliament until the 1640 Short Parliament—transformed the conditions for political knowledge making, Crown officials continued to rely on the same practices. But no longer pressed with the need to gain parliamentary approval, Charles's regime aggressively advanced the theory and practice of kingship that had taken root in the first years of his reign.

The axes of Charles's agenda during the Personal Rule included developing a fiscal policy that would keep the Crown on solid footing; regenerating aristocracy to maintain social stability; reorienting foreign policy away from religious alignments toward solidifying England's imperial authority; and invigorating the church by establishing an intensely hierarchical ecclesiology flourishing under royal supremacy.[69] These programs varied in their reliance on records, but Charles's counselors sought to discern precedents for each of them by compiling extracts unearthed from dusty and decayed sources. The activities of the primary functionaries at the Tower Record Office in these years—Keeper of the Tower Records John Borough and his deputy William Ryley—illuminate how Charles's regime relied on records of the past as crucial supports to develop a robust royal vision of the English state.[70]

* * *

By the advent of the Personal Rule, Borough was already emerging as one of the key figures anchoring Charles's emergent vision of kingship and English governance, and he would prove an exceptionally useful and loyal servant until his death in 1643.[71] Like William Bowyer, Borough did so primarily by capitalizing on his custody of the Tower records, using his mastery of them to construct resources legitimizing Caroline policies. In particular, he produced notes and historical treatises advancing Charles's priorities in the realms of Crown finance, international diplomacy, and aristocratic renewal.

Borough's path to the keepership after Bowyer's death had been grooved by support from Arundel and Cotton, who referred to him as "Cosen Borough" (which also may have been why Cotton did not support Knyveton's campaign for the position). Borough appears repeatedly in Cotton's lending lists; in 1621, for example, he had a "A Book of records gather concerning the sink ports," a "Parliament book of Richard 2, Henry 4, Henry the 5 bound in velom," and "Book of the Steward Marshall and Constable bound with my arms."[72] Other evidence from Borough's younger years suggest a wide-ranging education appropriate to those seeking to enter Crown governance.[73] He may have met Bacon during his time at Gray's Inn from 1611 to 1612, and by 1619 he was in the service of the Lord Chancellor. At Bacon's disgrace in 1621, Borough, too, was accused of corruption, but these charges fizzled, and within the year he was appointed Keeper, likely at Arundel's intercession, from which position he supplied archival material for Bacon's *History of Henry VII*.[74] The following year, Borough accompanied Lady Arundel to Venice, whence he provided updates to the earl and newsletters to Cotton before returning in late 1622.[75] Throughout the 1620s Arundel's support enabled him to steadily acquire positions such as Extraordinary Clerk of the Privy Council in 1623 and Norroy King of Arms in 1624, the same year in which he was knighted. He was also an MP in the Parliaments of 1621, 1624, 1625, and 1626, during which time he took detailed notes.[76]

Borough's activities in his first years as Keeper remain obscure. But as Crown and Parliament increasingly diverged on taxation policy in Charles's first years, Caesar commissioned Borough to produce a volume from Tower records concerning extraparliamentary measures to raise revenue. In January 1628, Borough delivered his notes concerning the "Means which Kinges have formerly used to rayse moneys," which became one of the most important among the aforementioned collections.[77] This compilation elaborated a range of methods, such as calling in old debts or farming or alienating Crown lands.[78] Like Cotton, Borough may have recognized that some of these tactics would be viewed as too rapacious, costly, or impractical to be pursued. But several of his suggestions were implemented in coming years, for despite Caesar's advanced age, he remained an important sponsor of Caroline projects.[79] Most notably, Borough appears to have stimulated Caesar's enthusiasm for distraint of knighthood, a fine levied against freeholders owning property worth more than £40 who did not attend the coronation to be knighted, which had been collected as recently as Mary's reign.[80] Caesar may have recognized the lucrative potential of this fine earlier, but either reminded or encouraged by Borough, Caesar spearheaded its introduction after 1630, and fines in distraint of knighthood would be one of the most successful mechanisms of revenue creation for the Caroline regime, raising around £170,000 before 1635.[81]

Borough's resurfacing of distraint in knighthood inaugurated a period of consistent work mobilizing the Tower records to develop and advance Charles's vision of government. In subsequent years, Borough used his heraldic and Tower expertise to contribute to the revitalization of the aristocracy and honors system—a priority of Arundel's that had languished during the Duke of Buckingham's ascendancy but that Charles heavily supported in the 1630s.[82] Charles wished to strengthen the aristocracy while drawing their interests closer to his; concurrently, he sought to resolve chronic issues of status and title that had arisen through the inflation of honors in previous years (compounded by the muddiness of genealogical knowledge exposed by Camden, Brooke, Vincent, and Knyveton). Among the measures of aristocratic renewal were in 1633 reviving heraldic visitations—which had not occurred for a decade—and, the following year, elevating the Court of Chivalry into a permanent court to adjudicate issues of status and honor, likely in response to an unwanted rash of dueling.

Borough was involved in both enterprises.[83] His involvement may have depended on his heraldic background, but it also suggests his rising status. Borough accompanied Charles's coronation trip to Scotland in 1633 and upon his return was commissioned, along with Sir Richard St. George, Clarenceux King of Arms, to reform the College of Arms. Within two months, Borough was elevated to Garter King of Arms and assigned sole oversight of the revived visitations.[84] Similarly, likely preparing for the regularization of the Court of Chivalry in 1634, Borough produced a manuscript of "The Forme of Proceeding upon an Appeale of Treason &c before the Constable and Marshall where the Combat was to be awarded."[85] This amounted to an English translation of a French collection assembled by Thomas of Woodstock, Duke of Gloucester, and

Constable under Richard II, supplemented with "annotations" drawn from "Records, Stories, Manuscripts, Collections, Statutes, and Common Lawe bookes" from Cotton's and John Coke's libraries and the Tower records.[86] While the volume appeared to crystallize the procedure for jousts—precisely what the Court of Chivalry hoped to avoid—the extracts likely sought to rebut common lawyers' suspicion of the court by sustaining the right of the Lords Constable and Marshall to convoke a permanent court of record.

Borough's tenure as Keeper was marked by the tightest entanglement between the College of Arms and Tower of the early modern period. As Garter King of Arms, Borough was the senior herald, and he considerably advanced the heraldic career of his main collaborator and clerk in the Tower, William Ryley. Ryley had been employed in the office since around 1618, and he would remain in this position for nearly fifty years, until his 1667 death.[87] Through Borough's influence, he was appointed Rouge Croix Pursuivant in 1630, Bluemantle Pursuivant in 1633, and Lancaster Herald in 1641.[88] Ryley's introduction to these offices was predicated on his Tower experience; as his 1630 petition for heraldic employment explained, he "hathe bene educated . . . in the Records of the Tower, as also in the study of Heraldry for the space of 12 yeares last past, wherein hee hath indeavoured to attaine to the knowledge of Pedigrees, Antiquityes, and decents."[89] In the late 1650s, Ryley would be appointed successively Norroy and then Clarenceux King of Arms.

Ryley's most significant work in this period, however, entailed poring through the Tower records for the materials that Borough shaped into memoranda and treatises guiding Caroline policy.[90] When, for example, Borough compiled a tract on the English nobility's history in the early 1630s—likely intended to serve as a reference manual for the Court of Chivalry—the first stage in the process was for Ryley to compile a series of notes.[91] Borough then compacted these notes into a lengthy treatise he dedicated to Lord Treasurer Weston entitled "Observations Concerning the Nobilitie of England, Antient & Moderne," which examined aristocratic names and titles, followed by examinations "Of the Power and Jurisdiction of the Auntient Nobilite in England," the patents of ennoblement, and other topics.[92] Discursive sections were supplemented by extracts from a wide array of records collected by Ryley.

Ryley also played a major role in Borough's best-known contribution to Charles's agenda: his "Sovereignty of the British Seas by Records, History, and the Municipall Lawes of this Kingdome," a manuscript treatise completed in 1633 that circulated in many copies before being printed in 1651.[93] The germ of this tract dated to 1631, when the French began to challenge English claims of ownership over the Channel. Reports circulated that French were demanding that English merchant ships in the Channel give salute and strike their flags, and rumors spread that the French were preparing to annex the waterway. Secretary of State Dudley Carleton, Viscount Dorchester, accordingly solicited support, and Clerk of the Counsel William Boswell wrote to him that Borough would be "able to produce an Originall concerning the first Instrument of La Rool D'Ooleron (under Seal by Edward 1)," referring to Law of Oleron, a set of thirteenth-century mercantile marine regulations concerning shipping in the English Channel and North Sea that, Boswell claimed, would also establish the Admiralty's supremacy in the Channel from at least 1286.[94] Intrigued, Dorchester requested that Borough send him materials. In turn, Borough deputized Ryley to comb the Tower for it and other appropriate records.

Borough likely recognized other advantages in establishing English maritime sovereignty, for not only could it be used as artillery in the battle for the Channel, but establishing these seas within English jurisdiction would enable control over North Sea fisheries. The uncertain legal status of these waters had provoked Hugo Grotius's famous 1609 *Mare Liberum*, which argued that the sea, as international territory, was not subject to any one authority and thus was open to use by all peoples. William Welwood and Selden had unsuccessfully sought to rebut Grotius, and Kings James I and Charles I had both struggled either to limit or to profit from Dutch fishing off English and Scottish coasts.[95] Asserting dominion over the seas, Borough recognized, might enable taxing or fining the Dutch while also benefiting Britain's fishing industry. Strengthening Charles's control over the Europe's northern seas could thus serve conjoined diplomatic and economic goals.

Ryley more than fulfilled Borough's hopes. He assembled a notebook containing rough copies of records demonstrating English sovereignty over the Channel, such as a license from Edward I letting Low Country fishermen work the Channel and a charter in which King Edgar "stiles himselfe Emperour and Lord of the Seas that environ the Brittish Islands."[96] Most significantly, Ryley noted a previously unrecognized Chancery suit recorded against the Genoese-born French captain Reyner Grimbald, who was accused of seizing the goods of English merchants in the first year of the fourteenth century.[97] The roll was endorsed "de superioritate Maris Angliae," and it contained numerous claims such as, "the Kings of England ... from time whereof there is no memory to the contrary, have been in peaceable possession of the Dominion of the Sea of England and of the Isles being in the same, in making and establishing Lawes and Statutes ... and in taking suretie and affording safeguard in all cases where need shall be in ordering of all other things necessary for maintaining of Peace Right and Equity amongst all manner of people, as well of other Dominions as of their own ... and in all other things which may appertaine to the exercise of soveraigne dominion in the places aforesaid."[98] As Ryley likely recognized, this document could be made the central pillar in Charles's claims to sovereignty of the seas.

Ryley did not deem all the extracts he had compiled as essential, and he delivered a selection of them to Borough in fair copy with table of contents under the title, "The soveraigntie of the English Seas Vindicated and Proved by Some few records (amongst many others of that kynd) remayning in the Tower of London, collected by William Ryley."[99] The case against Grimbald, now given the title "De superioritate Maris Angliae," was the volume's centerpiece. And indeed, "De superioritate Maris Angliae" quickly became essential to Charles's claim to sovereignty over the seas. Borough's response to Dorchester referred to the Laws of Oleron, as Boswell suggested, but emphasized that "there is likewise in the Tower amongst the Records in the little closset there a Record in French date in the tyme of Edward I or Edward II in which it is mencioned upon the depredacions of one Renauld Grimbald." As he explained, Grimbald had been convicted by a committee appointed by the English king consisting of representatives of the kings of Denmark, Sweden, and Portugal, the Duke of Burgundy, and from Holland, Zeeland and Flanders—thereby insinuating that all these polities also recognized the Channel as within England's imperial dominion. The memo concluded that "surely thoughe noe man be said to have the property of the sea because a man cannot say this water is myn which runns, yet it is manifest that the Kings of England have ever had the Soveraignty & Iurisdiction of those seas, that is power to give lawes, & redress meanes done on the same."[100]

Borough consolidated Ryley's research in his 1633 Latin "Dominium Maris Britannici," dedicated to Charles. Though associated with Borough's authorship, this was a hybrid volume, collaboratively produced by Borough and Ryley.[101] The text elaborated an expansive vision of British Empire, rooted in transcriptions or translations of documents Ryley had excavated. Though the first evidence of British domination came from Caesar's *De bello Gallico*, it quickly moved to transcriptions with commentaries, first of "De superioritate Maris Angliae" and then many others that Ryley had compiled, including the Laws of Oleron. Borough's explication of the "De superioritate Maris Angliae" proclaimed that English kings had held dominion of the sea "by immemorable prescription," that the title did not depend on possessing land on both shores, that these kings possessed sole authority to make laws and appoint admirals, and that this was assented to "by the Agents of most part of Christendome."[102] Borough also quickly translated the whole—lightly edited—into English as "The Soveraignty of the British Seas," which circulated in numerous manuscript copies before its 1651 print publication.

The impact of this text extended even more broadly. Most notably, in these years Selden returned to his unfinished manuscript rebutting Grotius, ultimately bringing it to publication as *Mare Clausum* in 1635. Selden had been intermittently imprisoned after the 1629 Parliament and was seemingly looking to appease the regime, and this text—newly dedicated to Charles—earned royal approbation.[103] While he had begun revising his manuscript as early as 1630, he consulted Borough's Latin "Dominium Maris Brittanici" during the process, and individual chapters of *Mare Clausum* translated and explicated "De superioritate Maris Angliae," which he accepted as a powerful testament to the Crown's dominion.

While Selden's and Borough's studies had considerable significance for foreign diplomacy, their ramifications for domestic policy were potentially extremely profitable as well, in particular because they could be turned to support Ship Money—a tax on inland counties for defense of the coasts. Charles had first sought to levy Ship Money in 1628, but opposition led him to withdraw the writ. In 1634, though, he issued another—first to the maritime counties before expanding it markedly the following year, when *Mare Clausum*, with its sweeping vision of royal maritime dominion, was published. Selden's volume was then cited several times in Hampden's Case, the 1637 case that declared Ship Money legal even in times of peace; one of these references centered on "De superioritate Maris Angliae."[104]

Borough may have recognized the possibility that "Dominium Maris Brittanici" might support Ship Money while composing it; indeed, the tract may have contributed to the Crown's move toward implementing it the following year. But Borough's involvement in Ship Money was substantial either way. This was despite his initial hesitation; Borough had not included Ship Money among his proposals of 1628, and a discouraging memo he produced for Caesar around this time, "Touching provision of ships & number in time of warre defensive before Edward III et devises," stated that tonnage and poundage had emerged under Edward III in lieu of the royal annexation of ships and soldiers, suggesting that they had not happened simultaneously.[105] But his mind was perhaps changed by the maritime records Ryley extracted from the Tower. And when Caesar asked Borough in 1634 to find precedents for Ship Money, he supplied twenty-four examples, all dating from before the advent of tonnage and poundage, but nonetheless now taken to substantiate Ship Money. The first, from a close roll from the twenty-third year of Edward I's reign, reported that "The King granted to them of Yarmouth, that those who have lands tenements & rents within that town though they dwell out of the towne shall be compelled to contribute towards the ships that were there, to be sett forth for furnishing the next fleet, so the king commanded to be made by the Kingdome for the sea."[106] Subsequent extracts extending up to the reign of Edward III included patents to raise soldiers in inland counties "to serve the king in the Fleet at sea,"[107] close rolls supporting impressment, tribute, and taxation, and further extracts decreeing that, for example, towns maintain their naval defense at their own expense and supporting the notion of "every man being bound to the guard of the kingdome."[108] This collection furnished an important legal fortification for Ship Money.

Under Borough's supervision, in short, the Tower Record Office became a formidable site for the generation and development of King Charles I's policies. Supported by such patrons as Arundel and Caesar, Borough's research was essential to the Caroline regime's priorities of aristocratic renewal, tightening control of British waters, and fiscal policy. Borough's labor in the records exemplifies how the practice of mobilizing inscriptions underlay a vision of English governance promising to reverse the attenuation of royal authority and enable a financially healthy Crown to revive England's aristocratic and imperial glory. But anatomizing the practices underlying this vision also emphasizes that the Caroline ideology of kingship was not simply recovered from the past. Rather, it was a new formation articulating an innovative and expansive model of royal authority, constructed by selective mobilization of past testimonies.

* * *

Borough's work in the early 1630s was vital to the initial success of the Caroline agenda, suggesting measures that stabilized Crown finances— provided its demands did not dramatically expand—while substantiating expansive visions of domestic and international order.[109] Selden's conversion to the court party, moreover, seemingly endorsed the stance that Charles's projects were not innovations but constituted a proper frame of government rooted in precedent. In the first years of the Personal Rule, in short, the Tower records appear to have been the engine room for a program of consolidating past measures into a robust vision of the state.

The mid-1630s, however, introduced increasing strains on the regime.[110] Despite its legal victories regarding Ship Money, the rapid and widespread circulation of manuscript materials by its critics contributed to the recalibration and hardening of new political perspectives.[111] Those frustrated by Charles's rule capitalized on the broader information ecosystem by flooding the public with pamphlets and other texts insisting on its illegality. This debate cleaved audiences, yawning a disagreement over its legality into a chasm separating those adhering to a vision of the state that dictated parliamentary control of taxation from those, like Borough, for whom Parliament's limitations on fiscal policy wrongfully impugned legitimate monarchical power.

Religion also proved a primary fault line, and the disagreements concerning the church in the late 1630s again highlight how the same records could furnish support for contradictory agendas, serving as their own hurdles to consensus and fueling discord. Archbishop Laud's vision for the English church mobilized past records to articulate a hierarchical ecclesiology dominated by a powerful episcopacy and bulwarked by royal supremacy.[112] This vision rejected the premise central to the Reformation that the medieval church had been characterized by papal and clerical tyranny. Instead, it depicted a vibrant medieval church increasingly threatened by anticlericalism and iconoclasm vested within the House of Commons, culminating in a Reformation that—while addressing some faults within the church—was marked by overreach. In Laud's view, both Puritanism and the Commons' challenge to Charles's ecclesiastical reforms in the late 1620s reproduced this threat, and during the Personal Rule, Laud promulgated reforms seeking to standardize the church in the image of the medieval glory and stability he envisaged.

Laud's vision was exemplified by a spectacular vellum manuscript he commissioned directly from Ryley, entitled "Iura et Privilegia Clero Anglicano Adiudicata ex Parliamentorum Rotulis deprompta" ("The Laws and Privileges Granted to English Clerics drawn from Parliament Rolls").[113] The volume had a majestic frontispiece, modeled after those of William Hole in the 1610s, extravagantly adorned in gold and lapis lazuli. This image depicted Laud's coat of arms near the top, with a portrait of Ryley—allegorized as "Industry"—pointing to the title, surrounded by the figures of Religion, Piety, Antiquity, and Truth. Below were the coats of arms for Laud's benefices at Oxford, Bath, London, St. David's (the Welsh diocese called Meneven in Latin), and Cambridge. Such profligate decoration recurred throughout the volume in the form of gilded initials, titles, and section heads, the coats of arms of previous Archbishops of Canterbury, and a rubricated index.

This material extravagance ornamented a spare text consisting predominantly of extracts from the "Placita Parliamentaria"—a manuscript that Ryley would publish in 1661, sometimes called the "Vetus Codex," which existed in copies in the Exchequer and in the Tower and which contained material from the pleadings in Parliament under Edward I and II before such material was integrated into the Parliament rolls. These

FIGURE 12. Frontispiece of William Ryley's 1637 "Iura et Privilegia Clero Anglicano Adiudicata." Ryley is likely the figure in the center pointing at the title. Lambeth Palace Library MS 323, frontispiece.

passages Ryley supplemented with additions from statutes and other records as well as a few coats of arms and brief biographies of the Archbishops of Canterbury under Edward I, and he also equipped the volume with an index.[114]

The extracts from past records Ryley curated collectively delimited the scope and limitations of the church's powers. For example, the first entry, from Edward I's reign, established that under certain circumstances, cases could proceed in ecclesiastical courts despite a royal prohibition, such as if the Lord Chancellor determined that royal courts could not "relieve the party."[115] Subsequent entries provided evidence, for example, of the role of archbishops in the coronation, Canterbury's prerogatives concerning wardships, and that "A Tax may not be layd upon Priests by the Commons but referred to the Convocation."[116]

As this suggests, the extracts were also dense with considerations of the church's liberties, in particular their affirmations in the face of challenges from the Commons.[117] For example, Ryley recorded that when the Commons petitioned Richard II to take measures against clerical absenteeism, Richard coldly responded, "It belongs to the Offices of Bishops, and the King will [sic] that they doe their office duely."[118] Similarly, the Commons' pleas that lands sold to clerics should not be bequeathed to the church elicited only the promise that the king would receive counsel on the matter.[119] The volume consisted of precedents indicating Crown support for the church's autonomy against a rancorous laity seeking to dictate its administration.

At the same time, the volume revealed, the church accepted appropriate discipline from the Crown. For example, it recounted the success of Parliamentary complaints in the last years of Edward I's reign against Bishop of Durham Antony Bek, who "doth devour and destroy all the woods belonging to his Bishoprick of Durham by gift and sale, and evill keaping and by making forges of Iron and lead and burning Coales."[120] In this case, Crown and church functioned in tandem to root out clerical avarice.

Ryley's extracts also portrayed the church as an important defender of the law of the realm. Under Edward III, for example, the clergy entered a massive petition complaining that the king's counselors had wrongfully imprisoned clerics in defiance of the liberty of the church. They petitioned for the keeping of "all the priviledges, franchises and free customs" granted by the king, and "that the Great Charter be publiquely seen, and by Oath de novo affirmed," to further reinforce these privileges. In fact, the petition maintained, violations of Magna Carta were rife throughout the realm, as "many of the people Justices and others are taken, & emprisoned & kept in prison against the points of great Charter, & the sentence of excommunication confirmed by the Pope, which was given against all those, that resisted the great Charter, in great perill of their soules." Accordingly, "they beseech that it may please our Lord the King to avoid the danger of his soule, to command that the lawes of this land be mantayned as they should be kept, & the deliverance of his said Clerks, and Laity which are so imprisoned."[121] Here, the church was presented as a great defender of the liberty of the subject. And in his approving response, the extracts noted, Edward III upheld the full gamut of clerical privileges.

The volume thus amassed a collection of records to delimit the rightful scope of powers for the church. In this way, it closely resembled the texts discussed earlier claiming to faithfully mediate evidence of the past while elaborating their own visions of appropriate institutional powers and procedures. The portrayal Laud endorsed as emerging from the records depicted a robust church devoted to beauty and order and sustained in harmony with royal supremacy against the factional antagonism most recently exemplified, to him, by Puritans in the Commons.

This interpretation starkly opposed that held by many people in England who since the Reformation had been steeped in the conviction that the medieval church was marked by tyrannical usurpation through Rome and its clerical minions, a message reinforced through print, proclamation, and pulpit. And Ryley's evidence was far from unequivocal. Indeed, in William Prynne's 1668 *An Exact Chronological Vindication*, many of the extracts collected by Ryley for Laud were used to substantiate a narrative in which medieval England was characterized by the clergy's lawless abrogation of rights, disdain for the well-being of English subjects, and contempt for the king and all other native institutions.[122] Most strikingly, Prynne used the first extract Laud had drawn from Edward I's reign—which Laud had interpreted as vindicating the jurisdiction of ecclesiastical courts—as a demonstration of the king's effort "to preserve the Jurisdiction of his own Temporal Courts against the Bishops encroachment."[123] Instead of establishing their formal jurisdiction, Prynne saw these extracts as evidence of the papal church's lawlessness and disregard for royal authority.

These extracts, that is, served as a Rorschach test. For those whose believed that the medieval papacy annexed power through ever-increasing exactions from subjects and laity, the materials collected in this volume documented the outrageous clerical usurpation that precipitated the Reformation. For those like Laud who perceived the medieval past as licensing an expansive scope of royal authority against perturbations fomented by rebellious subjects, Ryley's extracts demonstrated the righteousness of a vigorous king operating in concert with an assured, powerful clergy. The record itself carried authority, but its meaning was indeterminate.

Even as Laud's revision of the Book of Common Prayer provoked a new degree of Scottish resistance beginning in 1637, and Charles's government began to bend under the pressure that would lead to its disintegration, his counselors retained their faith in the records' ability to command authority and continually returned to them. When Charles, at Secretary Windebank's suggestion, wished to convene the Great Council of Peers at York—the first in nearly two centuries—Borough was asked to find precedents for its summoning.[124] Borough and Ryley continued to serve the regime faithfully; when this council counseled Charles to convoke a Parliament and negotiate a peace with the Scots, Borough served as a commissioner during the negotiations for the humiliating ensuing Treaty of Ripon, taking copious notes on the proceedings.[125] In January 1641 Borough and his clerks were recompensed £70 for "service in transcribing diverse coppyes of Records concerning the Scutage the last Somer, and for Coppyes concerning Attainders and other businesse to bee used in this present Parliament."[126] Littleton recommended Ryley's promotion to Lancaster Herald that September.[127] Both Borough and Ryley, in short, remained loyal subjects to Charles I as his rule threatened to dissolve.

In coming months, the anti-Caroline visions solidified in the Grand Remonstrance and then the Nineteen Propositions, which together codified a parliamentary vision of governance that asserted continuity with the English past by cutting a selective path through it, assigning legitimacy to certain past practices while tacitly omitting others. Charles's responses turned the same practices toward opposing ends, privileging different sources and interpretations to construct a past irreconcilably opposed to his adversaries'. Their shared practice of politics encouraged polarization, as all participants continually revised their historical understandings while insisting that they were restoring England's appropriate form of monarchical government rather than devising a new one. The regime of inscription thus conjured rival and incommensurable visions of the state, each simultaneously innovative though empirically grounded in the records of the past.

Conclusion

A common set of methods united political practice across the Jacobean and Caroline reigns, one in which polemicists and administrators mobilized an ambiguous inherited body of records to buttress reimagined visions of England's constitution. Their method of knowledge production stimulated expansive visions of the Crown's financial powers no less than it underlay Parliamentarian efforts to curb the resultant taxes. It was an elastic array of techniques that could be deployed to conjure noble lineages, county histories, and patterns of medieval taxation just as easily as it could be used to summon and certify celebratory histories of parliamentary rights.

Recognizing the ubiquity of such practices suggests a new context for those such as Edward Coke and John Selden, for instead of revealing them to be innovators devising techniques to discern a majestic ancient constitution, it reveals that they instead adopted and adapted widespread practices to construct it. Though their investigations often incorporated an unprecedented quantity of sources or displayed unusual mastery of their intricacies, they nonetheless relied on the same methods as ambitious projectors and valued administrators within Crown government, for such techniques provided the bedrock for the Caroline agenda. In all cases, inscriptions—whether the overwhelming mass inherited from medieval crowns or the staggering volume generated in this period—served as resources ripe for exploitation. And, like Thomas Wilson's, their argumentative mode also depended not on appeal to personal advancement or benefit but on the claim that their research communicated but did not construct past realities.

In such a terrain, the instruments used to conduct debate served less as a common repository of evidence than as weapons of division. An overpowering flood of inscription was mediated by distinct communities who promulgated their own articulations of the English past. This information ecosystem was constituted less by a generalized public sphere marked by a thrust toward moderation and rationality than by cacophony. It was nonetheless deeply empirical, reliant on a foundation of material evidence selectively culled from the chaotic and contradictory record of past political actions. Rather than provide a self-correcting environment, the proliferation of evidence thwarted consensus by enabling observers to consult and emphasize texts selectively. The material proliferation of new media ineluctably promoted fracture.

Through much of the Personal Rule of Charles I, his regime managed to smolder frustration by using the shared body of knowledge practices with sufficient success. Crown officials such as Sir Julius Caesar and John Borough capitalized on precedents of extraparliamentary taxation. Their findings were sufficient to fund Charles's program for nearly a decade, enabling the appearance of functionality and stability that, though precarious, withstood the frustration of those increasingly hardened in their conviction that the past prescribed a wholly distinct, rival hierarchy of institutions.[128] Overreach was not inevitable, but when it came, the Caroline system of fiscal extraction proved incapable of further expansion. The Scottish resistance to Laud's Book of Common Prayer and ensuing military disasters exposed its limits by forcing Charles to call Parliament, which granted leverage to proponents of another type of state system who for nearly ten years had endured and expanded through their agile manipulation of media spheres outside the government. The resulting conflict convulsed Britain as a whole, forcing the welter of distinct networks into unanticipated alignments and oppositions, arousing a world of multiple governments mapped upon rival information structures, and further fracturing the realm into a mosaic of ever-more-distinct tesserae.

5

Information Warfare

War forced early modern Britons to adapt how they deployed written materials for political ends. The methods they devised for the environment of combat did not disappear with the cessation of armed conflict, for even after the boil of violence had lowered into the Interregnum's simmering discontent, British politics remained characterized by the condition of information warfare.[1]

Those operating in this environment sought not only to reinforce their supporters and persuade their enemies but also to control the terms on which information circulated. Information warfare assumed three main guises: ensuring that one's own information remained inaccessible; procuring what one's adversaries tried to keep secret; and selectively communicating information to audiences and defining what should be public to serve a specific agenda. As this chapter shows, early modern Britons pursued these ends through many means. But they remained rooted in political inscriptions, for underlying this spectrum of practices was the acquisition, storage, and dissemination of papers. The Tower records, texts from the State Paper Office, and other political papers procured from friends and enemies became matériel ripe for information warfare.

While historians have examined the role of censorship, libel, petitioning, and polemic as forms of political conflict in early modern Britain, these were joined by other methods of waging war through texts and information, which this chapter examines by following the Interregnum and early Restoration activities of individuals linked by their formal offices and mastery of information.[2] Foremost among these are the central figures in the Tower Record Office during this period: William Ryley and his son William Ryley Jr. (in this chapter I refer to the father as "Ryley" and the son as "Ryley Jr."), both of whose work in the Tower was only briefly interrupted despite their conspicuous royalist affinities; and William Prynne, whose information mastery was critical to his prominence within the Parliamentarian cause but who became Keeper of the Tower

Records at the Restoration of Charles II. While these figures—and others such as Oliver Cromwell's Secretary of State John Thurloe—sometimes contorted the documentary record to serve their needs, their techniques at other moments were more subtle, aiming to pressure audiences by propagandistic use of print or obtaining documents outside their legal or customary purview. Examining their activities reveals something like a preliminary lexicon of the tactics of early modern information warfare.

Investigating these practices not only illuminates the remaking of British politics through the regime of inscription but reveals an additional insight into the relationship of archivization and historical knowledge. The sources those operating in perilous circumstances have left to historians were often inflected by misrepresentation and duplicity; many constitute unstable testimonies, their fidelity irrevocably compromised by the desperation and determination that motivated them. This condition may be unusually pronounced in evidence generated by moments of armed conflict but is not unique to it. Rather, the complex status of evidence from such moments exemplifies the broader point that archives and inscriptions are always conditioned by the habits, powers, interests, and ambitions of whoever generated and preserved them, and that those seeking historical knowledge must recognize how these mediations and exclusions inflect their lenses onto the past.

Destruction and Dissimulation

The practices of information warfare during the English Revolution and subsequent Interregnum governments left Britain's documentary landscape in bedlam, as contemporaries were intensely aware. Upon Joseph Williamson's appointment as Keeper of the State Papers shortly after Charles II's Restoration in 1660, he began to audit the records of the realm, both those that stretched back into the medieval past and those that had been produced during the previous years of devastation. The accounts he collected depicted two decades of information entropy little different from the Dissolution of the Monasteries, for invaluable materials had been mislaid, secreted away, or otherwise rendered inaccessible.

Williamson's task required discerning what papers still remained and mobilizing his authority to recover them. But some were permanently irrecoverable. In his notes from a 1663 interview with Edward Nicholas—who had served as Charles I's last Secretary of State, from 1640 to 1646, and then reprised this role after the Restoration before being pushed out shortly before their conversation—Williamson recorded that "His Papers, collected from that time viz while the King was in the North & till the surrender at Oxford, were by Sir Edward Nicholas designedly burnt at Oxford, upon a feare he had that the Rebelles intented, notwithstanding the Actes of Oxford, to seize him & his Papers." As Williamson reported, "Among his owne papers were mostly considerable the Treaties with those in Ireland & the passages relating to that Peace." This loss—for historians no less than contemporaries who might have desired precise knowledge of the negotiations with the Confederate Catholics leading to the secret "Glamorgan treaty" and any other pacts between the king and the Irish—were only the highlights of his archive turned to ash.[3] Williamson continued, "And with those he likewise burnt a faire cabinet of the Old Kings all full of Papers of very secreat nature, which had been left at Oxford by the King upon his retirement to the Scots, and were directed to be burnt by Sir Edward Nicholas rather then to fall into the Rebells hands. Amongste those of the kings were thought by Sir Edward Nicholas to be all the Queens letters to the King & things of very mysterious nature, but he looked not into one of them, to obey the Kings command."[4] Nicholas intentionally destroyed those materials deemed by Charles himself as most valuable and most damning if delivered into hostile hands.[5]

Destruction, in short, was the most effective means of ensuring secrecy.[6] Terrified of the Parliamentarian reaction to the papers they held, Charles and Nicholas annihilated materials that might otherwise have accumulated in bundles strewn across Nicholas's office before eventually being annexed by the State Paper Office. Theirs was neither an unusual nor an irrational response, and eventually those in Interregnum regimes confronted their own loss of power similarly. In the same interview, Nicholas described the fate of Cromwell's diplomatic papers upon the Restoration: "All of the Papers of State during the time of the last Usurpacion of Cromwell &c remained at his Majesty's returne in Thurlows hands, & Sir Samuel Morland did advise to a great Minister the seizing of them, being then privately buryed in 4 great decke chests, or burned, but that Minister (for reasons left to be judged) delayed to order it, & then Thurloe had time to burne them, that would have hanged a great many, tis thought, if they had been suffered to speake: and he did certainly burne them all except some principall ones culled out by himselfe."[7] Thurloe, in Nicholas's account, had been caught between the desire to preserve the papers and the danger of their availability to the restored government but had ultimately yielded to his instincts for survival and destroyed them. In fact, Thurloe's story was a misdirection, as almost forty years later, his papers were discovered hidden in a false ceiling in the attic of his chambers in Lincoln's Inn.[8] Thurloe used the plausibility of a strategy of burning to conceal the preservation of his papers.

It is worth pausing to consider what these episodes reveal about historians' capacity to know the past, not least because recognizing the significance of such dramatic interventions can sharpen the understanding of the more subtle ones discussed over the course of this chapter. The survival of documents over time depends on a precarious constellation of behaviors to counteract ephemerality, flux, fragility, greed, malice, neglect, self-interest, mendacity, carelessness, deterioration, animal appetites, fire, water, folly, accident, natural disaster, poor engineering, linguistic discontinuity, and more. And conditions as perilous as those experienced by Charles I in the 1640s and Thurloe in 1660 further jeopardize preservation. Not only are sources concerning the past most at threat precisely during moments of crisis, but those that contemporaries might have deemed most revelatory are—for that very reason—most likely to be intentionally destroyed. The survival of such records is not organic but rather predicated on a combination of effort and chance.

The uncertainty of information's survival from moments of crisis is only the most acute version of the greater problem that because writing has predominantly been an organ for establishing political and spiritual control, few human actions and thoughts have been deemed appropriate for inscription in the first place. No written evidence can perfectly capture the fullness of a world whose primary quality is its ephemerality; knowing the past entails seizing upon fleeting moments embodied in phantom traces. As early modern Britons seized by fear that their secrets might be exposed knew, calculated destruction could permanently shape and limit the possibilities of knowledge.

Disinformation and Spin

The logic behind destroying Charles's papers emerges powerfully when contrasted to the tactics of Prynne's campaign to bring down Archbishop William Laud. Prynne's methods included confiscating Laud's archive and selectively using his own writings and collections against him; Laud might well have preferred his papers burned than for Prynne to make them his tormenters.[9]

Prynne spent the 1630s stoking hostilities between Charles I and his detractors.[10] The antagonism toward the Laudian church expressed in his publications earned Prynne spectacular punishments from Star Chamber to the pillory, including the severing of both of his ears and the branding of both of his cheeks. But Prynne was not a cleric; his primary association was with Lincoln's Inn, and his Calvinism worked in concert with his command of Tower records and antiquarian collections of medieval sources such as those of Henry Spelman and John Weever.[11] The force of Prynne's claims emanated not only from his wit and aggression but also from his command of theological, historical, and legal idioms and his ability to portray scripture, custom, and the law as dovetailing around his preferred policies.

Over the course of the Interregnum, the thrust of radicalism left Prynne behind, and by the Restoration he was able to gain Charles II's favor, though many royalists continued to view him with suspicion. The form of reconciliation between the king and Prynne suggests Charles II's appreciation of the strategies that Prynne had been using for decades, for in 1660, Prynne was appointed Keeper of the Tower Records. This appointment recognized Prynne's years in the 1650s doggedly working through often obscure materials in the Tower—as discussed subsequently—but it also highlights that Prynne's archival sleuthings had earlier been elemental to the finding, extracting, and circulating of information characteristic of his anti-Laudian program.

Prynne's tactics of information warfare were on full display in 1644 as he prepared for Laud's trial in the House of Lords on the charge of treason. The State Paper Office constituted one source for materials; in early March, just before the trial began, Prynne wrote to Keeper of the State Papers Ambrose Randolph: "Sir I have have retorned some of Your Papers by the Bearer the risidue I shall keep a while for this Archbishopps Triall & Publicke Use. I pray send me the papers concerning Mr Gage his Negotiation at Rome, the Lord Digby & Calverts Letters about the Spanish Match, & the Warrant for distributing the lands in Spaine which I should have present use thereof."[12] While the precise papers Prynne had already acquired are unknown, the new requests likely would have been scoured for evidence that Laud had tried to orchestrate the Spanish match as a way to seduce Charles to Roman Catholicism. The State Paper Office was thus weaponized to forge a narrative of a conspiracy to Catholicize the witless prince.

Prynne secured even more valuable resources for his prosecution when, in May 1643, Parliament delegated him to lead a group of soldiers into the Tower of London, where Laud was imprisoned, to "search all the prisoners remaininge under restraint by order of either of the houses of Parliament or the Committee and to sease upon all letters and papers."[13] At the same time, Prynne was also appointed to search Laud's study in Lambeth Palace, where he found many more documents, including Laud's diary.

Prynne used the papers seized on these occasions to construct a narrative resembling a "secret history," a popular contemporary genre that claimed to use "politic" and sometimes conspiratorial reasoning to expose the diabolical intrigues and machinations that allegedly drove contemporary political and religious affairs.[14] The annexed materials were essential to the allegation that Laud had tricked Charles into swearing a coronation oath that subverted England's proper rule. During Prynne's deposition, he explained that Laud's diary recorded that in January 1626, "there was a speciall booke & forme for King Charles coronation compiled . . . extracted out of ancient bookes of the King's Coronation which the Archbishop had in his studdy."[15] Prynne reported that he had seized both the book containing Charles's oath and the volumes of previous coronations.[16] Close inspection of these, Prynne explained, revealed that Laud had manipulated and distorted his sources. Though Laud had claimed to follow the oath given to James, in fact he had strongly favored Edward VI's, which lacked several clauses establishing the Crown's sovereignty. In total, Prynne reported, Charles's oath differed in "21 particulars from that of King James, some whereof are of real concernment." For example, when describing how the king certified the law, Charles's oath read "performe" where James's had read "confirme" which, as Prynne emphasized, contradicted the directive articulated most clearly by Bracton that the law was external to the king. Even when Charles's oath seemed to uphold English traditions, Prynne noted that he was led to do so under alarmingly Catholic circumstances. His confirmation of Magna Carta, a horrified Prynne revealed, "twas done modo crucis, in the forme as at the Masse;" this meant that "the king was upon his knees at the unction" and that there had been "a crucifix over the alter."[17] The oath fashioned by Laud, Prynne maintained, had abnegated the king's duty to the law and replaced it with fealty to Roman Catholic tyranny—precisely the kind of subterfuge ubiquitous in secret histories.

The diary would supply some of Prynne's favorite evidence of Laud's mendacity, and he used it as the foundation of several publications in the 1640s.[18] Most notably, his 1644 slim quarto, *A Breviate of the Life of William Laud* was, as Prynne explained, "extracted (for the most part word for word) out of his [Laud's] owne Diary and Papers."[19] This volume claimed to vindicate Prynne and damn Laud through the allegedly faithful recitation of Laud's own words.

Prynne's strategy for distributing the book was designed to inflict maximum damage. Though the *Breviate* was printed in mid-August 1644, it was circulated on September 2—the precise day that Laud was intended to deliver his "recapitulation" to the House of Lords rebutting Prynne's prosecution. When he came to the bar that day, Laud later recounted, "I saw every lord present with a new thin book in Folio, in a blue coat. I heard that morning, that Mr Prynn had printed my diary, and published it to the world to disgrace me. Some notes of his own are made upon it. The first and the last are two desperate untruths, besides some others. This was the book then in the lords hands: and I assume myself that time picked for it, that the sight of it might damp me, and disenable me to speak."[20] The timing of its distribution was intended to magnify the effect of the text itself, which Prynne abridged from the diary but then equipped with a censorious commentary that blurred into Laud's own words.[21]

When Laud acquired a copy of the *Breviate* in the five months between its publication and his execution, he penned dozens of exculpatory annotations in its margins, perhaps hoping to use them as foundation for a formal rebuttal. In these notes, Laud recoiled at Prynne's accusation of his "uncleanness," tyranny, "reviving of the Scottish wars," and other treasons and heresies.[22] Similarly, he objected when Prynne criticized him for following royal commands or asserted that Laud's impieties had drawn providential punishment upon England.[23]

Above all, Laud was incensed by how Prynne's printed edition revised the diary, which by this time had been restored to him. These complaints expose Prynne's techniques of information warfare. Foremost among these tactics was the addition of details not found in the diary that reshaped the meanings of authentic entries. For example, where Laud recorded that he had proceeded to Bachelor of Divinity in July 1604, Prynne had added that his thesis "concerning the efficacie of Baptism, was taken verbatim out of Bellarmine," to which Laud responded in the margins "not possible."[24] Similarly, next to an anodyne entry that "Tuesday, I went to New-Hall to my Lord Duke of Buckingham, and came back to London on Friday," Prynne added, "It is credibly reported that the Duke made the Bishop at that time put off his Gowne and Cassocke, and then to Dance before him like an Hobgoblin to make him merry," prompting an appalled Laud to note, "Here by your self. But I solemnly avow there was never any such thing."[25] Such outrages were legion: Laud bristled at Prynne's comment that the commission that secured Archbishop of Canterbury Abbott's fall—enabling Laud's ascent—was "of his [Laud's] own procurement, in malice and envy against Archbishop Abbot," scribbling that "this is a most notorious scandal & slander cast upon me."[26] As Laud saw, Prynne edited the diary so that the archbishop seemed to incriminate himself.

Prynne also removed Laud's words to fit his agenda. For example, Laud noted, Prynne omitted entries showing that he had given up his previous post when chosen Bishop of St David's to avoid pluralism.[27] Worse, Prynne's claim that Laud resisted Buckingham's impeachment because of their shared Catholicism depended on such distortions; next to the printed passage discussing the impeachment, Laud noted, "Here my diary adds thatt if Pope & Spaniard would desier any thing acceptable for their ends they could not think of a better course then these distractions of his great Councell of the Kingdome. But Note that this is left out."[28]

Prynne's mistreatment of the volume extended to its physical state as well, for portions of the diary had burned while in Prynne's custody, allowing Prynne to substitute his own words for Laud's. For example, regarding his appeal to justice after his arrest in March 1641, Laud noted: "this passage burnt allso in part & made up by the Author."[29] To Laud's outrage, moreover, rather than acknowledging this, Prynne alleged that the archbishop himself had "burned most of his privy Letters and papers" and elsewhere called him an "Arch-Incendiary." In response Laud indignantly penned: "Mr Maxwell was by command of the Honorable House to be by me all the while. And he was not one minute from me & knows I did not burn any the paper."[30]

Prynne even sought to use the diary to fashion interpretation of the ongoing trial. At the time of its publication, it was clear that the Lords recognized that Prynne's evidence was insufficient to meet the standard of treason. Accordingly, Prynne used the diary to try to reshape memory of previous sessions, narrating his allegations as if they had commanded full assent. By contrast, Laud's note on Prynne's description of the coronation oath—"The whole business I have answered in Parliament"—expressed the belief that his testimony had exonerated him.[31] Laud's annotations repeatedly asserted this; for example, when Prynne derided him as a "poor vassal" of the Duke of Buckingham, Laud responded, "Not Vassall, but such a poor true Friend as that Honorable persons favours had made me. That which follows I have answer'd in Parliament."[32] His services to the Catholic Queen Henrietta Maria he similarly noted were, "objected & answered at my trial."[33] Prynne would not have agreed that the archbishop's testimony exonerated him, and Laud perhaps overstated the success of his defense. But the timing of the publication reveals that these passages were meant to remind the Peers of Laud's alleged treasons while claiming consensus for his guilt.

As Laud unhappily observed, Prynne's edition of the diary constituted a form of information warfare. He seized papers, excised and altered passages in ways deleterious to the archbishop, accused Laud of the unscrupulousness which he himself enacted, and circulated his narrative in a manner calculated to exert maximum impact. In response, Laud insisted that Prynne distorted his text using the exact practices which Prynne alleged him of using to construct Charles's coronation oath. They thus saw themselves as accused of the same dishonest methods distinctive—in their minds—to their enemies.

Prynne's *Breviate* used spin, disinformation, rumor, allegation, and innuendo to cast Laud as his own most incriminating witness. Ultimately,

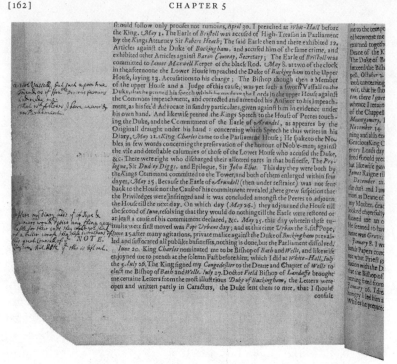

FIGURE 13. Archbishop William Laud's notes responding to William Prynne's *A Breviate of the Life of William Laud* (London, 1644). The Bodleian Libraries, University of Oxford, Laud. Misc.760, p. 8 (i.e., f. 14v).

Prynne failed to secure Laud's conviction for treason. But the antipathy embodied by his accusations prompted the House of Commons' turn to an ordinance of attainder and led to Laud's execution. Prynne's practices did not meet legal standards of proof, but that did not dilute their power as information warfare.

Spycraft and Impersonation

William Prynne's tactics were aggressive, his motivations obvious. At exactly this time, by contrast, William Ryley was embarking on a shadowy period in which he was likely involved in the information warfare of spycraft. But precisely because of the nature of espionage, his alleged acts produced only ambiguous evidence that frustrates any certainty not only regarding his underlying allegiances but also concerning the reality of his purported actions.[34]

In April 1642, four months before the initiation of combat, the House of Commons had ordered Keeper of the Tower Records John Borough to "give Order to Mr. *Ryley* to stay here and attend the Parliament with such Records as shall be required for the Service of the Commonwealth."[35] But Borough and Ryley, like most of the heralds, aligned with the Crown and accompanied Charles I when the king moved his court to Oxford. Ryley stayed there as the war ignited and spread, until in July 1643, Charles ordered him to return to the Tower "to preserve the Records and Bookes of the Office, and Officers Armes, in the absence of the other Kings, heralds, and Pursuivants of Armes."[36] The seeming truce between Parliament and Crown over the Tower records suggests that both viewed the archive as a neutral territory.[37] Ryley's tax burden was discharged by Parliament in September, and though John Selden was appointed Keeper of the Tower Records after Borough died that October, he treated the post as a sinecure; virtually all its responsibilities fell to Ryley.[38]

Ryley's return to London inaugurated a murky period. For the next decade, he faced allegations that he was a royalist spy, and after the Restoration, his son repeatedly listed these accusations in petitions for financial support. Ryley Jr.'s claims, however, should be viewed with caution, as they transparently intended to justify Ryley's service in Interregnum governments to the Stuart regime. Instead, the accusations levied against Ryley and then reiterated by his son should be seen as articulating contemporary perceptions of spycraft. At the same time, the opacity of Ryley's role reflects how wartime information practices obfuscated communication, created information asymmetries, and clouded the identity of individuals behind belligerent actions—and thus had the auxiliary effect of muddying the evidence relied on by historians.

Ryley Jr.'s petitions constructed a plausible history of Ryley performing intelligence services for Charles I. Upon his arrival in London in 1643, Ryley Jr. recorded, his father was immediately suspected, and the clerk Dancer Hancock "putt in Eight dangerous Articles against him, at the Committee of Examinations, charging him to carry Records to Oxford to maintaine and justifie the Commission of Array (which was very true, but could not bee proved) and that hee lay in London as a Lodger, Spye or Intelligencer, &c. And thereupon hee was committed in the most dangerous Custody for many weekes."[39] The Commissions of Array were Charles's means of raising an army in response to Parliament's Militia Ordinance; Ryley, on this account, had provided essential documentary tools for the king's military mobilization.

This was the first of many accusations levied against Ryley of passing information to the royalist camp—allegations which Ryley Jr. avowed as true but unproven by his father's antagonists.[40] The following year Robert Browne, Bluemantle Pursuivant, and William Crowne, Rouge Dragon Pursuivant, "revived Hancocks Articles, with additions of their owne, saying that hee made a Collection of all the Cornetts and Coullors both of Horse and Foote used in the Parliament service, together with the names of the Owners, and their Mottoes, all which were printed in a faire book, which hee sent to the late King to Oxford." As Ryley Jr. explained, his father had indeed procured for the king such valuable military intelligence, and in harrowing fashion. The messenger entrusted with delivering the book had been apprehended but had successfully hidden it in a secret panel in his horse's tack, and upon release, he had returned to Ryley, who then devised another plan to send the book to the king. This time the delivery succeeded, but Ryley—either unaware of the success or perhaps flush with new information—produced another volume and stole off to Oxford to deliver it directly to Charles himself. According to Ryley Jr., this proved a breach; several months later, John Lucas, a servant of William Le Neve, Clarenceux King of Arms, revealed this episode "to Browne and Crowne, for which and for sending Copys of Severall Records concerning the Commissions of Array, [Ryley] was again brought before the Committee of Examinations, where hee was highly prosecuted, and if Lucas had not then dyed, my father had been then tried for his life att a Council of Warre."[41] Ryley, in this account, again used his privileged place within the Tower to garner sensitive information about Parliamentarian armies which he transmitted to the king at profound personal risk.

According to Ryley Jr., his father continued to skirt disaster. In 1644 or 1645, Speaker of the House William Lenthall reprimanded him "for his affection and duty to his late Majetie, and his Offences against the Parliament," likely reviving Hancock's articles because, as Ryley Jr. put it, Lenthall exhibited "eight dangerous Articles exhibited against hym, which they could not prove, yett were all true."[42] The collection of "Cornetts and Coullors" resurfaced again shortly after, and Ryley was "prosecuted very vigorously before the Committee of Sequestration at Cambden house in London for sending and carying the said Cornetts and Coullors to Oxford and other his services for the King." This committee decided to punish him; as Ryley Jr. explained, "hee was sequestred and his study att the Heralds Office sealed up by order of that Committee. At the doore of which the words following were written and putt up, and entred in their Bookes also. That Ryley told the King that hee had Records to prove the Parliament Traitors."[43] Once again Ryley was released, though Ryley Jr. did not explain why. Then in 1650 he was again prosecuted, this time by the Committee for the Advance of Money, "and the old charge revived, and other Articles preserved against hym, as adhering, and maintaining the Kings right to the Militia, and sending Records to Oxford."[44] Three years later, Ryley Jr. attested, he was prosecuted by the Committee of Indemnity for serving in the king's army between 1642 and 1645. Later in

1653 the Barebones Parliament questioned him. Only with his absolution by Cromwell's Act of Grace in 1654 was Ryley indemnified.

Ryley's allegiances prior to 1643 and actions after the Restoration make his son's account plausible, and the few glimpses of his activities in these years other than those described by his son supply supporting evidence too. For example, Ryley continued to correspond with Catholic royalist exiles, and when Lord Treasurer Thomas Howard, Earl of Arundel, died in 1646, Ryley composed a Latin inscription for his funeral plate and then sent notes on the office of the Earl Marshall to his son, who had succeeded to the position.[45] Ryley's seeming rapprochement with Parliament in the late 1640s, furthermore, suggests that it required Ryley not just to accept its authority but to sever his royalist connections. After his return, he had continued to perform his clerical duties, and in 1646 he was even elevated to Norroy King of Arms, likely to provide appropriate ceremony for the funeral of the Parliamentarian Robert Devereux, 3rd Earl of Essex.[46] But Ryley was infrequently paid, and he petitioned for wages in arrears in 1645 and then again in 1648, noting that he "hath diligently attended the service of the Parliament."[47] His 1648 petition proved successful, as within a week Parliament voted him £200, with an additional £50 for repairs to the Tower records. The conditions of this award, however, were telling; he was to be paid "out of such Delinquents Estates as he shall discover to the Committee at Habberdash'rs Hall [the Committee for the Advance of Money])."[48] Ryley, that is, would be paid only with funds taken from royalists he incriminated. Finally, though Ryley Jr. did not record it, his father was brought before the Committee for Compounding with Delinquents in late 1651 and interrogated by them again in 1653.[49]

In his son's portrayal, in short, Ryley posed as a neutral clerk in the Tower to obtain justification for the king's raising of an army and information concerning the enemy force. For more than ten years he worked to penetrate Parliamentary secrecy, susceptible to potentially lethal consequences if discovered. Though operating under a cloud of mistrust, he repeatedly averted exposure. His espionage thus reflected the imperative to commandeer any advantage in the belligerent information terrain of the 1640s.

* * *

There is reason, however, to be skeptical of William Ryley Jr.'s portrayal of his father. It has long been recognized that Dancer Hancock's allegations were directed toward Theophilus Ryley, a coconspirator in the plot centered around Basil Brooke, rather than William Ryley.[50] Closer inspection of the dispute with Browne, moreover, further clouds Ryley Jr.'s assertions. Like William Ryley, Robert Browne and William Crowne had accompanied the king to Oxford, and they returned separately in summer 1644, a year after Ryley.[51] Browne did tell the Sequestrations Committee around January 1646 that Ryley "hath held Intelligence with the Enemy att Oxford and had a speciall dispensation under his Majesty's hand to reside heere in London, giving him alsoe power to looke to thee Records in the Tower and the Heralds office."[52] The committee, accordingly, sequestered Ryley and sealed his study. Ryley, however, responded by accusing Browne of a series of "delinquencies" such as that he "hath bene an Actor against the parliament," embezzled and sold records from the college, and devised coats of arms for "some persons of inferior condition." Moreover, Ryley maintained that when Browne "was in service against the Parliament he proclaimed the Parliament Traitour. And had a warrant from the King for one hundred pounds for his service done in the Kings Army."[53] Ryley even listed Crowne as a witness who would corroborate Browne's inappropriate grant of arms. In Ryley's account, Browne was the spy.

When the House of Lords summoned Browne the following week, Browne argued that Ryley's petition had been borne from "recrimination" and "malice," while professing his innocence and insisting he had "served the state with all faithfulnesse & Integrity."[54] In response, the Lords requested the Book of Accounts from the College of Arms and scheduled further questioning.[55] But the charges seem to have fizzled, as the Lords did not further pursue the case. Similarly, when the Sequestrations Committee called the case a week later, it requested answers to questions at its next meeting, but if these answers were ever provided, the records have not survived; certainly there is no testimony that Ryley was "prosecuted very vigorously," as Ryley Jr. maintained.[56] Ryley and Browne even collaborated on heraldic business that summer, though Browne died later that year.[57]

Ryley Jr.'s account of this episode, in short, is riddled with conflations and half-truths. Whereas it is possible that Ryley was a spy and that Browne wished to demonstrate his loyalty to Parliament by exposing him, other options are equally plausible: that Ryley's allegiances had shifted and the genuine spy Browne was creating misdirection, as Ryley suggested; that both were spies and that the dispute was part of their cover—or that neither knew about the other; or neither were spies and instead the episodes constitute a typical squabble among heralds, refracted through the darkness of the moment.

Ryley Jr.'s mention of the volume of "Cornetts and Coullors" similarly conflated disparate episodes. As in the previous case, Ryley Jr. portrayed his father as assuming great risk to supply intelligence to Charles I. But closer inspection clouds Ryley Jr.'s clarity. Lucas—who Ryley Jr. claimed had exposed his father's transmission of the volume—in fact compiled a 1646 collection entitled "London in Armes displayed," which he proudly sent to Parliamentarian leaders.[58] Perhaps Lucas copied this collection from Ryley and took credit; perhaps Ryley copied it from Lucas and sent it to the king's camp; perhaps Ryley's was a separate volume altogether. In all cases, Lucas's explicit claim of authoring this text fits oddly with the claim that he exposed Ryley's volume.

Moreover, Ryley had indeed performed the task his son described—but for Parliament. After routing royalist forces at the Battle of Naseby, Parliamentarian forces had secured a trove of the king's letters and papers, many of which were read publicly. The House of Commons then ordered that "the Ensigns and Cornets sent up now by Sir Thomas Fairfax, and all other Ensigns and Cornets, that have at any time formerly, or shall at any time hereafter, be taken from the Enemy, shall be brought into the Heralds Office," where they should be "registred, and preserved in some convenient Place there" by Ryley, who would then supply them when either house demanded.[59] Ryley Jr. appears to have jumbled these episodes, whether intentionally or accidentally. The episode perhaps illuminates the imagination of spycraft—concealment of identity, procuring and transmission of papers—more than it establishes Ryley's actions.

Finally, the prosecutions touted by Ryley Jr. as substantiating his father's loyalty to the king are more equivocal than he allowed. For example, his 1653 prosecution by the Committee of Indemnity was initiated by Thomas Nightingale, who considered Ryley's clerkship in the Tower to violate the Act for Disabling Delinquents to Bear Public Office of the previous October. Nightingale's petition provided as evidence that Ryley had been sequestered and alleged that he had been "in Actuall Armes" with the king from 1642 to 1645.[60] But the committee found the "particulars" Nightingale provided of Ryley's movements "uncertain," and he appears to have dropped the case after being instructed to gather more evidence.[61] Rather than testifying to Ryley Jr.'s continuing services, this prosecution suggests only how the churn of governments jeopardized those who had initially sided with the king.

* * *

One viable interpretation of Ryley's career after returning to London in 1643 is that he was not a spy covertly operating for Charles I's interest but that his royalist past was used against him intermittently. His son's assertions, from this perspective, do not prove his spycraft so much as reveal how intelligence work was conceived: as a matter of concealing allegiances while infiltrating positions from which one could obtain and transmit valuable information to allies.

But recognizing the imperative for secrecy ironically suggests that Ryley Jr.'s account should not be discarded so quickly. If Ryley had been a successful spy—even if only for a few years—he would have covered his tracks by measures such as burning his own papers.[62] That Ryley Jr.'s particulars were inaccurate does not invalidate his whole description; Browne's information could have been genuine, and Lucas could surely have copied a guide to Parliamentarian armies Ryley had produced and then claimed it as his own. The uncertainty over Ryley's actions might be less an accident than motivated, a consequence of a spycraft where deception was essential to discover and expose enemy information. Ryley's imposture may have been his service as a Parliamentarian bureaucrat, or it may have been his posthumous reconstruction as royalist spy. That no definitive answer is possible is not merely a matter of historical distance but rather a consequence of practices of information warfare endemic to a bellicose political environment fearfully aware of the power and possibilities of written materials.

Surveillance and Perception

The execution of Charles I did not remove the imperative for information warfare. Instead, the problems posed by individuals such as Ryley became central to the Commonwealth, whose stability rested on maintaining a base level of acceptance of its rule and disabling plots hatched by foreign powers, unreconstructed royalists, disgruntled Parliamentarians, Irish Catholics, and disillusioned Levellers. Distinguishing actively hostile individuals from the merely disaffected or formerly belligerent posed a thorny problem. Those charged with assessing such loyalties labored not only to obtain intelligence but also to control how events were described, recorded, and circulated in the effort to maintain peace among Britain's fractious populace.

Under Oliver Cromwell, the task of managing threats to the regime fell predominantly to Secretary of State John Thurloe.[63] His practices were finely attuned to a shadowy environment in which the prevalence of disguised identities and false accusations created the risks of too quickly dismissing viable threats or overreacting to fake ones. Thurloe rooted his mastery of this information landscape in surveillance: asserting asymmetrical control over the sphere of information by observing potential dangers without himself being observed. But this surveillance formed part of a comprehensive system of information management, for the reports he gleaned from informers and double agents were part of a broader agenda of legitimizing Cromwell's rule by creating and controlling public perception through acts and texts alike.[64]

* * *

As the Interregnum governments struggled to establish footing, they relied on many of the same administrative practices as their predecessors. The immediate aftermath of the execution of Charles I was marked, as Sean Kelsey has observed, by "the fundamentally preservationist impulse of Commonwealth political culture."[65] Even as the Commons moved forward with the trial of Charles in early 1649 on the charge of treason, it requested "an Account, where the Books and Records of this House are" and outfitted a room for them; later that year a committee was appointed to manage such records along with those of the House of Lords, which had come under Commons' control with the upper house's abolition.[66] John Milton was one of many who was intended to receive papers from the various committees and commissions that had sprung up as the Commonwealth sought to improvise a functional government into place.[67] The control of records, paperwork, and information retained its same centrality under revolutionary governance.

Thurloe ascended to the position of Secretary to the Council of State in spring 1652 and maintained prominent roles for the next seven years. During this time, he consulted the Tower records and State Paper Office in the same way as had previous administrators and counselors, such as to prepare for diplomacy.[68] His information work assumed many other dimensions as well. He actively oversaw the press, for one, ensuring the distribution of proclamations and other government statements, supplying news favorable to the regime, collaborating with authors and printers to ensure positive discussion of Cromwell's measures, and determining whether to license publications.

Thurloe's primary work, however, was the orchestration of an extensive communication network. He received print and manuscript newsletters from correspondents throughout Europe, but more strikingly, his surviving papers are saturated with cyphered letters of intelligence. These correspondents were often directed to infiltrate hostile communication networks, and accordingly they provided a steady flow of intercepted letters. To gain access to domestic communication, similarly, he was appointed Postmaster General in 1655, and Samuel Morland created a device for opening and resealing packets so that Thurloe's clerks could read the posts.

Maintaining Thurloe's invisibility was vital to his work, and penetrating enemy communication networks was necessary therefore not only to obtain intelligence but also to reveal when Thurloe's own networks and practices were exposed. Accordingly, his correspondence swirled with reports about what potential enemies at home and abroad knew and how they knew it. For example, in 1653 he received a stern letter from one of his spies in the Netherlands enclosing a letter which, his correspondent explained, revealed "howe it is in Holand discovered by letters from their deputies here, what intelligence the councel of state has here. If this be not avoided, you will have noe more from thence, and whoseover tells the deputies here thus much, tells it to keepe you from intelligences; and belike tells at least all he knowes to the deputies to their advantag and your disadvantadg."[69] Thurloe's information network had been breached. But at the same time, this letter informed Thurloe of Dutch practices whose secrecy the Dutch would have preferred to preserve, which he could then use to his own benefit.[70] This was an information ecosystem of universal spydom, with all parties watching one another not only to secure intelligence but also to assess the effectiveness of their own concealments.

When credible threats were identified, Thurloe worked quickly; for example, discovery of the plot to assassinate Cromwell spearheaded by John Gerard in 1654 led to an abrupt change in Cromwell's routines and immediate arrest of the conspirators.[71] Thurloe, however, acknowledged the impossibility of comprehensive oversight. To address this problem, he encouraged not just surveillance itself but its presumed appearance—a strategy of simulation and misdirection similar to his later claim to have destroyed his papers.

Thurloe's handling of Miles Sindercombe's plot encapsulates his methods.[72] This attempt to assassinate Cromwell was perhaps the narrowest escape of the Protectorate. Sindercombe was a Leveller soldier with a record of plotting against the army leadership he saw as debasing the ideals of revolution, most notably participating in the 1654 Overton Plot to seize control of the army in Scotland, with the broader goal of deposing Cromwell and restoring the English Republic. After the plot's discovery, Sindercombe fled to Flanders, where he met the radical Leveller Edward Sexby, who stoked his interest in assassinating Cromwell. Sindercombe returned to England in September 1656 under the alias of John Fish, at which point he recruited coconspirators including John Toope, a member of Cromwell's guard. The group designed but could not consummate at least five efforts on Cromwell's life, and it was plotting to blow up Whitehall with Cromwell inside in January 1657 when Toope betrayed them. Within the day, Thurloe apprehended the conspirators.

That Sindercombe's plot had persisted so long did not reflect Thurloe's failure to acquire information but rather his miscalculated response to alleged threats, for he had been apprised of Sindercombe's presence shortly after his arrival. A Savoyard minister-soldier in London named Jean-Baptiste Stouppe almost immediately received intelligence from Brussels that Sindercombe had recently arrived in Westminster with designs to assassinate Cromwell, and had hastened to Whitehall to give the report, including naming the street where Sindercombe was lodging. To Stouppe's surprise, Thurloe dismissed him, explaining that "they had many such advertisments sent them, which signified nothing but to make the world think the protector was in danger of his life; and the looking too much after these things had an appearance of fear, which did ill become so great a man." When Stouppe suggested that they search the street in question, Thurloe answered, "If we find no such person, how shall we be laughed at?"[73] Thurloe was confident in his ability to distinguish real threats from substanceless rumors. Moreover, he considered maintenance of the public's impression of the Protectorate's surveillance as a goal in its own right, and conspicuous embarrassments posed their own threat by suggesting the regime's fragility and incompetence. Thurlow thus aimed to perpetuate a cycle of perception in which the assumption of surveillance would inhibit plots, and the absence of plots would confirm the success of Thurloe's surveillance apparatus.

When Toope confessed, Cromwell was told of Stouppe's report and, enraged at having not been alerted, summoned Stouppe. When Stouppe explained that he had informed Thurloe, an incredulous Cromwell sent for the Secretary of State. But Thurloe remained unperturbed: "nor did he deny any part of it, but only said, that he had many such advertisements sent him, in which till this time he had never found any truth." This was untrue—as the Gerard plot testified—but was intended to deflect Stouppe, for after he left, "Thurloe shewed Cromwell such instances of his care, both for his honour and quiet, that he pacified him intirely." That is, Thurloe demonstrated that his apparatus was capable of distinguishing real from illusory threats, which he hoped would "justify his not being so attentive as he ought to have been" in Sindercombe's case.[74] By revealing his success in protecting the Protector, Thurloe regained Cromwell's trust.

Thurloe's attention not only to collecting information but also to controlling perception precluded the regime from conspicuously addressing every rumored conspiracy, which risked impugning Cromwell's honor. Rather, it required conspicuously acting against reports only when successful intervention was guaranteed. Unlike Charles I's papers, unwanted rumors could not be burned. But they could be delegitimized.

When conspiracies were real, moreover, Thurloe shifted strategies and publicized their successful exposure to maximize political benefit.

In January 1657, Thurloe reported to the Commons of the thwarting of Sindercombe's and two other plots, which ultimately led to an order for a day of public thanksgiving and strengthened the movement to restore the monarchy to Cromwell, which Thurloe strongly advocated.[75] Three pamphlets were published within the month exalting the foiling of the conspiracy as testimony of Cromwell's blessed rule. These were almost certainly completed with Thurloe's assistance—most obviously the pamphlet printed after Sindercombe's death in prison by Thurloe's regular collaborator, Thomas Newcombe, contained numerous official depositions likely provided by Thurloe, including one from Sindercombe's mother affirming that her son had committed suicide.[76] Thurloe thus converted a covert conspiracy to assassinate Cromwell into a public celebration of Cromwell's rule.

* * *

Thurloe's practice of surveillance entailed orchestrating networks that supplied intelligence about potential threats. This aspect of its functioning relied on maintaining information asymmetry: protecting Thurloe's secrecy while penetrating enemy communications. But circulating the perception of effective surveillance was also essential to foment fear among the disaffected and inhibit their capacity and motivation to devise plots. His tactic of surveillance, counterintuitively, entailed judiciously revealing its operations, both by ensuring that public confrontations with plots were staged to succeed and through strategically circulating communications to control public perception—selecting what should be aired and what should be suppressed in the streets and presses of Cromwellian Britain. Surveillance was thus a means of obtaining information one's adversaries might prefer to keep secret, but in Thurloe's hands it also fed his efforts to manage public knowledge of the political landscape.

Appropriation

While John Thurloe's acquisition of intelligence demanded subtlety and calculation, other operatives proclaimed dubious authority to assert control over papers, seizing them by force or against custom or legal agreement. After the execution of Charles I, the two William Ryleys were involved in several appropriations of records, and they supported this species of information warfare by enlisting tactics ranging from fraud to tendentious argumentation.

If he had not before, the elder Ryley seemingly reconciled himself to the new regime after the regicide, though he remained under occasional suspicion. After the Council of State inspected the Tower records in early December 1650, it proposed that Ryley receive an annual salary of £200 to perform his traditional duties.[77] Ryley Jr. joined his father working in the Tower in 1651, shortly after sustaining injury fighting alongside royalist forces at the Battle of Worcester.[78] Although it is possible that they concealed the cause of the injury—or that Ryley Jr. lied about how he had received it—more likely the Commonwealth allowed Ryley to employ his son because of the value of his expertise.

For the next two decades, the Ryleys served as Deputy Keepers.[79] Most notably, they were central to the heretofore unresolved saga of the Scottish state papers, which began under Cromwell and stretched into the Restoration. These papers had been traditionally kept in Edinburgh Castle, but upon its fall in 1650 to Cromwell's forces, the records were secreted to Stirling Castle. When this castle was captured in August 1651, the papers were seized and sent to England. In October, Parliament dictated that they should be sent to the Tower of London, with orders to pay Ryley £50 for "defraying" them.[80] By the following January, a portion of the confiscated collection had been registered, inspected, and stored in the Tower.

In late 1653, the Scots petitioned the Barebones Parliament asking that the records be returned. Parliament agreed to a limited repatriation restricted to records concerning private parties, such as deeds of conveyance. By contrast, it decreed that "such as are of the publick concernement, and for the benefit and advantage of the commonwealth bee preserved and kept here, and that the councell of state doe likewise take care of the safe keepeing of the records in the tower." The Ryleys would supervise these, with all the fees and perquisites that entailed. The order was implemented, and the Ryleys oversaw the gradual return of many of the private records while the public records remained in the Tower under their control.[81]

The Ryleys were thus the agents of the Cromwellian appropriation of the Scottish public records. After the Restoration, however, their role seemed poised to change. Charles II was far more sympathetic to Scottish interests than any of the regimes of the previous decade, and not long after his ascension, a delegation from Scotland arrived in London expecting to recover the papers. The initial negotiations would have encouraged the Scots, as in August 1660, Charles agreed to convey all the remaining Scottish records to Archibald Primrose, Lord Carrington. A warrant issued at this time entrusted Ryley with delivering them and dictated that he was also "to take his oath if itt were required that none of the said Records and writings had bin put away or abstracted since they came into his keeping. And if any of them had bin put away, he was to declare upon oath and under his handwriting when and how they were disposed of. And whose hands the same."[82]

The Scots surely recognized that they were requesting powerful documents, but so did the Ryleys, and they—and Ryley Jr. in particular—acted to prevent damaging documents from being delivered to the Scots. As Ryley Jr. later noted, while inventorying the records he uncovered "the Originall of the Solemn League & Covenant of Scotland, together with the Concessions at Breda, both signed by his Royall Majestie that now is."[83] These were the official documents testifying Charles II's agreement to the Solemn League and Covenant—which would remake the English church on the Scottish presbyterian model—as part of the Treaty of Breda in 1650, a condition the Scottish had insisted on for joining their forces to his. The king's desperate measure from a decade before, however, now constituted a major embarrassment and—if the Scots sought to enforce the agreement—a looming crisis. Ryley Jr. surreptitiously removed these documents from the papers slated for return.

The Scots envoys, unsurprisingly, were particularly interested in retrieving these items. When this group discovered that they were missing, Ryley Jr. claimed, "the Scotch men then in Towne intrusted for the sending of the Registers into Scotland, offered mee £2000, if I would have delivered the paper (as they called it) into their possession, but I replyed, I would never betray my King and Country for any reward." Instead, he reported, "This Covenant and Confession I gave to the Lord Chancellor, having no opportunity to present them to his Majesties owne hands."[84] Despite the legal agreement concerning the records' return, Ryley appropriated and then delivered these documents to the new regime.

The Ryleys' reversal mirrored the Crown's, for by early September Charles's regime had decided not to restore the documents to the Scots, and the Ryleys became embroiled in another plot to keep significant documents in England. On September 7, Ryley Jr. wrote to his father concerning his meetings the day before with London MP John Robinson; James Livingston, 1st Earl of Newburgh; and others. After promising to fulfill payments the Ryleys were owed, the group praised Ryley Jr.'s previous actions; he enthused that "they highly commended me for finding the Covenant, and sayed that the king should gratifie me for it, before they went away to Scotland, for they had heard that I found it, and sayed that it should be burnt by the hang man very shortly."[85]

Ryley Jr.'s companions also promised to reward him handsomely if he performed additional services. First, they asked that he inform them what records had already been returned to Scotland. They also asked that he provide them with a note, contravening his father's oath, maintaining that

"I know not of any stopt now from goeing to Scotland."[86] This last point was especially salient, because the group insisted that, like the Covenant and Breda concessions signed by Charles II, the four books of Parliamentary Acts of Scotland between 1639 and 1650 should not be returned. Instead, Ryley was to "have those 4 bookes carryed to Sir Edward Nicholas and to have the Kings warrant antedated for the delivery of them," which would justify the separation of these volumes from those that were to be returned.[87] This forged warrant was drawn up shortly thereafter, dictating that Ryley deliver to Nicholas "foure Bookes, or Volumes, concerning the Acts, Ordinances & other Transactions of severall Parliaments of our said Kingdom viz from the 15th day of May 1639 till the 8th of March 1650."[88] This was only the first element of a spurious paper trail. A warrant remanding the August order dated September 5 was also fabricated and a new warrant reissued in November, explaining that the prior one had been revoked "for some speciall reasons best knowne to us."[89] Robinson was appointed to oversee the return of the remaining papers, and on December 3 Charles ordered Ryley to deliver "one hundred and seaven Hogsheads, twelve chests, five trunks, and fower Barrells of Registers, Bookes, Warrants, Papers, and other writings, which are the Records of our Kingdome of Scotland," from which the four parliamentary registers were excluded.[90]

Whereas under Cromwell the Ryleys had sorted and supervised appropriated records, in this case the Ryleys fraudulently annexed compromising material. But ironically, the Ryleys' act of concealment and appropriation turned out be one of preservation. The absence of the four volumes went unnoticed in Scotland, for when one of the two ships each returning half the Scottish records sank in late 1661, they were assumed to have been among the lost cargo. Meanwhile, the books likely passed from Secretary Nicholas into Williamson's care in the State Paper Office, where they were forgotten. Not until 1826 were they found in the office, their removal to this location assumed to have been an "accident."[91] But though the survival of these papers was serendipitous—and offers a case study in the ironies and contingency of preservation and loss—it was also an unintended consequence of appropriating political records as acts of information warfare.

* * *

As the activity surrounding the Scottish records suggests, the reestablishment of monarchy initiated a moment of exceptional business for the Ryleys. Some tasks fell to the elder Ryley in his capacity as herald: for example, he was one of four entrusted with making the public announcement when the Convention Parliament declared Charles II king in May 1660.[92] In preparation for the coronation, further, Ryley was named clerk of a commission empaneled to judge the flood of claims of nobility and gentry who wished to attend.[93] In the Tower, meanwhile, both Ryleys were occupied by royalist landowners seeking evidence that would allow them to reclaim lands confiscated during the previous years; in 1661, nearly a third of the office's revenue came from fulfilling inquiries for the royalist earls of Arundel, Oxford, Ormond, Carbery, and Cork, and for James Norfolk, the Sergeant-at-Arms entrusted with finding and disinterring the corpses of regicides.[94] And in 1661, Ryley Jr. "did through my industry and care find out that Originall memorable Recognition of the Kings Royall Grandfathers Title to the Empire of greate Brittaine, which I presented to his Majestie my selfe."[95]

Throughout the 1660s, the Ryleys ministered to the documentary backbone of the realm, fulfilling requests from Council and Parliament such as when in 1667 the Lords requested precedents for the imminent trial of Edward Hyde, Earl of Clarendon.[96] One major element of this was an effort, parallel to Williamson's, to acquire the paperwork of the Interregnum governments. For example, in the immediate aftermath of the Restoration, Ryley requested a warrant to appropriate the books of the Committee on Sequestration, which, he claimed, if properly analyzed, would properly reveal a £20,000 debt still owed the king.[97] Similarly, in 1662 he sought a warrant to retrieve the books of John Marsh, clerk to the Committee of Arrears.[98] They also petitioned to retrieve the writings that had been confiscated from bishoprics, deans, and chapter houses, now stored "in a promiscuous and disorderly way, and made altogether useless" in the Excise Office.[99]

While maneuvering to secure these materials, the Ryleys faced a comparable effort to seize papers that had come under their control. In 1660 the new Lord Chief Justice in Eyre, Aubrey de Vere, Earl of Oxford, demanded that the papers of his predecessor Henry Rich, Earl of Holland, be delivered to him from the Tower, where they had been deposited when Rich was imprisoned there before his 1649 execution.[100] In response, Ryley wrote a blistering attack against de Vere which created a robust history of England's archives and conceptualized the records as essential lineaments binding Crown and polity.

Ryley's argument centered on the assertion that there was longstanding precedent and unassailable reason to make the records accessible. As he explained, "The Publick Records doe so much concern the King and his People as they are in a Petition of the Commons of England in parliament in 46 Edward III stiled the Peoples Evidence, and were so precious unto them as they had in the 14th year of that Kings Reign made it their humble suit in Parliament (and obtained an Act of Parliament thereupon) that they might not be denied any accesse unto them to search and take copies of any their concernments therein."[101] Ryley here invoked two medieval parliamentary acts that had previously gone unnoticed but that subsequent record keepers would repeatedly invoke to defend the dignity of their role.[102]

Though neither act mentioned the Tower, Ryley seized upon them to highlight the role of his office. Subsequent kings had recognized the records' value, Ryley maintained, and had funneled them to the Tower or Westminster archives to ensure their accessibility—otherwise "they would have been left to the unsafe and careless custody of executors & administrators, or private or unconcerned men, which would have bereaved posterity of all those many great lights and Assistances which the Public Scrinia or Archives have almost dayly upon important occasions and emergencies afforded."[103] Because de Vere's office, Ryley argued, was not equipped to make records accessible nor could guarantee their deposit in the Tower after his death, giving him the records would sever bonds between Crown and subject: "to have the Public Records of the Nation kept in any private or particular custody betwixt which and the publick there will be as great a difference as there is between safety and danger."[104] Ryley's sanguine administrative history depicted England's archives as preserving a comprehensive body of records that proved the foundation for political stability by ensuring subjects' access to them. He thus argued for his control over the eyre records on the basis that his office was the long-standing institutional auxiliary of the public good.

This novel argument was not without appeal at a moment in which the new monarchical regime sought to incorporate certain Commonwealth ideals, and in this instance it did prevail.[105] But it was also strategically misleading. The eyre records had come into Ryley's hands because of Rich's imprisonment, not on the basis of any institutional procedure. Moreover, records of such recent vintage had never been stored in the Tower but typically had been kept in the offices of those who oversaw them—in this case de Vere. Ryley's celebratory history assumed for the Tower the role of a functioning administrative archive, simultaneously distorting custom and invoking a tendentious logic of the public good to justify his own retention of the eyre records.

Ryley, moreover, was arguing for the importance of public access to the eyre papers at precisely the same time that he and his son were plotting to appropriate the Scottish parliamentary records, manifestly violating the principles he wielded against de Vere (who, to be clear, was also trying to acquire papers with uncertain ownership). As this suggests, the

Ryleys were less motivated by conviction than operating within an environment conducive to aggressive annexation of materials, which only occasionally demanded justification.

The violence and chaos of the Interregnum period created a free-for-all that encouraged the commandeering of politically valuable papers. This environment endured after the return of the monarchy, as those navigating the new regime sought to capitalize on the dislocations of the previous era, strengthen their own positions, and punish their enemies. Such appropriations were blunt exhibitions of power, but they reflected methods of information warfare acknowledging the power that came from possessing records and documents. And in this case, the logic of preserving records and making them publicly accessible was not its own end but a means to accrue personal and institutional authority.

Print, Polemic, Public

William Ryley's argument against Aubrey de Vere constituted one way of mobilizing the public for political ends—in his case, by conjuring the notion of the public good as rationale for maintaining custody over documents of uncertain ownership. But more frequently—as in John Thurloe's case—the public was conceptualized as a community of readers, and efforts to fashion opinion through the dissemination of texts proliferated in early modern Britain. These efforts capitalized on the possibilities of the printing press, for while manuscript circulation could direct texts both to specific audiences and down unexpected channels of readership, print enabled dissemination on a far larger scale.[106] And as William Prynne's publications both before and after his 1660 appointment to the keepership testify, the records of the realm could be readily enlisted in print projects of information warfare.

* * *

In 1661, the Ryleys—likely with Ryley Jr. in the lead—oversaw the publication of the *Placita Parliamentaria*. Ryley Jr. later claimed that the rationale for its publication was that it "did vindicate the Militia for the King, as his iust right belonging to hym, and his Royall predecessors."[107] As Ryley emphasized in his introduction, however, this political end was served by using print to replicate manuscript records throughout the realm. As he explained, "Of what great content and benefit the archives and memorials of former have been to succeeding times, constant experience hath so much shewed. . . . And that the communicating of such things to the World hath found an acceptance no lesse esteemed than so great a benefit doth well deserve, hath long since been, and is still seen from those many excellent Collections... which by the favour and industry of divers worthy persons versed in History and Antiquity, and learned in our Laws, are of late years brought to light."[108]

Ryley Jr.'s approach, while reminiscent of Matthew Parker's, also evoked the strategies of the recently appointed Keeper of the Tower Records, for in the late 1650s Prynne had launched a program of printing the Tower records. In these works, Prynne argued that the records' inaccessibility had enabled outrageous distortions of England's political past that underlay the mistaken revolutionary movements of recent years. Converting the archive into print, Prynne suggested, would expose and debunk such errors. He thus projected Tower records across the realm as a form of ideological combat, seeking to create an information public that would assent to his political views.

As one of early modern Britain's most prolific authors from the late 1620s until his 1669 death, Prynne had long used print as a political weapon. In the years leading up to the English Civil War, his works were predominantly anti-Laudian polemics. As punishment for his 1633 *Histriomastix*, Prynne's cheeks were branded with SL for "Seditious Libeller," but he continued to issue acerbic tirades in staggering numbers. At the outbreak of civil war he argued for the Commons' sovereignty, relying predominantly on Edward Coke's arguments, and Prynne's 1643 *The Soveraigne Powers of Parliament and Kingdomes* was one of the most significant assertions of Parliament's sovereignty and right to arms. But in subsequent years Prynne recoiled against radicalization and became convinced of the need to reform rather than overthrow the monarchy. In the mid-1640s he issued pamphlet screeds against Presbyterians, Independents, and Levellers in addition to invectives against Charles I. He became an MP for the first time in 1648, but his efforts to negotiate a settlement between Parliament and king led the Rump Parliament to seclude him, which he protested in broadsheets and pamphlets.[109] His imprisonment in 1650 slowed his rate of publication, but he resumed after his release three years later, authoring condemnations of Cromwell's regime and the extent of its religious toleration. With the Restoration, he transformed from inveterate critic to royalist propagandist. Print, in short, was Prynne's preferred mode of politics.

Printing the Tower records constituted an effort to project his own experience to a broader audience, for Prynne claimed that they had been instrumental to his abandonment of radicalism and commitment to monarchy. The impetus for this transformation, he maintained, was reading Robert Filmer's 1648 *The Freeholders Grand Inquest*, which rebutted *The Soveraigne Powers of Parliament* by arguing that the England shrouded by the mists of time had not possessed an assembly of the Commons. Though he did not embrace the ardency of Filmer's royalism, Prynne's acceptance of much of Filmer's criticism completed his conversion from Cokean promoter of the sovereignty of Parliament to a proponent of an English constitution in which the king worked in cooperation with two houses, with Lords preeminent.

Filmer insisted that the authority of the Commons could only be delimited by close readings of records, especially those from the Crown to the sheriff licensing the election of MPs.[110] As he explained, "The meanes to know what Trust, or Authority, the Country or Free-holders confer, or bestow by their election, is in this, as in other like cases, to have an eye to the words of the Commission, or Writ it selfe."[111] Accordingly, he began *The Freeholders Grand Inquest* with a Latin transcription and English translation of a generic parliamentary writ, which revealed that "we doe not find that the Commons are called to any part of the *Common Councell* of the Kingdom," or were given legislative authority. While it did specify that "the King would have *conference* and *treat* with the *Prelates, great men, and Peers*," there was "not a word of treating or conference with the Commons."[112] Indeed, he continued, "The duty of Knights, Citizens, and Burgesses, mentioned in the Writ, is only *ad faciendum, & consentiendum*, to *perform* and *consent* to such things as should be ordained by the *Common Councell* of the Kingdome."[113] According to the official form of its creation, the Commons' inherent powers were highly circumscribed. Moreover, against Prynne's attribution of authority to the Commons on account of its antiquity, Filmer maintained that "if Mr Pryn could have found so much antiquity, and proof for the Knights, Citizens, and Burgesses, being of the Common Councel: I make no doubt but we would have heard from him in Capitall characters: but alas! He meets not with so much as these Names in those elder ages." Instead, Filmer noted "the generall silence of antiquity which never makes mention of the Commons coming to Parliament" until Henry I's time, and argued that it was only formalized as an independent house under Henry III.[114] Against the view of British and Saxon kings governing in concert with assemblies including commoners, Filmer argued that the King's Council only included peers and high clerics until well after the conquest, and that the House of Commons was an institution belatedly introduced to English politics with no independent authority.

Filmer's argument rested on the stance that the absence of records of Commons' participation in Parliament before Henry I was not a problem to be explained away, as Coke and others had by exegetical interpretation or by placing great weight on slight evidence; rather, he saw the records themselves as deliberate legal instruments. Prynne accepted this belief in the autonomy and sufficiency of records more strongly than any other element of Filmer's work. In his 1648 *A Plea for the Lords*, which announced his conversion to Filmer's view, Prynne posited that ignorance of records had allowed reasonable complaints about Charles I to degrade into Leveller calls for abolishing the House of Lords. This ignorance he attributed to two causes. First, he argued that records necessary to place England's government on a secure foundation were extant, but disorder and carelessness had rendered them inaccessible. Second, he asserted that this obfuscation of the records compounded a general lack of record literacy, lamenting that there were "very few members in either House well read or versed in ancient Parliament Rolls, Pleas, or Journalls." As he explained, were these

> faithfully transcribed, and published in print to the eye of the world, as most of our Statutes are, by authority of both Houses of Parliament ... it would not only preserve them from imbezelling, and the hazards of fire and war, to which they are now subject, but likewise eternally silence, refute the Sectaries and Levellers ignorant false Allegations against your Honors' Parliamentary Iurisdiction and Iudicature, resolve and cleare all or most doubts that can arise concerning the power, iurisdiction, and priviledges of both, or either House ... chalke out the ancient regular way of proceedings in all Parliamentary affairs whatsoever ... cleare many doubts, and rectifie some grosse mistakes in printed Statutes, Law-Books, and our ordinary Historians ... and make all Lawyers, and the Members of both Houses farre more able then now they are, to manage and carry on all business in Parliament.[115]

Prynne thus proposed that the Lords finance the printing "of such a necessary publike worke."[116]

Much of Prynne's subsequent career was devoted to using print to redress the inaccessibility and illiteracy of the records and, in turn, advance his political agenda. He described his 1648 *Irenarches Redivivus*, for example, as a "concise refutation" of Coke through "a briefe collection of some concealed usefull Records, Petitions and Acts of Parliament (not hitherto Printed and almost quite buried in oblivion)."[117] Similarly, his 1649 *First Part of an Historicall Collection of Parliaments* was the result of spending "some vacant Hours in gathering into one or two small Bundles the scattered Histories and Records of our ancientest Parliaments and Great Councels (which are strangers and unknown to most)" to rectify "the grosse ignorance of the ancient constitution of our English Parliaments, and fanatick dream of a Supreme Parliamentary and absolute Legislative Authority in the House of Commons Alone."[118]

Prynne's conviction that the records supported a strong monarchy and disproved the Commons' sovereignty provoked antagonism toward the records themselves, and some Commonwealth radicals disavowed them altogether. Radical groups such as the Levellers and Diggers rejected the authority of such materials in favor of scripture, natural law, and other sources. For the independent preacher Hugh Peter, the Tower records were not aspects of a noble ancient constitution but evidence of the monstrousness of England's medieval despots. To Prynne's horror, Peter recommended, "it is verie advisable to burn all the old Records; yea, even those in the Tower, the Monuments of tyrannie."[119]

Such threats likely only motivated Prynne to embrace them more strongly. In 1657 he published an *Exact Abridgement of Parliamentary Records in the Tower of London* from a collection he attributed to Robert Cotton, explaining that "the records themselves being yet unprinted, unknown to most men, which this Epitome in good measure will now acquaint them with."[120] His preface outlined how he had corrected Cotton's text against other sources and criticized Coke for simply accepting what he found in commentaries, arguing that as a result Coke proceeded from corrupted foundations.

This volume also audited the state of the Tower records, suggesting that Prynne had begun to research them directly. He explained that there were "no Records in the Tower (except some few antient Charters, or Exemplifications of them) antienter than the first year of King John, all the rest from William the First his reign till then (except some few in the Exchequer, not relating to Parliaments) being utterly lost."[121] Many records from subsequent periods that should have been there, he noted, were "perished and quite lost, either though the Negligence of the Record-Keepers," during the Barons' Revolt against King John or the Wars of the Roses, or because of the tendency of Crown officers to borrow records and not return them.[122] By consulting other records and medieval chronicles, however, he maintained that much hidden past political activity could be recovered.

From this time onward, Prynne increasingly resorted to the Tower and published texts of the records—especially parliamentary writs—equipped with commentaries that framed them as supporting his politics. His 1659 *The First Part of a Brief Register, Kalendar and Survey of the Several Kinds, Forms of all Parliamentary Writs*, he claimed, addressed one of the "grand defects" of the records: the "great lack of diligent faithfull Collections and Publications of all the choicest Records, Proclamations, Writs, Letters, Charters, Patents, Commissions &c in the Tower."[123] He described his book as a model for an expansive program of printing unpublished or corrected editions of records, further describing it as "a rich cabinet, and Compendious Treasury of the chiefest, and most precious Parliamentary Jewels, Rarities, Records, ever yet presented to the world in print," and insisting that the printed version would replace the "very defective" manuscript aids in the Tower.[124] And again Prynne described the volume as refuting Coke, as he embedded commentaries adumbrating how the hundreds of writs in the register supported Prynne's vision of the supremacy of royal authority and the House of Lords over the Commons.

Prynne's appointment as Keeper enabled more sustained exploration of the Tower's holdings. His third volume on parliamentary writs—the 1662 *Brevia Parliamentaria Rediviva*—was also closely connected with his political program; as he explained, it aimed "to vindicate the indubitable inseperable Prerogative of the Kings of England to summon and dissolve Parliaments upon all emergent Occasions, to sit in them, and give their Royal assent to all Acts or Ordinances," among other royal powers.[125] This volume also was the product of years of communion with the space of the Tower. As he explained in his dedication to King Charles II, "No sooner received I your Royal Patent... for the Custody of your antient Records in your Tower of London... but I designed, endeavoured the rescue of the Greatest part of them from that desolation, corruption confusion, in which (through the Negligence or Sloathfullnesse of their Former Keepers) they had for many years by past layed buried together in one confused Chaos under corroding, putryifying, Cobwebs, Dust, Filth in the darkest corner of Caesars Chappel in the White Tower, as mere useless Reliques, not worthy to be calendred, or brought down thence into the Office amongst other Records of use."[126] His explorations revealed, to his surprise, that many materials he had assumed were lost had in fact survived.[127] In particular, he discovered that the writs Filmer had taught him to treasure had been treated with less care than rolls and other records. As he explained, "in raking up this Dung-heap I found many rare antient Precious Pearls and Golden Records," including "97 parcells of original writts" along with other records that allowed him not only to detail the scope of parliamentary duties but also to catalog members of previous Parliaments with unparalleled precision. And he again reiterated, "One principal meanes to perpetuate them to Posterity, and preserve them from the casualties of Fire, violence of Warre, and all-devouring lawes of Time, is to publish in Print those of greatest use."[128]

Prynne continued to publish the fruits of his inquiries, and similar practices and concerns underlay Prynne's 1662 *Antiquae Constitutiones*, his 1664 *The Fourth Part of a Brief Register, Kalender and Survey... of Parliamentary Writs*, and his 1668 *Aurum Reginae*. His activities reflected more than a deep faith that the records reflected the ancient constitution;

his new claim was that properly restored, they would wholly constitute it, and that printed editions of the records could simulate an ordered archive for the Restoration public.

* * *

Contemporaries recognized that Prynne's publications themselves mediated the archive.[129] When Denzil Holles brought his copy of Prynne's *Exact Abridgement* to the Tower to check its text—likely preparing for parliamentary debates concerning the jurisdiction of the Lords in the 1670s—he discovered that Prynne had not corrected his source manuscript, which ironically magnified the Commons' power beyond what the originals implied; Prynne had thus, in Holles's view, unwittingly overstated the Commons' power.[130] By contrast, William Petyt, Keeper of the Tower Records under William and Mary, devoted many years to finding and circulating records he claimed revealed the longevity of the Commons and correcting the perceived misapprehensions of Filmer, Prynne, and Petyt's great rival Robert Brady, Keeper under James VII and II. To this end, Petyt amassed an enormous body of records, which he used as a foundation for many printed and manuscript works. Similarly, he kept in the Tower a copy of Prynne's *Fourth Part of a Brief Register*, purchased from the clerk Ralph Jennings, which he assiduously covered with annotations identifying what he saw as Prynne's errors.[131] Across these texts and notes, he characterized Prynne's limited archival mastery as producing a diminished view of the power of the lower house, which Petyt saw as pushing his fellow subjects to dangerous obeisance.[132] Prynne's collections, in short, were recognized as their own interpolations.

Prynne's publications inflected the historical record in another way as well. While he repeatedly decried the condition of the Tower records, the Ryleys did not experience the archive as disordered; their decades-long success at surfacing documents and making collections of notes and their disinclination to revamp the Tower spaces suggest the opposite.[133] Prynne's claims instead might reflect his frosty relationship with the duo. They did at times execute projects for him; for example, Ryley Jr. collected extracts for Prynne's *Exact Chronological Vindication*, as discussed earlier in this chapter, but this work may not have been collegial, for the volume directly opposed the view of the church set forth by Ryley's collection for William Laud.[134] And the Ryleys portrayed Prynne as an interloper; warrants for searches were addressed to Ryley, and they complained that Prynne rarely appeared in the Tower.[135] Prynne's depiction of archival chaos may have been hyperbolic, spiteful, self-aggrandizing, or a consequence of an inability to collaborate with the Tower's long-serving clerks. But it has long been accepted at face value, erasing the steadfast work of the Ryleys and many others to make the Tower a usable archive.

* * *

Prynne's publications reflected a series of practices anchored in the Tower archive. After reading Filmer, he came to see the archive as authoritative, and he anticipated that projecting the records throughout the realm would delegitimize the seditious fantasies of his enemies. Initially he collected extracts from various sources, but especially after his appointment as Keeper, he investigated the Tower's neglected corners for materials to mobilize in his campaign to create and convince a public. While the revelation of obscured or forgotten records had spurred previous Keepers to reform the office in pursuit of personal advancement, it sparked in Prynne a program of print publication. The resultant texts constituted a virtual archive, replicating the physical Tower Record Office so that readers could traverse it with Prynne as guide.

Though framed as a tour through the archives, however, Prynne's works constituted a species of polemic that also controlled the information with which his readers constructed their visions of the past. He saw the records as the preeminent resource with which to construct the proper shape of Britain's constitution, but capitalizing fully on their power required turning to the technology of inscription, which could provide him an audience of the scale he sought. Print was accordingly the method by which he brought the authoritative archive to the public, and it was thus the weapon with which Prynne fought for the minds and souls of Britain.

Conclusion

As inscription and archivization permeated the political and intellectual life of early modern Britain, information became both a terrain and a means of combat. The stories of William Prynne, John Thurloe, and William Ryley expose some of the practices devised to seize control of information in the tempestuous and uncertain environment unleashed by the breakdown of England's political system in the 1640s that persisted throughout the Interregnum. Their tactics by no means encompass the full spectrum of methods of information warfare; the mediascape of their time also generated propaganda, forgery, cryptography, clandestine printing, and more. In all these methods, operatives sought to assert power by protecting their own materials, penetrating the communication and storage networks of their enemies, and controlling the messages and patterns of their circulation. Such information warfare predominantly entailed controlling paperwork as the material embodiment of information.

Recognizing the pervasiveness of practices of information warfare, however, constitutes something of a caution to historians, as it exposes their dependence on resources whose survival or destruction—and not just their production—reflect intention and motivation as well as fortune. While Edward Nicholas's bonfire of Charles I's papers, Prynne's contortion of William Laud's diary, Ryley's alleged subterfuges, Thurloe's surveillance regime, William Ryley Jr.'s appropriation of Scottish materials, and Prynne's virtual archive all reflect distinct strategies of information warfare, each not only intervened in the contemporary documentary landscape but also reverberated down to later generations, shaping what could be known and believed about the past as well as determining the accessibility of materials. Sometimes their practices were designed to make texts—or certain interpretations of them—conspicuous; other times they were intended to mystify.

Acknowledging that the visibility and invisibility of past sources is both structured and contingent draws attention to the need for those investigating the past to understand how their evidence has come down to them. This is particularly true of both public records (meaning official government records) and public discourse, for as the examples provided in this chapter indicate, the determination of what whether specific texts and events qualify as meriting public interest cannot be divorced from the personal and political factors underlying such decisions.

At its core, finally, the emergence and proliferation of information warfare signals how inscriptions were increasingly central to—and indeed constitutive of—politics in the emerging media society of early modern Britain. Under such circumstances, information became a battleground, and the horrific violence wrought on people's bodies was paralleled by another type, one of deception, distortion, misinformation, and intimidation. Such tactics of conflict articulated and perpetuated the intense imbrication of information and inscription in politics, prosecuted by other means.

6

Centralization and Orchestration

By the late seventeenth century, inscription had infiltrated the everyday habits of Britain's political sphere so deeply that it transcended its status as a tool and became a form of life.[1] Under King Charles II, administrators, diplomats, and clerks maintained communication networks and converted the influx of information into operational knowledge with unprecedented scale and coordination, crystallizing the state as an organ of political knowledge transformed from its predecessors. And as paperwork came to dominate the epistemic infrastructure of political action and knowledge, those within this world developed conventions and routines geared toward perpetuating its production and circulation, for this constituted the essence of governance.

Though inscription practices were ubiquitous throughout Restoration governance, the individual most responsible for enlarging and integrating them was Secretary of State Joseph Williamson.[2] Over the 1660s, Williamson emerged as the "information master" of Charles II's regime.[3] His ascent rested on his skill in distilling the pandemonium of human affairs into orderly collections of texts, as he and his clerks generated and collected reams of paperwork, devised textual instruments, and constructed material infrastructure to manage the resulting abundance. Letters, archives, and notebooks formed the substance of his political knowledge, as he apprehended newly received texts by coordinating them with other materials in his possession. He thus presided over a globalizing paperwork system of knowledge anchored in a center that aspired to generate political expertise and prepare the state for action by recontextualizing received reports amid its accumulated information resources.

Williamson's practices intensified the reliance on inscription so prevalent throughout early modern Europe. His methods resembled those of the French Minister of State Jean-Baptiste Colbert, who relied on a similar repertoire seeking to burnish the French crown's absolutist power, and thus suggests an important commonalty between Charles II's government and that of Louis XIV.[4] Moreover, the epistemic dimensions of this practice were not unique to politics, and the techniques Williamson and his clerks used were similar to those of contemporaneous scholars—most notably, antiquarians and natural philosophers.[5] Indeed, between 1677 and 1680, Williamson was the president of the Royal Society, whose members worked to replicate the world of nature by filling their notebooks with endless data drawn from observation. While natural philosophers' efforts aimed to reveal laws in the natural world, Williamson's were oriented toward political demands. But they shared a structure of practice manifested in analogous systems of information management that transformed the conditions of knowledge and politics. For the Royal Society it anchored an empirical, experimental, and operational philosophy; in Williamson's case—as in Colbert's—it was the foundation of an information state.

This chapter anatomizes Williamson's epistemic infrastructure.[6] Many of its elements were shared by individuals discussed previously in this book, and he thus represents an exemplar of the inscription-minded early modern statesman. But his information network also possessed unmatched size, coordination, and complexity, which allowed him to capitalize differently paper's availability, durability, mobility, and recombinability. Williamson was little concerned with the constitution-forming elements of his archive that obsessed his predecessors. Instead, he directed its possibilities toward forging a centralized, coordinated apparatus that pursued information asymmetries in the hopes of generating the privileged knowledge and communicative authority that facilitated expertise in governance. Observing Williamson's practice at work thus reveals the dynamics of an information state that inexorably sought to capture, know, and reshape a protean world.

* * *

Williamson's ascent to the secretaryship office built on the practices that had brought him into the government. He had been educated in his native Cumberland, but in his early teens accompanied his local MP to London as a clerk and, using this connection, gained admission to the Westminster School, which he attended for two years before moving to Queen's College, Oxford, in 1650. Likely during this period, he developed an appreciation for working with crumbling and obscure texts, honed by collaborating with some of England's foremost antiquarians; frustrated by the faltering negotiations in Cologne in 1673, Williamson wrote to his friend—and William Dugdale's son-in law—the herald Elias

Ashmole, ruing that among the "satisfactions" he missed in England, the "principall one would be to be with you & your worthy Father in law in our Rolls & Records, which I hope once found I have more time to employ than hitherto it has been my fortune to be master of."[7] His earlier experience working with the dusty mottled records would eventually enhance Williamson's suitability for his later roles.[8]

The lament to Ashmole also may have reflected a forlorn look back to a moment when his trajectory seemed more oriented toward scholarship than statecraft. After completing his degree at Queen's in 1654, he tutored royalist children on the Continent, where he also frequented Parisian scholarly salons and translated Francis Bacon's *New Atlantis* into Dutch. When he returned to England in 1658, he took up a fellowship at Queen's. Although he was an unsullied royalist, his early career exhibited little orientation toward political office.

Nonetheless, his activities during this period further prepared him for the positions Williamson would eventually hold. His time on the Continent refined his skill with languages, and it brought him into contact with many of the learned men and scholarly diplomats who would later feature in his correspondence networks.[9] And under the new regime, Williamson ascended through a series of positions that capitalized on his talent for information management. He was appointed Undersecretary of State to Edward Nicholas in 1660 and then Keeper of the State Papers in 1661. Though his position became tenuous with Nicholas's fall and the ascendancy of Henry Bennet, Earl of Arlington, to Secretary of State, Williamson quickly proved himself indispensable to Arlington, and the two developed a formidable partnership. From these earlier years he played a major role in coordinating the secretary's correspondence. He also assumed the daunting project of finding the records scattered during the Interregnum. Gradually, he accrued more responsibilities such as overseeing the state newspaper, serving as Postmaster General, and participating in the Council of Trade overseeing England's nascent empire. Success led to higher offices. In 1672 Williamson was appointed Clerk of the Privy Council, and in 1673 he was chosen as plenipotentiary to the Congress of Cologne, where he sought to rescue an advantageous peace to conclude the Third Anglo-Dutch War. When Arlington fell the following year, Williamson was elevated to Secretary of State of the Northern Department and placed on the Privy Council. Over the next five years Williamson wielded extensive power, accrued a large fortune, married Katherine Stewart, Baroness Clifton, and orchestrated England's maneuverings at the Congress of Nijmegen in 1677–78.

Williamson's fall was swift, however, and his information apparatus was directly implicated. In late 1678, he provoked public and parliamentary outrage by remaining skeptical of the Popish Plot—a rumored conspiracy that Catholics intended to assassinate Charles II and put his Catholic brother, the future King James VII and II, on the throne—likely because his massive network of information production provided no evidence to substantiate the panic. Shortly after, it was revealed that he had signed forms exempting Irish Catholics from the Test Act, which he claimed was an accidental action committed while overwhelmed by paperwork, but which his enemies interpreted as signaling complicity in the plot. Parliament's outrage led to his brief imprisonment in the Tower of London in early 1679, and though Charles II quickly freed him, the king removed him from service. Williamson retired to Kent, where he remained through the 1680s, but after 1690 he enjoyed a renaissance, serving as MP in both England and Ireland. In the late 1690s he was appointed plenipotentiary to the deliberations at Rijswick, staying afterward as ambassador to The Hague, before returning to England for his last years before his 1701 death.

The apex of Williamson's career, however, began at the Restoration and endured until his fall, and during this period he most thoroughly refined and executed his methods of political knowledge formation. These methods were paper intensive, generating unprecedented volumes of materials and unsurpassed capacity for managing flows of information. The scale and integration of his system, moreover, was its own end, for rather than seeking revelatory or consensus-producing texts, he prized its volume and dynamism as inherently advantageous, and he shaped its structure and labor accordingly. This chapter maps that process over his career, excavating the practices—and privileged epistemic position they created—that Williamson saw as the foundation of governance.

Scribbling

Joseph Williamson's was a life of inscription. He was an inveterate scribbler who kept pen and paper perpetually on hand, ready to scrawl passages from readings, snippets of conversation, or fleeting ideas. Though his rushed jottings were often barely decipherable, such notes constituted the foundation of a complex system of political knowledge and action.[10]

Williamson fanatically committed his own experience to writing. His official duties were saturated by paperwork, and he initialed and annotated the manuscript volumes he collected, scrawled comments on documents that passed across his desk in transit to other offices, and was likely the most prolific correspondent in Europe in the period between his first employment under the Crown and his fall. He kept daybooks and loose sheets close by to record notes during his daily tasks; for example, his surviving notes on Council of Trade meetings document a flurry of information drawn from letters, oral reports, documents, and other streams, as discussion spun from Tangier to Surinam to Barbados to Newfoundland.[11]

Williamson also used such volumes to record conversations, desiderata lists, and other casual communications. As this suggests, Williamson directed to his oral communications and lived experience the same techniques of culling, summarizing, and consultation that contemporaries typically directed at books. Most of his notes, however, originated in texts, and Williamson assiduously recorded his own reading, hurriedly transcribing into daybooks noteworthy pieces of information, rhetorical flourishes, names and titles, aphorisms, and all manner of extract. For example, one daybook interspersed notes drawn from "Records that I have" (including transcriptions of many Tower records) alongside extracts from Henry Foulis's *History of Romish Treasons and Usurpations* and notes concerning the pedigrees of ambassadors and nobles, as well as notes on the military, the papacy, Spain, Jewish learning, Poland, ecclesiastical matters, the cabalistic art of gematria, sovereignty, money, prerogative, the form of treaties, Sir Gawain and the Canterbury Tales, spas, guns, water, hemp, canvas, the proper styles for addressing the king, Lancashire, the length of a furlong, the duties of a steward, mills, ragmen, and Parliament.[12] These collections reflected the flurry of topics pelting Williamson's attention as he wrestled with the Restoration political landscape.

Williamson devised ways to quickly peruse the wild thickets of seemingly disconnected notes this system deposited in his daybooks. He typically inscribed the extract in the middle of the page, with a subject heading in the left margin and a reference to the source text in the right. The labeling method sought to instill order within the whiplash of his daily reading.

The daybooks were only the first stage in the compilation of notebook miscellanies resembling those produced by both ordinary and elite readers throughout early modern Europe. The headings assigned to extracts not only described their contents but also directed the flow of passages into second-order notebooks organized by theme rather than by sequence of reading. Williamson created scores of notebooks in this fashion, often crossing out passages from his daybooks after transcribing them into other volumes, occasionally razoring out slivers out to paste directly into the notebooks.[13]

His practices of transcription often enabled him to navigate back to the sources; for example, he observed of one volume that "The authorityes & Quotacions inserted in this Collection are taken out of the

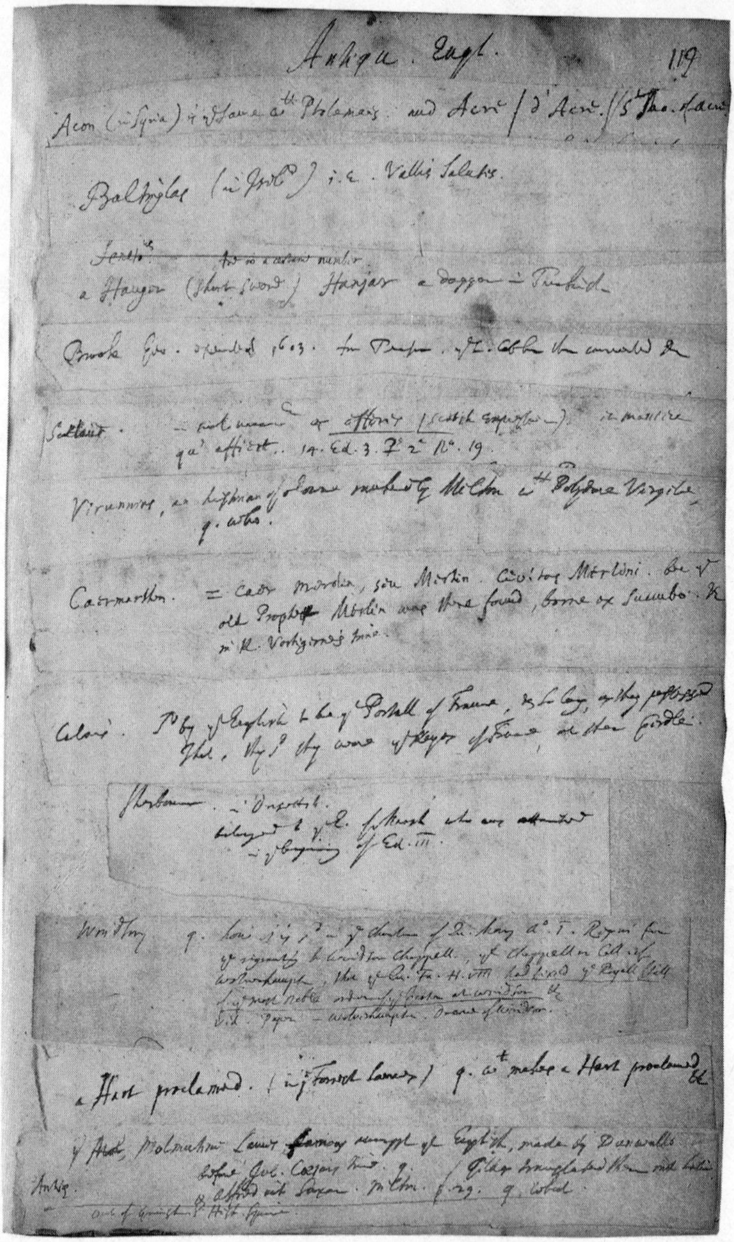

FIGURE 14. Joseph Williamson Notebook. Although in most cases Williamson transcribed extracts from his daybooks into collected volumes, here he has cut slips concerning English antiquities from them and pasted them into this notebook. The National Archives, Kew, SP 9/14, f. 119r. Contains public sector information licensed under the Open Government Licence v3.0.

underwritten Authors in their several subiects, & bi them the pages cited are to observe."[14] The primary function of such volumes, however, was not to refer to the original but to bring related extracts together. Williamson operated with a relatively stable set of categories, such as trade, rhetoric, and war. But these seem more improvisational than systematic; some may have been suggested by contemporary commonplace books, while others stemmed from his own experience. For example, the aforementioned notebook had a category for "Secretary's Office," which contained items such as the proper modes of addressing nobles and lists of European secretaries drawn from State Paper Office materials.[15] This category also served as rubric for subcategories, and a few notes under "Secretary's Office" were labeled as concerning "records." These extracts described various types of records but also praised predecessors who had recognized their value; for example, he commended the "great & exemplary diligence used by Cardinal Ximenez in Spaine 1518 to recover out of private hands public papers."[16] The notebooks thus created collections of related extracts whose later uses often were not immediately clear. On the other hand, some notes stimulated action, which often amounted to pursuing other texts, such as when he wrote, "quare what is become of the Repositorie or Entry Books of the Court of Requests. For such were kept, & I have seen them."[17]

Williamson's notebooks were his most essential tools for calming the maelstrom of paper blowing through the Restoration political sphere, and they showcase the discrete practices constitutive of Williamson's form of life: recording or collecting textual testimony of experience, parsing and cleaving it, reordering it according to loose designations, and using the processed texts to structure actions which in turn stimulated more writing. He and his clerks processed an immense quantity of material through this method, for each circuit of collecting, recording, reconfiguring, and circulating texts could reinstigate the cycle anew.

Accumulation: Collection and Excavation

In addition to recording his experience, Joseph Williamson's practice of knowing the world required the collection of texts. This was a collaborative effort, and he directed his clerks and correspondents to amass virtually all manner of politically oriented writing, regardless of immediate utility. The first stage of Williamson's political career was particularly marked by predilection for such acquisition.

Williamson succeeded Thomas Raymond as Keeper of the State Paper Office in November 1661. Raymond was the nephew of Sir William Boswell, who had become Keeper jointly with Ambrose Randolph upon the death of Thomas Wilson, Randolph's father-in-law, in 1629.[18] When Boswell died in 1650, the office reverted to Randolph and Raymond, a fervent royalist who had spent much of the previous twenty years on the Continent.[19] Throughout the 1650s, Raymond intermittently performed the office's duties.[20] The uncertainty that came with Cromwell's death mandated new attention to the office, and in 1659 Raymond composed a memorandum outlining its role. Its value, he insisted, remained constant despite England's political vicissitudes: "The Policie & Management of Affairs with forreyne Princes & State being (for the most part) the same that it hath beene formerlie, notwithstanding the change of Governement within our selves, this Office wilbe of greate & constante use as wherein is contayned president for, or light into, almost any forraigne affaire that occurred." Raymond also cataloged the requirements of the Keeper, which included capacity to maintain secrecy, skill in languages, industry in finding materials, and "exact, & minute methodizing, & daylie peruseing the severall Papers."[21]

In the first months of the Restoration, Raymond fulfilled these responsibilities.[22] But the emphasis of the keepership soon shifted to the recovery of the dispersed state papers of Interregnum governments. In October 1660 Nicholas dispatched a warrant ordering Oliver Cromwell's Secretary of State John Thurloe and Lord President of the Council of State John Bradshaw to return "all those paper bookes, & records of state" in their possession to Raymond.[23] As Thurloe's claim to have burned his papers suggests, voluntary bequests were resisted, and five months later the Council issued Raymond a warrant to recover their materials.[24] But Raymond seems not to have relished this role, and he complied as Williamson pushed for the office, yielding in November 1661.[25]

Williamson was an unusual choice as he was already an Undersecretary of State for whom the keepership might have appeared of small consequence. But Williamson perceived that integrating the two offices—and wielding the power Raymond was reluctant to exercise—would enhance the information infrastructure at his disposal. Moreover, Williamson's antiquarian skills suited him for the project of reassembling materials dispersed through the Interregnum. Within days of his appointment to the keepership, Nicholas issued him warrants to recover materials from places ranging from the Haberdasher's Company—whose building had hosted the Committee for Advance of Money—to the widow of the Clerk of the Council William Jessop. When Nicholas fell, Arlington quickly reissued similar warrants.[26]

Williamson threw himself into this enterprise, taking extensive notes on interviews, reports, and rumors to map how Interregnum papers had fanned out across the realm. Every movement of such materials was charted; for example, one set of notes observed that a Mr. Cotton, servant to Serjeant-of-Arms James Norfolk, reported that some of Bradshaw's papers were still being held by Sir William Gerard, while a "Scotch Maior and a widow woman in Kingstreet" reported that Gerard also held some of the regicide Edmund Ludlow's papers.[27] Even when books had been secured, Williamson cataloged their whereabouts, noting, for example, that Keeper of Council Records John Wooley had acquired the two Council Books that had been produced under the various experiments in government during the nearly two-year period from Oliver Cromwell's death to the Restoration.[28] Williamson enlisted his own clerks and others' to this end; for example, he had William Ryley prepare a catalog of "The Committees and Commissions that acted in the late tymes of Rebellion from Anno 1643 to 1649," which traced the movements of the records produced by committees in Camden House, Worcester House, Goldsmiths Hall, Haberdashers Hall, and Drury House.[29] He continued these enterprises into the mid-1660s.[30]

Williamson, in short, aggressively fulfilled the Keeper's responsibility of recovering the records of the Interregnum governments. Moreover, he assumed a similar strategy to understand his own positions. He drew up extensive notes concerning the history of the State Paper Office, including lists of Keepers, their oaths, and the costs they incurred.[31] He also composed memoranda establishing precedents for its requisitions, citing the seizures of the papers of Edward Coke; Dudley Carleton, Viscount Dorchester; and Walter Ralegh.[32] These notes established protocols for the office, but they also revealed specific texts that Williamson wished to recover. For example, he took notes on "papers imbezilled," and in several memoranda he noted that Bradshaw had taken away more State Paper Office materials than anyone else during the Interregnum.[33] In the mid-1660s, similarly, Williamson constructed a desiderata list of "Transactions of state worth enquiring after for storing the Paper Office," which included Thurloe's papers and the correspondence Nicholas had taken when forced from office. Shortly after, he recorded another desiderata list registering his hope to acquire the "Usurpers Papers" as well as "The original treaties between Usurpers & Holland for excluding the Prince of Orange" and several treaties which, according to Thurloe, were at that point held by Edward Hyde, Earl of Clarendon.

Williamson also took copious notes tracing the collections of predecessors in his office and other statesmen from prior to the 1640s. For example, he recorded that the papers of the Elizabethan statesman Robert Dudley, Earl of Leicester, had been procured by Leicester's secretary Richard Browne, and they had conveyed down this family line until reaching his great-granddaughter Mary Browne, who had married John

Evelyn. Williamson reported visiting them in Deptford, where he had inspected the materials, "though a great part of them had perished by time & the distruction of the Warres, & being left in England by Sir Richard Browne during the Rebellion, many had been abused to the meanest uses."[34] Similarly, he consulted Sir Symonds D'Ewes's collections, and in 1676 he visited Colonel Charles Caesar and made a complete copy of the catalog compiling tables of contents that Sir Julius had made four decades prior.[35]

Over the 1660s, Williamson applied these practices to all corners of Charles II's government, and, in particular, instruments of diplomacy. His desiderata lists increasingly named items such as recent treaties, correspondence from diplomats from Bombay to Ireland, and commissions and instructions for Caribbean Governors.[36] He used secretarial funds to obtain such materials; for example, in 1668 or 1669 he directed Peter du Moulin's purchase in Paris of nearly one hundred diplomatic manuscripts.[37] In early 1669 Williamson was also given wide-ranging authority to transcribe the treaties, leagues, and commissions in the Exchequer at no cost.[38] Moreover, from this time, original treaties were deposited in Williamson's archive rather than to the Exchequer, and in the 1670s he created space for them in the State Paper Office.[39]

Williamson was keen to gain knowledge of the regime's ordinary operations as well, especially in the 1670s as his power increased. He paid particular attention to the entry books—registers that briefly summarized correspondence and formal acts—maintained by various offices; for example, in the mid-1670s he visited the Signet Office to abridge its twenty-seven entry books.[40] He also conducted extensive correspondence with offices such as the Chancery to arrange transcription of documents.[41] In contrast to those who relied on "Books of Office" to learn the government, Williamson sought to know it through each office's communications.

Arlington's fall not only opened an opportunity for promotion to Secretary of State but also swelled Williamson's collections. Williamson had overseen Arlington's correspondence for long stretches, and as Keeper of the State Paper Office, he had occasionally received deposits of Arlington's materials.[42] But within days of the resignation, Williamson retrieved the remaining papers that the earl had accumulated over his twelve-year tenure, and State Paper Office clerk Henry Ball quickly completed a "Catalogue of Letters and other Papers received out of the Earle of Arlington's Office" enumerating 582 bundles, including 27 entry books.[43] These resources would have helped his secretarial duties in subsequent years as well as fulfilling the charter of the State Paper Office. Similarly, at William Ryley Jr.'s death, Williamson purchased the bulk of his papers, including many of the Tower's reference tools, from his widow, Elizabeth.[44]

Williamson was endlessly concerned with retrieving papers produced by previous governments, and he was likely the driving force behind an ad hoc "Committee about Records" convened in late 1676, which examined the Tower of London, the Exchequer, the Rolls Chapel, Court of Requests, and Star Chamber—though not the State Paper Office. To understand the Tower, he generated a questionnaire likely intended to be adapted for other collections. It began by querying the offices, names, duties, and salaries of the staff, then requested information concerning the "sorts, titles, yeares, contents" of the holdings, as well as whether the rooms and furniture were appropriate to maintain them and in "what condition of repair or decay" the papers lay. Finally, the committee asked for "what methode used in searches, copyeing, of private persons allowed to take entire copyes of the Rolls."[45]

Williamson, in short, used the keepership to integrate a political practice predicated on rabidly accumulating materials produced by previous governments. He navigated the terrain of inscription in an aggressively extractive manner, adapting preexisting scholarly and administrative methods to bring new texts, records, and collections into his orbit. He hoped, through acts of excavation, reconstruction, and coordination, to restore integrity to a compromised documentary terrain. And while this effort was initially focused on resolving Interregnum chaos, his efforts to acquire knowledge of Charles II's regime led him to direct these techniques to his present as well.

Accumulation: Correspondence

Joseph Williamson's ability to trace Interregnum records depended on a network of informers who also transmitted intelligence concerning rumored plots, troop movements, public gossip, migrations of papers, and more. Their correspondence sought to inform Williamson of events in all corners of the world. They thus constituted essential input for his global epistemic system, and accordingly he devised practices to enhance the usability of their missives.

Williamson began to build his correspondence network upon his appointment as Undersecretary of State. While its growth temporarily halted with Nicholas's fall, Arlington quickly recognized Williamson's value and restored him, deputing Williamson to conduct most of the secretariat's correspondence. The State Paper Office facilitated this element of Williamson's work as well, for he used its clerks to process incoming letters and compose responses.

Some of Williamson's correspondents operated under the condition of paid secrecy. Soon after his appointment as Undersecretary of State, Williamson began to distribute regular disbursements to domestic and foreign informants such as the former Fifth Monarchist William Pestell, the spy Edward Potter, and Theodore van Ruyven, secretary to the Prince of Orange. He also paid some individuals for occasional services such as acquiring newssheets.[46] The size of the disbursements varied; van Ruyven several times received £100, and Potter eventually earned £10 per information, while others received only a pound or two. In his first two years as secretary, Williamson paid nearly £1,500 for their collected intelligence. Over the next two decades, he continued to devise means of covertly extracting information; most notably, upon his appointment as Postmaster General in 1667, he deputed postmasters to open letters at will and transmit crucial findings.[47]

These clandestine communications, however, were only a small part of Williamson's colossal correspondence network, as he was poised at the epicenter of a buzzing machine delivering a constant flow of paper and information into his purview.[48] His network of diplomats, consuls, aspiring administrators, spies, ship captains, and informants supplied news and rumor reporting on everything from European diplomacy to the movements of goods in the Caribbean to Mediterranean battles to reputed miracles in Welsh villages. The majority of letters came from around 215 male correspondents with whom he maintained regular communication for extended stretches. Williamson's most frequent correspondents were such figures as the diplomats Richard Bulstrode and William Temple, the English agent in Paris William Perwich, the spy Ignatius White, and the Cologne news broker Hendrik van Bilderbeeck.[49] As this assortment suggests, European politics played a prominent role in his correspondence. But Williamson also received prolific numbers of dispatches from well-placed individuals such as the Postmaster at Deal Castle in Dover Richard Watts, colonial governors including Thomas Modyford, and diverse others such as the resident agent in Constantinople John Finch and the ship's surgeon Richard Browne, as well as occasional missives from Continental scholars such as Jean Mabillon.[50]

Though the correspondence predominantly concerned political matters and was almost exclusively from men, it was not homogeneous. It came from wide array of geographical locales, even before Williamson became involved in the Board of Trade in the 1670s. Equally notably, it came from men of a range of social positions, ranging from highborn aristocrats to ordinary men in urban locations or whose employment—as postmasters or lighthouse keepers, for example—made them hubs for news. These correspondents were sometimes compensated, while other times they supplied intelligence hoping to earn Williamson's favor. And his portfolios were distinct for particular places. While he maintained brisk correspondence with many locals permanently resident in Continental Europe, the missives he received directly from North America, the Caribbean, and the Mediterranean typically came from a narrower range of sources; for example, his letters from Jamaica came only from appointed officials or from Browne, who had started as a local informant at the Suffolk port of Aldeburgh before relocating to Jamaica.

The epistolary corpus this network produced was enormous. Alexandre Tessier's recent survey estimated its intake alone at around at least 18,000 and probably closer to 23,000 letters for his two decades of political activity. This number dwarfs those of contemporaries famed for their correspondence such as Henry Oldenburg, Gottfried Wilhelm Leibnitz, and Nicolas-Claude Fabri de Peiresc, and it likely makes Williamson's correspondence the largest in Europe among that generation of graphomanic diplomats and letter writers.[51] This estimate, furthermore, constitutes an understatement—perhaps a drastic one—as it omits most of Williamson's colonial correspondence and some of his regular domestic exchanges, such as those from Watts, who sent Williamson nearly a thousand letters between 1664 and 1678.

The contours of the communications operation with which Williamson managed this immense flow emerges most lucidly from memoranda produced before his departure for Cologne in 1673. At this time, he wrote to reassure Arlington that all aspects of their work would continue uninterrupted in his absence. While Williamson had previously overseen the clerks John Richards and William Bridgman's handling of Arlington's personal correspondence, they would now report directly to Arlington. With Williamson unavailable to conduct Arlington's official correspondence, it would be turned over to the clerk John Swaddell, who was "well versed in all your Lordship's forms of ordinary domesticke dispatches, in the books of entries and their indexes, in the papers that lye either bound up or bundled relateing to what has passed the office these many years."[52] Arlington's communications would thus remain on solid footing.

Williamson also promised the earl that his own operation would also continue unperturbed, as the clerk Robert Yard was poised to assume Williamson's duties. Most important, this meant Yard would "attend constantly at that post for the extracting, copying, translating etc all matters of correspondence just in the same manner I and my people now doe, and when prepared to present them to your Lordship through your secretaryes hands or immediately to your owne as it falls to be readiest and quickest."[53] Williamson's role, this emphasized to the earl, entailed determining the significance of incoming materials, deciding what form of them should be circulated, and specifying which audiences—with Arlington as priority—should receive the new assemblages.

Yard also received a memorandum directly from Williamson reinforcing that his own primary duty was sustaining the correspondence; as Williamson implored: "Above all bee hourly at the deske, working at the correspondence businesse, acknowledging, encourageing and provokeing our correspondants every where to be diligent." In the new configuration, Yard was responsible not only for caretaking the perpetual motion of the correspondence machine but also for filtering its flow of information to Williamson abroad; as he instructed, "Let me be sure to have every post all extracts: Inland, Foreigne, Copyes of papers &c." By this arrangement Williamson continued to receive summaries of all materials directed to his home office just as he had in England. Yard would also be responsible for the State Paper Office, and Williamson instructed him "to understand perfectly the Paper Office by running over all the classes, to see you noticed the contents & principal matters of the Papers. First to informe yourself, next to be able to give a reasonable account to my Lord Arlington in any occasion what papers & lastly, as you have time, to take me short notes of things, to lye by for my use."[54]

These instructions illuminate how Williamson merged his secretaryship and the State Paper Office to create a scribal workshop sustaining an immense communications operation, with his role being its maintenance and coordination. And they expose how the filtration and movement of texts constituted its cardinal operation, for both the receipt of letters and explorations of the archive provoked a cycle of reinscription and circulation to Williamson, Arlington, and others. Williamson thus presided over an information juggernaut in which the labor of clerks synthesized incoming materials to ensure a coordinated, consistent system of inflow and outflow.

* * *

Williamson's immense correspondence was designed to mitigate the immutable problem of distance by translating experience into text. But epistolary communications were not frictionless. The materials he elicited were periodic accounts of what was often professedly gossip, presented by individuals frequently self-interested to the point of unreliability, generated through complex chains of mediation, on sheets of paper susceptible to water damage or loss, whose tempo of transmission varied widely. Each letter reflected ephemeral moments that might have changed while in transit, if their descriptions had ever obtained in first place. Assessing each was thus an intricate endeavor; even more complex was coordinating the reports so that collectively they might produce meaningful knowledge.

These problems were widely recognized, and to ameliorate them, correspondents adhered to specific conventions shared with other complex early modern communications networks.[55] First, much space was devoted to describing conditions of communication—when previous letters had been sent and received, which newssheets had been received and which not, if weather, shipwreck, or other factors had caused delays. Virtually every letter from regular correspondents began with a recitation of the letters they had recently exchanged with Williamson. This practice confirmed whether Williamson's were successfully arriving while also perhaps facilitating his ability to situate the reports in context. Most diligently elaborated whence the news they communicated had originated, using formulas such as "From Warsaw wee hear."[56] The knots of mediation they described were often complex; for example, Watts sent a letter to Williamson in 1667 reporting that he had received "a letter from a merchant in Middleburrow directed to a merchant in Dover assuring him it was there strongly reported the Spanyards had entred on Jamaica & possess themselves of it & massacred men women & children of the English."[57] Finally, correspondents often communicated according to a regular schedule, as frequently as three times a week.

Second, many of Williamson's correspondents—and especially those abroad—included enclosures, transcriptions or abstracts of other documents. These were occasionally material such as printed pamphlets but were most commonly gazettes, the printed and manuscript newssheets that churned throughout Europe. Perwich, for example, frequently sent these or laced his letters with passages transcribed from them.[58] He also sent official documents containing lists of army officers and troop sizes; similarly, Robert Southwell sent transcriptions of foreign treaties.[59] Such formal government documents were the other most common class of enclosure. Colonial correspondents, for example, typically adhered to regulations requiring them to send the journals of assemblies, meetings for council minutes, and other government writings, and while Williamson was abroad, several individuals sent him parliamentary journals.[60] The missives he received were thus frequently hybrid packets compiling previously written materials with newly textualized observations made by the writer.

Third, while the secretariat did not issue instructions structuring the letters as Elizabethan counselors used the *artes apodemicae*, there were clear expectations—shared with other news networks—concerning what observations to include and how to frame them. The material transmitted adhered to the notion of "particulars" resonant in natural philosophical circles at the same time, consisting of descriptive, but often disconnected, reportage of discrete items.[61] For example, Perwich's letter which included news from Warsaw conveyed accounts of Polish religious politics amid items describing petitions from French Huguenots, a new tax in Paris on candles, shipments of corn to Bourgogne, the appointment of a Jesuit as the new Inquisitor of Spain, Spanish support for the siege of Crete, the marriage the Count of Schomberg, and more.[62] These reports were presented sequentially in staccato fashion without topical hierarchy; often they were extracted from printed and manuscript newssheets simply in the order received.[63]

Although the letters were not organized systematically, correspondents selected observations to send according to a recognized rationale. Military affairs, diplomatic negotiations, court politics, and ship departures and arrivals were prioritized. Perwich's letters, for example, were filled with items such as that "the brother of the bishop of Munster is at the court incognito" and that he had seen guns being brought out of the arsenal.[64] Often he reported about papers that he had seen or heard of. For example, one letter of July 1669 exclusively concerned Perwich's acquisition of a book printed by the Dutch but prohibited by the French, a letter sent from Madrid to the Savoyard ambassador which described Godolphin's negotiations with the Dutch minister in Spain, and a report that "I am now perusing all the catalogues of manuscripts formerly the Cardinal Mazarine's & now in the King's Library, & what things are curious I marke downe & shall send to you, for your approbation, that I may have them copyed."[65]

Information that met the parameters of inclusion could be transmitted regardless of its distance from the letter writer, and correspondents in European capitals gathered news concerning the rest of the globe, while those stationed beyond Europe similarly relayed what they had heard of locations closer to England. For example, Williamson received reports of events in Jamaica from correspondents in Britain and Europe beginning in 1655 at the latest, and the letters he received from officials in Boston, Barbados, and other Atlantic world locales consistently contained news and rumors of the island.[66]

Finally, because his correspondents could not be certain of how Williamson would assess their news, they typically reported information of potential interest without judging its credibility or asserting its significance. Despite Perwich's relatively elevated position, notably, he rarely evaluated the information he communicated. Occasionally he might describe a rumor as foolish, invoke "probable reason," or observe that multiple sources aligned in their descriptions of events.[67] Nonetheless, such statements were rare, for Williamson's correspondents conceptualized their roles as serializing particulars acquired from an array of sources without subjecting them to sustained assessment.[68]

As a result of this division of labor, statements reflecting anxieties concerning credibility that scholars have often characterized as critical to early modern communication networks were almost entirely absent from the letters.[69] Correspondents did not tie their reports to their social standing or veracity, news items that proved mistaken were infrequently defended or explained, and correspondents were not punished for inaccurate information. Even though the alleged massacre in Jamaica that Watts reported in 1667 never happened, for example, Watts continued to correspond with Williamson regularly for more than ten years after.

Clear conventions thus ensured that Williamson's correspondents delivered usable information and strengthened his information network. To be sure, frustration permeated these communications: Williamson's correspondents begged him to write more frequently, apologized for their inability to secure news, bemoaned the disappearance of letters, hastily scribbled additional notes in completed letters reporting late-arriving missives, and misrepresented their roles in local squabbles. In turn, he admonished them for jejune letters, expressed impatience with their failures to navigate local politics, played them off against one another, and withheld reports when he considered it advantageous.[70] But the correspondents nonetheless operated with a secure sense of how to convert their experience into inscription for him. This process entailed consolidating texts that they had obtained, framing their own readings and observations as discrete items, and providing Williamson with the context to situate their missives within his broader web of communication.

These practices aimed to fulfill multiple of Williamson's goals. First, correspondents enabled his familiarity with action distant from the bustle at Whitehall or negotiations at Cologne. They did so in a vein of neutrality, presenting themselves as vehicles of information with the assumption that Williamson's secretariat would decide how to make sense of their letters, and structuring the communication to facilitate such interpretation by reporting information in regularized and modular form easily coordinated with other missives. Similarly, the network had massive but profitable redundancy, as correspondents reported news independent of whether they thought Williamson would already know it, providing a means of blind corroboration. Williamson's correspondents, in short, operated as conduits of potentially powerful information. But they presented it in a form designed to be disaggregated by the secretarial machine and thus more easily processed to centralize political knowledge.

Spatial and Material Organization

Joseph Williamson and his secretariat faced a spiraling tornado of letters, enclosures, books, registers, notes, and memoranda. Calming the swirling flurry of paper and ensuring the ability to find desired information demanded deliberate techniques of material and spatial organization.[71] While he and his clerks built on preexisting methods, their adaptations illuminate both the power and the limitations of these information management practices.

In many respects, Williamson's practices of processing incoming documents followed those long established by state administrators. As his directives before leaving for Cologne indicate, letters were endorsed and docketed, after which they were appended to preexisting bundles or used to initiate new ones. Loose notes were treated similarly, and periodically his clerks bound loose papers into fixed volumes; for example, at Christmas 1677, he directed his clerks to bind up papers and documents produced since 1674. The resulting compilations were ordered on the pattern of previous administrative collections, as they yielded volumes such as "Sir William Temple from Holland, 1674–6."[72] Occasional projects of binding thus secured papers and imposed thematic continuities.

Binding was generally effective for storing individual items, and Williamson's practices largely explain the scope of seventeenth-century materials surviving in the National Archives today; more than any other person, Williamson is responsible for the preservation of the state papers of his period and that preceding him. The more formidable challenge that Williamson confronted, as a result, was one of scale. Enumerating the material under his purview helps illuminate both the contours of his collection and the difficulty of imposing order on it.

Not long after Williamson's death, the papers still in his possession were deposited in the State Paper Office, and his successor as Keeper, John Tucker, embarked on the project of cataloging them along with the rest of the office's holdings.[73] Tucker began his audit of Williamson's bequest with the materials that lay on three presses, totaling fifteen shelves, in the inner of the two main rooms of the office. Many were bound books, and Tucker categorized forty-four as "Extracts of the Rolls in the Tower & the Exchequer."[74] This category formed only a selection of the books on the shelves, and Tucker also registered forty-one volumes collecting the materials produced through diplomatic negotiations, twenty-one volumes concerning precedence and ceremonial styles of address, twenty-one volumes on law, fourteen books of Admiralty matters, and nine volumes of newsletters or extracts from them, as well as twenty-three *relazioni* and similar items, including a "Book of Offices." The shelves also held smaller sets of books concerning ecclesiastical matters, genealogies, grants, the royal household, Parliament, proclamations, and the Signet Office. Williamson, furthermore, had not bound up a good deal of his collection, and in addition to the two hundred or so bound volumes on these shelves, Tucker identified more than 180 bundles, only one-third of which he perceived as having thematic continuities, and only six of which he calendared before giving up.

Moreover, only a small fraction of Williamson's archive fit in these presses. A closet in the room held almost three hundred volumes of treaties, commissions, instructions, letters, notes, and advices concerning foreign negotiations. Even this did not come close to exhausting Williamson's collection, as another closet off the same room held more items ranging from entry books to bundles to individual proclamations, including ten entries on ecclesiastical matters, sixteen on Admiralty, almost fifty items on Ireland, twenty-seven volumes of letters, twenty-two on military matters, twenty-six on Parliament, fifty-four on trade, twenty-five on treaties, and smaller ones on commissions, caveats, warrants and other themes or classes of documents. And these were only the materials in this space that Tucker could easily categorize, as in the same closet he also cataloged 115 bundles of "miscellany papers relating to the secretarys office," mostly minutes and dispatches.[75]

Tucker's catalog reveals the enormity of Williamson's archive—well over five hundred bound books and well over five hundred bundles—which compelled him to confront questions of large-scale archival organization. Across his collections, Williamson had experimented with physical modes of introducing order. Though discernible only through occasional notes strewn across his manuscript corpus, these indicate that he and his secretariat sought to merge multiple symbolic systems and spatial arrangements. More strikingly, they expose how his macroorganizational tools struggled to contain the multiplicity of papers he collected and to integrate their logics of compilation.

By 1667, Williamson had developed a system for labeling his bundles, daybooks, and what he called his "Books of Collections"—bound volumes containing transcriptions of treaties, instructions, negotiations, and other materials. Each of these assemblages he gave alphabetical identifiers starting with *A*. As the volumes piled up, he increased them at least as far as *DDD*, including some nonrepetitive formulas such as *EF*.[76] He also expanded beyond Latin alphabetical symbols, labeling some volumes with Delta (Δ), silcrow (or section sign, i.e., §), clover (♣), and other such marks.

This practice, however, was not systematic. Individual letters were not keyed to specific categories; for example, one bound book labeled

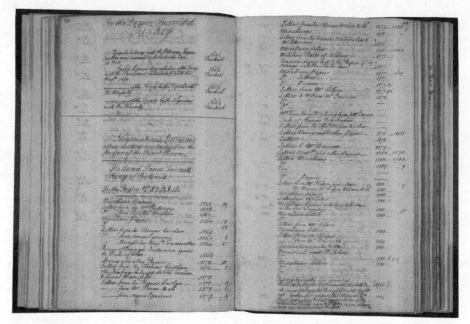

FIGURE 15. John Tucker's Catalog of the State Paper Office, c. 1705. This page outlines the contents of a drawer devoted to Turkey and several presses devoted to the Low Countries. Tucker's effort to create a comprehensive catalog of materials in the office was frustrated by its sheer scale, and he frequently resorted to describing volumes as miscellany and other expedients, such as repeatedly writing Do (ditto). British Library Lansdowne MS 1051, f. 14v–15r. By permission of the British Library.

A contained Scottish matters of all kinds, as was another collection exclusively of "Instructions and Negotiations" concerning the Low Countries.[77] Nor does there seem to have been a convention of following a specific sequence so that, most obviously, the first book in each category might share a symbol such as *A*. Moreover, many of the volumes were miscellaneous rather than topical; surviving table contents lists for volumes of "Commissions and Instruments" marked Δ and *O* reveal a bewildering variety of materials ranging across geographies, chronologies, and offices.[78] Similarly, a later calendar of treaties between England and France that Williamson owned show that they were distributed across scores of volumes with a range of identifying marks, including the Delta, the silcrow, and the Greek letter pi (π).[79] Finally, these markers do not appear to correspond to physical locations within his archive. Rather, he evidently labeled volumes in the order they were produced, or perhaps

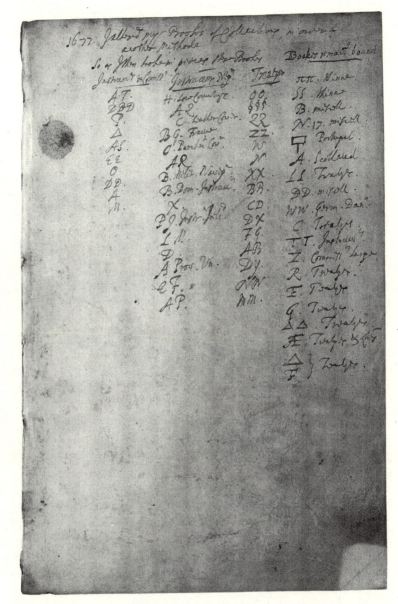

FIGURE 16. Joseph Williamson's notes on his "Books of Collections," 1677. On this page Williamson listed collections of treaties and political papers he had previously bound and labeled with a variety of numbers and symbols, which he had recently rebound. The National Archives, Kew, SP 9/132, f. 1r. Contains public sector information licensed under the Open Government Licence v3.0.

only when using them for specific projects to keep a running list of what he had consulted.[80]

The spatial organizations Williamson designed were slightly more stable. Notes from 1675 mapping the collections in the Secretary of State's office show that he had adopted Robert Cotton's method of arranging his books under the busts of emperors; for example, under Julius Caesar he kept materials concerning "Military. Admiralty. Soveraignty. Publica. Philosophia," while Augustus oversaw parliamentary materials, and Tiberius housed "Domestica," including ecclesiastical and London matters. Other busts were devoted to foreign polities; for example, Vitellius overlooked Spain, Flanders, and Portugal.[81] This plan suggests that Williamson adapted the scheme Thomas Wilson had introduced to the State Paper Office for his secretarial archive: although there were minor modifications, the categories and nomenclature align relatively closely, so that, for example, Caesar's bust oversaw the materials Wilson had labeled as *regalia* and *militaria*. Williamson, moreover, adapted this schema by devising appropriate categories for newly significant topics; for example, the bust of Claudius presided over the categories of "plantations" as well as "trade"— a new element within Wilson's *mechanica*.

Nonetheless, even with such additions, this ordering system contained disjunctures; for example, although Williamson classified many of his books as "Negotiations and Instruments," this was not a category outlined within the space of the archive itself. This discordance reflected two persistent problems: first, that of integrating incoming papers that did not easily fit into preexisting taxonomies; and second, that of finding the space, time, and energy to sort them.

These challenges were especially acute in the State Paper Office, as an anonymous description from between 1679 and 1682 entitled "Speculum Chartophylacii Regii" reveals. This document was most likely produced by John Brydall, an absolutist legal pamphleteer and occasional client of Williamson also in the patronage of Archbishop Sancroft.[82] As Brydall noted, "The paper office at Whitehall consists of 2 Roomes of Chambers, & 4 Towres; whereof one is a Stair-case."[83] The presses in the front room were predominantly devoted to "Negotiations with forrain Princes, & States," divided by realm. Brydall registered the correspondence in each drawer, which revealed that bundles had continued to be integrated at least in some fashion up to 1650s. Other presses in the same room were devoted to categories that mapped onto Wilson's designations, and it suggests that his system of classification largely remained in force.

The second room, however, revealed inadequacies within Wilson's arrangement. It continued to hold what Brydall described as "bundles of papers, indors'd Antiqua," from Henry VIII's to Mary's reigns, but it also now contained "Bookes & papers, belonging to the Government of the Usurpers." As this description suggests, some collections had been deposited here but not integrated into Wilson's system. This lack of integration was even more conspicuous in Brydall's description of the remaining rooms. In addition to "Old leagues, & treaties, bound up in books," Admiralty matters, papers related to trade, and heraldic materials, "The Tower, that looks to the Privy Garden" contained collections relating to Ralegh, the Overbury affair, and "All the Books, & papers, that concern the sequestracions at Haberdashers, & Goldsmiths Hall under the usurpers."[84] Whereas the first group hewed to the thematic organization, the latter did not. This hodgepodge was even more pronounced in the Tower closet facing Charing Cross, where bundles with such titles as "why a man shal not pay for his Wive's recusancy" and "the Whipping of 2 Dray-Men, that ran against the Earl of Exeter's Coach" abutted more conventional bundles concerning military and trade.[85]

As this account suggests, the proliferation of papers resisted and compromised the taxonomy of the archive. Williamson and his clerks evidently deposited the materials likely intending to file them later but were frustrated by lack of opportunity and their inherited filing system's inability to absorb individual items swiftly.

The difficulty of integrating papers remained an obstacle even when time was allotted to the enterprise. After his fall, Williamson retained his post as Keeper of the State Papers, and in late 1681, Leoline Jenkins and Edward Conway, now the two Secretaries of State, asked him to bring the office "into order." In response, he mapped and cataloged the archive while also consolidating some materials.[86] This consolidation was particularly necessary because Robert Montague, 3rd Earl of Manchester had commandeered two of the office's closets, and, Williamson reported, "they have not Roome enough for the paper" that had been moved into the main rooms.[87]

Almost a year later, he produced a plot and brief description of the compacted archive. Williamson's map, entitled "The Order of the Paper Office," depicted a smallish room lined by furniture for storing books and papers. His account revealed that many individual drawers had been at least roughly organized; for example, he noted that the French materials were "digested at least as to decades, least only because some of the papers of Gallia are left lesse perfect by the haste I hapned to be in."[88] While the outer room was largely unchanged from Brydall's description, the enforced influx of overflow records from the closets had altered the inner room. It still contained the ancient records and Interregnum materials.[89] But the space had been rearranged. Two presses containing six shelves were now devoted to "Letters from & to Kings, Princes, bound

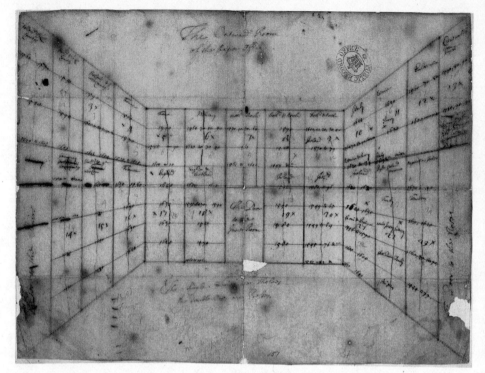

FIGURE 17. Drawing of State Paper Office's front room, produced for Parliament's Committee on Records, c. 1705. The National Archives, Kew, SP 45/21, f. 151. Contains public sector information licensed under the Open Government Licence v3.0.

or in bundles," and Williamson had shelved the incoming papers according to categories such as diplomatic correspondence—undifferentiated by locale—and "Household," "Offices," and "London."[90] Remaining drawers were devoted to older Signet and Council books and to treaties, negotiations, and commissions. The papers incorporated from the closets into the inner room, that is, were not integrated into the system of classification. While the outer room thus reflected the persistence of Wilson's scheme, the inner room exemplified the difficulty in capturing proliferating paperwork within abstract categories.

While Williamson sought to use spatial and material techniques and adaptable categories to impose order, these only worked at particular scales and could not achieve comprehensive coverage. This epistemological and classificatory tension was exacerbated by limitations on time, space, and energy. Success in obtaining papers created new problems; as Tucker's description reveals, when Williamson's collections were

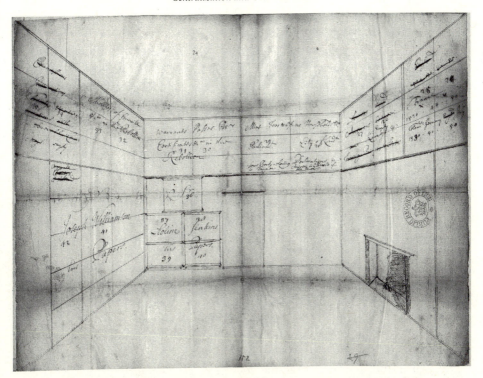

FIGURE 18. Drawing of State Paper Office's interior room, produced for Parliament's Committee on Records, c. 1705. The National Archives, Kew, SP 45/21, f. 152. Contains public sector information licensed under the Open Government Licence v3.0.

bequeathed to the office after his death, the influx spilled anew into the closets adjacent to the main room, unintegrated into existing schema—another index of the untamable abundance of paper. Physical organization was essential to Williamson's epistemic infrastructure, but the frenetic pace of production and accumulation led to an overburdened space and a pastiche of archival logics.

Navigation and Abstraction

The scope and scale of Joseph Williamson's collection thus posed their own hindrances as well as advantages. His spatial and material forms of organization might allow ready location of documents that fell into inherited categories or were part of collections related to discrete events. But finding specific information and coordinating knowledge across disparate volumes posed a more complex challenge, for which Williamson's practices of information management assumed heightened importance. Rather than relying on conventional registers or catalogs, Williamson adapted his note-taking technique to create volumes that served as para-archival reference tools. These notebooks balanced the functions of the compilation, commonplace book, and index—sometimes serving as guides to the sources, other times as new assemblages replacing them.[91] Above all, they reveal how the knowledge he wished to build from his archives depended on his techniques of information management.

Williamson and his clerks created these volumes using the methods discussed at the outset of this chapter: taking notes, supplying a heading for each extract, and then pasting or transcribing apposite materials into notebooks united by a common theme and, in these cases, typically organized alphabetically. These notebooks both consolidated the archive and facilitated maneuvering through it. Many were topical indexes to large numbers of texts. For example, at the front of one devoted to "Instruments," Williamson listed forty-seven volumes from which he had compiled it. Inside, at the end of each entry, he briefly cited the source: a typical example instructed that "for a Writt to Remoove Records," one should "vid EE 126."[92] Similarly, Williamson and his clerks constructed a notebook condensing instructions to English diplomats from about sixty collections of "Instruments and Treaties," divided geographically.[93] Entries briefly summarized the document to which they referred and named their source; a representative entry under Spain read "1577 Dr Wilson was sent to expostulate some matter with the Governor of Flanders in relation to the trade & entercourse with the Spanish Dominions to procure reduction," citing folio 226 of a volume labeled *C*.[94]

Such fine-grained guides to the archive could be directed toward virtually any topic, document type, geography, or office. Williamson made dozens of them, including twenty-six which Tucker listed as "Alphabetical Books and Indexes." These included three indexes to Tower records, as well as a chronological index of patents, grants, and commissions that may have covered Tower materials. Tucker also noted six collections covering "Historical, Geographical & Political Remarks" for specific European polities and two more of chronological notes covering the years 1670–76.[95]

These volumes were unified by shared practices of construction that could service malleable thematic frameworks. Similarly, the entries were generated by a common method modifiable to vastly different scales and forms, from summarizing grand generalities to transcribing minute details verbatim, while accommodating multiple types of information. An alphabetical volume concerning trade, for example, was peppered by

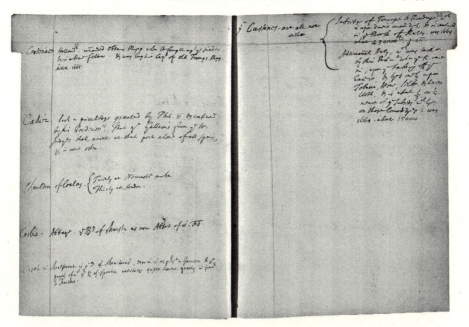

FIGURE 19. One of Joseph Williamson's notebooks formed by transcribing extracts from letters, newssheets, and other readings. The absence of references to original sources suggests that the collection served as a self-sufficient reference tool of miscellaneous information—note the categories of Cadiz, "Chauldron of coals," and customs—concerning trade. The National Archives, Kew, SP 9/28, 32v–33r. Contains public sector information licensed under the Open Government Licence v3.0.

instrumental notes concerning measurements, trade practices, money, and shipping. But others focused on the cultural and diplomatic elements of commerce, and extracts defining the "Asper" as a "small coyne in Turky, 232 make a piece of 6/8 in Tunish. 52 Aspers make a dollar" were as common as those such as "The King of Morocco turned Christian, & having lived nere then 12 yeeres in Spain, went back to Rome to embrace that Religion."[96]

Such matter-of-fact notes reveals another possibility of the notebooks, for in this one Williamson rarely recorded the sources for each passage. Its extracts likely contained the essential information those consulting them might need: anyone seeking to learn about an "Asper" would probably be satisfied with the digest entry without referring to the original source.

Omitting the source, however, transformed the volume's functioning, for rather than pointing the reader to another volume, it fused particulars from across Williamson's collections into a thematic surrogate for the archive. The series of notebooks concerning foreign polities, which Williamson referred to as "Persons, Things, Familyes &c," best illuminates this type.[97] Individual notebooks were devoted to Italy, Germany, France, and the Low Countries; another to Spain, Flanders, and Portugal; a last to Sweden, Denmark, Poland, Russia, and Turkey. Williamson began to compile these volumes in Cologne in 1673, likely trying to grasp the whirlwind of information that underlay the peace negotiations, added to them until at least 1678 as he sought to keep pace with the frenetic discussions in Nijmegen, and then made occasional entries in the 1690s.

These notebooks largely consisted of clipped biographies of Europe's diplomatic class in the late seventeenth century, most likely produced from transcribing extracts from letters upon their receipt. His volume for France, for example, was larded with such entries as "Colbert, was son to a Cittizen, a merchand de Rheims," and "Monsieur de Schomberg is borne somewhere up about the Palatinate, of an English mother, has a sone that serves with him."[98] He registered institutions and offices similarly; for example, he noted that an "Archimandrite was the name for the Abbot Superior in the Greek Church, like the Basilians in Messia, where the Archimandrite is Cardinal Sforza" and that "The Colledge of Commerce in Sweden as that Councill is called consists of A President, Vice President. 12 Attendants."[99]

Since Williamson's notes in such digests did not include citations, the provenance of each is unclear. But they likely originated in missives from those such as the agent Perwich, who embedded news about places far from where they were stationed and whose voluminous correspondence would have made it extremely difficult to navigate back to any specific point of information. The notebooks, this suggests, were designed to resolve the problem of relocating particulars within Williamson's archive by providing a topical volume where they could be recorded on first read, thus removing the need to find the source in the future. Moreover, such notebooks were designed to accommodate the ongoing influx of information, as the extracts were strewn throughout sizable prebound books—for example, only sixty of the nearly eight hundred pages of the Sweden volume contain any notes. This promiscuity of empty space characterized many of Williamson's volumes, a by-product of a notebook designed both for expansion and for navigation.[100]

Notebooks structured in this way served as digests of essential information, bringing together descriptions of people, customs, and institutions. But because the extracts did not record the original sources, the volumes could not help find them in the archive; rather they were their own compendia. This strategy of managing information consolidated the archive to replace it.

Williamson's notebooks concerning English governance similarly occupied the entire spectrum from digest to finding aid. Toward the latter end, one alphabetical notebook compiled by a clerk from Exchequer records entitled "Index of Commissions, powers, grants &c out of the Rolls of King James [&] Charles I" included citations to the records but provided limited information, beyond the date commissions were issued.[101] However, its categories—for example, admiral, auditor, attorney general, and apprentices—overlapped with those of another alphabetical volume on the other end of the spectrum: a catalog of English officeholders that did not include citations but only straightforward particulars without citation, such as that the king's "Great Seale may alter any ones name," or the rat killer "Randolph Holden is paid his Bills signed by Lord Chamberlain out of the Treasury Chamber."[102] Much like a "Book of Offices," this volume provided an overview of the government, but distributed alphabetically rather than by office. And some notebooks balanced the function of guide and surrogate, such as a notebook on "Parliamentary Powers &c," which provided citations for pasted-in scraps of notes from journals of both houses, Edward Husband's 1646 *A Collection of all the Publicke Orders, Ordinances, and Declarations of Both Houses of Parliament*, and Williamson's notebooks. This volume constituted both a compendium of parliamentary powers and a guide to the sources underlying its construction.[103]

Williamson's management of the chaos of paper in his office was structured by his practice of fragmenting sources into discrete particulars and recombining them into hybrid texts. The cross sections of the archives afforded by the resultant notebooks countered obstacles generated by the scale of Williamson's collecting. While his spaces overflowed with bundles, daybooks, and letters assembled according to various logics, the notebooks were thematically coherent, situating each extract alongside comparable particulars from other sources. In response to inescapable influx, they were designed for constant updating. Most crucially, they compiled extracts of related particulars from newsletters whose contents ranged widely. This practice, it should be emphasized, underlay the modular logic of correspondents' practice of reportage.

Such notebooks might serve as guides to the archive or surrogates for it. But in either case, the volumes dictated Williamson's access to and grasp of his collections; they were crucial tools mediating the heavy correspondence he solicited and the piles of books he accrued. In this sense they were simultaneously para-archival tools, translations of the archive, and new instruments of knowledge.

Center and Circulation

Joseph Williamson's notebooks were only one of many texts produced in his archive. As the volumes discussed above indicate, these served a range of functions. Though some had no immediate purpose, many were designed with predetermined uses in mind, including developing exigent knowledge, massaging political perception, and facilitating action. Williamson and his clerks designed these volumes carefully and circulated them to designated audiences ranging from fellow statesmen to an expansive public. Such transmissions used hybrid texts forged in the archive to promote a shared political perspective and to control and coordinate others' possession of information. And this practice propelled a symbiotic cycle of inscription, circulation, and collection intended to place Williamson in a privileged position, simultaneously enhancing his authority and enriching his political knowledge.

* * *

Williamson's massive archive facilitated the production of writings intended to assist administrative and diplomatic work. As was frequently the case, Williamson's practices resembled those of his predecessors, but on a grander scale and with tighter integration. His management of the copies of treaties supplies an exemplary case of centralization and coordination.

While Williamson attempted to assert control over diplomatic materials from the mid-1660s onward, he sought more intensively to harmonize the work of Britain's diplomatic corps after England entered the Triple Alliance with the Dutch and Swedish in 1668. Most significantly, he devised a core of transcriptions sent on virtually all embassies for the next few years—with additional items specific to their missions—consisting of the Triple Alliance treaty and its separate articles, along with a brief memorial he entitled "The method of Pressing Spain to yield to pay the subsidy."[104] The commonality of sources facilitated coordination across ventures, providing firm ground for England's stance and a blueprint for discussions. This fixed core was subsequently augmented with copies of the auxiliar agreements devised to strengthen the alliance and statements by the governor of the Hapsburg Netherlands, Francisco de Moura, 3rd Marquis de Castelrodrigo.[105]

Responsibility for preparing diplomatic packets also helped grow the State Paper Office. For several years Williamson had been pursuing this goal; in 1664, for example, when Arlington ordered him to provide treaties concerning Sweden to George Downing, Williamson acquired them from Philip Meadows and recorded copies for the office, which he later recopied for subsequent embassies. This practice accelerated after 1668 when, to help Williamson coordinate diplomacy, Arlington issued a warrant allowing him to copy treaties held in the Exchequer in bulk.[106] His production of notebooks concerning treaties and instruments also appears to have grown rapidly in these years. And increasingly during this time, the originals of treaties flowed into the State Paper Office rather than to the Exchequer.[107]

Such acquisitions would be integrated into compilations Williamson produced as resources for England's rapidly shifting diplomacy. The 1670 Secret Treaty of Dover with France abandoned the Triple Alliance and put England on tenuous ground that would ultimately lead to the Third Anglo-Dutch War and the Congress of Cologne. In response, Williamson embarked on a program of archival consolidation, ultimately producing a gigantic codex that he labeled "Generall Calendar of Treatyes with Foreigne Princes, &c. as it is drawn out of the Bookes of Treatyes remaining either in the Office of his Majesty's Papers of State, or out of my own Collections."[108] This volume compiled inventories such as a 1671 list of the "Originall Treaties remaining in the Paper Office" and a register of treaties in the Tower recently produced by the Ryleys. The bulk of it, however, consisted of extracts drawn from his notebooks, recording the year, signatory parties, negotiators, and conditions of treaties, with a reference to the source. The entries were organized haphazardly: those involving England came first but were not grouped by treaty partner, after which followed all pairings not involving England. None were arranged chronologically. To help navigate this morass, a clerk produced an index organized by the parties to treaties.[109] The "Generall Calendar" thus served as a disarrayed but invaluable reference tool for England's snarled diplomacy, consolidating European treaties past and present.

Similar compilations formed a significant component of the baggage accompanying Williamson to Cologne, which included at least eighteen "Books of Treatyes," many of which were produced for the occasion.[110] Most were designed to prepare for negotiations, but Williamson also collected volumes concerning diplomatic duties and protocol; for example, one derived from State Paper Office sources enumerated the proper forms of address for dignitaries.[111] This volume also mined seventy warrants from the previous century for "Allowances made to Ministers Abroad" such as advancements and reimbursements.[112] Such volumes translated his sprawling archive into compact miscellanies equipping him to comport himself appropriately in Cologne and navigate the Exchequer bursary upon return.

These collections were frequently consulted in Cologne.[113] As expected, preexisting treaties anchored negotiations, and those with whom Williamson was negotiating had their own copies. The archive he transported also helped him explain the unfavorable direction negotiations took to the dissatisfied Arlington, for these missives often referred to documents he had brought with him (whose originals or other copies Arlington could access in England's archives); for example, Williamson equipped a copy of the disadvantageous treaty provisionally advanced in March 1673 with notes elaborating how it followed precedents.[114] Previous treaties set the conditions of diplomacy; copies facilitated understanding—and managed expectations—between Cologne and Westminster.

Williamson's desire to operate as a central hub again directed his practices two years later as he remained at Whitehall while Jenkins went as English representative to the negotiations between the French and the Dutch at Nijmegen. Rather than equip Jenkins with an archive like the one he brought to Cologne, Williamson renovated his own: for example, he updated and neatened his "General Calendar" by incorporating new lists of treaties assembled in the interval, calendaring more notebooks of treaties, and expanding the index.[115] He tried to use these refreshed collections to influence the negotiations from afar. At the outset, he sent Jenkins a series of questions for the other delegations concerning Charles II's role. The desired outcome was clear, as the missive was accompanied by precedents from treaties explaining why Charles II should serve in the specific role of mediator—and with instructions that Jenkins then use the ostensible conflict of interest to extricate England from its 1667 Treaty of Breda with the Dutch.[116] After this had been achieved, however, Williamson found England's influence still inadequate. Accordingly, he requested that a clerk search "in treatyes mediated, Quaere, if the Mediator be not found named in the Treaty it selfe, & if so, quare if in the Preamble or in the Body." In response the clerk sent extracts from a handful of treaties between European powers indicating the placement of the name of the mediator, while noting that in the Treaty of Breda, "the King of England was named before the King of Denmark even & his ambassador before the ambassador of this latter"—a clear effort to use the notion of precedence between states to reverse Denmark's seeming ascendancy over England in the deliberations.[117] Williamson's possession of treaties thus enabled him to try to orchestrate Jenkins's moves. And he also viewed Nijmegen as an opportunity to expand his own collections, directing that "wee must keep a Journal of all those peoples at audiences, counselors, &c" in imitation of the Dutch practice, using the subsequent lists to update his geographical notebooks.[118]

Williamson's archive lay at the core of his campaign to coordinate and centralize resources for diplomats, for by using the labor attached to his offices to recombine its texts, he provided agents abroad with collections that unified and directed England's diplomatic stance. Previous embassies had often received preparatory archival materials, but Williamson's provision of a unified core for many of them, and its orchestration from a single office, was distinct, reshaping the practice of circulating materials even if it did not strengthen England's weak diplomatic position. And, no less significantly, this program spurred the delivery of new materials to his office, perpetuating the cycles of inscription and archivization, recombination and circulation, to both coordinate and strengthen the stances of those in his network.

* * *

By the time Williamson began to assert control of diplomatic resources, he had for several years been issuing hybrid texts to targeted audiences with the goal of influencing Britain's news landscape.[119] Williamson's practices in this sphere again synthesized those of his predecessors at an expanded scale: he centralized collection of information in his unified offices, directed his clerical labor to recombine incoming paperwork, and circulated new assemblages to targeted audiences, who in turn transmitted texts and papers back to him, reigniting the cycle. And again the texts he circulated shaped the boundaries of political knowledge.

This enterprise provided a different challenge from coordinating diplomacy, however, for the public's appetite for news and its established scale of circulation limited his—or anyone's—ability to control it fully. Accordingly, Williamson sought more to moderate a fractious and potentially seditious populace than to dictate political orthodoxy.[120] In fact, the structure of news exchange appears to have been designed less to extinguish opposition than to enhance the dynamic of perpetual circulation that, Williamson hoped, would place him in a position of privileged knowledge.

Restoration England was characterized by spaces laced with political discussion, as theaters, coffeehouses, and taverns hosted debates provoked by books, newssheets, and rumor. As a result, it has been characterized as a Habermasian public sphere in which political discussion took place free from government interference.[121] Like many others, Williamson perceived this flourishing media sphere as breeding dissension, and in particular identified unfettered news circulation as responsible. Printed newsletters first circulated on the Continent in the late sixteenth century, and they had begun to spread throughout England in the 1620s. Domestic production as well as importation of newssheets proliferated in the 1640s, but as newssheets were increasingly associated with domestic criticism, the industry became subject to repeated crackdowns—most notably Oliver Cromwell's 1655 suppression of all but two, and their subordination to Thurloe. But though efforts to regulate the production of news were widespread in Britain and on the Continent, governments found their measures incapable of stanching the influx of manuscript and printed newssheets from beyond their borders.

Williamson's experience in Cologne confirmed the power of news, as public sentiment against Charles II's pro-French policies and the war undermined his position and ultimately forced the unfavorable peace. During his time there, London quivered with discussion of both the war and the faltering negotiations, and his clerks constantly reported "the newes of the town."[122] Sir Thomas Player, for example, bitterly claimed, "There is not a place in the world soe fruitfull in liing storyes as London, and though the falsenesse of these storyes is usually within two or three dayes laid open to the world, yet the people are ready to receive new ones, and to beleeve them till they alsoe are detected. From hence it is that our enemyes gather stubbornnesse, for these reports are usually framed to the disadvantage of our owne affaires, and to the advantage of the Dutch."[123] As his complaint suggests, public opinion was frequently swayed by rumors derived from interpretation of foreign newssheets, in particular the *Haarlem Courant*. Indeed, as Helmer Helmers has argued, newsletters often formed a species of public diplomacy through which governments might pressure opinion abroad.[124] The *Courant* was a source of particular concern to those with Williamson's affinities, as its reportage often aligned with a Whig perspective critical of Charles II's regime.[125]

This vexed environment was familiar to Williamson long before he arrived in Cologne, as from the early 1660s, he had begun devising measures to mitigate the dangers posed by the flow of news to a British populace incompletely reconciled to the Restoration experiment. Above all, this effort entailed constructing a multitiered network disseminating texts that would curtail rebelliousness by shaping public perception of events. As Jason Peacey has observed, the *Courant* was already embedded in nascent Whig circles and British news culture more broadly, and thus counteracting its effects demanded a strategy of management rather than elimination. Accordingly, Williamson designed his newsletters not as propaganda insisting on a single Crown-sanctioned perspective but instead as a collection of diverse reports fulfilling an appetite for news, endorsing some but predominantly aiming to inhibit provocative interpretations of contemporary events.

Williamson's office produced both printed and manuscript newsletters. Initially after his appointment, Williamson was one of several sources providing extracts from their correspondence for Henry Muddiman's and Roger L'Estrange's monopoly-holding printed newsletters, but as early as 1662 Williamson was working to displace them and centralize printed news in his offices. In 1665, while the royal court was in Oxford to escape the plague, he partnered with Muddiman to launch the biweekly *Oxford Gazette*. When the court returned to London the following year, he wrested it from Muddiman and rechristened it the *London Gazette*, and it enjoyed a monopoly on printed news until the lapse of the Licensing Act in 1679, shortly after Williamson's fall. At this point the *Gazette* was selling roughly seven thousand copies per issue and distributing many more for free, and even with the lapse and emergence of competing newspapers, its paid circulation neared five thousand. After the 1682 restoration of the Licensing Act its circulation resurged, and it remained England's dominant newspaper into the eighteenth century.[126]

Williamson's assumption of control over the *Gazette* marked the vertical integration of the printed news industry; rather than supply copy to Muddiman or L'Estrange, Williamson now oversaw printing of extracts drawn from materials sent to his office.[127] As before, its text consisted of the particulars characteristic of his network: shipping news, troop movements and reports of battles, the proceeding of legislative bodies, the perambulations of diplomats, and other items transmitted by his correspondents. Though issues typically began with an item of domestic news and might print royal proclamations, they concentrated on Continental events, again arranging items likely in the order received, without an underlying geographical or chronological logic. The *Gazette* was, in essence, a printed hybrid selection of the letters Williamson received.

In addition to this pastiche construction, the *Gazette* also resembled Williamson's correspondence in that, though the paper had the imprimatur of state authority, it lacked editorializing or overt statements of ideology.[128] Nor did its items favor one media network; much of it originated from sources unsympathetic to Charles II's politics—most strikingly, the *Courant*, and even more strikingly, epistolary newsletters directly from the *Courant*'s founder and printer Abraham Casteleyn—and the text did not indicate the source of each passage to hint whether it warranted belief.[129] The *Gazette*, then, sought neither to compel adherence nor to advance a specific ideological perspective. Rather, it sought to create an official body of news to counterbalance, dilute, and moderate criticism sparked by the circulation of other news publications through Britain.

Williamson and his secretariat directed the same practice of recombining his correspondence to produce a separate, more exclusive body of news they disseminated: standardized manuscript newsletters sent to a network of officials, customs officers, postmasters, spies, and informants both within the realm and abroad. For this audience, the emphasis was domestic. The copy was more frequently gossipy and less concertedly neutral than the *Gazette*'s, though not overtly ideological: rumors of court scandals, potential matches, and popular discontent were mixed with reportage on parliamentary affairs, proclamations, and other official government actions. Foreign news was included as well, and this newsletter sometimes contained more sensitive items than did the *Gazette*. These newsletters thus consolidated Williamson's correspondence into an informed, though not intimate, perspective on the domestic politics. Much as his diplomatic packets strove to coordinate resources across multiple embassies, they distributed a standard packet of knowledge concerning the government to many working in it.

While scores of these newsletters survive, the best remaining evidence for the operation derives from a 1674 memorandum penned by the clerk Henry Ball in preparation for Williamson's return from Cologne, which elaborated how the office had functioned in Williamson's absence. As Ball explained, the scribal workshop consisted of four clerks employed in the State Paper Office, and he frequently contributed when the volume of material outstripped their capacity. Thrice a week two of the clerks went to the Rolls Office to copy relevant extracts while the other transcribed passages from "the foreign pacquet." During the other three workdays the staff as a whole "all attended in the Office to doe the letters, which were so many that if some part of them were not prepared the preceeding night, wee could not compass them."[130] Over each week, they produced eighty copies of weekly newsletters and almost two hundred shorter ones containing news of the previous two days. Many—likely most—were accompanied by free copies of the *Gazette*.

These manuscript newsletters went out to roughly 120 correspondents.[131] The foreign posts went to ambassadors and foreign diplomats such as Sir William Godolphin in Spain and Perwich in Paris. The "inland" post went to a wider audience, including nobility such as the Earl of Bath, clerics such as the bishop of Carlisle, municipal officials such as the mayor of Newcastle, military men, gentry, secretaries, and clerks in the Restoration regime.[132] Moreover, Williamson sometimes forwarded specific letters to individuals, who sometimes further circulated them, expanding the reach of their own curated selection of news.[133] As this practice suggests, access to this exclusive news network was its own form of social capital, and Williamson often compensated customs agents and postmasters with newsletters rather than money.[134]

The dynamic of exchange illuminates another critical dimension of

Williamson's system: many recipients also supplied Williamson's office with news.[135] His network, that is, flowed both ways, and it was enhanced by the number of participants incorporated into it. Williamson's newsletters thus stimulated the current of information; while they were instruments for shaping knowledge, they also galvanized the flow of particulars through Williamson's office, where they were subject to filtration and recirculation.

How newsletters operated in the economies of circulation for those like Perwich who were stationed abroad also illuminates the contours of Williamson's information system. Such individuals typically acquired information by exchanging newsletters with other diplomats and news gatherers, who then used them to scrutinize England's politics and drive further news exchange. This process underlay the frustration frequently voiced by correspondents when Williamson's newsletter contained items viewed as overly provocative; participants in this network worried that disseminating inappropriate information might lead to crackdowns and limit their ability to exchange news. For similar reasons, diplomats objected when the news they received contained unflattering portrayals of those with whom they were negotiating. The constant demand for news, that is, dampened the possibility that Williamson's newsletters might articulate the sharpest edge of English perception or policy, since doing so would imperil access to information. This imperative for the anodyne shaped the milquetoast *Gazette* even more strongly. The maelstrom of reports that blew through these texts and across these networks, in short, balanced the desire for information with the countervailing imperative to denude it of provocation.[136]

As the aforementioned complaints suggest, Williamson's newssheets sometimes inspired speculation and hostile interpretation despite his effort to keep them bland. But his circulation of news was not intended to infuse public spaces with intense political fervor or ideological unanimity; it was intended to satiate an existing desire for news by distributing an official version relatively favorable to the Restoration goals, muted in its tone and inclusive in its content. Reassembling the fragments of news he received in such abundance, his secretariat sought to keep audiences moored to an ongoing, constantly refreshed news spectacle while at the same time shaping and constraining public discourse—thereby managing the threats posed by potentially destabilizing publications such as the *Courant*.

Williamson's role in Restoration news production compromises any sense that it constituted a distinct sphere purely free from government interference; instead, it showcases government participation in the public sphere. And more, the distinct benefits this system conferred on Williamson reveal how the putative public sphere and the information state were deeply interrelated and coproduced by the same practices.[137] Like many of his correspondents, he used the bait of news to lure information. His place at the center of the networks and its integration with his collections, however, differentiated his position from theirs. In an information environment characterized by mediation, delay, rumor, error, and misdirection, the correspondence he received, the notebooks he maintained, and the archive he inherited supplied him with unprecedented resources to assess incoming reports and discern valuable slips of information.[138] This system relied on continual influx, as it was strengthened by every expansion of his network and the concomitant traffic of paper and particulars into his office. Williamson's privileged position, in short, depended on a superior flow of paper through his office.

* * *

Though the practices underlying the production of newssheets resembled those of preparing diplomatic packets, their differences illuminate distinct but interrelated dimensions of Williamson's epistemic system. While providing diplomats with a shared set of materials helped coordinate their action, dictating and fixing public opinion in comparable fashion was recognized as an unrealistic goal. Nonetheless, his news production aspired to establish and moderate the horizons of public opinion, dulling its predilection for the sharpest interpretations of contemporary events. His hybrid texts in both cases sought to capitalize on his role as information hub to influence political action and perception.

At the same time, such acts were structured to ensure the ongoing kinesis of his system. While providing resources to diplomats encouraged the delivery of papers into his secretariat, Williamson's newssheets were an essential means of lubricating news exchange and were sent out in large measure to yield information in return. His practices of coordination and distribution thus symbiotically enhanced his epistemic infrastructure, driving the generation and circulation of information with which he sought to grasp and shape the chaos of the world. And, more than any effort to dictate political allegiance and sentiment, this dynamic of perpetual transmission transformed the structure of British government—not by provoking constitutional or ideological change but by recasting it as an information state, dominated by practices of information collection, knowledge production, and textual circulation, which radiated local knowledge produced in its archives outward to reshape the world beyond it.

Conclusion: The Epistemology of the Archive

Joseph Williamson sat at the epicenter of a gigantic information machine whose constant whirring and endless paroxysms delivered an inexorable flow of paper into his purview. This paper constituted the terrain in which he maneuvered, furnishing the masses of particulars that he aspired to mobilize toward political understanding and authority.

Williamson's was a fundamentally empirical epistemology, for it allowed him to ignore any writer's personal credibility in favor of correlating their claims with evidence in the papers brimming in his archive. By consolidating and ordering the particulars that coursed through his offices, he could use passages scrawled in his digests to assess the likelihood of rumors about foreign dignitaries; calculate the value of foreign trade by his notes on monies; explain battlefield outcomes by his extracts on military structures; contextualize diplomatic reports according to the long histories of treaties; and check gossip concerning domestic conspiracies against his informants' pool of intelligence. His information infrastructure generated an unmatched database with which to compare incoming materials in the hope of verifying propositions, detecting falsehoods, identifying weaknesses, gauging the unlikely, and seeing the hidden. It formed its own technology for knowing the world.

This technology also created the boundaries on his knowledge, for the world Williamson saw was dictated by the flow of papers and mediated by his practice of note-taking, which splintered the texts that streamed across his desk and then sorted and compiled their shards into an archive embodying the present. Williamson's information Leviathan, in fact, proved his undoing. In 1678, as panic spread about the rumored Popish Plot, Williamson's dismissive response enraged the coalescing Whig party in the House of Commons. The phases of his fall highlight dual weaknesses within his epistemic system. First, his indifference to the English clergyman Titus Oates's claims likely reflected a conviction that his informants would have revealed evidence of the conspiracy had it been real; he was undone by the confidence in the information world he had constructed, which could not always exorcise the power of rumor or command others' beliefs. Second, in early 1679 he was vilified and briefly consigned to the Tower by Commons after hastily signing a series of warrants excusing Irish Catholic officers from the Test Act, which Williamson claimed he had distractedly done while overwhelmed by his exhausting burden of paperwork. His ruin marked the breaking point of his ability to manage the information behemoth that had enabled his rise.

That even his downfall reflected the tensions of inscription exemplifies its crystallization as a form of life, for Williamson's practice entailed constantly replenishing the body of inscription that rooted his knowledge of the world. He habitually copied, borrowed, spied, and wheedled to bring extant documents under his purview; at the same time he and his clerks constantly inscribed their own experiences, converting ephemeral moments into notes no less significant to them than copies of official records. Theirs was a collaborative project of reducing texts and experience into particulars and then recombining them into new forms. The notebooks produced by this process were highly flexible, and they could be used to navigate the archive, to create authoritative reference manuals or digests obviating the need to consult sources, or to form hybrid texts for transmission to external audiences. Indeed, the newssheets disseminated by Williamson are best thought of as a regular species of notebook integrating recent correspondence that he circulated more broadly than his other volumes. In all cases, the new assemblages were themselves inscriptions for managing an excess of inscription.

This abundance emerged by design, for Williamson's office and its archive constituted the mainframe in a tangle of networks designed to engineer the perpetual circulation of information. Together, they formed the site where all the inscriptions proliferating along his networks came into contact—the engine room of a nascent information state. The space of the archive embodied the perspective Williamson strove to attain, one which, by recontextualizing inscriptions in new volumes, ideally reimposed continuities on realities fractured by their transmission through space and time. The world was inscribed in the texts he generated and collected, but as chaos; his new revelatory configurations, he hoped, would expose paths to order and power. He aspired to use the simulacrum built in the archive to understand the world's dynamism. And by drawing the world into his archive to be remade and projected back out, he struggled to reform the world of his audiences as the specter of his archive.

Epilogue
The World of the Archive

Joseph Williamson's fall did not leave a vacuum at the top levels of authority. While no individual assumed his full portfolio of responsibilities, offices across the realm accumulated ever-growing archives whose consultation was abetted by the production of entry books, registers, and indexes. Correspondence churned through the post, weaving individuals in far-flung locales into dense communications webs before entering into the complex process of filtering and retransmission. Clerks and secretaries in these offices continued to fuse their archives and communications into hybrid texts—policy papers, diplomatic packets, newssheets—targeted to distinct audiences. These tasks were often introduced and spread by individuals who had worked under Williamson. Though Britain's information infrastructure was less integrated and more decentralized than it had been during his ascendancy, the emphasis on paperwork had become robust and self-perpetuating, a vehicle of stability leading to the convergence and routinization of practices within and across offices. The thickened communications networks and increased bureaucracy of late Stuart Britain reflects the permeation of the techniques exemplified by Williamson throughout the state.[1]

The spread of this mode of governance was facilitated by another paper boom. After 1620 the volume of imports hovered around 80,000 reams annually, but by the late 1660s more than 100,000 reams were regularly imported, and some years more than 150,000 reams. At the turn of the century, when domestic production finally started to reduce imports, customs records suggest that England annually imported 200,000 reams.[2] In the late seventeenth century, more paper flowed through British society than ever before.

Numerous aspects of Britain's contemporary political and historical environment reveal the persistent impact of the surge of paper and the rapid spread of inscription expertise. Even under Algernon May's absentee keepership, as noted in the introduction to this book, the Tower archive in the 1670s remained a site of considerable activity.[3] Its holdings continued to germinate polemical visions of the state; when Robert Brady and William Petyt reprised William Prynne's debate with Edward Coke over the antiquity of the House of Commons in the early 1680s, they competed to unearth ever more obscure records from it—which, drawing on the idiom of contemporary natural philosophers, they called "matters of fact"—and argued over who most faithfully transcribed them.[4] Moreover, they not only published copies of their favored evidence as a matter of information warfare—as Prynne had—but engaged in subterfuges to outmaneuver each other; for example, Brady received from Clerk of the Tower Records Laurence Halsted reports of what Petyt had consulted as well as transcriptions of records.[5]

The internalized devotion to these practices had unanticipated consequences. Petyt's certainty of the antiquity of the House of Commons rested on the assumption that definitive evidence had been destroyed or lost. At the same time he argued that had the introduction of the Commons taken place in 1265, as his opponents claimed, such dramatic change would surely have elicited comment at that time, and the Crown would have checked for precedents by sending officials to consult what he assumed would have been its robust archive concerning past Parliaments.[6] Petyt's vision of the murky past as possessed of a bureaucratic latticework of records, which he declared had been obliterated over time, reflects the perverse undercurrent of the internalization of inscription as a form of life: his contemporary mediascape colonized his historical imagination, leading him to conjure phantom records supporting his desired past.

This pursuit of envisioned records structured politics of the period, too, for the Popish Plot and subsequent rumored and real conspiracies provoked feverish pursuit of incriminating or exculpatory papers.[7] The updates that Secretary of State Leoline Jenkins received in Cologne during the frenzy of the plot largely consisted of reports concerning the movement and exposure of papers.[8] This practice shaped his own secretaryship after he succeeded Williamson, for his focus on pursuing plots provoked surveillance and investigations generating ever-more-voluminous paperwork, which then came to suffuse his archive.[9] By 1681 such domestic intelligence work had reversed the wave of Whig anti-Catholicism that had felled Williamson.

The recalibration of Britain's politics by inscription, moreover, directed attention toward its legacy of archives. While Williamson's Privy Council committee to oversee the records had little effect, in the first years of the eighteenth century Queen Anne's principal counselors spearheaded a comparable endeavor in Parliament. That Parliament rather than the Privy Council was given custody over state archives reflected that body's newfound ascendancy in Britain's postrevolutionary parliamentary monarchy. And though the committee focused on supporting the material infrastructure of the office by funding architectural improvements, it also led to new textual instruments for establishing order. Under its charge, for example, Petyt created the first handbook describing the form and function of each distinct type of Tower record.[10] This committee was also the catalyst for John Tucker's catalog of the State Paper Office's contents, and the weaknesses revealed through this process spurred him to devise an abstract taxonomic system that anticipated Melville Dewey's of two centuries later.[11]

The absorption of the regime of inscription thus reshaped the political and historical imagination, stimulated novel approaches to classification and abstract systems of knowledge, and gave new dimensions to assumptions about public benefit. But above all, it underlay the emergence of an information state that was simultaneously its own media sphere, a participant intermingling in a broader public cosmos of information, and a political and administrative organ dependent on inscription to absorb external information and emanate messages into the world. Its capacity to manage information underlay what Michael Braddick has termed the "actions without design, patterns without blueprints" that drove the process of state formation.[12] And it was a predicate to state formation's various modalities, enabling the coordination of action and communication between center and locality, the institutionalization and routinization of fiscal-military record keeping, and the monitoring of constituent populations. These forms were not directed by rationalization but borne of individuals within governance perceiving opportunities for advancement or expertise by using paper to forge new patterns of communication, information storage, and authoritative texts. Their contingent acts ultimately precipitated a structural change in the practice of governance.

The circulation and reception of papers, this suggests, was not merely a feature of Britain's political life but rather was constitutive of it. News, letters, archives, and more did not merely translate an external reality for public consumption but instead mediated the perception of reality, and even—or especially—statesmen and dignitaries performed a mode of existence that experienced the world through a prism of text.

* * *

A political practice rooted in inscription was essential to the realm's imperial project, the most distinctive element of Britain's eighteenth-century politics. A robust information infrastructure was crucial to ensure communication and coordination across an expansive geography.[13] The contours of this network also structured the distribution of power and knowledge between Whitehall, provincial authorities, and colonial subjects. But it also introduced profound limitations that in turn have directed and constrained the focus of subsequent historians.

After Williamson's fall, his role was most closely replicated by William Blathwayt, who started out as part of diplomat William Temple's embassy to The Hague and then in 1675, with Williamson's support, earned a clerkship in the Plantation Office. Blathwayt's efficient handling of correspondence and financial matters led to his ascent through more important and lucrative positions: he became Secretary of the Lords of Trade and Plantations in 1679, Surveyor and Auditor General of royal revenues the following year, and Undersecretary of State to Edward Conway the year after; purchased the office of Secretary of War in 1683; and was appointed Clerk of the Privy Council in 1686. His role as nerve center made him indispensable, and though he had been integral to James II's rule, he was quickly reconciled to the Williamite regime after the Glorious Revolution. Throughout the 1690s he accompanied the king on Continental campaigns while maintaining his offices, in particular advancing his colonial expertise. In 1696 King William III appointed him to the revived Board of Trade, and he became one of its most prominent members. He continued in many of these roles until 1707, when the vicissitudes of party politics brought him down.[14]

Blathwayt was more focused on war and trade than Williamson had been. But his practices signaled the imbrication of similar methods, for he was an inveterate notetaker, record keeper, and correspondent, and he fulfilled his responsibilities through the constant circulation of letters and maintenance of instruments documenting the activity of the offices he served. Although he may have absorbed these tools under Temple, his appointment to the Plantation Office under Williamson was central to his development of them, and a site where he developed and expanded their usage.[15]

Williamson had not held an official role in the Council of Trade before his appointment to a reconstituted version in 1675—one which was designed to seize power from the companies that had long run many of the colonies. But as undersecretary to Secretary of State Henry Bennet, Earl of Arlington, Williamson had often performed its secretarial work. Throughout the 1660s and early 1670s, he corresponded directly with colonial governors such as Thomas Lynch and Edmund Andros and mediated other imperial communications by drafting letters or annotating incoming letters for Arlington and the king. He was also responsible for composing charters, instructions, and other official communications, which he constructed by drawing on precedents in his archives. Williamson seems to have introduced his standard practices to the Plantation Office to manage the paperwork flowing into it from colonial dominions, and under his custody its volumes included the council's journal, compilations of orders, entry books, collections of petitions, references, and reports.[16]

Blathwayt maintained the volumes he inherited while developing new ones to create a web of overlapping texts minutely documenting the office's activity. His clerks produced journals of meetings by taking rough copies in real time, which Robert Southwell or Blathwayt then corrected for transcription into a cleaner version.[17] From 1683 to 1688 they also maintained a "Journal of All that Passes in the Office," which registered items such as minutes of meetings, memoranda concerning daily business, and records of posts.[18] Entry books proliferated further; while there previously had been two entry books "relating to the forraign Plantations in general," under Blathwayt's supervision the office maintained seventeen, devoting each to more specific units such as Barbados, Virginia, Newfoundland, and the Royal African Company. His clerks also compiled collections of formal documents such as "Jamaica Journal and Laws" or "State Council Books of Maryland"; many began with the charter establishing the colony, much as the reports from embassies had long begun with the formal commission.[19] After the letters were copied into these entry books, the originals were archived in volumes with names such as "Papers of Barbados," that also included lists and other informal papers.[20] Similarly, specific types of documents such as commissions and patents were bound together. Finally, from 1678 to 1688, the office also maintained a "Book of Occurrences" containing snippets drawn from incoming letters that resembled Williamson's idiosyncratic notebooks.[21] Under Blathwayt, the office thus developed a fine-grained system of information management that distributed incoming materials by colony and type. The increasing complexity of the organization reflected heightening sensitivity both to the specificity of each locale and to a rising tide of incoming paperwork.

Like Williamson, Blathwayt viewed ongoing communication as necessary to resolve problems of distance and uncertainty, and he implemented means of encouraging communication and confronting its challenges; for example, he oversaw the provision of paper to the colonies.[22] Similarly, his correspondence, like Williamson's, was rife with references to the transmission of other papers, but his correspondents also frequently reported on the status of duplicates that they were encouraged to send. This productive redundancy sought to secure the regularity of communication despite the hazards of the sea and rival empires' regular seizure of papers.[23]

The texts that Blathwayt's colonial correspondents sent him in duplicate, moreover, had often been produced in response to specific requests from the Board of Trade or the Privy Council, and thus also signaled their priorities. For example, Governor of Bermuda Isaac Richier, writing to Blathwayt in January 1692, began, "In October last I enclosed to you Duplicate of the Lawes and what els was sent your Majesty before by way of Barbados. I have enclosed a duplicate of my letter then writt to the Lords Committee for Plantations, and if the original be not come to hand I praye (sir) that their Lordships may see this."[24]

Richier's provision of Bermuda's laws responded to the charge issued to colonial governors that they send to England the documentary output of imperial administration. Such texts had been solicited from the 1660s but required after 1675.[25] Colonial administrators were charged with sending unofficial documents as well. Most strikingly, the Privy Council periodically ordered governors to send missives elaborating the "state of" the colony, with accompanying prescriptions dictating what they observe and record according to specific "Heads of Inquiries."[26] These reports constituted another iteration of the *artes apodemicae*, as they requested basic information concerning the geography, population, commodities, legal structures, military capacities, and other features of the colonies.[27] They were often ordered in batches at moments of crisis or transfer of power. For example, in August 1675, as the Privy Council looked to seize control from the companies that oversaw many of the colonies, circular requests of this sort were sent to Virginia, Barbados, and Jamaica; eight more were sent the following April.

Blathwayt both solicited and collected such texts; for example, he owned a collection of notes produced in 1669 entitled "An account of the Carybee Islands," which accumulated extracts out of the Privy Council journal to produce brief overviews of each island, as well as a copy of Governor Richard Dutton's account of Barbados.[28] Such requests could be more focused as well. In December 1696, Governor of Bermuda John Goddard wrote to Blathwayt explaining that "I have likewise sent home the state of the Island by their Lordshipps particular order, and of the number of the slaves, to all officers, and an account of all the Publick lands belonging to the King."[29] Similarly, colonial administrators often sent lists of officeholders: for example, around 1692, Surveyor General of Customs Edward Randolph sent to Blathwayt "The names of the Present Collectors & Surveyors of His Majesties Customs in the Plantations on the continent of America & Islands adjacent who are upon the Establishment as also of the Navall officers in the severall districts."[30] Blathwayt, in short, used constant and closely structured communication to thicken his colonial connections and ensure regular and regulated knowledge.

Blathwayt elicited more information than had Williamson, and his correspondence with colonial figures expanded on Williamson's pattern as well. Whereas Williamson tended to correspond only with colonists holding offices, Blathwayt fomented endemic contestation within colonial administrations and maintained correspondence with various factions in each locale. This strategy allowed him to gain multiple perspectives on events and exert leverage over their actions. Colonial officers, accordingly, provided requested materials to signal not just competence but also trustworthiness, and those writing to Blathwayt often complained about their rivals and predecessors. For example, Governor of Bermuda Robert Robinson, responding to a solicitation for a wide body of materials, wrote to Blathwayt in March 1689 that he would send home lists of the names of all military, political, and commercial officers and of recent court sessions. But, he explained, "Theres one thing may hinder the Lords satisfaction that is thee Book of Records (which I have severall things out of which shall also bee sent home) is put out of the way & so lost to me being not to bee found. Tho I have demanded it severall times as likewise other Recordes."[31] Colonial officials curried metropolitan goodwill by presenting themselves as addressing the failures of their rivals, generating a surge in communication between Whitehall and its colonial administrators and informants that enabled Blathwayt to enhance his information resources.

Finally, like Williamson, Blathwayt's office extracted, recombined, and recirculated texts received from colonial dominions, often for other officials in the regime.[32] Most notably, the instructions, commissions, and warrants generated and archived by previous Councils were adapted for the formation of new iterations, a practice which facilitated administrative continuity while localizing the Plantation Office archive as the central bank of imperial authority. As Asheesh Siddique has argued, the paperwork it promulgated functioned as an imperial constitution from the Restoration well into the eighteenth century.[33]

In short, the practices devised for administering and knowing Britain and the Continent were also directed toward colonial territories: imperial knowledge was forged by the structured circulation of texts. When these texts cycled into the offices in London, they were subject to the collection, categorization, extraction, recombination, and dissemination fundamental to early modern British administration. This constellation of practices enabled Whitehall's centralized knowledge of Britain's colonies and its efforts to coordinate political action in them.[34]

Blathwayt's system, however, permitted only specific ways of knowing the colonies, for despite its volume, regularization, and centralization, his network's structure constrained what entered the system. The administrative procedures introduced by Blathwayt ensured the constant replication of an official perspective by the projection of past precedents and circulation of official laws and acts throughout the empire. Similarly, the focus on receiving journals, laws, and other formal texts from the colonies tethered imperial knowledge to the correspondents who provided them. The right to participate in imperial knowledge making was thus reserved to an exclusive body of people and texts. Indeed, it is striking how absent direct testimony from ordinary colonists was from Blathwayt's archive—let alone from Indigenous or enslaved African-descended peoples, whose interests and experience went fully unrepresented. These silences were a consequence of restricting regular communication to a select and exclusionary few in competition with others, rather than soliciting local informants or galvanizing a broader public through which to circulate information.[35] The information was dense, but the network was concentrated.

Moreover, the competitive terrain Blathwayt encouraged influenced the information he received. Colonial correspondents operated with strong incentives to conceal unpleasant local circumstances and suppress unwanted communications. Accordingly, they demonized their enemies, conflated personal and imperial interests, and concealed interactions with local informants—further narrowing the vision of the imperial network. Such practices also devalued the pointillist recitation of news characteristic of Williamson's regime. The result was a court politics conducted at a distance, in which the closed-circuit structure and the tenor of agonistic communication restricted what colonial phenomena were transmitted into metropolitan view.

Blathwayt's imperial knowledge depended on the lens of his network to observe colonial events and experiences, and through it, he developed a grasp of the early English empire without parallel among administrators of his day. But like all lenses, his introduced refractions that reinforced the perspective it privileged.[36] His information system catalyzed an autonomous body of imperial writing—a cosmos of texts—distinct from the world and shaped as a literary exercise from the center.[37] It was extremely unrepresentatively white, male, Protestant, and elite, and little concerned with those external to it in practice or in theory. And the omissions, occlusions, objectifications, and distortions of this blinkered information system—during a period in which Britain's involvement and dependence on the horrors of the Atlantic slave trade was rapidly accelerating—have reverberated through and been amplified by those subsequent historians who have taken its communications as transparent evidence of the colonial past.[38]

Inscription perpetuated inscription. But as Blathwayt's cracked lens suggests, the material and sociological conditions for generating information stipulated a systemically partial knowledge of the world, one which reinforced and exacerbated preexisting hierarchies and exclusions.

* * *

Though William Petyt died in 1707 before the reforms he had suggested to the parliamentary commission were finished, his deputy George Holmes oversaw their completion and then remained a conscientious steward until his death in 1749 as the keepership fell to a series of figures who treated it as a sinecure. Continuity brought order, and in the last decade of the century, Keeper Thomas Astle's response to inquiries from the Lords Commissioners of the Treasury reveal that the Tower of London Record Office remained a model of organization. As he explained, the records were "in the most excellent Order, and are lockt up in Eighteen Close Presses, beginning with King John in 1199 and ending with the 22nd of Edward the fourth in 1483, in exact chronological Order, each Year in each Reign having the Records of such year in Separate Partitions, with complete Calendars and Indexes of people and places [*Virorum et locorum*] alphabetical to the same, in as much as professional men and Historians have said that they never consulted an office more ready for the production of any things required."[39] To the Lords' questions of its specific needs, Astle explained that a few calendars needed recopying; the roof needed reinforcement; it could use a rug, some chairs, and a new fireplace fender; and it had been five years since its last paint job.[40] Overall, the Tower was a comfortable place to work.

By contrast, the State Paper Office experienced virtual abandonment. Its keepership, too, became a sinecure, often attached to Undersecretaries of State but without clerks. According to the colonial administrator William Knox, in 1764 Secretary to the Board of Trade John Pownall inquired after a book of pre-Restoration Privy Council orders and was surprised to learn that "there were no books there of so old a date" in the Council office. However, "one of the clerks told him, there were several old books in a room over the gateway into Privy Garden, which was then standing, and that it was probable he might find what he wanted there." As he continued, "My indefatigable friend immediately climbed up the rotten staircase, and finding the door of the room fastened by a lock, which had not been opened for many years, and to which there was no key to

FIGURE 20. Image of Tower of London Record Office in 1801, drawn by Charles Tomkins. © The Trustees of the British Museum. By permission.

be found, procured a smith to break it open with his sledge-hammer; which being done, he was covered with a cloud of dust, raised by a flock of pigeons, who had long made that room (the windows being broken) their dwelling pace. When the cloud was dissipated, he removed the filth, and there found the books he was in search of, with many ancient and public records." According to Knox, Pownall contacted Prime Minister George Grenville about his discovery, and the two hatched a plan for an office that would rectify "the little care which had been taken of public documents" produced in the reigns prior to George III.[41] The State Paper Office evidently required reinvention.[42]

As the divergent fates of the Tower and the State Paper Office suggest, there was not a linear and universal improvement or rationalization of British archives in the eighteenth century.[43] But the careers of those involved in restoring the forgotten Paper Office expose how inscription-based practices of forging political knowledge had become irreversibly entrenched. Pownall was a tireless seeker of administrative precedents, Knox published this recollection within a compilation of state papers, and both along with Grenville had lengthy careers amid the relentless correspondence and paperwork of high offices. While specific institutions might shrink into obscurity, the constellation of practices examined in this book became ubiquitous, essential to governance and the public dimension of British politics throughout the British archipelago, North American and Caribbean colonies, and subcontinent. Administration remained dependent on material technologies for the production, replication, and comparison of information. The post office, packet ships, and new roads combined to facilitate the ease and dependability of correspondence and news. The empire was supported by a military and strengthened by a complex regime of taxation, which both demanded voluminous paperwork. And the collected body of instructions, commissions, patents, and correspondence supplied the constitution of imperial and domestic governance.[44]

At the same time, publications such as Thomas Rymer's *Foedera*, a collection of England's treaties with foreign powers compiled from the Tower and Exchequer—the vast majority of whose twenty volumes were edited by Holmes—marked a singular achievement in European diplomacy. Similarly, works such as Thomas Madox's *History of the Exchequer* and the six-volume collection of parliamentary records in the Tower issued between 1766 and 1777—which Astle helped bring to completion—testify to a thriving antiquarian community.[45] The institutional and textual incarnations that embodied the regime of inscription shifted, but the practices and values endured, further suffusing political life in constantly evolving forms.[46]

* * *

From the mid-sixteenth to the late seventeenth century, the technology of paper and the practices of inscription, preservation, and circulation it enabled revolutionized the structure of politics in Britain. This replicable, durable, transportable material enhanced the capacity to convert experience into writing, reproduce existing texts, communicate over space, sustain thoughts and observations over time, and compare, collate, and recombine inscriptions into new forms. The practices it inspired traversed spheres from a public ravenous for news to a modern information state characterized by bureaucratic institutions wedded to past practice, to scholarship that resuscitated the past to reenvisage the present and future, to imperial administrators who dreamed of using paperwork to control those they sought to govern.

While the visions of the world erected through inscriptive practices challenged custom, memory, and orality as modes of authority, their avatars also used the writings they collected to espouse alternative social organizations and political constitutions. The specific forms they recommended, however, were not predetermined. Rather, paper and inscription provided resources that individuals mobilized and manipulated in the efforts to secure power, patronage, and authority.[47] The importance of such social forces accounts for some of the ironies throughout this book—how, for example, an individual such as Thomas Wilson proclaimed the objectivity of the collection of sources he had carefully curated, or how he crystallized an image of a long-standing institutionalized state by binding together texts proposing provisional solutions. The papers individuals collected and solicited did not control their visions of politics—though these might shape possibilities—but stimulated creative adaptations of the regime of inscription fitted to local circumstances.

William Petyt's and William Blathwayt's experiences exemplify the epistemic benefits and limitations of this regime. For both, a thirst for information endowed them with robust knowledge. At the same time, their practices posed their own pitfalls. Petyt's confidence in his erudition led him to project his own present into the past, conjuring an illusory ancient history of medieval administration that made his Whiggish history a watchword for anachronism. Blathwayt's densely concentrated imperial networks furnished him with unprecedented volumes of information but also obscured many aspects of colonial experience—compounding his systemic disinterest in the experience of those who suffered under it. Inscription was a powerful tool, but it created a model of the world rather than a mirror to it, and the transformations it engendered often resulted from replicating and magnifying what was already seen rather than leading to discovery or diversification of knowledge.

The long trajectory of early modern Europe highlights the challenge of today's media landscape, when novel technologies boast that they can capture and connect the world in full. For all their power, speed, accessibility, and scale, and despite the breathless prophecies of their advocates and engineers, they convey a profoundly limited selection of recent and contemporary experience, and one that has thus far proven deeply susceptible to deliberate manipulation and exploitation. And for all the novelty of such technologies, their epistemic problems stem from quandaries that confronted early modern record keepers: Who has the right to access the materials? What do they make visible and what do they obscure? How can they be instilled with value and meaning? What qualifies as meriting public interest? How can proper use be distinguished from misuse, and how can this line be maintained? The dangers resulting from specific responses to these problems—or, worse, lack of engagement with them—also resonate across time: that texts not transitioned to new formats will simply disappear, that communities without access to them will operate at increasingly severe disadvantage, that meaningful knowledge not foregrounded in them will be marginalized and forgotten, and above all, that systemic errors and deliberate distortions will be amplified and reinforced. For record keepers and media managers in both past and present, the social dominance and concomitant epistemic limitations of their technologies threaten to wash the past into a sea of forgetting, carrying away the means to understand not only the present but the trajectory of human history.

Media revolutions, however, no matter when they occur, do not have inevitable effects. Rather, they create opportunities that can be seized upon, whether to forge communal ties and understanding or to obscure, deepen, or exploit inherited fissures in our social bonds. The stranglehold contemporary technologies are rapidly asserting over communication, information, and knowledge intensifies the urgency for those who recognize their hazards as well as their possibilities to devise methods to capture humanity's place in the world responsibly, cognizant—in a way early modern Britons rarely were—of distortions they risk introducing and people, labor, and knowledge they might efface. The imperative of our moment entails discerning the sounds and silences in the archive of the past and present we have, and salvaging and protecting those most vulnerable to political and technological threat from harmful and deliberate perversion or the prospect of perpetual oblivion—or, put another way, preventing technologies from imprisoning us in a benighted simulacrum of our world. Such self-consciousness concerning the media we rely on to know, to communicate, and to act is utterly essential as we engage in the perpetual project of reimagining humanity's past and future.

Abbreviations

BL   British Library, London
Bodl.   Bodleian Library, Oxford
CCST   *A Complete Collection of State Trials and Proceedings for High Treason and Other Crimes and Misdemeanors*, ed. Thomas Bayly Howell, 34 vols. (London: Hansard, 1816–28)
CD, 1621   *Commons Debates, 1621*, 7 vols., ed. Wallace Notestein, Frances Helen Relf, and Hartley Simpson (New Haven, CT: Yale University Press, 1935)
CD, 1628   *Commons Debates, 1628*, 6 vols., ed. Robert C. Johnson, et al. (New Haven, CT: Yale University Press, 1977–83)
CEB   *The Colonial Entry Books*, ed. C. S. S. Higham (London: Society for Promoting Christian Knowledge, 1921)
CJ   *Journal of the House of Commons, 1547–1830*, 85 vols. (London: H. M. Stationery Office, 1837–)
CoA   College of Arms, London
CP   Cecil Papers, Hatfield House, Hertfordshire, United Kingdom
CW   John D. Rockefeller Jr. Library, Colonial Williamsburg, Williamsburg, Virginia
DWP   *The Despatches of William Perwich, English Agent in Paris, 1669–1677*, ed. M. Beryl Curran (London: Royal Historical Society, 1903)
EHR   *English Historical Review*
FSL   Folger Shakespeare Library, Washington, DC
G&C   Gonville and Caius College Library, Cambridge
HEH   Henry E. Huntington Library, San Marino, California
HJ   *Historical Journal*
HLQ   *Huntington Library Quarterly*
HR   *Historical Research*
ITL   Inner Temple Library, London
JBS   *Journal of British Studies*
JEMH   *Journal of Early Modern History*
JHI   *Journal of the History of Ideas*

JMH	*Journal of Modern History*
JSA	*Journal of the Society of Archivists*
LJ	*Journal of the House of Lords, 1509–1832*, 64 vols. (London: H. M. Stationery Office, 1767–1830)
LPL	Lambeth Palace Library, London
PA	Parliamentary Archive, Palace of Westminster, United Kingdom
PH	*Parliamentary History*
P&P	*Past & Present*
SP	State Paper Office Records, the National Archives, Kew, United Kingdom
TNA	The National Archives, Kew, United Kingdom
WC	*Letters Addressed from London to Sir Joseph Williamson While Plenipotentiary at the Congress of Cologne in the Years 1673 and 1674*, 2 vols., ed. W. D. Christie (London: Camden Society, 1874)
WCRO	Warwickshire County Record Office
WMQ	*William and Mary Quarterly*
YBL	Yale Beinecke Library, New Haven, Connecticut

Manuscripts and Manuscript Collections Cited

The National Archives (TNA), Kew, UK

C (Chancery Records)
CO (Colonial Office Records)
CRES (Records of the Crown Estate)
E (Exchequer Records)
IND (Indexes to Various Series)
OBS (Obsolete Lists and Indexes)
PC (Privy Council Records)
PRO (Public Record Office Records)
SP (State Paper Office Records)

Bodleian Library (Bodl.), Oxford

Additional MS
Ashmole MS
Carte MS
Eng. Hist. MS
Eng. Let. MS
Gough MS
Laud Misc. MS
Rawlinson MS
Tanner MS
Top. Gen. MS

British Library (BL), London

Additional MS
Cotton MS
Egerton MS
Hargrave MS
Harley MS
Lansdowne MS

Sloane MS
Stowe MS

College of Arms (CoA), London

MS B1
MS B4
MS B5
MS B15
MS B 32
MS M5c
MS Vincent 3

Folger Shakespeare Library (FSL), Washington, DC

MS V.a.99
MS V.a.182
MS V.b.1
MS V.b.113
MS V.b.117–121
MS V.b.368

Gonville and Caius Library (G&C), Cambridge

MS 330/582
MS 331/583
MS 332/584
MS 580/685

Hatfield House, Hertfordshire, UK

Cecil Papers

Henry E. Huntington Library (HEH), San Marino, CA

BL (William Blathwayt Papers)
EL (Ellesmere Collection)
HM (Historical Manuscripts)
ST (Stowe Collection)

Inner Temple Library (ITL), London

Petyt MS

Lambeth Palace Library (LPL), London

LPL MS 323
LPL MS 1093
LPL MS 2000

London Metropolitan Archive, London

CLC/270/MS03342

National Library of Jamaica, Kingston

MS 159

Newberry Library, Chicago

Ayer MS 827

Parliamentary Archive (PA), Westminster, UK

PA HL/PO/JO/10/1/199
PA HL/PO/JO/10/6/67/2029
PA HC/LB/1/102

John D. Rockefeller Library, Colonial Williamsburg (CW), Williamsburg, VA

William Blathwayt Papers

John Rylands Library, Manchester, UK

Ryl. Lat. MS 318
Ryl. Lat. MS 319

Sheffield City Archives, Sheffield, UK

WWM/Str P 32

Society of Antiquaries, London

MS 72/22
MS 125

Staffordshire Record Office, Stafford, UK

MS D(W)1778/V/1413

University of Illinois–Champaign Rare Book and Manuscript Library, Urbana, IL

Pre-1650 MSS 0100

Warwickshire County Record Office (WCRO), Warwick, UK

CR 2017/C97/1-3
CR 2017/C48/101
CR 2017/C48/145
CR 1998 Large Carved Box No. 67

Yale Beinecke Library (YBL), New Haven, CT

GEN MS 418
Osborn MS fb 60
Osborn MS fb 84
Osborn MS fb 212
Osborn MS 370
Osborn MS 1287

Notes

All translations are my own unless otherwise noted. Dates are given in the new style of the Gregorian calendar, with the year beginning on January 1. While I have retained the original capitalization and spelling in quotations, I have silently expanded abbreviations and contractions, modified some punctuation for purposes of clarity, removed superfluous italicization, and silently corrected dates to the Gregorian calendar. Only shortened citations are used in the notes; corresponding full citations appear in the bibliography.

Introduction

1. For recent overviews of studies of early modern archives, see Yale, "The History of Archives"; Walsham, introduction to "The Social History of the Archive." For European archives, see the classic Bautier, "La Phase Cruciale"; more recently, see Head, "Knowing Like a State"; Blair and Milligan, "Toward a Cultural History of Archives"; de Vivo, *Information and Communication in Venice*; Head, "Mirroring Governance"; Head, "Archival Knowledge Cultures in Europe"; Sternberg, "Manipulating Information in the Ancien Régime"; Soll, *The Information Master*; Rule and Trotter, *A World of Paper*; de Vivo, Guidi, and Silvestri, "Archival Transformations in Early Modern European History"; Brendecke, *The Empirical Empire*; Corens, Peters, and Walsham, "The Social History of the Archive"; Friedrich, *The Birth of the Archive*; Head, *Making Archives in Early Modern Europe*. For archives in early modern England, see Wernham, "The Public Records in the 16th and 17th Centuries"; Ross, "The Memorial Culture of Early Modern English Lawyers"; Slack, "Government and Information in Seventeenth Century England"; Yale, "With Slips and Scraps"; Popper, "From Abbey to Archive"; Halliday, "Authority in the Archives"; Starza Smith, *John Donne and the Conway Papers*. For colonial archives, see epilogue, n 37.

2. BL Harley MS 6751, f. 69v.

3. SP 29/143, f. 265. Many of the original records concerning early modern British archival management have been printed in the appendix to the *Thirtieth Annual Report of the Deputy Keeper of the Public Records*. Comparably, many records

related to Italian archives are now available in de Vivo, Guidi, and Silvestri, *Fonti per la storia degli archivi*.

4. SP 29/143, f. 265.

5. TNA C 272/1, f. 109.

6. SP 29/143, f. 265.

7. TNA C 272/1, f. 64r.

8. TNA C 272/1, f. 130.

9. Similarly, see Shapin, "The Invisible Technician;" Hunt, "The Early Modern Secretary and the Archive"; Blair, "New Knowledge-Makers."

10. They were not the only women present in the Tower. A contemporary register record two visits by a "Mrs Morley," who visited on behalf of "Mr Bernard of the Treasurer's Remembrancers Office" (TNA C 272/1, f. 8r, 9r.; TNA C 272/1, f. 14r). Mrs. Morley may have been married to "Esquire Morley," who visited the Tower in October of that year and was noted as "Mr Petyt's friend"; William Petyt was a frequent visitor and would become its keeper (TNA C 272/1, 8r, 9r). The register also notes occasional visits by male agents employed by women; for example, in August 1670, "Mr [Nicholas] Hooke of the Subpoena Office in Chancery" came on behalf of Lady Alice Lisle (TNA C 272/1, f. 9r, 10r). Similarly, Henry Champion was a frequent visitor to the Tower, sometimes as solicitor for the Countess of Northumberland (TNA C 272/1, May 1673, June 1674, November 1674, January 1764). These women were both widows and thus likely controlled their own economic affairs. For women in the Plantation Office, see Emanuel, "'Great weights hang by small wires.'"

11. For the extent and limitations to which archives illuminate early modern British women's lives, see Jewell, *Women in Medieval England*, 1–18; Mendelson and Crawford, *Women in Early Modern England*, 345–429; Wood, *Riot, Rebellion, and Popular Politics*, 100–111; Daybell, *Women and Politics in Early Modern England*, esp. 1–20, 114–31; Stretton, "Women, Legal Records, and the Problem of the Lawyer's Hand"; Shepard, "Worthless Witnesses?"; Popper, "Inscription and Political Exclusion." Women, especially those of high status, had strategies to exert some agency in law courts and other public forums; see Stretton, *Women Waging Law*; Chalus, "Elite Women, Social Politics, and the Political World"; Mendelson and Crawford, *Women in Early Modern England*, 345–430; B. Harris, *English Aristocratic Women*, 175–209.

12. Trouillot, *Silencing the Past*; Stoler, *Along the Archival Grain*; Fuentes, *Dispossessed Lives*. On paperwork as a gendered epistemic technology, see Daybell, "Gendered Archival Practices"; Gowing, "Girls on Forms"; Bittel, Leong, and Von Oertzen, *Working with Paper*.

13. Popper, "Archives and the Boundaries of Early Modern Science."

14. My primary reference point here is Latour and Woolgar, *Laboratory Life*, though the inscriptions I examine differ from theirs by being more consistently textual than graphic, collected rather than manufactured, and older rather than new.

15. Clanchy, *From Memory to Written Record*.

16. The best overview of England's administrative output for the period remains Elton, *England, 1200–1640*.

17. More attention has recently been called for in Bellingradt and Reynolds, *The Paper Trade*, especially Bellingradt's introduction, 1–27. See also Mueller, *White Magic*; Williams, "Unfolding Diplomatic Paper and Paper Practices." Among major publications reflecting aspects of the increased availability of paper, see Febvre and Martin, *L'apparition du livre*; Eisenstein, *The Printing Revolution*; Love, *Scribal Publication in Seventeenth-Century England*; Blair, *Too Much To Know*.

18. See Lyall, "Materials: The Paper Revolution." Small quantities were imported earlier; see da Rold, "Networks of Paper in Medieval England."

19. See D. Coleman, *The British Paper Industry*, 24–88; Bland, "The London Book Trade in 1600." A *ream* is about five hundred sheets of paper; the import records do not indicate the size of the paper. Printers would likely have purchased *folios* with the option to fold them into *quarto*, *octavo*, and *duodecimo* sized sheets; individuals tended to purchase *quires* of twenty-five sheets of variable sizes.

20. Elton, *Policy and Police*.

21. This total includes 303 from SP 1–7, 49, 60; there are others scattered in classes such as SP 46/6, but not in such quantities as to change these numbers significantly.

22. Lake and Questier, "Puritans, Papists, and the 'Public Sphere'"; Lake, "The Politics of 'Popularity' and the Public Sphere."

23. For some related materials, see Stallybrass, "Little Jobs"; Gowing, "Girls on Forms"; more broadly, see Groebner, *Who Are You?*

24. For early modern petitioning, see the Brody Waddell–led project "The Power of Petitioning in Seventeenth-Century England" (https://petitioning.history.ac.uk/about/team), which includes many resources. For the vertical connections, see in particular Lake, *Bad Queen Bess?*; Chou, "Parliamentary Mind"; Coast, "Speaking for the People." For the material aspects of petitions, see Dabhoiwala, "Writing Petitions in Early Modern England."

25. Grafton, *What Was History?*; Popper, *Walter Ralegh's "History of the World"*; Gajda, *The Earl of Essex and Late Elizabethan Political Culture*.

26. Grafton and Siraisi, *Natural Particulars;* Pomata and Siraisi, *Historia*; Pomata, "Observation Rising."

27. For secretarial practice, see Dover, *Secretaries and Statecraft in the Early Modern World*.

28. Harold Love memorably has described early modern England as a culture of transcription (Love, *Scribal Publication*, 200).

29. Findlen, *Possessing Nature*; see also Swann, *Curiosities and Texts*. For collecting papers as a political practice, see Popper, "Archives and the Boundaries of Early Modern Science"; Halliday, "Authority in the Archives"; Millstone, *Manuscript Circulation and the Invention of Politics*; Yale, *Sociable Knowledge*.

30. R. Yeo, *Notebooks, Virtuosi, and Early Modern Science*.

31. For a later media society, see Darnton, "An Early Information Society"; see also Ghobrial, *The Whispers of Cities*.

32. BL Harley MS 1857, f. 42v–43r.

33. Society of Antiquaries MS 125.

34. University of Illinois–Champaign Rare Book and Manuscript Library Pre-1650 MSS 0100. BL Egerton MS 3370 has the same note.

35. I have located almost 120 and consulted nearly 100, relying in part on consultations with Alan Nelson, Holger Syme, and archivists at many institutions.

36. This partial updating was characteristic—for example, Lewis Lewkenor was created Master of the Ceremonies in 1603, but he does not appear in any "Book of Offices" I have seen until 1608. As a result, copies sometimes contain notes by scholars and archivists struggling to figure out their dates of creation; see, for example, HEH EL 1198.

37. Buckhurst's is FSL MSS V.a.99; Egerton's are HEH EL 6206b, HEH 3042b, and HEH EL 1198; Caesar's are in BL Lansdowne MS 171, BL Add. MS 11405, and TNA CRES 40/191; Strafford's is Sheffield City Archives WWM/Str P 32; Dodderidge's is BL Sloane MS 3479; Legge's is Staffordshire Record Office MS D(W)1778/V/1413. Carleton's is listed in an inventory of his books, SP 16/473, f. 237.

38. *Trevelyan Papers, Part III*, 47–57.

39. Preceded by the Latin equivalent "Omnia cum retines manibus mirabile si non / Officium obtineas multis e millibus unum. Si non tibi saltem amicis." This ditty is in BL Harley MS 1848 and FSL MS V.b.113.

40. Peers's are FSL MSS V.b.117–121.

41. FSL MSS V.b.117.

42. For the political culture of scribes, see Millstone, *Manuscript Circulation*.

43. Though there is little evidence explaining the halt in production of such manuscripts after the 1630s, they continued to circulate, and late seventeenth-century antiquarians such as Peter de Neve (BL Add. MS 12508 and BL Add. MS 12512) and George Maynwaring, Richmond Herald (HEH HM 174) owned copies.

44. For a later parallel, see Slauter, "Write Up Your Dead."

45. Haward, *The Charges Issuing forth of the Crown Revenue* (1647), A3r.

46. See similarly Bulman, "Introduction: Post-Revisionism," though my approach draws more on the field of the history of knowledge.

47. I should acknowledge that prioritizing these two archives may have led me to emphasize the centralizing and statist elements of early modern British governance, but part of my argument here is that such archives created the reality of that kind of state.

48. For paper practices in modern political work and epistemology, see Becker and Clark, *Little Tools of Knowledge*; Vismann, *Files*; Kafka, *The Demon of Writing*; Gitelman, *Paper Knowledge*. For scholarship ascribing causal power to information flows, see Headrick, *When Information Came of Age*; Cortada, "Shaping Information History"; Cortada, "The Information Ecosystems of National Diplomacy."

49. Brewer, *The Sinews of Power*; Hindle, *The State and Social Change*; Braddick, *State Formation in Early Modern England*; Ash, *The Draining of the Fens*.

Chapter One

1. For Burghley's practices, see Alford, *The Early Elizabethan Polity*; N. Jones, *Governing by Virtue*. For his secretariat, see A. Smith, "The Secretariats of the Cecils."
2. Peltonen, *Classical Humanism and Republicanism*.
3. SP 45/20, f. 22r.
4. Cf. BL Lansdowne MS 48, f. 78v–79r.
5. Notably, Burghley held that better attention to record keeping would ameliorate the persistent tumult in Ireland. See CP 153/103, in which Burghley's minutes from a Privy Council meeting recommend "to take order that the records, both of the crowne and of the revenue, be better kept," and SP 63/33, f. 48, in which Burghley recommended the printing of the statutes in Ireland in 1571. For Irish "Books of Offices," see SP 63/64, f. 5; SP 63/165, f. 3; SP 63/218, f. 82; SP 63/222, f. 159; SP 63/231, f. 202; SP 63/237, f. 197; SP 63/344, f. 5.
6. For Beale's collection, see *Catalogue of the Additions to the Manuscripts: The Yelverton Manuscripts*. For Beale, see Taviner, "Robert Beale and the Elizabethan Polity"; Collinson, "Servants and Citizens"; Gehring, *Diplomatic Intelligence*.
7. For the Parker circle, see Grafton, "Church History in Early Modern Europe"; Grafton, "Matthew Parker"; McMahon, "Matthew Parker and the Practice of Church History." For Flacius, see Lyon, "Baudouin, Flacius, and the Plan for the Magdeburg Centuries"; Bollbuck, "Searching for the True Religion." For medieval sources in early modern history writing, see McKisack, *Medieval History in the Tudor Age*; Summit, *Memory's Library*.
8. For the impact of the Dissolution, see Carley, "Monastic Collections and their Disposal"; Carley, "The Dispersal of the Monastic Libraries and the Salvaging of the Spoils"; Harding, "Monastic Records and the Dissolution."
9. Graves, *Thomas Norton*, esp. 55–57, 62.
10. For the textualization of political knowledge in Europe, see Head, *Making Archives in Early Modern Europe*; Teuscher, *Lords' Rights and Peasant Stories*; Dover, *Information Revolution*. For the authority of writing in early modern England, see A. Fox, "Custom, Memory, and the Authority of Writing"; A. Fox, *Oral and Literate Culture in England*; Wood, *Memory of the People*, 247–86.
11. For the Tower records, see Hallam, "The Tower of London as Record Office"; see also Wernham, "The Public Records in the 16th and 17th Centuries." Much of the work on English archives has focused on municipal or personal archives; see Cain, "Robert Smith and the Reform of the Archives of the City of London"; Griffiths, "Secrecy and Authority"; Griffiths, "Local Arithmetic"; Wood, *Memory of the People*, 256-71; Bishop, "The Clerk's Tale"; Wood, "Tales from the 'Yarmouth Hutch.'"
12. Clanchy, *From Memory to Written Record*.
13. Norman Jones has observed that the map in HEH HM 160, discussed subsequently, is likely by Lawrence Nowell, which would suggest a long-continuing relationship between the two.

14. Anderson, "Henry, Lord Stafford." For the full context, see C. Coleman, "Artifice or Accident?" For the duke's record keeping, see Rawcliffe, "A Tudor Nobleman as Archivist."

15. See Youngs, *The Letter-Book of Henry, Lord Stafford*.

16. SP 12/33, f. 2.

17. BL Lansdowne MS 113, f. 103r. SP 12/33, f. 2 is a slightly different version.

18. BL Lansdowne MS 113, f. 103r.

19. BL Lansdowne MS 113, f. 107v. "Et cum perciperem quanta tibi fuerat voluntas videndi et intelligendi Acta, ceteraque Archiva intra Turrim (ut illis cognitis maior foret Reg[is] maiestatis servitus)."

20. BL Lansdowne MS 113, f. 108r. "Cepi omnia mea studia et laborem in Registeriis compilandis consumere."

21. BL Lansdowne MS 113, f. 107v. "Sic meas studias, curas et cogitationes postea destinavi ut intra unius Anni curriculum ante mortem illius prestantiss. viri omnia Chartarum scrinia a primo Anno R[egis] John usque ad ultimum annum R[egis] edwardi quarti in breve compendium sive Repertorium compilarem."

22. BL Lansdowne MS 113, f. 108r. "Et ea omnia in ex magna volumina congessi. Quae opera quam sunt necessaria R[ege] Maiest[ate] et quam utilia tot Reip[ublicae] tuae Censurae subiiciam."

23. BL Lansdowne MS 113, f. 108v. "Promittam de mea fide quod intra quatuor Annos (si tam diu vivens permansero) fiscalem sive feodaricum librum exhibebo Regi Maiest[ate] qui omnia feoda militum per universos Comitatus regni complectatur."

24. SP 12/42, f. 101. I thank Norm Jones for informing me that they were never delivered.

25. For Cordell's objection, see SP 12/43, f. 6r. For Bowyer's response, BL Lansdowne MS 113, f. 109r–112v, quote at 112r.

26. Copies of this text include BL Harley MS 94, f. 41r–45r, which belonged to Sir Simonds D'Ewes; John Borough's is TNA OBS 1/1273 (copied in BL Add. MS 48008, f. 396r–408v); Elias Ashmole's is Bodl. Ashmole MS 861, f. 227r–230; William Petyt's is SP 46/167, f. 296r; Ralph Jennings's is TNA OBS 1/1271; and Thomas Astle's is BL Stowe MS 543, f. 1r–27r.

27. For the relationships between written instruments and forms of archival organization, see Head, *Making Archives in Early Modern Europe*.

28. For Bowyer's, see TNA OBS 1/1273 (copied in BL Add. MS 48008, f. 396r–408v); for Jennings's, see TNA OBS 1/1271.

29. For the importance of the materiality of early modern archives, see Stallybrass and Wolfe, "The Material Culture of Record-Keeping in Early Modern Archives."

30. CoA MS B15.

31. CoA MS B1. He added additional paratextual elements in others; he gave one of the two collections he made of extracts of charter rolls a table of contents at the end. CoA MS B4 (Charter Rolls from John to Henry III), f. 129; the second half is CoA MS B5.

32. SP 12/42, f. 101.

33. BL Add. MS 21923. As a herald, Bowyer knew how to compose and interpret arms (cf. CoA MS B22).

34. HEH HM 160, online as https://hdl.huntington.org/digital/collection/p15150coll7/id/44656. I thank Norman Jones, Vanessa Wilkie, and Heather James for stimulating conversation and insights concerning this manuscript.

35. HEH HM 160, f. 3v. "Quam quidem operam meam in tres partes ita diduxi, ut Authentice quaedam, Historice nonulla, caeteris Poetice descripserim. Nam cum praecipua argumenti huius portio ex actis Regiis excerpatur, Authenticum illud iure dici meretur. Historice autem non solum maiorum tuorum vitas, et res gestas easque breviter perstrinxi, Sed et illorum Regum, quorum liberalitate has illi dignitates percepereunt. Poetarum autem illud misterium, quod illorum Regum et Principum effigies atque insignia pictura expresserim, carmine effinxerim."

36. HEH HM 160, f. 10v.

37. HEH HM 160, f. 15v.

38. HEH HM 160, f. 20r–v, f. 24r–34r; f. 44r–59v, f. 60r–83r.

39. SP 12/43, f. 139.

40. BL Lansdowne MS 25, f. 116r.

41. BL Stowe MS 543, f. 53r–v.

42. These three volumes are now TNA OBS 1/249–251. It is possible that these volumes were produced by Bowyer or even Stafford. They continued to be used into the late seventeenth century, when Bishop Edward Stillingfleet copied them into one volume, equipped with a massive index (BL Harley MS 744).

43. Copies include BL Cotton MS Titus B VI, f. 247; Bodl. Rawlinson MS B. 384, f. 21r; BL Sloane MS 262, f. 35v; ITL Petyt MS 538.19, f. 149v ff.

44. BL Stowe MS 543, f. 58r–v. For Lambarde, see "William Lambarde's Reading, Revision and Reception."

45. BL Stowe MS 543, f. 55r–57v. Four days later, Lambarde presented his "Pandect" to the elderly queen in her Privy Chamber in Greenwich. Because, upon encountering the name of Richard II, she reportedly declared, "I am Richard II. Know ye not that?" scholars have examined this event as a potential reference to the staging of Shakespeare's play *Richard II* that allegedly inspired a revolt by the Earl of Essex's men (one swiftly quashed by the queen's forces). But this was a digression, and the event's rationale was to present an index to the Tower records to Elizabeth, who responded by asking questions about her government's records.

46. CoA MS B 32, f. 52 ff. The relevant pages of the volume are unpaginated.

47. These fees only applied to records for which there were decent calendars—for others, as the lawyer Thomas Powell explained, "your fees must answer the Clarkes extraordinarie paines." Powell, *Direction for Search of Records*, 14–15.

48. BL Lansdowne MS 25, f.117; for the expenses, see BL Cotton MS Titus B VI, f. 247.

49. SP 75/1, f. 11r–14v. For further perusals for Danish treaties under Elizabeth, see HEH HM 4546 and CP 38/51.

50. BL Cotton MS Galba C VIII, f. 102r–v.

51. BL Add. MS 48129, f. 92. See S. Adams, "Elizabeth I and the Sovereignty of the Netherlands."

52. For the Elizabethan Society of Antiquaries, see Van Norden, "The Elizabethan College of Antiquaries"; Kennedy, "Those Who Stayed."

53. For Thynne, see Carlson, "The Writings and Manuscript Collections." For the diversification of materials seen as conducive to historical knowledge, see Woolf, *The Social Circulation of the Past*.

54. Kewes, Archer, and Heal, *The Oxford Handbook of Holinshed's Chronicles*.

55. See, for example, HEH EL 1137 and BL Stowe MS 1047.

56. For Thynne's similar volume on the history of the lord treasurer, see BL Stowe MS 573.

57. HEH EL 26/a/6.

58. Thynne disagreed with those who dated the origins of this office to after the eleventh-century Norman Conquest because "I have warrantes of Recordes and historyes which name certene Chauncellors longe before that tyme" (HEH EL 26/a/6, f. 6r). Though Thynne acknowledged that critics might argue that these texts "were "counterfetted by religious persons when they had landes & knewe not who gave yt to them," he insisted that "everye one maye easely condempne all Antiquitye and recordes and with one blast at one instant overblowe the credytte of everye thinge" (HEH EL 26/a/6, f. 6v).

59. HEH EL 26/a/6, f. 11r.

60. HEH EL 26/a/6, f. 9v.

61. W. Jones, *The Elizabethan Court of Chancery*. For the increasing centrality of paperwork and secretariats to Elizabethan government, see Andreani, *The Elizabethan Secretariat and the Signet Office*.

62. TNA C 275/5—index to record class C 54—has, exceptionally, a calendar of the close rolls and an index.

63. TNA C 275/12, f. 20r.

64. Cf. TNA C 274/1; index to record class C 66.

65. TNA IND 1/1430; index to record class C 33.

66. TNA C 274/9.

67. TNA E 14/5.

68. Riordan, "'The King's Library of Manuscripts.'" For a speculative treatment of its early history, see Platt, "The Elizabethan 'Foreign Office.'"

69. BL Stowe MS 162. For this source see Tu, "The Dispersal of Francis Walsingham's Papers"; Williamson, "Archival Practice and the Production of Knowledge."

70. BL Harley MS 6035, f. 107v–111r.

71. BL Stowe MS 162, f. 2v–3v.

72. BL Stowe MS 162, f. 47r–50v.

73. For the practices of secretariats in early modern England, see A. Smith, *Servant of the Cecils*; A. Smith, "Secretariats of the Cecils"; Hammer, "The Uses of Scholarship"; Andreani, *Elizabethan Secretariat*; Hunt, "The Early Modern Secretary and the Archive." See also Dover, *Secretaries and Statecraft*.

74. For Elizabethan spycraft, see R. Adams, "A Most Secret Service"; R. Adams,

"The Service I am Here for"; Alford, *The Watchers*. My approach here more closely resembles Hammer, "Essex and Europe."

75. For the regimes of observation in early modern Europe, see Blair, "Reading Strategies for Coping with Information Overload"; Blair, "Note Taking as an Art of Transmission"; Daston, "On Scientific Observation."

76. SP 12/77/10. The letter is reprinted in Warneke, *Images of the Educational Traveller*, 295–98, quote at 295.

77. For Manners in this context, see Mears, *Queenship and Political Discourse*.

78. Potter, *Foreign Intelligence and Information*, 23–120. Burghley also likely supplied Edward de la Zouche with a copy of the instructions given to Rutland before Zouche's Continental journey in 1587. See Bodl. Tanner MS 103, f. 230–32. BL Cotton MS Nero B IX, f. 138r–142r, also contains anonymous instructions for Zouche.

79. *The Correspondence of Sir Philip Sidney and Hubert Languet*, 196–200.

80. Read, *Mr. Secretary Walsingham and the Policy of Queen Elizabeth*, 1:20.

81. For *relazioni*, see Queller, "The Development of Venetian *Relazioni*"; de Vivo, *Information and Communication*; de Vivo, "How to Read Venetian *Relazioni*."

82. See Stagl, "The Methodising of Travel in the 16th Century"; Rubies, "Instructions for Travellers."

83. For the continued importance of such works under King James I, see Millstone, "Seeing Like a Statesman."

84. For this distinction, see Williamson, "Fishing after News." For the authorship of this letter, see most recently Williamson, "A Letter of Travel Advice?" and the discussion in Bacon, *The Early Writings*, 1006–13.

85. Bacon, *The Letters and the Life of Francis Bacon*, 2:17.

86. BL Add. MS 48062, ff. 184r–227v. The text is now edited and published in Gehring, *Diplomatic Intelligence*.

87. See *Catalogue of the Additions to the Manuscripts: The Yelverton Manuscripts*.

88. Danvers, for example, in 1593 sent roughly forty *relazioni* to England from Venice (CP 170/2, ff. 1–2).

89. For such works, see Shapiro, *Political Communication and Political Culture*.

90. C. Hughes, "Nicholas Faunt's Discourse." For this text, see Taviner, "Robert Beale and the Elizabethan Polity," 125ff. See also the similar advice by Beale for Edward Wotton printed in Read, *Mr. Secretary Walsingham*, 1:423–42, and Thomas Wilkes's tract in BL Stowe MS 296, ff. 7r–19v.

91. C. Hughes, "Faunt's Discourse," 502–3.

92. C. Hughes, "Faunt's Discourse," 507.

93. Some aspirants produced analytic descriptions of England; see Wilson, "The State of England"; Davison, *The Poetical Rhapsody*, 1:xlix–li.

94. See similarly Sobecki, "John Peyton's 'A Relation of the State of Polonia'"; Sobecki, "'A Man of Curious Enquiry.'"

95. For Powle, see Stern, *Sir Stephen Powle of Court and Country*; Scott-Warren, "Reconstructing Manuscript Networks;" Popper, "An Information State for Early Modern England."

96. Bodl. Tanner MS 169, f. 262r.
97. Bodl. Tanner MS 169, f. 149r.
98. Bodl. Tanner MS 309, f. 17r.
99. Bodl. Tanner MS 231.
100. Bodl. Tanner MS 309, f. 97r–115v.
101. Stern, *Sir Stephen Powle*, 65.
102. Bodl. Tanner MS 309, f. 16v–17r.
103. Printed in Stern, *Sir Stephen Powle*, 214.
104. Bodl. Tanner MS 169, f. 36v–39v.
105. SP 12/122/112; SP 12/222/126; SP 12/223/2; BL Lansdowne MS 75, f. 132r. He also petitioned Egerton (Bodl. Tanner MS 309, f. 57r).
106. Bodl. Tanner MS 309, f. 12r and f. 115v.
107. Bodl. Tanner MS 169, f. 206r–210r. Another copy is in BL Egerton MS 3876, f. 34v–37v.
108. BL Add. MS 48017, f. 200r–207v.
109. Gehring, *Diplomatic Intelligence*.
110. For printed editions of such works with invaluable commentaries, see Heffernan, "Six Tracts on 'Coign and Livery'"; Heffernan, *Reform Treatises on Tudor Ireland*; Maginn and Ellis, *The Tudor Discovery of Ireland*. For the broader context for such recommendations, see Crawford, *Anglicizing the Government of Ireland*; Brady, *The Chief Governors*; Brady, "From Policy to Power."
111. Heffernan, *Debating Tudor Policy*.
112. BL Add. MS 48015, f. 291v–306v. For these tracts (except Beale's), see Heffernan, "Six Tracts."
113. For Beales's copies of Tremayne and Sherlock, see BL Add. MS 48015, f. 274r–284v, copied from Walsingham's versions in BL Cotton MS Titus B XII.
114. BL Add. MS 48015, 184v; also in BL Lansdowne MS 229.
115. BL Add. MS 48015, f. 264r–265r; 284v–290v.
116. BL Add. MS 48105, 176r–v, ff. 188r–205v, 210r–211r).
117. BL Add. MS 48015, 216r.
118. BL Cotton MS Domitian A XVIII, f. 100r.
119. Maginn and Ellis, *Tudor Discovery*, 35–41.
120. BL Add. MS 47311.
121. See Read Foster, "The Painful Labour of Mr. Elsyng."
122. CoA MS B1.
123. For Bowyer's borrowings from Cotton, see BL Harley MS 6018, f. 148v, 154v, 158r.

Chapter Two

1. Among many works examining the causal influence of media in early modern England, see Croft, "The Reputation of Robert Cecil"; Bellany, *The Politics of Court Scandal*; J. Raymond, *Pamphlets and Pamphleteering*; Sharpe, *Selling the Tudor Monarchy*; Kyle, *Theater of State*; Peacey, *Print and Public Politics in the English*

Revolution; Millstone, "Seeing Like a Statesman"; Millstone, *Manuscript Circulation*; Shapiro, *Political Communication*; Kyle and Peacey, *Connecting Centre and Locality*.

2. Before his appointment, Bowyer had angled for several clerkships, generally unsuccessfully, but since 1599 had been acting as secretary for Thomas Sackville, 1st Earl of Dorset. Kyle, "Robert Bowyer."

3. For the condition of information overload in early modern Europe, see Blair, *Too Much to Know*.

4. ITL Petyt MS 538.17, f. 270r.

5. ITL Petyt MS 538.17, f. 273r.

6. ITL Petyt MS 538.17, f. 274r.

7. ITL Petyt MS 538.17, f. 279r.

8. ITL Petyt MS 538.17, f. 272r.

9. ITL Petyt MS 538.17, f. 281r.

10. For parliamentary archives more generally and Bowyer's role more particularly, see Bond, "The Formation of the Archives of Parliament"; Thrush, "The House of Lords' Record Repository"; Thrush, *The House of Commons 1604–1629*, 1:217–18; Kyle, "Robert Bowyer."

11. ITL Petyt MS 538.17, f. 315r–318r.

12. Pulton's warrant is reproduced in BL Add. MS 4572, f. 86r; the quote is from the description of his endeavor, BL Cotton MS Titus B V, f. 279r. For the role of the archives in early modern English legal culture, see Ross, "Memorial Culture of Early Modern English Lawyers"; Halliday, "Authority in the Archives."

13. BL Cotton MS Titus B V, f. 279v.

14. BL Cotton MS Vespasian F IX, f. 252r–v.

15. HEH EL 1963; see also Pulton's request for money where he also suggests that Egerton had approved the project even before he had obtained the warrant to search the records (HEH EL 1964); BL Cotton MS Julius C III, f. 310.

16. HEH EL 2979.

17. Pulton, *A Collection of Sundrie Statutes*.

18. For Cotton specifically, see Sharpe, *Sir Robert Cotton*. The preponderance of work in this context has focused on Cotton, Coke, and John Selden without—for the most part—recognizing the ubiquity of their practices. See Pocock, *The Ancient Constitution and the Feudal Law*; L. Fox, *English Historical Scholarship*; Parry, *The Trophies of Time*; Christianson, *Discourse on History, Law, and Governance*; Barbour, *John Selden*; Cromartie, *The Constitutionalist Revolution*; Toomer, *John Selden: A Life*; Vine, *In Defiance of Time*; D. Smith, *Sir Edward Coke and the Reformation of the Laws*.

19. On copying in early modern England, see Gordon, "*Copycopia*"; Daybell, *The Material Letter in Early Modern England*, 175–216; Gordon, "Material Fictions."

20. See most broadly Zaret, *The Origins of Democratic Culture*; as well Levy, "How Information Spread amongst the Gentry"; Cust, "News and Politics"; Watt, *Cheap Print and Popular Piety*; A. Fox, "Popular Verses and Their Readership in the Early Seventeenth Century"; Halasz, *The Marketplace of Print*; J. Raymond,

Pamphlets and Pamphleteering; Peacey, "Print Culture and Political Lobbying"; Lecky, "Archiving Ordinary Experience"; Lecky, *Pocket Maps and Public Poetry*. Much of this literature is concerned more with the formation of a public sphere than democratization per se; see particularly Lake and Pincus, "Rethinking the Public Sphere"; Lake and Pincus, *The Politics of the Public Sphere*.

21. For manuscript circulation in seventeenth-century England, see Love, *Scribal Publication*; Woudhuysen, *Sir Philip Sidney and the Circulation of Manuscripts*; Beal, *In Praise of Scribes*; Starza Smith, *John Donne and the Conway Papers*; Millstone, *Manuscript Circulation*.

22. For Starkey, see Millstone, *Manuscript Circulation*.

23. For this world, see Beal, *In Praise of Scribes*; and Daybell, "The Scribal Circulation of Early Modern Letters." There are now invaluable online resources cataloging and, in the latter case, transcribing such materials: Catalogue of English Literary Manuscripts (https://celm-ms.org.uk/); Manuscript Pamphleteering in Early Stuart England (https://mpese.ac.uk).

24. Grafton, "Matthew Parker"; Knight, *Bound to Read*.

25. The register of visitors is SP 14/200, f. 116r–123r; the list of transcribed documents is SP 14/200, f. 126r–138v. There is a convention of stating that Bowyer and Elsynge left the office in 1612, but I find no record of anyone else assuming the role until John Borough in 1621 or 1622 (Woolf, "John Selden, John Borough, and Francis Bacon's 'History of Henry VII'").

26. SP 14/200, f. 131v, 134r.

27. SP 14/200, f. 126v, 128r, 130v, 131v, 132v.

28. Merritt, "Power and Communication."

29. For this practice, see Hurstfield, "The Profits of Fiscal Feudalism"; Questier, "Sir Henry Spiller"; Cramsie, *Kingship and Crown Finance*. For Nicholson, see Sandall, "Custom, Common Right and Commercialisation." Cotton, too, used his expertise to such ends; see Manning, "Antiquarianism and the Seigneurial Reaction."

30. BL Cotton MS Titus B V, f. 308r; SP 14/50, f. 47. For the 1607 payment, see *Issues of the Exchequer*, 78.

31. BL Cotton MS Titus B V, f. 309r.

32. SP 14/50, f. 46.

33. BL Add. MS 36767, f. 46.

34. For Proby's effort to keep the post by invoking precedents from Tower records, see SP 14/9A, f. 34, 38; for examples of his searching in the Tower, see SP 14/6, f. 50r, 108r; CP 107/69; CP 107/70; CP 107/102.

35. BL Lansdowne MS 161, f. 82r.

36. Tite, *The Early Records of Sir Robert Cotton's Library*; see also C. Wright, *Sir Robert Cotton as Collector*.

37. BL Harley MS 6018, f. 148r, 149v, 170r, 178r, 179r. Cotton's list of his loans have been published in Tite, *The Early Records of Sir Robert Cotton's Library*; see also in this context, C. Wright, *Sir Robert Cotton as Collector*.

38. BL Harley MS 6018, f. 161r.

39. BL Harley MS 6018, f. 151r has a list likely compiled around 1617; see also BL Cotton MS Julius C III for his correspondence.

40. Toomer, *John Selden: A Life*.

41. BL Harley MS 6018, f. 148v, 154.

42. On Cotton's circulation of such materials, see also Millstone, "Evil Counsel"; Millstone, "Sir Robert Cotton, Manuscript Pamphleteering, and the Making of Jacobean Kingship."

43. BL Harley MS 6018, f. 148r, 149v, 153v, 155v, 160r.

44. For Agarde, see Hallam, "Arthur Agarde and the Domesday Book"; Yax, "Arthur Agarde, Elizabethan Archivist"; Popper, "From Abbey to Archive."

45. For Exchequer archives in this period, see K. Wright, "The Exchequer of Receipt."

46. Agarde may have been the driving force behind a 1573 reorganization of Exchequer records (BL Harley MS 94, f. 41r–42r). For his performance of routine Exchequer activities, see HEH ST 3; BL Egerton MS 2598, f. 117r, 119v, 202r, 226r.

47. Agarde borrowed many volumes from Cotton (BL Harley MS 6018, f. 155r, 176r). See also his letter thanking Cotton for help him with a search (BL Cotton MS Julius C III, 1r).

48. For the notebooks, see John Rylands Library, Ryl. Lat. MS 318. For a similar volume furnished out of notes received from Cotton, Camden, Cope, Spelman, and many others, see Ryl. Lat. 319. For the authentication, see HEH ST 39. The 1590s Tower register notes frequent visits from Jeffs (CoA MS B 32).

49. Hearne, *A Collection of Curious Discourses*, 2:43–44.

50. CP 79/2. Arthur Throckmorton referred to Agarde as "my fathers owld servant." Because the elder Throckmorton served as chamberlain of the Exchequer until his death in 1571, this account corroborates Agarde's claim to have worked there since around 1570.

51. BL Cotton MS Julius C III, f. 75r.

52. For the register of this search, see LPL MS 2000, ff. 56–81.

53. LPL MS 2000, f. 82r ff. Because the date of this inventory is unknown, the recipient archbishop could be either Richard Bancroft or George Abbot.

54. For its starting point, see his note dated to 1586 on searching Norfolk records, HEH EL 34/c/4, f. 10r. For its delivery, see BL Lansdowne MS 171, f. 374r; HEH EL 35/b/60, f. 18v. Because the date of its completion is unclear, the recipient justice could have been John Popham, Thomas Fleming, or, most likely, Coke.

55. HEH EL 34/c/4, front matter. "Excerpsi ex libro statutorum manuscripto Mr Grimston de Grays Ynne 1590. Et confirmit per Registrum Coventer 1595."

56. HEH EL 34/c/4, f. 7v. "Quere pro libro nuncupato Swatham qui est apud Peterborough." This is the chronicle of Robert of Swaffham.

57. For such strategies more broadly, see Blair, *Too Much to Know*.

58. TNA IND 1/17089. This volume and TNA IND 1/17088 are among the few volumes definitely produced by Agarde in the nearly fifty items labeled "Agarde's indices" by nineteenth-century archivists. Most are in the hands of later seventeenth-century figures such as Peter La Neve and John Lowe, though it is possible that

they recopied collections initially made by Agarde. The suggested date of 1606 reflects the collection of papal bulls at the end of one of them and the focus of the transcriptions on questions of ecclesiastical property; they were likely produced during the Oath of Allegiance Controversy. TNA IND 1/17088 has the same principles as TNA 1/17089 but covers the reigns from Richard I to Edward III. BL Add. MS 25173 is a fair copy. Several notes in Egerton's papers suggest that Egerton consulted Agarde's books when taking notes on the history of the Star Chamber (HEH EL 485).

59. HEH EL 35/c/36.

60. Agarde adopted a similar method, likely beginning in the 1580s, when making abridgments of records concerning the King's Bench in Westminster between the reigns of Edward I and Henry V. Twenty years later, after obtaining many new relevant items, he created an abridgement of the omitted material organized in the same fashion (HEH EL 35/c/36; second pagination). A later copy is in ITL Petyt MS 538.7, f. 347ff. There are also partial copies in BL Add. MS 25159 and BL Add. MS 25160.

61. Agarde completed a draft of this collection roughly a decade prior; see BL MS Lansdowne 171, f. 367ff.

62. For example, in 1609 Agarde delivered to Chancellor of the Exchequer Sir Julius Caesar "Records touchinge matters of ireland," and "Two bundells of letters of advertisements to the king and counsaile of the state of Ireland," that "are to be found in a bag intituled Hibernia being in the Kings Majesty's Treasury." BL Lansdowne MS 156, f. 201r. Similarly, at some point he compiled a "Compendium of papal bulls formerly sent in to England" taken from bundles as they lay throughout the treasury. LPL MS 2000, "Bullarum Pontificiarum in Angliam olim missarum compendium," 1v–35v; see BL Add. MS 48008, f. 376–395v for a contemporary copy.

63. BL Harley MS 604, f. 219.

64. CP 252/1, f. 1r.

65. CP 252/1, f. 1r.

66. CP 252/1, f. 1r–v.

67. CP 252/1, f. 8v.

68. CP 252/1, f. 9r.

69. CP 252/1, f. 9r.

70. CP 252/1, f. 9v.

71. CP 252/1, f. 2v–4v.

72. These offices were the front room for those searching Exchequer archives where they might consult with the Deputy Chamberlains. I thank Kirsty Wright for this point.

73. BL Stowe MS 138, f. 9r, 13r, 24v, 34r–v, 40r, 49r, 52r, 55r, 59r–v, 78v. This and TNA IND 1/17126 appear to have been working copies of the manuscript.

74. BL Stowe MS 138, f. 13r, 24v, 34r.

75. BL Lansdowne MS 137. Caesar also had another copy: BL Lansdowne MS 151, f. 211r.

76. HEH EL 35/b/60.

77. As Starkey explained, holders of this office needed to be able to read Latin and French, to read the tallies used in accounting, and to "understand the records and to know the diversity of the natures." Further, he recommended, when copying from the Domesday Book, "you must write itt as neere you can to the letter thereof observering both the greate letters and the points therein which are prickt with a penn." HEH EL 35/b/60 [unpaginated]; for these extracts see also BL Sloane MS 262, f. 35v–36r.

78. HEH EL 35/b/60, f. 17r–20v.

79. See for example ITL Petyt MS 538.19, f. 122r–127v.

80. BL Add. MS 25256, BL Sloane MS 262; Bodl. Rawlinson MS B. 384; BL Harley MS 94; BL Add. MS 48008; BL Lansdowne MS 799; BL Cotton MS Vespasian C XIV, f. 205r–214v.

81. Powell, *Direction for Search of Records*, A3r; for the manuscript version, see FSL MS V.a.182.

82. Powell, *The Repertorie of Records*.

83. SP 45/20, f. 173v–181v.

84. At Cecil's death, Wilson accessioned 24 domestic books, 22 on Scotland and the borders, 21 on France, 5 packets and bundles on Italy, 9 on Spain, 23 on the Low Countries, and 73 on Ireland, and subsequently a further 90 books, bundles, packets, boxes, and commissions generated by Cecil's private affairs (SP 45/20, f. 170r–172r).

85. SP 45/20, f. 184r–188r.

86. SP 45/20, f 200v–201r.

87. SP 45/20, f. 198r–206r.

88. For the architecture of early modern archives, see Head, *Making Archives in Early Modern Europe*; Stallybrass and Wolfe, "Material Culture of Record Keeping."

89. For Caesar, see Hill, *Bench and Bureaucracy*; Sherman, *Used Books*, 127–50.

90. See, e.g., Fulke Greville's solicitation of a register for Barking Abbey (SP 9/55/5); Caesar's report of a "diligente serch" of Admiralty records for Walsingham shortly after appointment as a judge in the Admiralty (SP 12/175, f. 45); and instances where Caesar circulated information necessary to recover debts (CP 128/104) or oversaw the confiscation of books (CP 195/20; SP 14/75, f. 41, 62).

91. CP 93/54; CP 192/93; CP 107/112; CP Petitions 1708; CP 95/79; CP 91/26.

92. SP 46/67, f. 123; SP 14/40, f. 144.

93. BL Harley MS 6018, f. 157. Caesar's name is listed as a borrower of books, but no lists itemize his borrowings.

94. BL Lansdowne MS 151, f. 164v–165r.

95. BL Add. MS 6038. See Sherman, *Used Books*.

96. BL shelfmark C.20.f.15–58.

97. BL Lansdowne MS 161, f. 47.

98. Secretaries seemed to have expected that patiently searching the shelves and rolls would yield desired materials. For example, six weeks after Burghley's death, Auditor General of the Court of Wards William Tooke, responding to a

request from Robert Cecil for his father's book "wherein are collected and sett downe the names of the Chiefeste Gentlemen in England," reported that he had "perused the Cathalogue of your Lords Bookes, and made diligente searche besydes the bagges amongst diverse papers" but had been unable to find this volume. He had thus asked Burghley's secretary Michael Hickes, who responded that he "hath not harde of any such thinge, and yet he thinkes it maye verye well be amongest some of those bagges that are not yet sorted, which (being manye) will aske a longer tyme of searche." That these men had been unable to find such a document among his overspilling archive is less remarkable than their confidence that they would find it with time (CP 64/31).

99. The latest papers date from 1635, but there are only a scattered few from immediately preceding years.

100. BL Add. MS 9045; BL Add. MS 15235.

101. BL Add. MS 36969; BL Add. MS 36970; BL Add. MS 12495.

102. See the collection of eleven books bound together later in TNA CRES 40/19A; BL Add. MS 12501.

103. BL Add. MS 4190.

104. Cf. BL Add. MS 15208; BL Add. MS 12505; BL Add. MS 5664; BL Add. MS 12506; BL Add. MS 12507; BL Lansdowne MS 150; BL Lansdowne MS 148; BL Lansdowne MS 140; BL Lansdowne MS 139; BL Lansdowne MS 154; BL Lansdowne MS 141.

105. BL Add. MS 11405.

106. Nor was there chronological continuity in the volumes, whose contents often flitted across decades. Later purchasers of his materials, frustrated by the chronological disharmony, would occasionally unbind and then rebind his collections in chronological order (Cf. BL Add. MS 38170).

107. BL Lansdowne MS 141.

108. BL Lansdowne MS 151, f. 168r–210v.

109. See also Paterson, *Catalogue of the Manuscripts*, 68–69.

110. BL Add. MS 10113, f. 2r. Accordingly, Snelling produced another, more complete table of contents.

111. BL Add. MS 34324.

112. BL Lansdowne MS 124, f. 2r.

113. BL Lansdowne MS 124, f. 4r–6v.

114. See most recently the introduction to Kyle and Peacey, *Connecting Centre and Locality*, 1–21.

Chapter Three

1. Few secondary works capture this dynamic for the period, but see Collinson, "The Monarchical Republic of Queen Elizabeth I"; Collinson, "Puritans, Men of Business and Elizabethan Parliaments"; Graves, *Thomas Norton*; Goldie, "The Unacknowledged Republic"; Cramsie, *Kingship and Crown Finance*.

2. For projects in early modern Britain, see Ash, *Power, Knowledge and Exper-*

tise; McCormick, *William Petty and the Ambitions of Political Arithmetic*; Keller and McCormick, "Towards a History of Projects"; Ash, *The Draining of the Fens*; Yamamoto, *Taming Capitalism Before Its Triumph*. For a parallel literature on alchemical projects and the state, see Harkness, *The Jewel House*; Nummedal, *Alchemy and Authority*; Keller, "Mining Tacitus"; Amundsen, "Thinking Metallurgically." For a similar argument concerning revolutions effected by clerks, see Zakim, *Accounting for Capitalism*.

3. For English state formation, see Brewer, *The Sinews of Power*; Braddick, *State Formation in Early Modern England*; Hindle, *The State and Social Change*; Ash, *Draining of the Fens*.

4. Agarde produced a Latin version of this treatise as well: BL Cotton Vitellius C IX, f. 229r–233v.

5. BL Cotton MS Vitellius C IX, f. 238v.

6. Hallam, "Arthur Agarde and the Domesday Book"; Hallam, "Annotations in Domesday Book since 1100," 41.

7. The abstract of the Great Domesday is BL Add. MS 74948; the abstract of Little Domesday is BL Harley MS 5167.

8. Bodl. MS Top. Gen. C 22. Similarly, Agarde may have been involved in the production of a glossary for the Red Book of the Exchequer (HEH EL 2206).

9. BL Cotton MS Vitellius C IX, f. 236v.

10. Hearne, *A Collection of Curious Discourses*, 2:43–50.

11. BL Cotton MS Vitellius C IX, f. 235v.

12. BL Cotton MS Vitellius C IX, f. 236r.

13. BL Cotton MS Vitellius C IX, f. 236v.

14. For a later account of Agarde's reasoning, see the account likely by Henry Powle in BL Lansdowne MS 232, f. 6r.

15. Agarde's Domesday materials were copied by Camden and fellow member of the Society of Antiquaries Joseph Holland, and they were acquired by Robert Cotton (BL Cotton MS Faustina C XI, ff. 61–161; BL Cotton MS Julius C I; see also BL Lansdowne MS 329.) Sir Simonds D'Ewes also came to own some of them (BL Harley MS 139, f. 126ff.).

16. Pocock, *The Ancient Constitution and the Feudal Law*; and alternatively Brooks and Sharpe, "History, English Law, and the Renaissance"; Chou, "Parliamentary Mind"; Gajda and Cavill, *Writing the History of Parliament*.

17. Gajda and Cavill nicely encapsulate this process for Parliament, arguing that studying its history "altered perceptions of parliament's role in the polity, both among members and among those whom they represented. When contemporaries historicized parliament, it ceased to be a one-off 'event' and came instead to be regarded as an institution, a permanent presence in the body politic's imaginary" (Gajda and Cavill, *Writing the History of Parliament*, 2).

18. BL Lansdowne MS 145, f. 22v.

19. The manuscript has been collated and published as Hill, *The Ancient State Authoritie, and Proceedings of the Court of Requests*. Quotation at BL Lansdowne MS 125, f. 25r–v; Hill, *Ancient State Authoritie*, 3.

20. BL Add. MS 36111, f. 42r ff.

21. Hill, *Ancient State Authoritie*, xlv–xlvii.

22. BL Lansdowne MS 125, 9r.

23. It is worth noting that Caesar also exaggerated the antiquity and institutional stability of the Privy Council.

24. BL Lansdowne MS 125, f. 9v.

25. Caesar also gave uncorrected copies to William Lambarde, William Bowyer, and likely others (Bowyer's is Bodl. Tanner MS 264, Lambarde's is BL shelfmark 1380 g 21). Caesar continued to edit his own copy until the 1620s or 1630s; see Hill, *Ancient State Authoritie*, xx; BL Lansdowne MS 125, f. 4v–42v, 167v–168r.

26. BL Lansdowne MS 125, f. 10r–11v.

27. BL Lansdowne MS 125, f. 3r–8v.

28. BL Lansdowne MS 160, f. 268r.

29. BL Lansdowne MS 160, f. 270r.

30. BL Lansdowne MS 160, f. 264r.

31. BL Lansdowne MS 160, f. 264r.

32. Caesar and Coke failed to acquire the position; Lord Montagu was named Lord President in 1621 mainly to give him a soft landing after relinquishing the position of Lord Treasurer to Cranfield.

33. Cf. BL Lansdowne MS 145, f. 3r.

34. Slack, "Government and Information." For a recent case of Elizabethan bureaucratization (and its tensions), see Kyle, "'A Dog, A Butcher, and a Puritan'"; see also A. Hughes, "Diligent Enquiries and Perfect Accounts."

35. For an Elizabethan instance, Matthew Parker's son John tried to create an office that would perform some of the fee-generating copying traditionally done by the Six Clerks, who angrily rebuffed it (HEH EL 2849–2852). See W. Jones, *Elizabethan Court of Chancery*, 70–76.

36. For Egerton's intellectual world, see Knafla, *Law and Politics in Jacobean England*; Knafla, "The Law Studies of an Elizabethan Student."

37. Lambarde was one of several clients to provide him with copies of medieval documents as gifts. See, for example, HEH EL 2649 and HEH EL 2649B, which are Lambarde's gifts of the Black Book of the Exchequer, outfitted with an index. For Egerton's patronage, see Knafla, "The 'Country Chancellor.'" In 1609 Egerton, along with the Privy Council, insisted that "a fit place be assigned and proper receptacles be provided for the safe custody of the public records" in Ireland (*Calendar of State Papers, Relating to Ireland, of the Reign of James I*, 3:148).

38. Egerton also oversaw the assembly of a volume containing abstracts of records in the collections of George Robson and Henry Clyffe, Clerks in the Tower under the Heneages (HEH EL 1120).

39. HEH EL 1170. Similarly, in the first years of James I's reign, Egerton compiled a list of "The Propositions I have made for relieveinge the king upon state as it now stands," which cited, among other sources, close rolls from Edward III's and Henry IV's reigns (HEH EL 1216).

40. See, for example, HEH EL 121, 137, 290, 291. See also HEH HM 66348, a guide to household management predicated on the vertical integration of notebooks recording household practices.

41. TNA IND 1/1878, index to record series TNA C 38.

42. TNA C 31/1A. The earliest extant volume collecting written affidavits dates from 1611, though it seems likely that the first few volumes were lost.

43. TNA C 31/1. The earliest of these is from 1607/8, suggesting that the first few volumes of the compiled affidavits have been lost or destroyed.

44. TNA IND 1/7245.

45. TNA C 41/1.

46. *Orders of the High Court of Chancery*, 1:101.

47. BL Add. MS 10038, f. 19r–22r.

48. BL Add. MS 10038, f. 19r, 20v. Licensing projects and projects to manage financial instruments were also predominantly concerned with maintaining paperwork.

49. SP 14/93, f. 170.

50. SP 14/93, f. 173.

51. Cope was a collector of medieval manuscripts, in addition to his roles as client of Burghley and Cecil, member of Parliament, and after 1612 Master of the Court of Wards. See Watson, "The Manuscript Collection of Sir Walter Cope."

52. *A True Transcription and Publication of his Maiesties Letters Pattent*, B1r–v.

53. *True Transcription*, B1v.

54. *True Transcription*, C4r–v.

55. *True Transcription*, C4v.

56. For Wilson, see Pollard, "Wilson, Sir Thomas"; A. Stewart, "Familiar Letters and State Papers." Wilson had come to the attention to Burghley by 1583 when Burghley recommended him for a fellowship from St. John's College, Cambridge; in 1594 Burghley recommended Wilson for a fellowship at Trinity Hall Cambridge (BL Lansdowne MS 77, f. 20).

57. Much of the information from the following section comes from draft letters and commissions in Wilson's hand, often addressed to a patron, but it is often unclear whether he sent them. Thus the account here may reflect in part a fantastical imagination of his life in draft responses he angrily penned but never had the nerve to send.

58. For early modern British scholarly services, see Sharpe, *Sir Robert Cotton*; Jardine and Grafton, "'Studied for Action'"; Jardine and Sherman, "Pragmatic Readers"; Sherman, *John Dee*; Popper, *Walter Ralegh's "History of the World"*; Mishra, "In the Company of Merchants."

59. For his 1590s collections, see SP 14/11, f. 137ff. For collections of his *relazioni*, which date from this period and then were consulted and augmented later, see SP 9/100, SP 9/105, SP 9/200, Bodl. Rawlinson MS D. 1035, and his collection in SP 9/195, which also included an English "Book of Offices." He bequeathed this collection to his son-in-law and successor as Keeper Ambrose Randolph, despite their tempestuous relationship (SP 14/171, f.123).

60. For examples of Wilson's newsletters, see SP 96/1, SP 85/2, f. 94; CP 182/13, CP 182/14; SP 29/283a.

61. SP 12/278, f. 255. Buckhurst continued to receive them (SP 81/8, f. 197).

62. SP 12/280, later published as Wilson, "The State of England (1600)."

63. Cecil had long relied on secretaries to order paperwork. For example, likely in 1601, he had his clerks compile lists of correspondents over the previous years (CP 243/2); in 1602 they collected a packet of thirty-nine treaties and other materials from the Exchequer for his own copying (CP 141/223); and at some other time they created a catalog of documents in his possession ranging from 1569 to 1586 (CP 140/40).

64. For example, in one he discounted the value of his own intelligence: "My letters from Spaine mentioned in my laste save one to your Lordship are now come to my hands but they are old of age and sillie of devise most being stale and common matters." CP 191/20 and SP 14/15, f. 49.

65. SP 9/105. Similarly, around 1606, Wilson compiled "The state of the Germaine Empire." SP 9/201/5, f. 6r ff.

66. For example, sometime before Cecil's death, Wilson compiled a list of "Papers which concern the augmentacion of the kinges revenues found confusedly dispersed amongst my lords papers" (CP 140/48).

67. CP 112/2.

68. Typical entries included "A pacquett to Mr Winwood wherein his Majesties letter to the States, concerning the busynesss of Embden, sent by Thomas Stanbanck," and "The Ratification of the Treaty of France sent under the great Seale of England with a dispatch to Sir George Carew" (Bodl. Rawlinson MS D. 1035, f. 6v, 9r).

69. CP 140/40 is a working document of these categories, likely originally made under Thomas Lake's supervision and then shared between Lake and Wilson; upon Cecil's death in 1612, Wilson also compiled a similar list, CP 140/48.

70. SP 45/20, f. 128r; CP 243/1,2,5,6,7.

71. There were occasional efforts to improve it, such as the 1597 efforts of Wilson's predecessor John James and Thomas Lake to prepare space in the Banqueting House for the office (CP 56/24).

72. SP 45/20, f. 27r.

73. The only sign of significant labor concerning the State Paper Office possibly from these years is an undated "Catalogue of Collection of the particular Instructions and Letters remaining in the Office of the Kings papers Chamber at Whitehall," BL Add. MS 11595, f. 2r ff.

74. For the straits Wilson found himself in upon Cecil's death, see SP 14/69, f. 105.

75. For the first letter, see SP 14/96, f. 159; for the later reminiscence, see SP 14/111, f. 201.

76. SP 14/99, f. 5. It is almost certain that he had black hair rather than was of African descent.

77. SP 14/103, f. 19. Wilson was employed in bizarre interrogations on other

occasions as well. In April 1626, along with Bishop of Durham Richard Neile he interrogated Lucy Martin, who had hurled what seemed to be a seditious prophecy, wrapped around a stone, at the king as he listened to the Palm Sunday Sermon at Whitehall. To their relief, they discovered that she was a danger only to herself: she merely wanted one of the king's guard to accompany her pilgrimage to London sites where she could abjure her former harlotries, since her tactic of casting her own blood on those sites had not rid London of iniquity (SP 16/24, f. 105). For this episode, see Cressy, *Charles I and the People of England*, 1–7. The choice of Wilson may have recognized his recent service to Neile, for two months prior, he had translated between Neile and the French ambassador after a riot nearly broke out when the ambassador's supporters tried to protect English Catholics celebrating Mass with them from constables who had a warrant to arrest them (SP 16/21, f. 92r–95r).

78. SP 14/103, f. 107r–v; the library catalog was recorded in Ralegh's notebook (BL Add. MS 57555).

79. SP 14/104, f. 161.

80. SP 14/111, f. 91.

81. Bodl. Rawlinson MS D. 1035, f. 2r [reverse pagination].

82. Bodl. Rawlinson MS D. 1035, f. 18r [reverse pagination].

83. Among Wilson's drafts of letters to Carr are vitriolic notes condemning sodomy (Bodl. Rawlinson MS D. 1035, f. 5v).

84. Bodl. Rawlinson MS D. 1035, f 3r–v.

85. Bodl. Rawlinson MS D. 1035, f. 3v.

86. He also offered Carr "a summary catalog of such things as ar in charge in the office of the papers." Bodl. Rawlinson MS D. 1035, f. 3r.

87. For the petitions, see SP 14/84, f. 95 (Trinity Hall) and SP 14/105, f. 101 (Gonville and Caius).

88. For his petitions for plantations in Ireland, see SP 63/234, f. 187 (1618) and SP 45/20, f. 164r (1629). In the 1618 petition, he hinged his suitability for the grant on a proposed history of Ireland to be written using the Paper Office's records, which he claimed had impressed James (SP 45/20, f. 73r; SP 14/107, f. 24).

89. SP 45/20, f. 110r.

90. SP 45/20, f. 121r; for his other communications with Reid, see SP 45/20, f. 110r, 119r.

91. SP 14/94, f. 188r.

92. SP 14/94, f. 188v.

93. SP 14/104, f. 154. For two successful similar projects from the period, see the indexes of royal grants made by James (BL Lansdowne MS 222) and registers of knighthoods (CoA MS M5c).

94. See SP 14/104, f. 148; the official petition is SP 14/104, f. 145. Wilson was knighted in July 1618, evidently at his request for some token of appreciation despite the consistent failure of the regime to pay or reimburse him (SP 45/20, f. 88r), and it seems to have prompted the idea of the register. Six months later, he made a list of "Knights made after me," likely with an eye toward his proposed register (SP 14/105, f. 105).

95. Wilson may have derived this idea from Continental models, but he had also observed Marin de Boislore's effort to monopolize the printing of broadsides, which sparked protests from the Stationers Company (SP 14/83, f. 2, 106).

96. SP 14/124, f. 230r.

97. SP 14/124, f. 231r. Pory and Wilson presented themselves as suited to this role because they received news from "Antwerpe Brussels Hague Colloyn Francford Prage Vienne Gratz Venice Florence Rome Naples Genoa Spayne Paris & Lyons." They requested £20 each plus an additional £20 to procure the newssheets from abroad. But they suggested that it would also serve Crown counselors, for Wilson proposed that "I shold alwayse keep an historical register allwaise ready of what soever shall pass in the world" for their consultation.

98. SP 14/124, f. 231r.

99. SP 14/88, f. 83. For petitions for Mastership of the Requests into the mid-1620s, see SP 14/93, f. 291; SP 14/94, f. 188, 189; SP 14/135, f. 19; SP 14/90, f. 212r; SP 45/20, f. 110r. See also his petition to Thomas Howard, Earl of Suffolk, in 1618; Suffolk's response was encouraging, but he fell from grace shortly afterward (SP 45/20, f. 60r).

100. SP 14/93, f. 231r–v.

101. Wilson described the office's formation as a consequence of accelerating political inscription: "After Secretaryes began to be great (as they did first in the time of Queen Elizabeth) and that the papers growe to that bulke that not a chest nor scarse a great roome could contain them and that secretaryes began to have all the busines of the kingdom (and of Christendome also) lyeing upone them whereby there servants which they employed in writing were soe overcharged with busines that they could not keepe them in order by reason of the multitude of the papers and the straight roomes that were allowed to keepe them in court, and by reason of the often changing of Secretaryes whereby the papers began to be embessled by those servants when there Masters died or left there places then it was thought necessarie that a certaine place should be appointed for them, and a fitt man chosen for regestring and keepeing them in order upon all occasions of seizure when they should be called for." SP 15/42, f. 150v.

102. In addition to Cecil's and Lake's materials discussed previously, Wilson received at least forty-one bundles from Naunton and at least sixty-eight from George Calvert (SP 45/20, f. 170r ff.). He also badgered those who had borrowed materials to return them (SP 45/20, f. 108r, 112r), succeeding primarily with those secretaries whose favor he held, but noted that many resisted (SP 14/94, f. 191 and SP 14/135, f. 20). For his audit of Lake's missing papers, see SP 45/20, 54r–v.

103. For Wilson's efforts to acquire Agarde's books (which he worried that Cotton would obtain first), see SP 14/81, f.120, 121. Wilson also recorded that he found Agarde after the latter's death, and he recommended that his son-in-law Ambrose Randolph pursue the vacant deputy chamberlainship in the expectation that Cotton would as well. For his listing of Coke's papers, see SP 45/20, f. 93r; for the warrant, TNA PC 2/31, f. 233; for Starkey's, BL Harley MS 286, f. 286. Wilson also made registers and catalogs of other repositories' holdings, including Cotton's library

and the Exchequer (SP 9/94). Wilson and Cotton have generally been portrayed as rivals, but they also cooperated for many years; for example, before Cecil's death, Cotton lent Wilson volumes including "The calendar of the Papers at Whitehall from 4 Elizabeth to 1589," and the two exchanged volumes several times over the next two decades, including "one of my calendars of the treatises original in the Escheker gathered by Mr Agarde" (BL Harley MS 6018, f. 176r; see also BL Harley MS 6018, f. 149r, and BL Cotton MS Julius C III, f. 404r). At some point Wilson even asked Cotton to recommend him to the Lord Treasurer, probably James Ley (BL Cotton Julius C III, f. 406r.)

104. SP 45/20, f. 56r. Even with this success, Wilson pushed to enlarge the scope of the office, proposing that it be given a library of "all suche bookes of the generall lawes of kingdomes & states cronological History and Policy as I have sett downe in a catalogue her unto annexed," which Wilson would consult for the Crown or counselors when it "may be any light or helpe to present consultacions."

105. SP 45/20, f. 47r; SP 14/96, f. 75r. James also licensed his favorites to approve or reject such requests and to support Wilson (SP 14/86, f. 6; SP 14/137, f. 33). Despite James's intervention, Wilson later complained that Privy Counsellors routinely did not return papers taken from him (BL Stowe 548, 7r; SP 45/20, f. 131r).

106. Expanding the office also required space, so to acquire the rooms under the Paper Office from the Earl of Worcester, he gave Worcester several books (SP 45/210, f. 57r).

107. Bodl. Ashmole MS 826, f. 144; an earlier draft is SP 45/20, f. 33r. The claim of eight years likely refers to his appointment as Keeper, but he had probably had not directly confronted the office's disorder until Cecil's death.

108. SP 9/94, f. 24r ff.

109. SP 45/20, f. 171r.

110. Bodl. Ashmole MS 826, f. 144.

111. This system of classification resembled those used by certain German archives, and it is possible that Wilson had learned of them during his time on the Continent, or that he derived this system from the *artes apodemicae*. Nonetheless, even his categories were not comprehensive, and at the end he included a category of "Mixta" (BL Add. MS 48008, 7v).

112. Copies include BL Add. MS 48008, f. 3r–6r, and SP 45/20, f. 62r–67v; and a later copy at SP 45/20, f. 165r; other later copies include BL Stowe MS 548, f. 2r–7v, and BL Harley MS 1579.

113. SP 9/94, ff. 42r, 54r, 115r, and 129, which contain Low Countries registers updated until 1618. Similarly, see "A register of the papers of Germany as they now lye in order" (SP 9/90, f. 90r).

114. BL Add. MS 48008, f. 3v.

115. BL Add. MS 48008, f. 4r.

116. Head, *Making Archives in Early Modern Europe*; more generally, see Grafton, "The World of the Polyhistors"; Hotson, *Johann Heinrich Alsted*; Nelles, "The Library as an Instrument of Discovery."

117. SP 14/88, f. 82.

118. For Conway's, see SP 14/137, f. 62. Coke's is referred to in Bodl. Rawlinson MS D. 1035, f. 86r–v. Barrett's was copied for BL Harley MS 1579; see also Wilson's draft letter to him in Bodl. Rawlinson MS D. 1035, f. 36v.

119. SP 14/94, f. 189.

120. SP 45/20, f. 76r.

121. SP 45/20, f. 50r. He did not include collections for Privy Counsellors in his bills, though during the time frame of this one, he did produce compilations such as precedents on Dutch trade for Egerton (HEH EL 1672, 1673, 1692).

122. SP 14/96, f. 75r–v.

123. SP 45/20, f. 74r.

124. SP 45/20, f. 135r.

125. SP 9/94, f. 125. For this alleged debt, see SP 45/20, f. 50r, 54v, 85r, 99r, 135r, 146r; SP 14/104, f. 146; SP 14/113, f. 35. Robert Naunton and perhaps others did investigate by consulting the treaty in question; see BL MS Stowe 138, f. 13r (Fig. 10).

126. SP 77/18, f. 40.

127. SP 14/118, f. 106.

128. BL Harley MS 4272; FSL MS V.b.368; YBL Osborn MS fb60, f. 180r; Bodl. Rawlinson MS D. 718, f. 123r. For a draft of this treatise with "abstract" of the foreign revenues at the end, see SP 9/105, f. 185. See also Wilson's draft of the letter to Ley (Bodl. Rawlinson MS D. 1035, f 38r).

129. BL Harley MS 4272, f. 18r.

130. Wilson relied on Cotton heavily in this enterprise, obtaining from him "your abstracte of prince Arthurs treaty" while reminding Cotton that "you have promised me to denye me nothing noe more will I ever doe to you" (BL Cotton MS Julius C III, f. 403r). In exchange, he offered Cotton a copy of the final product and to commend Cotton to Carr.

131. See, in this vein, Dooley and Baron, *The Politics of Information*.

132. SP 45/20, f. 52r.

133. BL Add. MS 11576; another copy of the dedicatory epistle is SP 14/94, f. 189.

134. SP 45/20, f. 141r.

135. BL Add. MS 11576, f. 2r.

136. SP 14/87, f. 183.

137. SP 45/20, f. 99r. Wilson repeatedly implored Buckingham to use these tracts more (SP 14/135, f. 22; SP 14/124, f. 206; SP 45/20, f. 146r).

138. SP 45/20, f. 105r.

139. SP 15/42 f. 150r; see also the earlier draft in SP 45/21, f. 102r. Calvert ultimately used the office as heavily as any other counselor.

140. SP 45/20, f. 137r, 139r, 158r.

141. Bodl. Rawlinson MS D. 1035, f. 87v–88r.

142. Bodl. Rawlinson MS D. 1035, f. 87r.

143. Overall, the volume was intended to use the seeming neutrality of past records to spur anti-Spanish sentiment (Bodl. Rawlinson MS D. 1035, f. 24r, 25r).

144. Bodl. Rawlinson MS D. 1035, f. 29v.

145. Bodl. Rawlinson MS D. 1035, f. 38v.
146. Bodl. Rawlinson MS D. 1035, f. 29v.
147. Weber, *The Theory of Social and Economic Organization*.
148. Elton, *The Tudor Revolution in Government*; Aylmer, *The King's Servants*; Aylmer, *The Crown's Servants*; Levy Peck, *Court Patronage and Corruption*; Stewart, *The English Ordnance Office*. See also the dismantling of Elton's claims in C. Coleman and Starkey, *Revolution Reassessed*.
149. Weber, *Theory of Social and Economic Organization*, 332.
150. Becker and Clark, *Little Tools of Knowledge*; Vismann, *Files*; Kafka, *The Demon of Writing*; Gitelman, *Paper Knowledge*; Felten and von Oertzen, "Histories of Bureaucratic Knowledge."

Chapter Four

1. For other revolutionary moments as media events, foundational works include Eisenstein, *The Printing Revolution*; Newman, "The World Made Print"; Popkin, *Revolutionary News*; Chartier, *The Cultural Origins of the French Revolution*; Hesse, *Publishing and Cultural Politics in Revolutionary Paris*; Warner, *The Letters of the Republic*; Scribner, *For the Sake of Simple Folk*; Darnton, "An Early Information Society." For seventeenth-century Britain through this lens, see A. Hughes, *Gangraena and the Struggle for the English Revolution*; J. Raymond, *Pamphlets and Pamphleteering*; Peacey, *Print and Public Politics*; Millstone, *Manuscript Circulation*.

2. For aristocratic logics of power in early modern Britain, see James, *Society, Politics and Culture*; Cust, "Honour and Politics"; Adamson, *The Noble Revolt*; Kane, *The Politics and Culture of Honour*; Cust, *Charles I and the Aristocracy*; Bulman, *The Rise of Majority Rule*.

3. Some of these originated with Agarde. Though Squyer directed little energy to describing the spaces as a whole that had preoccupied Agarde, sometime in the 1620s he produced a brief summation of the conditions of treasuries (SP 14/180, f. 130). For Squyer, see Taylor, "The Books and Manuscripts of Scipio le Squyer"; Ovenden, "Scipio le Squyer and the Fate of Monastic Cartularies."

4. BL Add. MS 14262. A decade later, in 1617, he produced a similar armorial (BL Harley MS 6126).

5. SP 12/42, f. 101. For the College of Arms in this period, see Ramsay, *Heralds and Heraldry in Shakespeare's England*.

6. BL Lansdowne MS 126.

7. WCRO, CR 1998 Large Carved Box No. 67.

8. BL Harley MS 4286 contains several collections of Knyveton's notes. See BL Harley MS 3374 (Villiers family); BL Add. MS 5701 (Cope); BL Harley MS 6697 (Curzons); BL Harley MS 3375 (Frescheville). BL Harley MS 6833 is a later transcription of this last. For this type of history, see Heal and Holmes, *The Gentry in England and Wales*; A. Fox, "Remembering the Past in Early Modern England"; Broadway, *"No historie so meete"*; Woolf, *The Social Circulation of the Past*; A. Fox and Woolf, *The Spoken Word*; French, "The 'Remembered Family.'"

9. CoA MS Vincent 3, f. 1r. "Habes iam tandem (Clarissime Comes) has qualescunque de antiquissimis Arundeliae Comitibus observantes ab adventu Normannorum in Angliam in hunc usque diem continuatas. Que ex diplomatibus archiviis Scriniisque Regiis et historicis fide dignis summa cum fide colliguntur et celsitudini tuae eiusdem nobilissimi censerantur." (You have here at last these certain observations concerning the ancient Earls of Arundel, from the coming of the Normans into English continued to this day, which were collected faithfully from the royal records, archives and chests and trustworthy histories.) Another copy of this is BL Harley MS 4840.

10. CoA MS Vincent 3, f. 1r. In the original Latin: "Tuo merito, et omnium Judicio, nec inter nobiles doctior, nec inter doctos nobilior quam tu us, quisquam reperiri queat." This was followed by a "Carmen Censorium" which again exalted Arundel, while making clear that producing the volume entailed reducing a "confused chaos" into order. CoA MS Vincent 3, f. 2r. In the original Latin: "Confusum nimium Chaos nihilque / Quod vel iudicium sapit vel arte, / Quam scriptori opus est laboriosum."

11. BL Harley MS 6018, f. 148v, 151v, 155r, 159r, 176v.

12. Arundel had commissioned Cotton to produce a text of this sort in 1613 (Broadway, *"No historie so meete,"* 40). For Northampton's patronage, see Levy Peck, *Northampton*.

13. BL Cotton MS Julius C III, f. 228r.

14. BL Cotton MS Vespasian, F XIII, f. 249, 330r; see SP 12/287, f. 110, for Knyveton writing to Agarde in 1603.

15. For Camden's notebook containing many extracts from Tower records, see YBL Osborn MS 370.

16. For this episode, see Kendrick, *British Antiquity*; Rockett, "*Britannia*, Ralph Brooke, and the Representation of Privilege"; Herendeen, *William Camden*, 445–92.

17. Vincent also borrowed chronicles, records, and a volume of Thynne's from Cotton (BL Harley MS 6018, f. 150r, 164v, 173r); the Thynne collection had also been borrowed by Knyveton. Indeed, Vincent was a diligent antiquarian, as his massive extant collections in the College of Arms testify. Strikingly, Knyveton's collection on the Arundel family ended up in Vincent's collection (CoA MS Vincent 3).

18. Vincent, *A Discoverie of Errours*, a1v. I have consulted the later transcription of Knyveton's notes made by Peter Le Neve at the Folger Shakespeare Library, shelfmark STC 24756 copy 2 (hereafter cited as Knyveton's Vincent). The original is Bodl. Gough MS Top. Gen. 213.

19. Knyveton's Vincent, insert between 476/477.

20. Knyveton's Vincent, 122.

21. Knyveton's Vincent, 125. Similarly when Vincent cited a ballad to trace the descent of Richard, Duke of York, Knyveton marveled, "I am ashamed on your behalf that live most among & by the records in your Custody yet can not prove the Descent but by an old Ballad Song, so many years ago & perhaps false." Knyveton's Vincent, 622.

22. Knyveton's Vincent, 87.
23. Knyveton's Vincent, 78.
24. Knyveton's Vincent, 151.
25. Knyveton's Vincent, 293.
26. Knyveton's Vincent, 266.
27. Knyveton's Vincent, 416.
28. Knyveton's Vincent, 327.
29. See similarly Peacey's *The Madman and the Churchrobber*, which was published too late to be appropriately integrated into this book.
30. Tite, *Impeachment and Parliamentary Judicature*. For this episode in a similar context to that presented here, see Hunneyball, "The Development of Parliamentary Privilege."
31. *Commons Debates, 1621* (hereafter cited as *CD, 1621*), 4:120.
32. *CD, 1621*, 2:337–38; 3:123ff.
33. Cotton, *Cottoni Posthuma*, 347; the original, which is addressed to Montagu, is BL Harley MS 6810.
34. For Coke in this context, see Boyer, *Sir Edward Coke*; Cromartie, *The Constitutionalist Revolution*.
35. *CD, 1621*, 3:183.
36. *CD, 1621*, 3:229.
37. Toomer, *John Selden: A Life*, 1:322–24; Sharpe, *Sir Robert Cotton*.
38. BL Stowe MS 354, f. 62r–v.
39. Gajda and Cavill, *Writing the History of Parliament*; Read Foster, "The Painful Labour of Mr. Elsyng."
40. In this context, see Pocock, *The Ancient Constitution and the Feudal Law*; Parry, *The Trophies of Time*; Christianson, *Discourse on History, Law, and Governance*; Greenberg, *The Radical Face of the Ancient Constitution*; J. Somerville, "King James VI and I and John Selden"; McGee, *An Industrious Mind*.
41. Cust, *The Forced Loan*; Cogswell, "The Politics of Propaganda."
42. HEH EL 1169, f. 16r.
43. HEH EL 1169, f. 16v.
44. BL Cotton MS Vespasian C XIV, f. 216r–v.
45. Vernon, *Considerations for Regulating the Exchequer*, 58; for Vernon and Cotton in this context, see Gray, "Exchequer Officials and the Market in Crown Property"; Hoyle, "'Vain Projects.'"
46. HEH HM 30662. Kevin Sharpe, in his notes to this manuscript, comments that it had frequently been conflated with Cotton's 1609 collection but that it more likely dated to 1626–28. Given its focus, I agree that it was part of the abortive 1628 Ship Money campaign. Another copy is BL Lansdowne MS 209/9, f. 183 ff.
47. HEH HM 30662, f. 49r.
48. HEH HM 30662, f. 8r.
49. HEH HM 30662, f. 9.
50. He had taken a similar approach in his 1609 tract; I thank Noah Millstone

for sharing his "Sir Robert Cotton, Manuscript Pamphleteering, and the Making of Jacobean Kingship" prior to its publication.

51. The Petition of Right itself was a consummate example of a political instrument emanating from past sources, most notably Magna Carta and its subsequent confirmation and extension in the *Statutum de tallagio non concedendo* under Edward I.

52. *Commons Debates, 1628* (hereafter cited as *CD, 1628*), 2:64.

53. *CD, 1628*, 2:74.

54. *CD, 1628*, 2:248.

55. This episode has proven the nexus of many debates concerning the Caroline regime and the merits of revisionism; see Guy, "The Origins of the Petition of Right Reconsidered"; Young, "The Origins of the Petition of Right Reconsidered Further"; Christianson, "John Selden, the Five Knights Case, and Discretionary Imprisonment"; Christianson, *Discourse on History, Law, and Governance*, 112–63; Kishlansky, "Tyranny Denied"; Lake, "From Revisionist to Royalist History."

56. *CD, 1628*, 2:211.

57. *CD, 1628*, 2:217–19.

58. *CD, 1628*, 2:218.

59. *CD, 1628*, 2:229.

60. Kishlansky maintained that the Crown's decisions about registering the case pursued moderation by not elevating the case to a referendum on discretionary imprisonment (Kishlansky, "Tyranny Denied"). Further explorations of the process of enrollment and expectations for records have confirmed that the delayed enrollment was not unusual; see G. Yeo, "'Let Us See What Is Meant by the Word *Recorde*.'"

61. *CD, 1628*, 2:445, 448, 454–55, 457.

62. *CD, 1628*, 2:508.

63. Popofsky, "The Crisis over Tonnage and Poundage."

64. As was reported in Parliament, the king wished to have tonnage and poundage supplied such that "by passing the bill as my ancestors have had it, my by-past actions will be included, and my future proceedings authorized." *Commons Debates for 1629*, 11.

65. SP 16/133, f. 72r.

66. SP 16/133, f. 99r–v.

67. Rushworth, *Historical Collections of Private Passages of State*, 2:3–4.

68. D. Smith, *Sir Edward Coke*, exposes this as a false opposition.

69. See above all, Sharpe, *The Personal Rule of Charles I*.

70. The William Ryley (d. 1667) in this chapter was the father of William Ryley Jr. (d. 1675) mentioned in the introduction to this volume. Both are discussed extensively in chapter 5, with the elder referred to as William Ryley and the younger as William Ryley Jr.

71. Baron, "Borough, Sir John."

72. BL Harley MS 6018, f. 149r–v.

73. Manuscripts survive of his translations of the first books of Tacitus's *Annales* (Bodl. Rawlinson MS D. 58–59).

74. Woolf, "John Selden, John Borough and Francis Bacon's 'History of Henry VII.'"

75. BL Cotton MS Julius C III, f. 33r–35r.

76. BL Harley MS 6445, published as *Sir John Borough's Notes of Proceedings*.

77. Sharpe, *Personal Rule*, 13, and Cust, *Charles I and the Aristocracy*, 160, highlight the importance of this memo.

78. BL Add. MS 34324, f. 269–274v.

79. Note that at precisely this time Caesar's archive was reorganized, and it would prove a major a repository of precedents for the extraparliamentary revenue creation.

80. Citing a close roll from Edward I's reign, Borough described it as, "Such as after summons had not taken the order of knighthood having in possession 40l land per annum were fined," noting in the margin "fines for not taking knighthood." BL Add. MS 34324, f. 274v.

81. Leonard, "Distraint of Knighthood." Leonard judges it to have been the largest source of Crown revenue in the first decade of Charles's reign outside of parliamentary subsidies, sale of Crown lands, and the Forced Loan, more recently confirmed by Healy, "Crown Revenue and the Political Culture of Early Stuart England."

82. Cust, *Charles I and the Aristocracy*.

83. Borough did perform heraldic services in the 1620s, though in these years there was limited demand. See, for example, Bodl. Add. MS D 84, f. 176v.

84. Cust, *Charles I and the Aristocracy*, 160–61.

85. SP 9/10, f. 43r.

86. SP 9/10, f. 44v.

87. See Bailey, *The Troubles of William Ryley*.

88. In 1634, Ryley performed visitations to Buckinghamshire and Oxfordshire along with John Philipot, Somerset Herald. The Buckinghamshire visitation is printed: Philipot and Ryley, *The Visitation of the Country of Buckingham*.

89. SP 16/169, f. 119.

90. Ryley also frequently produced documents for the Court of Chivalry, and he brought a case there in 1639 when he felt he was dishonored by George Owen, York Herald. See Cust and Hopper, "572 Ryley v Owen."

91. SP 9/33, np.

92. Weston's copy is Bodl. Rawlinson MS B. 55. Another copy is BL Harley MS 1849.

93. For this text, see the apparatus to Borough, *The Sovereignty of the British Seas*.

94. SP 16/200, f. 10. The laws had not been intended to grant England wide-reaching sovereignty; whatever priority was granted to the English Crown reflected that most shipping at the time was done on English vessels. The French crown's power was at a low ebb at this moment.

95. For Grotius and Selden, see Tuck, *Philosophy and Government*; Armitage, *The Ideological Origins of the British Empire*, 123–36; J. Somerville, "Selden, Grotius, and the Seventeenth-Century Intellectual Revolution"; Brito Vieira, "*Mare*

Liberum vs *Mare Clausum*"; Thornton, "John Selden's Response to Hugo Grotius"; Toomer, *John Selden: A Life*, 2:388–435.

96. BL Harley MS 4819, f. 1–120. Previous observers have dated this collection to a later period, and it is clear that Ryley at least presented it to Charles II in 1662 and showed it to Denzil Holles in 1672, but for reasons articulated subsequently, it is more likely that this volume contains Ryley's rough notes, later repurposed for Charles's and then Holles's benefit.

97. The original of "De superioritate maris angliae" is TNA C 47/32/19.

98. Borough, *The Soveraignty of the British Seas Proved by records, History, and the Municipall Lawes of this Kingdome*, 30–31.

99. BL Harley MS 4314.

100. SP 16/208, f. 333v.

101. BL Harley MS 4914 is likely the presentation copy. This version is appended to the fair copy of records that Borough received from Ryley; it is unclear whether they were packaged together for Charles or subsequently.

102. Borough, *Soveraignty of the British Seas Proved by records*, 43–45.

103. Selden also published a much-expanded edition of his *Titles of Honor* in 1631, which covered similar ground to Borough's "Observations," though far more comprehensively. While this text has not typically been viewed as part of Charles's program of aristocratic regeneration, Selden likely hoped it would be. Toomer, *John Selden: A Life*, 1:126–68.

104. *A Complete Collection of State Trials and Proceedings for High Treason and Other Crimes and Misdemeanors*, 3:1023, hereafter cited as *CCST*.

105. BL Add. MS 34324, f. 284.

106. SP 16/276, f. 186r.

107. SP 16/276, f. 186r.

108. SP 16/276, f. 188v.

109. For the classic studies characterizing Charles's Personal Rule as initially, and potentially enduringly, successful, see Russell, *Parliaments and English Politics*; Russell, *The Fall of the British Monarchies*; Russell, *Unrevolutionary England*; Sharpe, *Personal Rule*.

110. Smuts, "Force, Love, and Authority."

111. Millstone, *Manuscript Circulation*, 238–74; Langelüddecke, "'I finde all men & my officers all soe unwilling.'"

112. Lake, "The Laudian Style"; Fincham, "The Restoration of the Altars"; Milton, *Catholic and Reformed*; Milton, "The Creation of Laudianism."

113. For this volume, see Milton, *Catholic and Reformed*, 318. The volume was likely the product of long gestation; at some uncertain moment, Laud compiled a list of "Things which I have projected to do, if God bless me in them." ([Laud], *The Autobiography of Dr William Laud*, 439.) Among the ensuing list of twenty-three items was "A book in vellum fair written, concerning the records which are in the Tower, and concern the Clergy." Laud returned to this list to note when these projects were fulfilled; next to this entry, "This book I got done at my own charge, and have left it in my study at Lambeth for posterity, July 10, 1637. Ab anno 20 Ed. I ad

annum IV." [Laud], *The Autobiography of Dr William Laud*, 442; Prynne, *A Breviate of the Life of William Laud*, 29.

114. Why Laud consulted Ryley rather than Borough is unclear, but in his capacity as Chancellor of Oxford, Laud had licensed Ryley and Philipot to scrutinize the colleges' coats of arms during their visitation to Oxford, which elicited resistance. They nonetheless completed their visitation, perhaps earning Laud's esteem (Society of Antiquaries MS 72/22; SP 16/271, f. 178–180).

115. LPL MS 323, f. 1r: "Dominus rex vult et precipit, quod cum Iudices Ecclesiastici per prohibicionem Regiam sibi porrectam supersedeant in casibus predictis, quod Cancellarius vel capitalis Iusticiarius ipsius Domini regis, qui pro tempore fuerit viso libello illius causa ad instanciam querentis si viderint quod per breve de Cancellaria querenti remedium suo caso non possit, sed quod ad Curiam ecclesasticam pertineat causam illam determinare, scribant Iudicibus coram quibus causa illa prius fuerit agitata, quod in causa illa procedant, non obstante Prohibitione Regia prius sibi inde directa." (The Lord King wills and commands, that Ecclesiastical Judges may sit in the above-mentioned cases, despite long-standing royal prohibition, if the Chancellor or the Lord Chief Justice of this realm has seen the writ of the complainant and determined that they cannot give redress to the party in this case, but that it pertains to the Ecclesiastical Court, they may write to the judges that they should proceed, notwithstanding the previous Royal prohibition.)

116. LPL MS 323, f. 224r.

117. LPL MS 323, f. 14r–v, 108r–v, 224r–v.

118. LPL MS 323, f. 105.

119. LPL MS 323, f. 102r.

120. LPL MS 323, f. 9r.

121. LPL MS 323, f. 19r–24v.

122. The extracts for Prynne's volume may have been collected by Ryley's son William Ryley Jr., though whether this should be interpreted as a historical irony or an act of malice by Prynne is unclear (BL Lansdowne MS 228).

123. Prynne, *The First [Third] Tome of an Exact Chronological Vindication*, 440.

124. SP 16/466, f. 181.

125. Bodl. Rawlinson MS D. 921.

126. SP 16/476, f. 75.

127. SP 16/484, f. 77.

128. It might be argued that the health and vigor of the Personal Rule portrayed by revisionist historians —such as Conrad Russell, Kevin Sharpe, and Mark Kishlansky—captures, if inaccurately universalizes, a media bubble inhabited by the more sanguine members of the Caroline regime.

Chapter Five

1. The category of "information warfare" is of relatively recent vintage and tends to have an extremely modern focus. The US Air Force's *Cornerstones of Information Warfare* defines the term as "any action to Deny, Exploit, Corrupt, or Destroy the

enemy's information and its functions; protecting ourselves against those actions and exploiting our own military information functions." (Fogelman and Widnall, *Cornerstones of Information Warfare*, 3–4.) Andrew Borden has influentially revised the categories to "degrade, corrupt, deny, exploit" (Borden, "What is Information Warfare?" 4). I adapt these definitions to a context in which participants were as concerned with allegiance as with military conflict and that possessed unique technological and communications features; it nonetheless remains a useful rubric for understanding elements of conflict in this increasingly information-dependent society. For the study of information, see now most essentially Blair et al., *Information: Historical Companion*.

2. There is a large literature on censorship in early modern Britain; major works include Patterson, *Censorship and Interpretation*; Lambert, "The Printers and the Government"; Mendle, "De Facto Freedom, De Facto Authority"; Clegg, *Press Censorship in Jacobean England*; McElligott, *Royalism, Print, and Censorship in Revolutionary England*; Clegg, *Press Censorship in Caroline England*; Como, "Print, Censorship, and Ideological Escalation." Scholarship on libel and polemic is too expansive to cite fully, but see Croft, "The Reputation of Robert Cecil"; Bellany; "'Railing Rymes and Vaunting Verse'"; Bellany, *The Politics of Court Scandal*; Knights, *Representation and Misrepresentation in Later Stuart Britain*; A. Hughes, *Gangraena and the Struggle for the English Revolution*; McRae, "Reading Libels"; Cogswell, "John Felton, Popular Political Culture, and the Assassination of the Duke of Buckingham"; Bellany and Cogswell, *The Murder of King James I*; Lake, *Bad Queen Bess?*; Lake, *All Hail to the Archpriest*. There is also a sizable literature on petitioning, especially during the English Civil War, but see particularly in this context Zaret, *The Origins of Democratic Culture*; Hirst, "Making Contact"; Weil, "Thinking about Allegiance"; Lake, "Puritans, Popularity and Petitions"; Peacey, *Print and Public Politics*; Worthen, "Supplicants and Guardians."

3. The Parliamentarians did capture a copy of the Glamorgan Treaty after the ambush and killing of the Archbishop of Tuam in 1645. For both Crown correspondence captured by Parliamentarians and the communication strategies used by Charles I and Queen Henrietta Maria at this time, see Bulman, "The Practice of Politics."

4. SP 45/20, f. 281r.

5. Clegg, "Burning Books as Propaganda"; Cressy, "Book Burning in Tudor and Stuart England"; Hunt, "'Burn This Letter'"; Smyth, *Material Texts in Early Modern England*. For somewhat similar issues, see Partington and Smyth, *Book Destruction from the Medieval to the Contemporary*; Ovenden, *Burning the Books*.

6. Despite Charles's efforts, many of his papers were captured. In November 1647, for example, Secretary of the Foreign Tongues Georg Rudolph Weckerlin deposited 115 letters and seven bundles and packets of "papers & letters intercepted," likely into the State Paper Office; another delivery from January 1648 deposited 124 letters (SP 45/20, f. 227r, 228r).

7. SP 45/20, f. 281v.

8. Birch, *A Collection of the State Papers of John Thurloe*, 2:v.

9. Gilbert Burnet claimed that Laud had burned his more incriminating papers; Anthony Milton notes that there is little to support this (Milton, Laud, William"). The study of historical disinformation is only gradually emerging; in this context see Coast, "Misinformation and Disinformation in Late Jacobean Court Politics"; W. White, "Parliament, Print, and the Politics of Disinformation."

10. For Prynne, see Lamont, *Marginal Prynne*; Weston and Greenberg, *Subjects and Sovereigns*; McRae, "Stigmatizing Prynne"; Kishlansky, "A Whipper Whipped."

11. For Prynne's library catalog, likely from his time at Lincoln's Inn in the 1620s, see SP 16/377, f. 207r–209v.

12. BL Sloane MS 2035b, f. 12.

13. SP 16/497, f.159.

14. For this literature, see Millstone, "Seeing Like a Statesman"; Bellany and Cogswell, *Murder of King James I*; Lake, *Bad Queen Bess?*; Cowan, "The History of Secret Histories." Though the most celebrated of such works vilified Catholics, this mode of reasoning could be directed toward any adversary. Information warfare was ubiquitous in them, as they regularly described evil counselors destroying incriminating documents, stealing papers, and circulating disinformation. Those who wrote the texts also often claimed to have acquired them through clandestine means. For example, Thomas Scott's 1620 *Vox Populi*—the best-known work in the genre—purported to transcribe a secret speech of Ambassador Count Gondomar to the Spanish Council of State, which described efforts to undermine the Bodleian Library and reveled at the prospect of breaking up Robert Cotton's library.

15. SP 16/499, f. 97r.

16. SP 16/499, f. 97r.

17. SP 16/499, f. 97v.

18. Two such works, Prynne's 1645 *Hidden Workes of Darkenes Brought to Publike* and then, the next year, *Canterburies Doom*, were published after Laud's execution.

19. Prynne, *A Breviate of the Life of William Laud*, 1.

20. *CCST*, 4:566.

21. Mark Kishlansky has noted that Prynne used a similar strategy in his famous *Histriomastix*, which earned him his public punishments; Kishlansky, "A Whipper Whipped."

22. Bodl. Laud Misc. MS 760, 29–31. For a printed edition of these notes, see Laud, *The Works of the Most Reverend Father in God, William Laud*, 3:259–72.

23. Bodl. Laud Misc. MS 760, 33–35.

24. Bodl. Laud Misc. MS 760, 2. For the diary entry itself see Laud, *Works*, 3:132.

25. Bodl. Laud Misc. MS 760, 4.

26. Bodl. Laud Misc. MS 760, 11.

27. Bodl. Laud Misc. MS 760, 2.

28. Bodl. Laud Misc. MS 760, 8. Similarly, Laud noted where Prynne had omitted pious phrases such as "God be merciful." Bodl. Laud Misc., MS 760, 26, 35, passim.

29. Bodl. Laud Misc. MS 760, 24.

30. Bodl. Laud Misc. MS 760, 24, 32.

31. Bodl. Laud Misc. MS 760, 7.

32. Bodl. Laud Misc. MS 760, 8.

33. Bodl. Laud Misc. MS 760, 19, 22, 28.

34. In part for reasons adduced subsequently, the literature on spycraft in early modern Britain is patchy. See Marshall, *Intelligence and Espionage in the Reign of Charles II*; Bossy, *Under the Molehill*; R. Adams, "A Spy on the Payroll?"; R. Adams, "A Most Secret Service"; Alford, "Some Elizabethan Spies;" Akkerman, *Invisible Agents*.

35. *Journal of the House of Commons, 1547–1830*, 2:515, hereafter cited as *CJ*.

36. SP 45/21, f. 78r.

37. Why Charles chose this moment is unclear; lack of access to such materials may have been a problem since his flight from London, but perhaps his attention only turned to this issue at this point. The appeal of Ryley's return for Parliament is no clearer, but perhaps its members desired someone with facility in the Tower records on hand and were willing to be flexible concerning that person's allegiances.

38. *CJ*, 3:233, 3:291. Ryley Jr named Selden as his godfather in a petition shortly after his father's death, in which he insinuated that it was Ryley's recommendation that earned Selden the Keepership (SP 29/251, f. 199r).

39. SP 29/251, f. 199r. This is the earliest and fullest of Ryley Jr.'s petitions; see also SP 29/66, f. 220; SP 45/21, f. 82r, and his wife Elizabeth's petition after his death (SP 29/387, f. 252r). Hancock worked alongside Ryley in the Tower Office, was granted a coat of arms by Borough's rival Richard St. George in 1635, and served in low-level bureaucratic positions during the Interregnum until his death in 1659. Guillim, *A Display of Heraldry*, 347; TNA E 215/568; *Calendar of the Proceedings of the Committee for Advance of Money, 1642–1656*, 2:904.

40. For such practices of transmission, see Britland, "'In the Hollow of His Wooden Leg.'"

41. SP 29/251, f. 199r.

42. SP 45/21, f. 78r.

43. SP 29/251, f. 199r–v.

44. SP 29/251, f. 199v.

45. SP 16/514/2 f. 1, 65. His reading continued to focus on aristocratic and honor-based concerns; his commonplace book, from around this time, predominantly concerned heraldry and honor culture (BL Harley MS 4991).

46. *Journal of the House of Lords, 1509–1832*, 8:542, hereafter cited as *LJ*.

47. SP 16/507, f. 15; Bailey, *The Troubles of William Ryley*, 11, 20–21.

48. *LJ*, 10:643.

49. *Calendar of the Proceedings of the Committee for Compounding etc, 1643–1660*, 4:2912.

50. Bailey, *Troubles of William Ryley*, 16.

51. Ailes, "'A Pair of Garters,'" 224.

52. PA HL/PO/JO/10/1/199.

53. PA HL/PO/JO/10/1/199.

54. *LJ*, 8:122; PA HL/PO/JO/10/1/199.

55. *LJ*, 8:130.

56. SP 201/2, f. 154; SP 29/251, f. 199.

57. SP 16/514/2, f. 66; BL Harley MS 1380, f. 27.

58. P. Daly, *The English Emblem Book Tradition*, 3:xxix–xxx; see BL Harley MS 14308 and Bodl. Rawlinson MS B. 48. There is also a draft in London Metropolitan Archive CLC/270/MS03342.

59. *CJ*, 4:184. Ryley also took custody of the standards captured from the Scots in 1650, whose display in Westminster he oversaw, and he presented "a perfect Registry of all the Colours taken from the *Scotts*" to the Commons. *CJ*, 6:465, 517; P. Daly, *English Emblem Book Tradition*, 3:xxvii–xxviii.

60. SP 24/66, f. 119r; SP 24/15, f. 17v.

61. SP 24/15, f. 126r, 186r.

62. Similarly, see Akkerman, *Invisible Agents*.

63. For Thurloe, see Peacey, "Cromwellian England"; Little, "John Thurloe and the Offer of the Crown to Oliver Cromwell"; Peacock, "Cromwell's 'Spymaster'?"; Venning, "Thurloe, John."

64. Peacey, "Cromwellian England."

65. Kelsey, *Inventing a Republic*, 18.

66. *CJ*, 6:108, 111, 168, 333; Kelsey, *Inventing a Republic*, 16.

67. SP 45/20, f. 230r.

68. SP 25/17, f. 26; SP 25/65, f. 18; Bodl. Tanner MS 114, f. 91r; Bodl. Tanner MS 114, f. 92r. Similarly, in April 1653, at the height of the First Anglo-Dutch War, Ryley was ordered to send to the Council of State records on English control of the Channel. SP 25/41, f. 36; SP 18/35, f. 69.

69. Birch, *Collection of the State Papers*, 1:377.

70. This mode of information warfare would reshape political institutions more broadly in the War of Spanish Succession; see Munda, "The Spyglass and the Mirror."

71. Underdown, *Royalist Conspiracy*, 97–104; *CCST*, 5:517–40.

72. Underdown, *Royalist Conspiracy*, 192–93; Fitzgibbons, "Hereditary Succession and the Cromwellian Protectorate"; *CCST*, 5:841–72.

73. Birch, *Collection of the State Papers*, 1:xiv; Burnett, *History of His Own Time*, 86–87.

74. Birch, *Collection of the State Papers*, 1:xiv. Burnett, *History of His Own Time*, 87–88.

75. See Little, "John Thurloe and the Offer of the Crown," and Fitzgibbons, "Hereditary Succession," which disagree on the specific strategy but agree on the broader point.

76. *The Whole Business of Sindercombe*, 23–24; Marshall, "Sindercombe, Miles"; *CJ*, 7:481.

77. SP 25/14, f. 39. The increased salary reflected the lack of requests and therefore fees available to the Tower clerks (SP 25/15, f. 29r).

78. As Ryley Jr. later put it, "Being a student at Oxford anno 1651 my Loyalty

commanded mee to make my escape to Worcester, and did ingage severall persons of quality to goe thither with mee." He reported that here he "received a shott in my knee and was taken prisoner, sent up to Peterhouse in Aldergate-street, and suffered many hardshipps, and am now soe disabled, that I am only fitt for a sedentary life." SP 29/251, f. 199v.

79. The Ryleys also engaged in the projecting characteristic of previous Tower Keepers, most notably in proposals in 1653 and 1654 to use Tower records concerning forest lands previously owned by the Crown to generate revenue (SP 18/40, f. 48r–48v; 56r–57v; Bodl. Rawlinson MS A. 21, f. 412r). At this point Ryley also appealed to Thurloe for support (Birch, *Collection of the State Papers*, 2:242). This effort resulted in Ryley Jr.'s appointment as agent of the commission for the sale of royal forests.

80. SP 25/23, f. 43; for subsequent orders, see Bailey, *The Troubles of William Ryley*, 23–25.

81. SP 25/134 contains a list of private bonds returned in 1654. In 1657 Ryley inventoried 1,609 volumes that were returned, delivering to Parliament "An inventory or Catalogue of those Registers which were sent into Scotland." SP 25/135, f. 1r, 63r. During this period, Ryley distilled these records for the use of John Rushworth (SP 25/136). Rushworth integrated these notes into his *Historical Collections*, on several occasions simply transcribing them. They remained essential as he composed the latter parts of his collection, as by that time the records summarized in Ryley's notebook had been lost at sea (Rushworth, *Historical Collections of Private Passages of State*, 4:383).

82. SP 29/21, f. 287r.

83. SP 29/251, f. 199v.

84. SP 29/251, f. 199v.

85. SP 29/14, f. 87v–88r. Though Ryley told them that this appropriation had incurred the outrage of John Maitlaind, Duke of Lauderdale, his interlocutors scoffed, "it was no matter If it were hanged about his necke If he were so much for the Covenant, and that shortly that Bishops and Common Prayer should be through all Scotland and in a better settlement than England."

86. SP 29/14, f. 88r–v.

87. SP 29/14, f. 88v.

88. SP 29/14, f. 89r. Note that accounts of these Parliaments were available in Scotland through printed acts, draft minutes, and more, but the texts in question were the official records.

89. SP 29/21, f. 287.

90. SP 29/23, f. 14; SP 29/24, f. 16.

91. *The Acts of the Parliaments of Scotland*, 4:i–ii.

92. SP 45/21, f. 78r.

93. SP 29/32, f. 48r.

94. In 1661 they charged nearly £138 in response to around 110 requests, and they were on a similar pace for the first five months of 1662, when the account book ends (SP 29/55, f. 51ff). Fabian Phillips and William Dugdale were frequently the agents

for such requests. In 1662 the Ryleys requested an annual salary of £160, suggesting that the fee structure for the Tower records had reverted back to its pre-1650 form (SP 45/21, f. 79r).

95. SP 29/251, f. 199v.

96. ITL Petyt MS 538 17, f. 466r. Ryley had died that July, but Ryley Jr. continued such services (SP 29/251, f. 200r).

97. SP 29/21, f. 284; it is possible that he worried that these books might show him in a poor light to the new regime.

98. SP 29/448, f. 47.

99. Bodl. Tanner MS 141, f. 109r–v.

100. In Ryley Jr.'s later petitions, he highlighted that his father "hath carefully preserved all the Records and Claymes of al the forests, parkes, chases and warrens on this side Trent, in the tyme of the late warres, and hath made Callendars of Indexes therunto for his Majeties advantage." SP 45/21, f. 78v.

101. BL Stowe MS 544, f. 108r. This is a later copy of SP 29/5, f. 139 ff.

102. "Edward III: November 1372," in *Parliament Rolls of Medieval England*, http://www.british-history.ac.uk/no-series/parliament-rolls-medieval/november-1372: "Also, the commons pray: that whereas records and so on received in the king's courts should by right remain there as permanent evidence and assistance for all those party to them and, when necessary, for all those to whom they relate in any manner; recently the courts of our said lord the king have refused to make a search or exemplification of anything that might fall in evidence against the king or to his disadvantage. May it please him to ordain by statute that such searches and exemplifications shall be made for all people on whatever record concerns them in any manner, whether it falls against the king or against other people."

103. BL Stowe MS 544, f. 108v.

104. BL Stowe MS 544, f. 109v.

105. Shortly after Prynne's death, de Vere issued a warrant to Ryley Jr. ordering the delivery of the eyre records he had previously been denied. The new Keeper, Algernon May, rebuffed the entreaty (SP 29/276, f. 220).

106. The literature on politics and publishing is far too voluminous to cite, but see in this context Knights, *Representation and Misrepresentation*; J. Raymond, *Pamphlets and Pamphleteering*; A. Hughes, *Gangraena*; Peacey, *Print and Public Politics*; Sharpe, *Rebranding Rule*.

107. SP 29/251, f. 200r; SP 45/21, f. 78v.

108. Ryley, *Placita Parliamentaria*, A2r, A2v. There are Latin and English versions of this epistle; I have relied on the English version while also incorporating some material that the Latin version excised from the English.

109. In late 1649 John Milton seized his papers and writings (TNA PRO 22/22).

110. For Filmer, see Pocock, *The Ancient Constitution and Feudal Law*; J. Daly, *Sir Robert Filmer*; Cuttica, *Sir Robert Filmer*.

111. Filmer, *The Free-holders Grand Inquest*, 1–2.

112. Filmer, *Free-holders Grand Inquest*, 4.

113. Filmer, *Free-holders Grand Inquest*, 5.

114. Filmer, *Free-holders Grand Inquest*, 13.
115. Prynne, *A Plea for the Lords*, A2v–A3r.
116. Prynne, *A Plea for the Lords*, A3v.
117. Prynne, *Irenarches redivivus*, A2r.
118. Prynne, *The First Part of an Historicall Collection of Parliaments of England*, A2r–A3v.
119. Peter, *Good Work for a Magistrate*, 33.
120. Prynne, *Exact Abridgement*, A4v. Whereas Prynne attributed it to Cotton, others have speculated that it may have been collected by William Lambarde or William Bowyer.
121. Prynne, *Exact Abridgement*, A3v.
122. Prynne, *Exact Abridgement*, A3v–A4r.
123. Prynne, *The First Part of a Brief Register*, B2v.
124. Prynne, *First Part of a Brief Register*, B1v–B2r.
125. Prynne, *Brevia Parliamentaria Rediviva*, A4v–A*1r. This volume consisted of extracts from the "the Records I newly rescued and raysed for the Grave, being unknown to, unperused by any of this or the former Generation," with brief commentaries, while also providing a catalog of past MPs that he argued should be used to structure parliament (Prynne, *Brevia Parliamentaria Rediviva*, A*4v). In early 1660, seemingly unaware that the army was paving the way for Charles II's return, Prynne published *The Second Part of a Brief Register* to contest the army's right to dissolve Parliament, criticizing in particular the legality of Pride's Purge.
126. Prynne, *Brevia Parliamentaria Rediviva*, A2v–A3r.
127. Prynne created his own lists, catalogs, and indexes, such as a collection of papal bulls (TNA OBS 1/1271). He also took advantage of his position to bring rolls to his lodgings; around Prynne's death, the clerk Ralph Jennings's audit revealed that in the previous three years, twenty-two rolls had gone missing, which he recovered from Prynne's chambers (TNA OBS 1/1271, f. 2r–v).
128. Prynne, *Brevia Parliamentaria Rediviva*, A4v.
129. For instances of access to archives being used as a political measure, see Griffiths, "Secrecy and Authority."
130. Holles was particularly sensitive to instances when the *Exact Abridgment* overstated the power of the Commons: for example, when Prynne claimed that the judgment on the fining of Henry le Despenser, Bishop of Norwich, had been delivered by "the Lords by assent of the Parliament," Holles noted that the record read "del assent des Contz, Barons, & autres Sr Temporelx presents en ce Parlement," which suggested not that the Lords were part of Parliament but rather constitutive of it (HEH Rare Books 433814, p. 293).
131. For example, Petyt claimed that Prynne had dated a large body of parliamentary writs to Edward III's reign that derived from Edward I's (PA HC/LB/1/102, p. 899). For Petyt's collections, which form the core of the Inner Temple Library's manuscript collection, see Davies, *Catalogue of manuscripts*.
132. For this controversy, see Pocock, *Ancient Constitution*; Weston, "Legal Sovereignty in the Brady Controversy"; Weston and Greenberg, *Subjects and Sov-*

ereigns; Greenberg, *The Radical Face of the Ancient Constitution*; Rose, "Robert Brady's Intellectual History."

133. The Ryleys do not seem to have reorganized the space, and the volumes they produced possessed little detail and few notes concerning the locations or descriptions of their sources, suggesting that they were for personal use and not to facilitate searching by others (TNA OBS 1/241). A catalog of their manuscripts, produced by Williamson after purchasing them at Ryley Jr.'s death in 1675, listed more than 140 volumes. Three types predominated: heraldic materials, transcriptions of records drawn from the Tower, and catalogs to record classes, such as a "Catalogus Cartarum Antiquarum" (SP 29/230, f. 175r–176r).

134. BL Lansdowne MS 228.

135. For the first, see Samuel Pepys's diary for May 13, 1664; for the second, see, for example, SP 29/246, f. 54. That said, in 1666 Prynne rebuffed an effort to evict the Ryleys from their Tower residence of sixteen years (SP 29/153, f. 127r).

Chapter Six

1. I have adapted the term from the usage in Shapin and Schaffer, *Leviathan and the Air-pump*, itself an adaptation from Wittgenstein. As will be clear, I do not see Williamson as sharing the same experimental form of life of Robert Boyle; rather, his emphasis on inscription and role as center of calculation more approximates that described in Latour, *Science in Action*, and Latour and Woolgar, *Laboratory Life*.

2. For Williamson, see Fraser, *The Intelligence of the Secretaries of State*; Marshall, *Intelligence and Espionage in the Reign of Charles II*; Marshall, "Sir Joseph Williamson and the Conduct of Administration"; Tessier, *Réseaux diplomatiques et République des Lettres*; Peacey, "'A Knowing but a Discrete Man'"; Popper, "Joseph Williamson and the Information Order of the Early English Empire."

3. Soll, *The Information Master*.

4. Soll, *Information Master*. Note that Williamson's archive evinces little trace of the mercantile practices and concern with political economy so central to Colbert. See also Brendecke, *Empirical Empire*, for the limitations of such practices and the archives they produced.

5. For such connections, see R. Yeo, *Notebooks, Virtuosi, and Early Modern Science*; P. Miller, *Peiresc's Mediterranean World*; R. Yeo, "Thinking with Excerpts"; Keller, *Knowledge and the Public Interest*; Yale, "With Slips and Scraps"; Yale, *Sociable Knowledge*.

6. Peacey, "A Knowing but a Discrete Man," calls for precisely this perspective on Williamson.

7. Williamson made good use of these relationships; for example, seeking to win favor in Cologne, he presented the Elector Palatine with Ashmole's *History of the Most Noble Order of the Garter* (Bodl. Ashmole MS 1131, f. 300r).

8. Bodl. Ashmole MS 1131, 299v. Williamson also consulted Ashmole concerning issues of precedence (Bodl. Ashmole MS 840, f. 323r).

9. He received, for example, congratulations on his appointment to the keeper-

ship from Vincent Placcius, then serving as Hamburg's envoy to England but who was better known as a polymathic jurist and who wrote an influential treatise on the art of excerpting (SP 82/10, f. 96r).

10. For such rough note taking, see Blair, "Note-Taking as an Art of Transmission"; R. Yeo, *Notebooks, Virtuosi, and Early Modern Science*; Vine, *Miscellaneous Order*. Williamson's career and notes show little direct uptake from the commercial practices of note-taking that often shaped similar note-taking practices; see Soll, *Information Master*; Vine, "Commercial Commonplacing."

11. TNA CO 324/3. For other daybooks, see, for example, SP 29/87; TNA 29/319a. For another example of a book mostly consisting of notes from meetings, see SP 29/366.

12. SP 9/17.

13. For early modern notebooks, see Moss, *Printed Common-Place Books*; Blair, *Too Much to Know*; Havens, *Commonplace Books*. For the epistemological dimensions of the practices of note-taking and notebook making, see also te Heesen, "The Notebook"; Müller-Wille and Charmantier, "Carl Linnaeus's Botanical Paper Slips."

14. SP 9/14, front matter.

15. SP 9/14, f. 12r.

16. SP 9/14, f. 10v.

17. SP 9/14, f. 11r; the following page had notes from such volumes.

18. Neither shared Wilson's energy for the keepership. Throughout Boswell's tenure, he was predominantly at The Hague, serving as the resident agent to the United Provinces. Randolph obtained some papers in the 1630s, but he did not promote the office. For Randolph's *relazioni* and notebooks of state documents, see SP 9/192, SP 9/195. All influx to the office apparently ceased in the 1640s.

19. Raymond had been granted the office in reversion in 1640. In 1636 he was in Florence and Rome, likely in the service of Basil Fielding, 2nd Earl of Denbigh, ambassador to Venice, whence he wrote to Boswell. The following year he had returned to Westminster and sent Denbigh occasional newsletters. Raymond was in Paris by 1641. See WCRO CR 2017/C97/1–3 for Raymond's correspondence with Boswell; see WCRO CR 2017/C48/145 and WCRO CR 2017/C48/101 for his newsletters to Denbigh. His experience in the State Paper Office is passed over in his autobiography; see T. Raymond, *The Autobiography of Thomas Raymond*.

20. Randolph continued to be paid until his 1660 death, but Raymond seems to have done the labor and in 1655 wrote to Randolph to solidify his claim to the office (SP 45/20, f. 233r). Raymond performed the same tasks as Wilson and Randolph, producing volumes such as a formulary of salutations and valedictions for addressing dignitaries (SP 9/189). For other similar collections of his, see SP 9/54; SP 9/154, SP 9/155; Bodl. Tanner MS 186. Williamson acquired these collections after Raymond's death.

21. Bodl. Tanner MS 80, f. 97.

22. For example, in 1661 he provided the governor of newly acquired Tangier, Henry Mordaunt, Earl of Peterborough, with twenty-three letters, instructions, minutes, patents, and more concerning "Morocco, Fez, or other part of Barbary"

(SP 45/20, 244r–245r). This was likely the entirety of the office's collections at that time concerning these polities (SP 45/20, f. 245; BL Lansdowne MS 1051, f. 25r). For other occasions of Raymond delivering packets to diplomats, see SP 45/20, f. 239r, f. 240r.

23. SP 45/20, f. 238r.

24. SP 45/20, f. 243. For the catalog, see SP 45/20, f. 248r.

25. SP 45/20, f. 249r. Shortly after relinquishing the keepership, Raymond prepared a sketch history of the office for Williamson. In this history, he acknowledged that it still relied on Wilson's classification but that only a schematic description of the offices could be given because of "the many taken out of the Office by the Secretaries of State & Privy Councellors & very often not returned, the discordes & losses in the Office produced by the late troubles of near 20 yeares continuance, & the takeing out of diverse papers by Bradshaw, Thurlowe, Milton, & which I am now endeavouring to recover" (SP 45/20, f. 273r, another copy at SP 45/20, f. 274r and BL Stowe MS 549, f. 1r). As late as 1673, Raymond continued to correspond with Williamson, occasionally sending books and papers that had come into his possession and seeking Williamson's support for his disabled son (SP 29/56, f. 174; SP 29/273 f. 270; SP 29/274, f. 192; SP 29/277, f. 237; SP 29/334, f. 209).

26. SP 45/20, f. 269r; SP 29/45, f. 43.

27. SP 45/20, f. 283r; see also SP 45/21, f. 104r, 105r, 107r.

28. SP 45/20, f. 282r.

29. SP 45/21, f. 111r.

30. In 1664, for example, warrants were still being issued directing Haberdashers Hall papers' return (SP 44/15, f. 65); for the recovered list, see SP 29/109, f. 109. That April, Williamson received an expansive warrant to collect from "thee hands of many persons severall Books Papers and writings releateing to matters ... during the late Warrs and times of usurpation" (SP 44/16, f. 87). For continuing acquisitions, see SP 29/120, f. 131; SP 45/20, f. 284r–286r. Such actions continued to be part of his portfolio, and he was centrally involved in confiscating Milton's "De doctrina christiana"; see Campbell et al, *Milton and the Manuscript of De doctrina Christiana.*

31. SP 45/21, f. 109v–110r.

32. SP 45/21, f. 106r.

33. SP 45/20, f. 281v.

34. SP 45/20, f. 282r. For the provenance of this collection, see S. Adams, "The Papers of Robert Dudley, Earl of Leicester, I." For Leicester's other papers, see S. Adams, "The Papers of Robert Dudley, Earl of Leicester, II" and "The Papers of Robert Dudley, Earl of Leicester, III."

35. SP 9/30; SP 9/32, f. 185r.

36. SP 45/20, f. 280r–281v; SP 45/20, f. 287r.

37. SP 45/21, f. 6r. Such gifts often also included *relazioni*, which he received several of in these years (SP 9/145, 9/147, 9/149, 9/125). For Williamson's patronage of such materials, see Bulman, *Anglican Enlightenment.*

38. SP 45/21, f. 5r.

39. SP 45/21, f. 72r, 74r.

40. SP 45/21 f. 85r.

41. See, for example, his correspondence regarding copying treaties held by the Chancery: SP 45/21, f. 17r; SP 29/63, f. 67; SP 29/70, f. 43, 97; SP 29/90, f. 113; SP 29/236, f. 109; SP 29/450, f. 235; SP 29/237, f. 25; SP 29/309, f. 2.

42. For example, in 1670 he received thirteen of Arlington's entry books (SP 45/21, f. 15r).

43. SP 45/21, f. 44r–56v. See also Tessier, *Réseaux diplomatiques*, 609–15. For the catalogs of entry books, see SP 45/21, f. 59r–60v. The following year, he had a clerk take succinct notes concerning entries registered in these volumes (SP 9/32, f. 314 ff.) Tessier numbers the former at 378, the latter at 24.

44. TNA PC 2/69, f. 454; for Williamson's list of the Ryleys' records, see TNA OBS 1/241. For Elizabeth Ryley, see Popper, "Inscription and Political Exclusion."

45. TNA 29/366, f. 128.

46. BL Egerton MS 2542, f. 115–16, reprinted in Tessier, *Réseaux diplomatiques*, 592–95.

47. For the post office, see Fraser, *Intelligence of the Secretaries of State*; Whyman, *The Pen and the People*.

48. For letter writing in early modern Britain, see Daybell and Hinds, *Material Readings of Early Modern Culture*; Daybell, *The Material Letter in Early Modern England*; O'Neill, *The Opened Letter*; Daybell and Gordon, *Cultures of Correspondence in Early Modern Britain*.

49. Tessier, *Réseaux diplomatiques*, 217.

50. For agents in news correspondence, see Peacey, "Written According to My Usual Way."

51. Tessier, *Réseaux diplomatiques*, 185.

52. SP 29/441, f. 127r, reprinted in Tessier, *Réseaux diplomatiques*, 601.

53. SP 29/441, f. 126r, reprinted in Tessier, *Réseaux diplomatiques*, 600–601.

54. SP 81/60–61, f. 138; Tessier, *Réseaux diplomatiques*, 602.

55. These were often mercantile, but the communications themselves were not necessarily concerned with specific commercial news. See, for example, the Viennese collection of sixteenth-century handwritten newsletters known as *Fuggerzeitungen* hosted by the Austrian Institute of Historical Research: Institut für Österreichische Geschichtsforschung, "About the Fugger Newsletters." See also Schobesberger, "Mapping the *Fuggerzeitungen*." For the development of norms and conventions in commercial communications networks in response to these challenges, see Trivellato, *The Familiarity of Strangers*.

56. *The Despatches of William Perwich*, 4, hereafter cited as *DWP*.

57. SP 29/196, f. 136.

58. For a limited sample, *DWP*, 19, 222, 321. On occasion Perwich acknowledged that the enclosure contained the full value of his epistle (*DWP*, 292).

59. The two-volume collection edited by W. D. Christie, *Letters Addressed from London to Sir Joseph Williamson*, hereafter cited as WC, contains such examples. See WC, 1:33, 1:187, 2:77.

60. WC, 2:111, 113, 124.

61. At times Perwich reported on natural philosophical news, such as a disastrous blood transfusion in Paris, which Perwich claimed would be "a great piece of news to the English Greshamites." *DWP*, 60; see also *DWP*, 48.

62. *DWP*, 4–5.

63. Similarly, see Slauter, "The Paragraph as Information Technology."

64. *DWP*, 40, 52, 75.

65. *DWP*, 25.

66. SP 18/101, f. 87r. He also acquired the earliest plat of Port Royal; see Vernier, "Maps for Intelligence Gathering?"

67. *DWP*, 19, 64, 106, 131.

68. Similarly, despite their contempt for public gossip, Williamson's clerks reported it to him while he was in Cologne, whether or not they deemed it credible. See, for example, WC, 1:63, 99.

69. This stance often generalizes from Shapin, *The Social History of Truth*; for one line of criticism of this approach, see Millstone, "Designed for Collection."

70. For Williamson's manipulation and usage of such tensions, see Tessier, "Un apprentissage diplomatique."

71. For the material strategies of archival organization in early modern Europe, see Malcolm, "Thomas Harrison and his 'Ark of Studies'"; Stallybrass and Wolfe, "The Material Culture of Record-Keeping in Early Modern Archives"; Friedrich, *The Birth of the Archive*; Head, *Making Archives in Early Modern Europe*.

72. SP 45/21, f. 87r, Tessier, *Réseaux diplomatiques*, 617.

73. BL Lansdowne MS 1051, f. 53v–78v.

74. BL Lansdowne MS 1051, f. 60r–v.

75. BL Lansdowne MS 1051, f. 69v–71v.

76. For their descriptions as "Books of Collections," see SP 9/132, f. 1. See other lists of them see, for example, SP 9/133, f. 3r, 151r.

77. SP 9/252, f. 143r.

78. SP 9/133, f. 415r–419r.

79. SP 9/133, f. 25r–39v.

80. In 1677 Williamson decided to move away from this system, noting that "I altered my Books of Collections, in order to another method," but it is unclear how his new method differed (SP 9/132, front matter). Williamson revisited such binding practices even after he left the Paper Office. In 1690, for example, he turned his attention to his collections of Tower records. He recommended that "all copies of records &c to be bound up in time, separating them according to their kinds ... & even undoing such as are stitched now together." The project aimed to consolidate diverse materials into crisper, new codices with their own "proper heads"; Williamson also dictated that "all Indexes, Repertoryes, & Abstracts of Rolls &c [are] to be bound up in time" (SP 9/20, back matter). He does not seem to have implemented this program, however.

81. SP 9/157, back cover.

82. Brydall was frequently deployed to make catalogs and take extracts from

various repositories, especially the State Paper Office. Williamson had a collection of Brydall's, which he described as "Extracts [by Mr Bridell] out of the Paper Office &c" (SP 9/212). In 1682, Brydall produced a "A Calendar of the Most Remarquable & Important papers (relating to Ecclesiastical Matters) to be found his Majeties Paper office at Whitehall," likely for Archbishop Sancroft (Bodl. Tanner MS 271, f. 56r). In 1692, he produced a massive calendar of notes from this office for longtime diplomat and Irish Principal Secretary Robert Southwell, which was copied by many contemporaries (FSL MS V.b.1 is likely the original; see also BL Add. MS 38536; SP 46/165; LPL MS 1093; BL Harley MS 1217; BL Stowe MS 548; YBL Osborn MS fb 84). He also cataloged the Duke of Ormond's papers when they came into the possession of Southwell (Bodl. Carte MS 276; Bodl. Eng. Hist. MS c. 38; Bodl. Eng. Hist. MS c. 39).

83. Bodl. Tanner MS 271, f. 55r.

84. Bodl. Tanner MS 271, f. 55r.

85. Bodl. Tanner MS 271, f. 55r–v.

86. For use of the office after Williamson's fall, see, for example, SP 87/1, f. 269; SP 44/339, f. 446; SP 44/341, f. 345; SP 90/1, f. 44; SP 44/337, f. 197.

87. SP 294/417, f. 34.

88. SP 45/21, f. 95v–96r.

89. BL Lansdowne MS 1051, f. 44v–45v.

90. SP 45/21, f. 95r.

91. There may have been registers to cabinets; see SP 45/21, f. 150r, 153r, 155r; see Tessier, *Réseaux diplomatiques*, 628–30.

92. SP 9/24, f. 184r. SP 9/27 appears to be a copy of this volume but was continually added to and thus differs from the original.

93. SP 9/252; front matter.

94. SP 9/252, f. 9r.

95. BL Lansdowne MS 1051, f. 60v–61r. For one of the notebooks concerning records, drawing from William Prynne's *Abridgement* as well as Tower rolls, letters, and gazettes, and updated as late as 1694, see SP 9/20.

96. SP 9/28, f. 1r, 153r–v.

97. SP 9/162, front matter.

98. SP 9/162, f. 9r [each section has separate pagination]. SP 9/158, f. 2v–3r [separate pagination].

99. SP 9/159, np. In the original: "Archimandrite: l'esta a dice l'abbe en superieur dans les abbeys de l'eglise Grecque, comme des Basiles a Messina, dont est Archimandrite de Cardinal Sforza"; SP 9/157, np.

100. For another model, in 1679 he began a new notebook similarly divided geographically but in which he and his clerks entered relevant notes from newssheets, creating a volume that resembled a chronicle rather than an alphabetical compendium (SP 9/160, f. 11r).

101. SP 9/16.

102. SP 9/25, np.

103. SP 9/18.

104. These materials were provided for embassies to Saxony, Constantinople, Monterey, and Spain (SP 45/21, f. 21r, 28r, 31r, 99r–100r). Williamson also sent this packet to future Secretary of State Henry Coventry earlier that year preparing for an embassy to Sweden (SP 45/21, 21r). He furnished Coventry with diplomatic packages on many occasions; for example, in 1667 when Holles and Coventry embarked to the Low Countries to negotiate a peace, Williamson equipped them with thirteen treaties (SP 45/21, f. 1r). As part of this endeavor, he ordered the Ryleys "to take brief noates" from all the treaties in the Tower (SP 29/195, f. 132). As Ryley Jr. later described it, he "made an abstract out of the Records in the Tower of all such Treatyes of Peace or Truces as have bin acted or done between the Kings of England and other Princes or States, now in the Custody of Mr Williamson" (SP 45/21, f. 78v).

105. Commercial negotiations were similarly facilitated by Williamson's labor (SP 45/21, f. 2r, 3r, 40r, 62r). The East India Company also received such materials (SP 44/35, f. 55).

106. SP 45/21, f. 5r.

107. Lansdowne MS 1051 begins with an expansive list of original treaties in the office, which is heavily weighted toward the 1660s and 1670s.

108. SP 9/133, front matter.

109. SP 9/133, f. 17r.

110. SP 9/133, f. 3r, back matter. Cf. the volume he labeled "England & Holland. The Two East Indy Companyes. Copyes of Papers put into my hands & otherwise layd by me together in Order to the treaty at Cologne. 1673." SP 105/219, front matter.

111. SP 9/156, f. 122, 128–130.

112. He also produced comparable notes concerning payments made by foreign crowns to their ambassadors (SP 9/156, f. 209–220, 229, 230).

113. His notebooks formed only part of the corpus of writings he had at his disposal, as he continued to use inscription to organize his experience upon arriving in Cologne. For example, he kept a list of the foreign posts to and from the city (SP 9/201/30), diaries in which he recorded meetings and entered incoming and outgoing dispatches, and daybooks describing daily negotiations and materials he read (SP 105/220). See similarly SP 9/215 for his diary for 1678. All these materials aided Williamson as he and Jenkins produced their regular reports for Arlington, which Williamson summarized in a series of "Journalle Bookes" (SP 105/221–230).

114. SP 105/223, f. 58r ff. Williamson and Jenkins reported to Arlington on oral conversations between diplomats, but documents, gazettes, and other texts were constantly noted, and treaties were invoked with a regularity that suggests that all parties had their own copies. Wynne, *The Life of Leoline Jenkins*, 1:235, provides an especially clear example.

115. The new version included Ryley's catalog of treaties in the Tower and one of Arthur Agarde's list of treaties in the Exchequer in which he—or more likely his clerks—entered an *x* next to those treaties they had consulted. The original list from which Williamson's version (SP 9/128) was copied is SP 9/129.

116. YBL Osborn MS fb 212 vol. 1, n.p.

117. SP 9/128, np; SP 9/138.

118. SP 9/128, n.p.

119. For Williamson in this context, see Fraser, *Intelligence of the Secretaries of State*; Peacey, "'My Friend the Gazetier'"; Peacey, "Managing Dutch Advices." For news more broadly, see J. Raymond, *The Invention of the Newspaper*; C. Sommerville, *The News Revolution in England*; Dooley and Baron, *The Politics of Information*; Pettegree, *The Invention of News*; J. Raymond and Moxham, *News Networks in Early Modern Europe*; Helmers and Van Groesen, "Managing the News in Early Modern Europe."

120. Peacey, "'A Knowing but a Discrete Man.'"

121. On London as a site of public discussion of politics, see T. Harris, *London Crowds in the Reign of Charles II*; J. Miller, "Public Opinion in Charles II's England"; Pincus, "'Coffee Politicians Does Create'"; J. Raymond, *Invention of the Newspaper*. For the notion of the public sphere, see Habermas, *Structural Transformation*; Cowan, *The Social Life of Coffee*, however, better resembles the dynamic described in this book.

122. WC, 1:102, 106, 112.

123. WC, 1:134.

124. Helmers, "Public Diplomacy in Early Modern Europe."

125. Peacey, "Managing Dutch Advices."

126. For the circulation of the *Gazette*, see Childs, "The Sale of Government Gazettes"; Glaisyer, "'The Most Universal Intelligencers.'" For continuing scribal publication, see Barber, "'It is not Easy What to Say of Our Condition'"; Scarborough King, "The Manuscript Newsletter and the Rise of the Newspaper."

127. Both remained closely tied to this sphere: Muddiman continued to oversee a successful manuscript newsletter, while L'Estrange continued in his roles as Licenser and Surveyor of the Press.

128. Fraser, *Intelligence of the Secretaries of State*, 54.

129. For Williamson's substantial collections of the *Courant*, see SP 119/56–80; for their correspondence, see Peacey, "Managing Dutch Advises," 428.

130. SP 45/21, 68r. Tessier, *Réseaux diplomatiques*, 605.

131. Williamson and his clerks had recorded comparable lists since 1661 and would continue to do so; this 1674 one was distinguished by its overall surveying of the office in preparation for Williamson's return. SP 45/21, f. 64r–68r; Tessier, *Réseaux diplomatiques*, 606–8.

132. SP 45/21, f. 64v; Tessier, *Réseaux diplomatiques*, 606.

133. WC, 2:116; Fraser, *Intelligence of the Secretaries of State*, 30–31.

134. Fraser, *Intelligence of the Secretaries of State*, 29.

135. Fraser, *Intelligence of the Secretaries of State*, 71.

136. *DWP*, 147. William Blathwayt levied similar complaints while at The Hague; see, for example, Bodl. Eng. Let. MS D 37, f. 95r.

137. I thank Steve Pincus, discussing work by Jacob Soll, for drawing this point out from me.

138. Similarly, Tessier shows that he established redundant epistolary networks to monitor whether his correspondents were concealing any news from him (Tessier, "Un apprentissage diplomatique").

Epilogue

1. For the "administrative revolution," see Brewer, *The Sinews of Power*; Braddick, *The Nerves of State*; Ogborn, "The Capacities of the State"; Aylmer, *The Crown's Servants*. The concept often rests on older studies of offices whose most recent iterations include Baxter, *The Development of the Treasury*; Roseveare, *The Treasury*; Chandaman, *The English Public Revenue*. See also Coleby, *Central Government and the Localities*. While the concept is often unacknowledged in histories of the period, it remains vital for social scientists broadly; see, for example, Kiser and Kane, "Revolution and State Structure"; Hodgson, "1688 and All That." See also Tadmor, "The Settlement of the Poor," for related changes driven by middling and provincial printers and scribes.

2. D. Coleman, *The British Paper Industry*, 13.

3. TNA OBS 1/1271; TNA OBS 1/127; TNA C 272/1; BL Harley MS 6751; BL Add. MS 34711, f. 6r; SP 29/397, f. 87; SP 29/398, f. 24; SP 29/418, f. 143.

4. For this controversy, see ch. 5, n. 132. See also T. Harris, *London Crowds in the Reign of Charles II*; Scott, "England's Troubles"; Zook, *Radical Whigs and Conspiratorial Politics*.

5. For Brady's collections, see G&C MS 330/582; G&C MS 331/583; G&C MS 332/584. For his correspondence with Halsted, see G&C MS 580/685, esp. f. 10r.

6. Petyt, *The Ancient Right of the Commons Asserted*, 11. Petyt continued to criticize Brady's use of records in unpublished responses; see ITL Petyt MS 512 L,M.

7. Knights, "Faults on Both Sides"; Weil, *A Plague of Informers*. For the media dimension of this moment, see Knights, *Politics and Opinion in Crisis*; Love, "The Look of News"; Knights, *Representation and Misrepresentation in Later Stuart Britain*; Clarke, "Re-reading the Exclusion Crisis"; Morton, "Intensive Ephemera"; Morton, "Popery, Politics, and Play"; Koscak, *Monarchy, Print Culture, and Reverence*.

8. For example, see HEH HM 30314, f. 21, 42, 48, 51, 56, 91, 108; HEH HM 30315, f. 148, 169, 170, 173, 176; BL Add. MS 72482, f. 20, 26.

9. For Jenkins's archives, see BL Lansdowne MS 1051, f. 79r–103v; SP 294/417, f. 34; SP 44/70, f. 229; BL Lansdowne MS, f. 53v.

10. ITL Petyt MS 528 25; BL Hargrave MS 126. BL Stowe MS 543, f. 39r, contains draft notes for this volume. For further evidence of his working with the commission, see PA HL/PO/JO/10/6/67/2029; *LJ*, 17.555–56; 17.574–75, 17.638; SP 46/167, f. 52r, 55r; BL Add. MS 34711, f. 21r; SP 34/5, f. 121.

11. For Tucker's catalog, see BL Lansdowne MS 1051; BL Add. MS 30191 is a copy; SP 9/49 is a partial copy; all three share the same pagination to coordinate use. The images in figures 17 and 18 in chapter 6 were almost certainly produced for the committee as well. For Tucker's communication with the committee, see

also SP 45/21, f. 113–134r; *LJ*, 18.69, 18.135. For his report, see Hallam, "Problems with Record Keeping in Early 18th c. London"; Popper, "Archives and the Boundaries of Early Modern Science." Tucker's proposed system devised an abstract taxonomy that would facilitate classification and consultation: as he explained, "Let each General head have a letter. For example Ecclesiastical A. Secretary's Office C. Councill B. Treasury D. Heraldry E. Military F. Admiralty G. Let each subdivision have a letter additional. For ex, Military Ordinance Fa. Military Establishment Fb. If those be again subdivided add a Letter." For example, papers related to "military ordnance Government of the Office" would be classified as "Fab" while military ordnance "estimates" would be "Fac." Within each category, moreover, he explained, "Let each Bundle or Books be numbered according to Order of time. A1. A2 A3. &c." (SP 45/21, f. 147r.) In a subsequent note he laid out the scheme in full, covering a gamut of ecclesiastical matters from "Kings Supremacy"—designated as Aa—to the "royal Chapel" (Ar); for civil matters, it ranged from the "royal prerogative" (Ba) to "Justice of the Peace" (Bw). Subcategories further nested institutions, document types, and themes. Tucker folded all foreign papers under the designation Br, with individual polities receiving their own letters (Spain, for example, was Brb) (SP 45/21, f. 143r). General indexes would further illuminate connections across categories.

12. Braddick, *State Formation in Early Modern England*, 427.

13. For other works on administration and paperwork in the early British Empire, see Steele, *The English Atlantic*; Ogborn, *Indian Ink*; Underwood, "Ordering Knowledge, Re-Ordering Empire"; Siddique, "Paperwork, Governance, and the Archive in the British Empire"; Siddique, "Governance through Documents"; Beaver, "Sovereignty by the Book." For other European empires, see Parker, *The Grand Strategy of Philip II*; Banks, *Chasing Empire across the Sea*; Bleichmar, *Visible Empire*; Friedrich, "Government and Information-Management"; Sellers-Garcia, *Distance and Documents at the Spanish Empire's Periphery*; Brendecke, *The Empirical Empire*; Houllemare, "Seeing the Empire through Lists and Charts."

14. For Blathwayt, see Jacobsen, *William Blathwayt*; Webb, "William Blathwayt, Imperial Fixer, 2 pts.: Part 1"; Webb, "William Blathwayt, Imperial Fixer, Part 2"; Murison, "The Talented Mr Blathwayt"; Emanuel, "'Great weights hang by small wires.'"

15. There is no evidence that Williamson directly instructed Blathwayt in their surviving correspondence, much of which dated from Blathwayt's tenure at The Hague; see Bodl. Eng. Let. MS D 37, f. 14r. See also Tessier, "Un apprentissage diplomatique."

16. Popper, "Joseph Williamson and the Information Order of the Early English Empire."

17. Jacobsen, *William Blathwayt*, 418. Eight journals remain from between 1675 and 1696 (*Colonial Entry Books*, 40–41, hereafter cited as *CEB*).

18. *CEB*, 40–41.

19. *CEB*, 43.

20. *CEB*, 42.

21. TNA CO 389/35. Blathwayt actively oversaw such collections; see HEH BL (William Blathwayt Papers), Box 2, BL 398; HEH BL, Box 3, BL 296.

22. Jacobsen, *William Blathwayt*, 418.

23. Blathwayt frequently received collections of extracts from letters sent within the colonies. See HEH BL, Box 3, BL 214, BL 235, BL 234, BL 237, BL 239, BL 240, BL 242, BL 291, and throughout the William Blathwayt Papers collection at the John D. Rockefeller Library, Colonial Williamsburg, in Williamsburg, Virginia (hereafter cited as CW).

24. CW, Vol.36, Folder 3.

25. Although these documents were supposed to be sent as they were produced, they were often sent only at the conclusion of an administration. For example, shortly after arriving in Maryland to assume its governorship, Francis Nicholson sent Blathwayt a lengthy list of all the materials produced during his time as governor of New York. HEH BL, Box 3, BL 64.

26. TNA CO 5/723, f. 21–22. For an example of a specific set of heads, see the letter sent from the Lords of the Trade and Plantations to Sir William Berkeley, governor of Virginia, in 1676, TNA CO 1/36, 80r–82. These were sent to at least seven colonies (TNA CO 5/723, 23–26). For a sample of responses, see TNA CO 1/42, no. 40; TNA CO 1/37, f. 48–55; TNA CO 1/47, f. 153–157. Many reports from the colonies clearly indicate their origins in similar instructions. The scale of descriptions of Jamaica are illustrative: Governor Thomas Lynch's account from the mid-1660s, which was published by Richard Blome in 1678, exists in multiple manuscript copies (Williamson's was TNA CO 324/1, f. 135r–182v, see also HEH HM 57346, f. 75r–92v; BL Harley MS 3361);see also the enclosure from Lynch's letter to Arlington shortly after returning to Jamaica in 1671 documenting the authority, offices, and officeholders of the island (TNA CO 1/27, no. 22 and TNA CO 138/2, f. 6r–38v). Governor Thomas Modyford provided one upon his return to England in 1671 (TNA CO 138/1, f. 96–119); for Deputy Governor James Modyford's, owned by Williamson, see CO 324/1, f. 253r–258v; BL Add. MS 11410, f. 151r–157v; and HEH HM 57346, f. 135r–146v. See also Edward Cranfield's 1675 "Observations on the present state of Jamaica, being answers to 21 queries, drawn out of his Majesty's Instructions" (TNA CO 138/2, f. 108r–121v) and one produced under Governor Vaughan in 1676 (TNA CO 138/2, f. 44r–96v; National Library of Jamaica, MS 159). For a brief discussion of these texts, see Siddique, "Governance through Documents," 276–78.

27. In the late seventeenth century, *artes apodemicae* were also deployed to compile knowledge of Britain itself. For domestic versions, see A. Fox, "Printed Questionnaires"; Yale, *Sociable Knowledge*.

28. HEH BL, Box 1, BL 368; Newberry Library Ayer MS 827.

29. CW, Vol. 36, Box 4. See also HEH BL, Box 6, BL 28, BL 204.

30. HEH BL, Box 3, BL 142.

31. CW, Vol. 36, Box 1, Folder 3.

32. HEH BL, Box 5, BL 340; SP 87/1, f. 269. Accounts were maintained this way, too; see, for example, Blathwayt's comprehensive overview of North American and Caribbean revenues, YBL GEN MSS 418.

33. Siddique, "Governance through Documents."

34. For studies of infrastructure and the imperial perspective in the late seventeenth and eighteenth century, see Steele, *English Atlantic*; Dierks, *In My Power*; Guldi, *Roads to Power*; Grandjean, *American Passage*; Dubcovsky, *Informed Power*; Edelson, *The New Map of Empire*; Zuercher Reichardt, "War for the Interior"; Pincus, Bains, and Zuercher Reichardt, "Thinking the Empire Whole." The ideal agent operating in the network Blathwayt envisioned resembled Edward Randolph, as described by Dierks, *In My Power*, 9–51.

35. Recent scholarship has exposed that the political, legal, and social structures of the British Empire offered fewer opportunities to petition, give testimony, and otherwise express themselves than did other European empires—a stance which has shaped the techniques necessary for historians find marginalized and oppressed voices in their respective archives. Compare, for example, Fuentes, *Dispossessed Lives*, with Premo, *Enlightenment on Trial*, and S. White, *Voices of the Enslaved*.

36. Dery, "'Papereality' and Learning in Bureaucratic Institutions."

37. Similarly, see Rama, *The Lettered City*; Ogborn, *Indian Ink*; Raphael, "In Pursuit of 'Useful' Knowledge."

38. The classic text exposing the immutably colonial nature of these archives remains Trouillot, *Silencing the Past*; see also Messick, *The Calligraphic State*. More recently, see Burton, *Dwelling in the Archive*; MacMillan, *Dangerous Games*; Stoler, *Along the Archival Grain*; Burns, *Into the Archive*; Raman, *Document Raj*; Hull, *Government of Paper*; Weld, *Paper Cadavers*; Fuentes, *Dispossessed Lives*; Tortorici, *Sins Against Nature*; Johnson, *Wicked Flesh*; Morgan, *Reckoning with Slavery*; Johnson, *Encyclopédie noire*.

39. BL Stowe MS 543, f. 46v.

40. BL Stowe MS 543, f. 47r.

41. Knox, *Extra Official State Papers*, 11–14; SP 45/21, f. 208r.

42. It should be noted that a decade prior, Thomas Birch quickly found records in the office, suggesting that it was less forgotten than Knox proclaimed (YBL Osborn MS 1287).

43. For these archives in the eighteenth century, see Mullett, "The 'Better Reception, Preservation, and More Convenient Use'"; Riordan, "Materials for History?"

44. Brewer, *Sinews of Power*; Bayly, *Empire and Information*; Ogborn, *Indian Ink*; Guldi, *Roads to Power*; Siddique, "Mobilizing the 'State Papers' of Empire"; Siddique, "Governance through Documents"; Siddique, "The Archival Epistemology of Political Economy." Such transformations have long been associated with a "Communications Revolution"; for this historiography, most associated with Harold Innis and Marshall McLuhan, see most recently Behringer, "Communications Revolutions."

45. Dugdale, *English Scholars*; Sweet, *Antiquaries*; Woolf, *The Idea of History*; Parry, *The Trophies of Time*.

46. For the importance of formwork in the eighteenth century, see Tadmor, "Settlement of the Poor"; for recent studies revealing the spread of archival prac-

tices, see Woolf, *Reading History*; Waddell, "Writing History from Below"; Peck, "'Of no sort of use?'"

47. This account thus better fits with Johns, *The Nature of the Book*, than with Eisenstein, *The Printing Revolution*, whose view was shaped by technological determinists such as Walter Ong, Marshall McLuhan, and Harold Innis.

Bibliography

The Acts of the Parliaments of Scotland. 11 vols. Edinburgh: Lords Commissioners of her Majesty's Treasury, 1870.
Adams, Robyn. "A Most Secret Service: William Herle and the Circulation of Intelligence." In Adams and Cox, *Diplomacy and Early Modern Culture*, 63–81.
Adams, Robyn. "'The Service I am Here for': William Herle in the Marshalsea Prison, 1571." *HLQ* 72, no. 2 (2009): 217–38.
Adams, Robyn. "A Spy on the Payroll? William Herle and the Mid Elizabethan Polity." *HR* 83, no. 220 (2010): 266–80.
Adams, Robyn, and Rosanna Cox. *Diplomacy and Early Modern Culture.* Basingstoke, UK: Palgrave Macmillan, 2011.
Adams, Simon. "Elizabeth I and the Sovereignty of the Netherlands, 1576–1585." *Transactions of the Royal Historical Society* 14 (2004): 309–19.
Adams, Simon. "The Papers of Robert Dudley, Earl of Leicester, I: The Browne-Evelyn Collection." *Archives* 20, no. 87 (1992): 63–85.
Adams, Simon. "The Papers of Robert Dudley, Earl of Leicester, II: The Atye-Cotton Collection." *Archives* 20, no. 90 (1993): 131–44.
Adams, Simon, "The Papers of Robert Dudley, Earl of Leicester, III: The Countess of Leicester's Collection." *Archives* 22, no. 94 (1996): 1–26.
Adamson, J. S. A. *The Noble Revolt: The Overthrow of Charles I.* London: Weidenfeld and Nicolson, 2007.
Ailes, Adrian. "'A Pair of Garters': Heralds and Heraldry at the Restoration." In *Revolutionary England, c. 1630–c. 1660*, edited by George Southcombe and Grant Tapsell, 218–34. Abingdon, UK: Routledge, 2017.
Akkerman, Nadine. *Invisible Agents: Women and Espionage in Seventeenth-Century Britain.* Oxford: Oxford University Press, 2018.
Alford, Stephen. *The Early Elizabethan Polity: William Cecil and the British Succession Crisis, 1558–1569.* Cambridge: Cambridge University Press, 1998.
Alford, Stephen. "Some Elizabethan Spies in the Office of Sir Francis Walsingham." In Adams and Cox, *Diplomacy and Early Modern Culture*, 46–62.
Alford, Stephen. *The Watchers: A Secret History of the Reign of Elizabeth I.* New York: Bloomsbury, 2012.

Amundsen, Karin. "Thinking Metallurgically: Metals and Empires in the Projects of Edward Hayes." *HLQ* 79, no. 4 (2016): 561–90.

Anderson, Andrew H. "Henry, Lord Stafford (1501–1563) in Local and Central Government." *EHR* 78, no. 307 (1963): 225–42.

Andreani, Angela. *The Elizabethan Secretariat and the Signet Office: The Production of State Papers, 1590–1596*. London: Routledge, 2017.

Armitage, David. *The Ideological Origins of the British Empire*. Cambridge: Cambridge University Press, 2000.

Ash, Eric. *The Draining of the Fens: Projectors, Popular Politics, and State Building in Early Modern England*. Baltimore: Johns Hopkins University Press, 2017.

Ash, Eric. *Power, Knowledge and Expertise in Elizabethan England*. Baltimore: Johns Hopkins University Press, 2004.

Aylmer, G. E. *The Crown's Servants: Government and Civil Service Under Charles II, 1660–1685*. Oxford: Oxford University Press, 2002.

Aylmer, G. E. *The King's Servants; The Civil Service of Charles I, 1625–1642*. New York: Columbia University Press, 1961.

Bacon, Francis. *The Early Writings, 1584–1596*. Edited by Alan Stewart with Harriet Knight. Oxford: Oxford University Press, 2012.

Bacon, Francis. *The Letters and the Life of Francis Bacon*. Edited by James Spedding. 9 vols. London, 1861–90.

Bailey, John E. *The Troubles of William Ryley, Lancaster Herald, and of His Son, Clerks of the Records in the Tower*. Leigh, Lancashire, UK: The "Chronicle" Office, 1879.

Banks, Kenneth. *Chasing Empire across the Sea: Communications and the State in the French Atlantic*. Montreal: McGill-Queen's University Press, 2002.

Barber, Alex. "'It Is not Easy What to Say of Our Condition, Much Less to Write It': The Continued Importance of Scribal News in the Early 18th Century." *PH* 32, no. 2 (2013): 293–316.

Barbour, Reid. *John Selden: Measures of the Holy Commonwealth in Seventeenth-Century England*. Toronto: University of Toronto Press, 2003.

Baron, Sabrina Alcorn. "Borough, Sir John (d. 1643)." In *Oxford Dictionary of National Biography*. Oxford University Press, 2004. Online ed., 2004, modified May 19, 2011. https://doi.org/10.1093/ref:odnb/2913.

Bautier, Robert-Henri. "La Phase Cruciale de l'histoire des archives: La constitution des dépôts d'archives et la naissance de l'archivistique." *Archivum* 18 (1968): 139–49.

Baxter, Stephen. *The Development of the Treasury, 1660–1702*. Cambridge, MA: Harvard University Press, 1957.

Bayly, C. A. *Empire and Information: Intelligence Gathering and Social Communication in India, 1780–1870*. Cambridge: Cambridge University Press, 1996.

Beal, Peter. *In Praise of Scribes: Manuscripts and Their Makers in Seventeenth-Century England*. Oxford: Clarendon, 1998.

Beaver, Dan. "Sovereignty by the Book: English Corporations, Atlantic Plantations, and Literate Order, 1557–1650." In Kyle and Peacey, *Connecting Centre and Locality*, 157–73.

Becker, Peter, and William Clark, eds. *Little Tools of Knowledge: Historical Essays on Academic and Bureaucratic Practices*. Ann Arbor: University of Michigan Press, 2000.

Behringer, Wolfgang. "Communications Revolutions: A Historiographical Concept." *German History* 24, no. 3 (2006): 333–74.

Bellany, Alastair. *The Politics of Court Scandal in Early Modern England: News Culture and the Overbury Affair, 1603–1660*. Cambridge: Cambridge University Press, 2002.

Bellany, Alastair. "'Railing Rymes and Vaunting Verse': Libellous Politics in Early Stuart England, 1603–1628." In *Culture and Politics in Early Stuart England*, edited by Kevin Sharpe and Peter Lake, 285–310. London: Macmillan, 1994.

Bellany, Alastair, and Thomas Cogswell. *The Murder of King James I*. New Haven, CT: Yale University Press, 2015.

Bellingradt, Daniel, and Anna Reynolds, eds. *The Paper Trade in Early Modern Europe: Practices, Materials, Networks*. Leiden, Neth.: Brill, 2021.

Birch, Thomas, ed. *A Collection of the State Papers of John Thurloe*. 7 vols. London, 1742.

Bishop, Jennifer. "The Clerk's Tale: Civic Writing in Sixteenth-Century London." In "The Social History of the Archive: Record Keeping in Early Modern Europe," edited by Liesbeth Corens, Kate Peters, and Alexandra Walsham. Supplement, *P&P* 11 (2016): 112–30.

Bittel, Carla, Elaine Leong, and Christine Von Oertzen. *Working with Paper: Gendered Practices in the History of Knowledge*. Pittsburgh, PA: University of Pittsburgh Press, 2019.

Blair, Ann. "New Knowledge-Makers." In *New Horizons in Early Modern European Scholarship*, edited by Ann Blair and Nicholas Popper, 167–82. Baltimore: Johns Hopkins University Press, 2021.

Blair, Ann. "Note Taking as an Art of Transmission." *Critical Inquiry* 31, no. 1 (2004): 85–107.

Blair, Ann. "Reading Strategies for Coping with Information Overload, ca. 1550–1700." *JHI* 64, no. 1 (2003): 11–28.

Blair, Ann. *Too Much to Know: Managing Scholarly Information before the Modern Age*. New Haven, CT: Yale University Press, 2010.

Blair, Ann, and Jennifer Milligan, eds. "Toward a Cultural History of Archives." Special issue, *Archival Science* 7, no. 4 (December 2007).

Blair, Ann, Paul Duguid, Anja-Silvia Goeing, and Anthony Grafton. *Information: A Historical Companion*. Princeton, NJ: Princeton University Press, 2021.

Bland, Mark. "The London Book Trade in 1600." In *A Companion to Shakespeare*, edited by David Scott Kastan, 450–63. Malden, MA: Blackwell, 1999.

Bleichmar, Daniela. *Visible Empire: Botanical Expeditions and Visual Culture in the Hispanic Enlightenment*. Chicago: University of Chicago Press, 2012.

Bollbuck, Harald. "Searching for the True Religion: The Church History of the

Magdeburg Centuries between Critical Methods and Confessional Polemics." *Renaissance Studies* 35, no. 1 (2021): 100–117.

Bond, Maurice. "The Formation of the Archives of Parliament, 1497–1691." *JSA* 1, no. 6 (1957): 151–58.

Borden, Andrew. "What Is Information Warfare?" Article IAW AFI 35-101 in *Aerospace Power Chronicles* (journal of United States Air Force, Air University, Maxwell Air Force Base), 1999. https://www.airuniversity.af.edu/Portals/10/ASPJ/journals/Chronicles/borden.pdf.

[Borough, John]. *Sir John Borough's Notes of Proceedings in Committees of the House of Commons, 27 February–23 March, 1626*. Edited by Christopher Thompson. Wivenhoe, UK: Orchard Press, 1988.

Borough, John. *The Soveraignty of the British Seas Proved by records, History, and the Municipall Lawes of this Kingdome*. London, 1651.

Borough, John. *The Sovereignty of the British Seas*. Edited by Thomas Callander Wade. Edinburgh: W. Green & Son, 1920.

Bossy, John. *Under the Molehill: An Elizabethan Spy Story*. New Haven, CT: Yale University Press, 2001.

Boyer, Allen. *Sir Edward Coke and the Elizabethan Age*. Stanford, CA: Stanford University Press, 2003.

Braddick, Michael. *The Nerves of State: Taxation and the Financing of the English State, 1558–1714*. Manchester: Manchester University Press, 1996.

Braddick, Michael. *State Formation in Early Modern England, c. 1550–1700*. Cambridge: Cambridge University Press, 2000.

Brady, Ciaran. *The Chief Governors: The Rise and Fall of Reform Government in Tudor Ireland, 1536–1588*. Cambridge: Cambridge University Press, 1994.

Brady, Ciaran. "From Policy to Power: The Evolution of Tudor Reform Strategies in Sixteenth-Century Ireland." In *Reshaping Ireland, 1550–1700: Colonization and Its Consequences*, edited by Brian MacCuarta, 21–42. Dublin: Four Courts Press, 2011.

Brendecke, Arndt. *The Empirical Empire: Spanish Colonial Rule and the Politics of Knowledge*. Berlin: De Gruyter Oldenbourg, 2016.

Brendecke, Arndt, ed. *Praktiken der Frühen Neuzeit: Akteure, Handlungen, Artefakte*. Cologne: Böhlau, 2015.

Brewer, John. *The Sinews of Power: War, Money, and the English State, 1688–1783*. London: Unwin Hyman, 1989.

Britland, Karen. "'In the Hollow of his Wooden Leg': The Transmission of Civil War Materials, 1642-9." In *Insolent Proceedings: Rethinking Public Politics in the English Revolution*, edited by Peter Lake and Jason Peacey, 88–106. Manchester: Manchester University Press, 2022.

Brito Vieira, Mónica. "*Mare Liberum* vs *Mare Clausum*: Grotius, Freitas, and Selden's Debate on Dominion over the Seas." *JHI* 64, no. 3 (2003): 361–77.

Broadway, Jan. *"No historie so meete": Gentry Culture and the Development of Local History in Elizabethan and Early Stuart England*. Manchester: Manchester University Press, 2004.

Brooks, Christopher, and Kevin Sharpe. "History, English Law, and the Renaissance." *P&P* 72(1976): 133–42.

Bulman, William. *Anglican Enlightenment: Orientalism, Religion, and Politics in England and Its Empire, 1648–1715*. Cambridge: Cambridge University Press, 2015.

Bulman, William. "Introduction: Post-Revisionism and the History of Practices in the Early Modern British World," in Bulman and Dominguez, *Political and Religious Practice in the Early Modern World*, 1–34.

Bulman, William. "The Practice of Politics: The English Civil War and the 'Resolution' of Henrietta Maria and Charles I." *P&P* 206 (2010): 43–79.

Bulman, William. *The Rise of Majority Rule in Early Modern Britain and its Empire*. Cambridge: Cambridge University Press, 2021.

Bulman, William, and Freddy Dominguez, eds. *Political and Religious Practice in the Early Modern World*. Manchester: Manchester University Press, 2022.

Burnett, Gilbert. *History of His Own Time*. London, 1724.

Burns, Kathryn, *Into the Archive: Writing and Power in Colonial Peru*. Durham, NC: Duke University Press, 2010.

Burton, Antoinette. *Dwelling in the Archive: Women Writing House, Home, and History in Late Colonial India*. Oxford: Oxford University Press, 2003.

Cain, Piers. "Robert Smith and the Reform of the Archives of the City of London, 1580–1623." *London Journal* 13, no. 1 (1987–88): 3–16.

Calendar of the Proceedings of the Committee for Advance of Money, 1642–1656. 3 vols. Edited by Mary Anne Everett Green. London: H. M. Stationery Office, 1888.

Calendar of the Proceedings of the Committee for Compounding &C, 1643–1660. 5 vols. Edited by Mary Anne Everett Green. London: Eyre and Spottiswoode for H. M. Stationery Office, 1889.

Calendar of State Papers, Relating to Ireland, of the Reign of James I. 5 vols. Edited by C. W. Russell and John P. Prendergast. London: Longman, 1872–80.

Campbell, Gordon, Thomas Corns, John Hale, and Fiona Tweedle, eds. *Milton and the Manuscript of De doctrina Christiana*. Oxford: Oxford University Press, 2007.

Carley, J. P. "The Dispersal of the Monastic Libraries and the Salvaging of the Spoils." In *The Cambridge History of Libraries in Britain and Ireland*, vol. 1, *To 1640*, 265–91. Cambridge: Cambridge University Press, 2006.

Carley, J. P. "Monastic Collections and their Disposal." In *The Cambridge History of the Book in Britain*, vol. 4, *1557–1695*, edited by John Barnard and Donald F. McKenzie, with the assistance of Maureen Bell, 339–47. Cambridge: Cambridge University Press, 2002.

Carlson, David R. "The Writings and Manuscript Collections of the Elizabethan Alchemist, Antiquary, and Herald Francis Thynne." *HLQ* 52, no. 2 (1989): 203–72.

Catalogue of the Additions to the Manuscripts: The Yelverton Manuscripts—Additional Manuscripts 48000–48196. 2 vols. London: British Library, 1994.

Chalus, Elaine. "Elite Women, Social Politics, and the Political World of Late Eighteenth-Century England." *HJ* 43, no. 3 (2000): 669–97.

Chandaman, C. D. *The English Public Revenue, 1660–88*. Oxford: Clarendon, 1975.

Chartier, Roger. *The Cultural Origins of the French Revolution*. Durham, NC: Duke University Press, 1991.

Childs, John. "The Sale of Government Gazettes during the Exclusion Crisis, 1678–81." *EHR* 102, no. 402 (1987): 103–6.

Christianson, Paul. *Discourse on History, Law, and Governance in the Career of John Selden, 1610–1635*. Toronto: University of Toronto Press, 1996.

Christianson, Paul. "John Selden, the Five Knights Case, and Discretionary Imprisonment in Early Stuart England." *Criminal Justice History* 6 (1985): 65–87.

Chou, Catherine. "The Parliamentary Mind and the Mutable Constitution." *HR* 89, no. 245 (2016): 470–85.

Clanchy, M. T. *From Memory to Written Record: England, 1066–1307*. London: Blackwell, 1993.

Clarke, Elizabeth. "Re-reading the Exclusion Crisis." *Seventeenth Century* 21, no. 1 (2006): 141–59.

Clegg, Cyndia. "Burning Books as Propaganda in Jacobean England." In *Literature and Censorship in Renaissance England*, edited by Andrew Hadfield, 165–86. Basingstoke, UK: Palgrave, 2001.

Clegg, Cyndia. *Press Censorship in Caroline England*. Cambridge: Cambridge University Press, 2008.

Clegg, Cyndia. *Press Censorship in Jacobean England*. Cambridge: Cambridge University Press, 2001.

Coast, David. "Misinformation and Disinformation in Late Jacobean Court Politics." *JEMH* 16, no. 4–5 (2012): 335–54.

Coast, David. "Speaking for the People in Early Modern England." *P&P* 244 (2019): 51–88.

Cogswell, Thomas. "John Felton, Popular Political Culture, and the Assassination of the Duke of Buckingham." *HJ* 49, no. 2 (2006): 357–85.

Cogswell, Thomas. "The Politics of Propaganda: Charles I and the People in the 1620s." *JBS* 29, no. 3 (1990): 187–215.

Cogswell, Thomas, Richard Cust, and Peter Lake. *Politics, Religion and Popularity in Early Stuart Britain*. Cambridge: Cambridge University Press, 2002.

Coleby, Andrew. *Central Government and the Localities: Hampshire, 1649–1689*. Cambridge: Cambridge University Press, 1987.

Coleman, Christopher. "Artifice or Accident? The Reorganization of the Exchequer of Receipt, c. 1554–1572." In Coleman and Starkey, *Revolution Reassessed*, 163–98. Oxford: Oxford University Press, 1986.

Coleman, Christopher, and David Starkey, eds. *Revolution Reassessed: Revisions in the History of Tudor Government and Administration*. Oxford: Clarendon Press, 1986.

Coleman, D. C. *The British Paper Industry, 1495–1860: A Study in Industrial Growth*. Oxford: Clarendon Press, 1958.

Collinson, Patrick. "The Monarchical Republic of Queen Elizabeth I." *Bulletin of the John Rylands Library* 69, no. 2 (1987): 394–424.

Collinson, Patrick. "Puritans, Men of Business and Elizabethan Parliaments." *PH* 69, no. 2 (1988): 187–211.

Collinson, Patrick. "Servants and Citizens: Robert Beale and other Elizabethans." *HR* 79, no. 206 (2006): 488–511.

The Colonial Entry Books. Edited by C. S. S. Higham. London: Society for Promoting Christian Knowledge, 1921.

Commons Debates, 1621. 7 vols. Edited by Wallace Notestein, Frances Helen Relf, and Hartley Simpson. New Haven, CT: Yale University Press, 1935.

Commons Debates, 1628. 6 vols. Edited by Robert C. Johnson, Mary Keeler, Maija Jansson Cole, and William B. Bidwell. New Haven, CT: Yale University Press, 1977–1983.

Commons Debates for 1629. Edited by Wallace Notestein and Frances Helen Relf. Minneapolis: University of Minnesota Press, 1921.

Como, David. "Print, Censorship, and Ideological Escalation in the English Civil War." *JBS* 51, no. 4 (2012): 820–57.

A Complete Collection of State Trials and Proceedings for High Treason and Other Crimes and Misdemeanors. 34 vols. Edited by Thomas Bayly Howell. London: Hansard, 1816–28.

Corens, Liesbeth, Kate Peters, and Alexandra Walsham, eds. "The Social History of the Archive: Record Keeping in Early Modern Europe." Supplement, *P&P* 11 (2016).

The Correspondence of Sir Philip Sidney and Hubert Languet. Edited by Steuart Pears. Farnsborough, UK: Gregg International Publishers Press, 1971.

Cotton, Robert. *Cottoni Posthuma*. London, 1672.

Cortada, James. "The Information Ecosystems of National Diplomacy: The Case of Spain, 1815–1936." *Information & Culture* 48, no. 2 (2013): 222–59.

Cortada, James. "Shaping Information History as an Intellectual Discipline." *Information & Culture* 47, no. 2 (2012): 119–44.

Cowan, Brian. "The History of Secret Histories." *HLQ* 81, no. 1 (2018): 121–51.

Cowan, Brian. *The Social Life of Coffee: The Emergence of the British Coffeehouse*. New Haven, CT: Yale University Press, 2005.

Cramsie, John. *Kingship and Crown Finance under James VI and I, 1603–1625*. Woodbridge, UK: Royal Historical Society/Boydell Press, 2002.

Crawford, Jon. *Anglicizing the Government of Ireland: The Irish Privy Council and the Expansion of Tudor Rule, 1556–1578*. Dublin: Irish Academic Press in association with the Irish Legal History Society, 1993.

Cressy, David. "Book Burning in Tudor and Stuart England." *Sixteenth Century Journal* 36, no. 2 (2005): 359–74.

Cressy, David. *Charles I and the People of England*. Oxford: Oxford University Press, 2015.

Croft, Pauline. "The Reputation of Robert Cecil." *Transactions of the Royal Historical Society* (1991): 43–69.

Cromartie, Alan. *The Constitutionalist Revolution: An Essay on the History of England, 1450–1642*. Cambridge: Cambridge University Press, 2006.

Cust, Richard. *The Forced Loan and English Politics, 1626–1628*. Oxford: Clarendon Press, 1987.

Cust, Richard. *Charles I and the Aristocracy, 1625–1642*. Cambridge: Cambridge University Press, 2013.

Cust, Richard. "Honour and Politics in Early Stuart England: The Case of Beaumont v. Hastings." *P&P* 149 (1995): 57–94.

Cust, Richard. "News and Politics in Early Seventeenth-Century England." *P&P* 112 (1986): 60–90.

Cust, Richard, and Andrew Hopper. "572 Ryley v Owen." In *The Court of Chivalry 1634–1640*, edited by Richard Cust and Andrew Hopper. British History Online. http://www.british-history.ac.uk/no-series/court-of-chivalry/572-ryley-owen.

Cuttica, Cesare. *Sir Robert Filmer (1588–1652) and the Patriotic Monarch: Patriarchalism in Seventeenth-Century Political Thought*. Manchester: Manchester University Press, 2012.

Dabhoiwala, Faramerz. "Writing Petitions in Early Modern England." In *Suffering and Happiness in England 1550–1850: Narratives and Representations: A Collection to Honour Paul Slack*, edited by Michael Braddick and Joanna Innes, 127–48. Oxford: Oxford University Press, 2017.

Daly, James. *Sir Robert Filmer and English Political Thought*. Toronto: University of Toronto Press, 1979.

Daly, Peter. *The English Emblem Book Tradition*. With Leslie Duer and Anthony Raspa. 5 vols. Toronto: University of Toronto Press, 1988–98.

Darnton, Robert. "An Early Information Society: News and the Media in Eighteenth-Century France." *American Historical Review* 105, no. 1 (2000): 1–35.

da Rold, Orietta. "Networks of Paper in Late Medieval England." In *The Book Trade in Early Modern Europe*, edited by Anna Reynolds and Daniel Bellingradt, 148–66. Leiden, Neth.: Brill, 2021.

Daston, Lorraine. "On Scientific Observation." *Isis* 99, no. 1 (2008): 97–110.

Davies, J. Conway. *Catalogue of manuscripts in the library of the Honourable Society of the Inner Temple*. 3 vols. London: Oxford University Press for the Masters of the Bench of the Inner Temple, 1972.

Davison, Francis. *The Poetical Rhapsody: To which are added, Several Other Pieces*. 2 vols. Edited by Nicholas Harris Nicolas. London: W. Pickering, 1826.

Daybell, James. "Gendered Archival Practices and the Future Lives of Letters." In Daybell and Gordon, *Cultures of Correspondence in Early Modern Britain*, 210–36.

Daybell, James. *The Material Letter in Early Modern England: Manuscript Letters and Culture and Practices of Letter-Writing, 1512–1635*. Houndmills, UK: Palgrave Macmillan, 2012.

Daybell, James. "The Scribal Circulation of Early Modern Letters." *HLQ* 79, no. 3 (2016): 365–85.

Daybell, James, ed. *Women and Politics in Early Modern England, 1450–1750*. London: Routledge, 2004.

Daybell, James, and Andrew Gordon, eds. *Cultures of Correspondence in Early Modern Britain*. Philadelphia: University of Pennsylvania Press, 2016.

Daybell, James, and Peter Hinds, eds. *Material Readings of Early Modern Culture: Texts and Social Practices, 1580–1730*. Houndmills, UK: Palgrave Macmillan, 2010.

Dery, David. "'Papereality' and Learning in Bureaucratic Institutions." *Administration & Society* 29, no. 6 (1998): 677–89.

The Despatches of William Perwich, English Agent in Paris, 1669–1677. Edited by M. Beryl Curran. London: Royal Historical Society, 1903.

de Vivo, Filippo. "How to Read Venetian *Relazioni*." *Renaissance and Reformation* 34, no. 1/2 (2011): 25–59.

de Vivo, Filippo. *Information and Communication in Venice: Rethinking Early Modern Politics*. Oxford: Oxford University Press, 2007.

de Vivo, Filippo, Andrea Guidi, and Alessandro Silvestri, eds. "Archival Transformations in Early Modern European History." Special Issue, *European History Quarterly* 46, no. 3 (July 2016): 421–589.

de Vivo, Filippo, Andrea Guidi, and Alessandro Silvestri. *Fonti per la storia degli archivi degli antichi stati italiani*. With Fabio Antonini and Giacomo Guidici. Rome: Ministero dei beni e delle attività culturali e del turismo, Direzione generale Archivi, 2016.

Dierks, Konstantin. *In My Power: Letter Writing and Communications in Early America*. Philadelphia: University of Pennsylvania Press, 2009.

Dooley, Brendan, and Sabrina Baron, eds. *The Politics of Information in Early Modern Europe*. London, Routledge, 2001.

Dover, Paul. *The Information Revolution in Early Modern Europe* Cambridge: Cambridge University Press, 2021.

Dover, Paul, ed. *Secretaries and Statecraft in the Early Modern World*. Edinburgh: Edinburgh University Press, 2017.

Dubcovsky, Alejandra. *Informed Power: Communication in the Early American South*. Cambridge, MA: Harvard University Press, 2016.

Dugdale, David. *English Scholars, 1660–1730*. London: Eyre & Spottiswoode, 1951.

Edelson, Max. *The New Map of Empire: How Britain Imagined America before Independence*. Cambridge, MA: Harvard University Press, 2017.

Eisenstein, Elizabeth. *The Printing Revolution in Early Modern Europe*. Cambridge: Cambridge University Press, 1983.

Elton, G. R. *England, 1200–1640*. Ithaca, NY: Cornell University Press, 1969.

Elton, G. R. *Policy and Police: The Enforcement of the Reformation in the Age of Thomas Cromwell*. Cambridge: Cambridge University Press, 1972.

Elton, G. R. *The Tudor Revolution in Government: Administrative Changes in the Reign of Henry VIII*. Cambridge: Cambridge University Press, 1953.

Emanuel, Phillip. "'Great Weights Hang by Small Wires': Households and the

Making of the British Empire, c. 1650–1713." PhD diss., College of William and Mary, 2022.

Febvre, Lucien, and Henri Martin. *L'apparition du livre*. Paris: A. Michel, 1958.

Felten, Sebastien, and Christine von Oertzen, eds. "Histories of Bureaucratic Knowledge." Special issue, *Journal for the History of Knowledge* (2020).

Filmer, Robert. *The Free-holders Grand Inquest touching our Soveraigne Lord the King and His Parliament*. London, 1648.

Fincham, Kenneth. "The Restoration of the Altars in the 1630s." *HJ* 44, no. 4 (2001): 919–40.

Findlen, Paula. *Possessing Nature: Museums, Collecting, and Scientific Culture in Early Modern Italy*. Berkeley: University of California Press, 1994.

Fitzgibbons, Jonathan. "Hereditary Succession and the Cromwellian Protectorate: The Offer of the Crown Reconsidered." *EHR* 128, no. 534 (2013): 1095–1128.

Fogelman, Ronald, and Sheila E. Widnall. *Cornerstones of Information Warfare*. Washington, DC: Office of the Chief of Staff, US Air Force, 1997.

Fox, Adam. "Custom, Memory, and the Authority of Writing." In *The Experience of Authority in Early Modern England*, edited by Paul Griffiths, Adam Fox, and Steve Hindle, 89–116. Basingstoke, UK: Macmillan, 1996.

Fox, Adam. *Oral and Literate Culture in England, 1500–1700*. Oxford: Clarendon, 2001.

Fox, Adam. "Popular Verses and their Readership in the Early Seventeenth Century." In *The Practice and Representation of Reading in England*, edited by James Raven, Naomi Tadmor, and Helen Small, 125–37. Cambridge: Cambridge University Press, 1996.

Fox, Adam. "Printed Questionnaires, Research Networks, and the Discovery of the British Isles." *HJ* 53, no. 3 (2010): 593–621.

Fox, Adam. "Remembering the Past, in Early Modern England: Oral and Written Tradition." *Transactions of the Royal Historical Society*, 6th ser., 9 (1999): 233–56.

Fox, Adam, and Daniel Woolf, eds. *The Spoken Word: Oral Culture in Britain, 1500–1850*. Manchester: Manchester University Press, 2002.

Fox, Levi, ed. *English Historical Scholarship in the Sixteenth and Seventeenth Centuries*. London: Oxford University Press, 1956.

Fraser, Peter. *The Intelligence of the Secretaries of State and their Monopoly of Licensed News, 1660–1688*. Cambridge: Cambridge University Press, 1956.

French, Henry. "The 'Remembered Family' and Dynastic Senses of Identity among the English Gentry, c. 1600–1800." *HR* 92, no. 257 (2019): 529–46.

Friedrich, Markus. *The Birth of the Archive: A History of Knowledge*. Translated by John Noël Dillon. Ann Arbor: University of Michigan Press, 2018.

Friedrich, Markus. "Government and Information-Management in Early Modern Europe: The Case of the Society of Jesus (1540–1773)." *JEMH* 12, no. 6 (2009): 539–63.

Fuentes, Marisa. *Dispossessed Lives: Enslaved Women, Violence, and the Archive*. Philadelphia: University of Pennsylvania Press, 2016.

Gajda, Alexandra. *The Earl of Essex and Late Elizabethan Political Culture*. Oxford: Oxford University Press, 2012.

Gajda, Alexandra, and Paul Cavill, eds. *Writing the History of Parliament in Tudor and Early Stuart England*. Manchester: Manchester University Press, 2018.

Gehring, David, ed. *Diplomatic Intelligence on the Holy Roman Empire and Denmark during the Reigns of Elizabeth I and James VI: Three Treatises*. Cambridge: Cambridge University Press, 2015.

Ghobrial, John-Paul. *The Whispers of Cities: Information Flows in Istanbul, London, and Paris in the Age of William Trumbull*. Oxford: Oxford University Press, 2013.

Gitelman, Lisa. *Paper Knowledge: Towards a Media History of Documents*. Durham, NC: Duke University Press, 2014.

Glaisyer, Natasha. "'The Most Universal Intelligencers': The Circulation of the *London Gazette* in the 1690s." *Media History* 23, no. 2 (2017): 256–80.

Goldie, Mark. "The Unacknowledged Republic: Officeholding in Early Modern England." In *The Politics of the Excluded, c. 1500–1800*, edited by Tim Harris, 153–94. Basingstoke, UK: Palgrave, 2001.

Gordon, Andrew. "*Copycopia*, or the Place of Copied Correspondence in Manuscript Culture: A Case Study." In Daybell and Hinds, *Material Readings of Early Modern Culture*, 65–81.

Gordon, Andrew. "Material Fictions: Counterfeit Correspondence and the Culture of Copying in Early Modern England." In Daybell and Gordon, *Cultures of Correspondence in Early Modern Britain*, 85–109.

Gowing, Laura. "Girls on Forms: Apprenticing Young Women in Seventeenth-Century London." *JBS* 55, no. 3 (2016): 447–73;

Grafton, Anthony. "Church History in Early Modern Europe: Tradition and Innovation." In *Sacred History: Uses of the Christian Past in the Renaissance World*, edited by Katherine Van Liere, Simon Ditchfield, and Howard Louthan, 3–26. Oxford: Oxford University Press, 2012.

Grafton, Anthony. "Matthew Parker: The Book as Archive." *History of Humanities* 2, no. 1 (2017): 15–50.

Grafton, Anthony. *What Was History? The Art of History in Early Modern Europe*. Cambridge: Cambridge University Press, 2007.

Grafton, Anthony. "The World of the Polyhistors: Humanism and Encyclopedism." *Central European History* 18, no. 1 (1985): 31–47.

Grafton, Anthony, and Nancy Siraisi, eds. *Natural Particulars: Nature and the Disciplines in Renaissance Europe*. Cambridge, MA: Harvard University Press, 1999.

Grandjean, Katherine. *American Passage: The Communications Frontier in Early New England*. Cambridge, MA: Harvard University Press, 2015.

Graves, Michael A. R. *Thomas Norton: The Parliament Man*. Oxford: Blackwell, 1994.

Gray, Madeleine. "Exchequer Officials and the Market in Crown Property, 1558–1640." In *The Estates of the English Crown, 1558–1640*, edited by R. W. Hoyle, 112–36. Cambridge: Cambridge University Press, 1992.

Greenberg, Janelle Renfrow. *The Radical Face of the Ancient Constitution: St Edward's "Laws" in Early Modern Political Thought.* Cambridge: Cambridge University Press, 2001.

Griffiths, Paul. "Local Arithmetic: Information Cultures in Early Modern England." In *Remaking English Society: Social Relations and Social Change in Early Modern England,* edited by Steve Hindle, Alexandra Shepard, and John Walter, 113–34. Woodbridge, UK: Boydell Press, 2013.

Griffiths, Paul. "Secrecy and Authority in Late Sixteenth- and Seventeenth-Century London." *HJ* 40, no. 4 (1997): 925–51.

Groebner, Valentin. *Who Are You? Identification, Deception, and Surveillance in Early Modern Europe.* Translated by Mark Kyzburz and John Peck. New York: Zone Books, 2007.

Guillim, John. *A Display of Heraldry.* 6th ed. London, 1724.

Guldi, Jo. *Roads to Power: Britain Invents the Infrastructure State.* Cambridge, MA: Harvard University Press, 2012.

Guy, John. "The Origins of the Petition of Right Reconsidered." *HJ* 25, no. 2 (1982): 289–312.

Habermas, Jürgen. *The Structural Transformation of the Public Sphere: An Inquiry into the Category of Bourgeois Society.* Translated by Thomas Burger with Frederick Lawrence. Cambridge: Polity, 1989.

Halasz, Alexandra. *The Marketplace of Print: Pamphlet and the Public Sphere in Early Modern England.* Cambridge: Cambridge University Press, 1997.

Hallam, Elizabeth. "Annotations in Domesday Book since 1100." In *Domesday Book Studies,* edited by Ann Williams and R. W. H. Erskine, 136–50. London: Alecto, 1987.

Hallam, Elizabeth. "Arthur Agarde and the Domesday Book." In *Sir Robert Cotton as Collector: Essays on an Early Stuart Courtier and his Legacy,* edited by Colin Tite, 253–61. London: British Library, 1997.

Hallam, Elizabeth. "Problems with Record Keeping in Early 18th c. London: Some Pictorial Representations of the State Paper Office, 1705–1706." *JSA* 6, no. 4 (1979): 219–26.

Hallam, Elizabeth. "The Tower of London as Record Office." *Archives* 14, no. 61 (1979): 3–10.

Halliday, Paul. "Authority in the Archives." *Critical Analysis of Law* 1, no. 1 (2014): 110–42.

Hammer, Paul E. J. "Essex and Europe: Evidence from Confidential Instructions by the Earl of Essex, 1595–6." *EHR* 111, no. 441 (1996): 357–81.

Hammer, Paul E. J. "The Uses of Scholarship: The Secretariat of Robert Devereux, 2nd Earl of Essex, c.1585–1601." *EHR* 109, no. 430 (1994): 26–51.

Harding, Vanessa. "Monastic Records and the Dissolution: A Tudor Revolution in the Archives?" *European History Quarterly* 46, no. 3 (2016): 480–97.

Harkness, Deborah. *The Jewel House: Elizabethan London and the Scientific Revolution.* New Haven, CT: Yale University Press, 2008.

Harris, Barbara J. *English Aristocratic Women, 1450–1550*. Oxford: Oxford University Press, 2002.

Harris, Tim. *London Crowds in the Reign of Charles II: Propaganda and Politics from the Restoration until the Exclusion Crisis*. Cambridge: Cambridge University Press, 1987.

Havens, Earle. *Commonplace Books: A History of Manuscripts and Printed Books from Antiquity to the Twentieth Century*. New Haven, CT: Beinecke Rare Book and Manuscript Library, 2001. Distributed by University Press of New England.

Haward, Lazarus. *The Charges Issuing forth of the Crown Revenue of England and Dominion of Wales*. London, 1647.

Haward, Lazarus. *The Charges Issuing forth of the Crown Revenue of England and Dominion of Wales*. London, 1660.

Head, Randolph, ed. "Archival Knowledge Cultures in Europe, 1400–1900." Special issue, *Archival Science* 10, no. 3 (2010): 191–343.

Head, Randolph. "Knowing Like a State: The Transformation of Political Knowledge in Swiss Archives, 1450–1770." *JMH* 75, no. 4 (2003): 745–82.

Head, Randolph. *Making Archives in Early Modern Europe: Proof, Information, and Political Record-Keeping, 1400–1700*. Cambridge: Cambridge University Press, 2019.

Head, Randolph. "Mirroring Governance: Archives, Inventories and Political Knowledge in Early Modern Switzerland and Europe." *Archival Sciences* 7, no. 4 (2007): 317–29.

Headrick, Daniel. *When Information Came of Age: Technologies of Knowledge in the Age of Reason and Revolution, 1700–1850*. Oxford: Oxford University Press, 2000.

Heal, Felicity, and Clive Holmes. *The Gentry in England and Wales, 1500–1700*. London: Macmillan, 1994.

Healy, Simon. "Crown Revenue and the Political Culture of Early Stuart England." PhD diss., Birkbeck, University of London, 2015.

Hearne, Thomas. *A Collection of Curious Discourses written by Eminent Antiquaries upon several heads in our English Antiquities*. 2 vols. London, 1773.

Heffernan, David. *Debating Tudor Policy in Sixteenth-Century Ireland*. Manchester: Manchester University Press, 2018.

Heffernan, David, ed. *Reform Treatises on Tudor Ireland, 1537–1599*. Dublin: Four Courts Press, 2016.

Heffernan, David. "Six Tracts on 'Coign and Livery,' c. 1568–1578." *Analecta Hibernica* 45 (2014): 1–33.

Helmers, Helmer. "Public Diplomacy in Early Modern Europe: Towards a New History of News." Special issue, *Media History* 22, no. 3–4 (2016): 401–20.

Helmers, Helmer, and Michiel Van Groesen, eds. "Managing the News in Early Modern Europe." Special issue, *Media History* 22, no. 3–4 (2016): 261–447.

Herendeen, Wyman. *William Camden: A Life in Context*. Woodbridge, UK: Boydell and Brewer, 2007.

Hesse, Carla. *Publishing and Cultural Politics in Revolutionary Paris, 1789–1810*. Berkeley: University of California Press, 1991.

Hill, Lamar M. *Bench and Bureaucracy: The Public Career of Sir Julius Caesar, 1580–1636*. Stanford, CA: Stanford University Press, 1988.

Hill, Lamar M., ed. *The Ancient State Authoritie, and Proceedings of the Court of Requests by Sir Julius Caesar*. Cambridge: Cambridge University Press, 1975.

Hindle, Steve. *The State and Social Change in Early Modern England, 1550–1640*. New York: St. Martin's Press, 2000.

Hirst, Derek. "Making Contact: Petitions and the English Republic." *JBS* 45, no. 1 (2006): 26–50.

Hodgson, Geoffrey. "1688 and All That: Property Rights, the Glorious Revolution and the Rise of British Capitalism." *Journal of Institutional Economics* 13, no. 1 (2017): 79–107.

Hotson, Howard. *Johann Heinrich Alsted, 1588–1638: Between Renaissance, Reformation, and Universal Reform*. Oxford: Oxford University Press, 2000.

Houllemare, Marie. "Seeing the Empire through Lists and Charts: French Colonial Records in the Eighteenth Century." *JEMH* 22, no. 5 (2018): 371–91.

Hoyle, Richard. "'Vain Projects': The Crown and its Copyholders in the Reign of James I." In *English Rural Society, 1500–1800: Essays in Honour of Joan Thirsk*, edited by John Chartres and David Hey, 73–104. Cambridge: Cambridge University Press, 1990.

Hughes, Ann. "Diligent Enquiries and Perfect Accounts: Central Initiatives and Local Agency in the English Civil War." In Kyle and Peacey, *Connecting Centre and Locality*, 116–32.

Hughes, Ann. *Gangraena and the Struggle for the English Revolution*. Oxford: Oxford University Press, 2004.

Hughes, Charles, ed. "Nicholas Faunt's Discourse Touching the Office of Principal Secretary of Estate, &c. 1592." *EHR* 20, no. 79 (1905): 499–508.

Hull, Matthew. *Government of Paper: The Materiality of Bureaucracy in Urban Pakistan*. Berkeley: University of California Press, 2012.

Hunneyball, Paul. "The Development of Parliamentary Privilege, 1604–1629." *PH* 34, no. 1 (2015): 111–28.

Hunt, Arnold. "'Burn This Letter': Preservation and Destruction in the Early Modern Archive." In Daybell and Gordon, *Cultures of Correspondence in Early Modern Britain*, 189–209.

Hunt, Arnold. "The Early Modern Secretary and the Archive." In Peters, Walsham, and Corens, *Archives and Information in the Early Modern World*, 105–30.

Hurstfield, Joel. "The Profits of Fiscal Feudalism, 1541–1603." *Economic History Review* 8, no. 1 (1955): 53–61.

Institut für Österreichische Geschichtsforschung, "About the Fugger Newsletters." FWF-Der Wissenschaftsfonds. https://fuggerzeitungen.univie.ac.at/en/about-fugger-newsletters.

Issues of the Exchequer, being Payments made out of his Majesty's Revenue during the Reign of James I. Edited by Frederick Devon. London: John Rodwell, 1836.

Jacobsen, Gertrude Ann. *William Blathwayt: A Late Seventeenth Century English Administrator.* New Haven, CT: Yale University Press, 1932.

James, Mervyn. *Society, Politics and Culture: Studies in Early Modern England.* Cambridge: Cambridge University Press, 1986.

Jardine, Lisa, and Anthony Grafton. "'Studied for Action': How Gabriel Harvey Read his Livy." *P&P* 129 (1990): 30–78.

Jardine, Lisa, and William Sherman. "Pragmatic Readers: Knowledge Transactions and Scholarly Services in Early Modern England." In *Religion, Culture and Society in Early Modern England: Essays in Honour of Patrick Collinson*, edited by Anthony John Fletcher and Peter Roberts, 102–24. Cambridge: Cambridge University Press, 1996.

Jewell, Helen. *Women in Medieval England.* Manchester: Manchester University Press, 1996.

Johns, Adrian. *The Nature of the Book: Print and Knowledge in the Making.* Chicago: University of Chicago Press, 1998.

Johnson, Jessica Marie. *Wicked Flesh: Women, Intimacy, and Freedom in the Atlantic World.* Philadelphia: University of Pennsylvania Press, 2020.

Johnson, Sara E. *Encyclopédie noire: The Making of Moreau de Saint-Méry's Intellectual World.* Chapel Hill: University of North Carolina Press, 2023. Published for the Omohundro Institute of Early American History and Culture.

Jones, Norman. *Governing by Virtue: Lord Burghley and the Management of Elizabethan England.* Oxford: Oxford University Press, 2015.

Jones, W. J. *The Elizabethan Court of Chancery.* Oxford: Clarendon Press, 1967.

Journal of the House of Commons, 1547–1834. 89 vols. London: H. M. Stationery Office, 1802–1834.

Journal of the House of Lords, 1509–1832. 64 vols. London: H. M. Stationery Office, 1767–1832.

Kafka, Ben. *The Demon of Writing: Powers and Failures of Paperwork.* New York: Zone Books, 2012.

Kane, Brendan. *The Politics and Culture of Honour in Britain and Ireland, 1541–1641.* Cambridge: Cambridge University Press, 2010.

Keller, Vera. *Knowledge and the Public Interest, 1575–1725.* Cambridge: Cambridge University Press, 2015.

Keller, Vera. "Mining Tacitus: Secrets of Empire, Nature and Art in the Reason of State." *British Journal for the History of Science* 45, no. 2 (2012): 189–212.

Keller, Vera, and Ted McCormick, eds. "Towards a History of Projects." *Early Science and Medicine* 21 (2016): 423–44.

Kelsey, Sean. *Inventing a Republic: The Political Culture of the English Commonwealth.* Manchester: Manchester University Press, 1997.

Kendrick, T. D. *British Antiquity*. London: Methuen, 1950.

Kennedy, Claire. "Those Who Stayed: English Chorography and the Elizabethan Society of Antiquaries." In *Motion and Knowledge in the Changing Early Modern World: Orbits, Routes, and Vessels*, edited by Ofer Gal and Yi Zhang, 47–70. Dordrecht, Neth.: Springer, 2014.

Kewes, Paulina, Ian Archer, and Felicity Heal. *The Oxford Handbook of Holinshed's Chronicles*. Oxford: Oxford University Press, 2013.

Kiser, Edgar, and Joshua Kane. "Revolution and State Structure: The Bureaucratization of Tax Administration in Early Modern England and France." *American Journal of Sociology* 107, no. 1 (2001): 183–223.

Kishlansky, Mark. "Tyranny Denied: Charles I, Attorney General Heath, and the Five Knights' Case." *HJ* 42, no. 1 (1999): 53–83.

Kishlansky, Mark. "A Whipper Whipped: The Sedition of William Prynne." *HJ* 56, no. 3 (2013): 603–27.

Knafla, Louis. "The 'Country Chancellor': The Patronage of Sir Thomas Egerton, Baron Ellesmere." In *Patronage in Late Renaissance England: Papers at a Clark Library Seminar 14 May 1977*, edited by French R. Fogle and Louis A. Knafla, 31–115. Los Angeles: Clark Memorial Library, 1983.

Knafla, Louis. *Law and Politics in Jacobean England: The Tracts of Lord Chancellor Ellesemere*. Cambridge: Cambridge University Press, 1972.

Knafla, Louis. "The Law Studies of an Elizabethan Student." *HLQ* 32, no. 3 (1969): 221–40.

Knight, Jeffrey Todd. *Bound to Read: Compilations, Collections, and the Making of Renaissance Literature*. Philadelphia: University of Pennsylvania Press, 2013.

Knights, Mark. "Faults on Both Sides: The Conspiracies of Party Politics under the Later Stuarts." In *Conspiracies and Conspiracy Theory in Early Modern Europe: From the Waldensians to the French Revolution*, edited by Barry Coward and Julian Swann, 173–95. Aldershot, UK: Ashgate, 2004.

Knights, Mark. *Politics and Opinion in Crisis, 1678–1681*. Cambridge University Press, 1994.

Knights, Mark. *Representation and Misrepresentation in Later Stuart Britain: Partisanship and Political and Culture*. Oxford: Oxford University Press, 2005.

Knox, William. *Extra Official State Papers*. London, 1789.

Koscak, Stephanie. *Monarchy, Print Culture, and Reverence in Early Modern England: Picturing Royal Subjects*. New York: Routledge, 2020.

Kyle, Chris. "'A Dog, a Butcher, and a Puritan': The Politics of Lent in Early Modern England." In Kyle and Peacey, *Connecting Centre and Locality*, 22–43.

Kyle, Chris. "Robert Bowyer." History of Parliament Online. Accessed January 25, 2023. https://www.historyofparliamentonline.org/volume/1604-1629/member/bowyer-robert-1569-1621. Originally published in Thrush and Ferris, *The House of Commons 1604–1629*.

Kyle, Chris. *Theater of State: Parliament and Political Culture in Early Modern England*. Stanford, CA: Stanford University Press, 2012.

Kyle, Chris, and Jason Peacey, eds. *Connecting Centre and Locality: Political Com-*

munication in *Early Modern England*. Manchester: Manchester University Press, 2020.

Lake, Peter. *All Hail to the Archpriest: Confessional Conflict, Toleration, and the Politics of Publicity in Post-Reformation England*. Oxford: Oxford University Press, 2019.

Lake, Peter. *Bad Queen Bess? Libels, Secret Histories, and the Politics of Publicity in the Reign of Queen Elizabeth I*. Oxford: Oxford University Press, 2016.

Lake, Peter. "From Revisionist to Royalist History; or, Was Charles I the First Whig Historian." *HLQ* 78, no. 4 (2015): 657–81.

Lake, Peter. "The Laudian Style: Order, Uniformity, and the Pursuit of the Beauty of Holiness in the 1630s." In *The Early Stuart Church, 1603–1642*, ed. Kenneth Fincham, 161–85. Basingstoke, UK: Macmillan, 1993.

Lake, Peter. "The Politics of 'Popularity' and the Public Sphere: The 'Monarchical Republic' of Elizabeth I Defends Itself." In Lake and Pincus, *The Politics of the Public Sphere in Early Modern England*, 59–94.

Lake, Peter. "Puritans, Popularity and Petitions: Local Politics in National Context, Cheshire, 1641." In Cogswell, Cust, and Lake, *Politics, Religion and Popularity in Early Stuart Britain*, 259–89.

Lake, Peter, and Stephen Pincus, eds. *The Politics of the Public Sphere in Early Modern England*. Manchester: Manchester University Press, 2007.

Lake, Peter, and Stephen Pincus. "Rethinking the Public Sphere in Early Modern England." *JBS* 45, no. 2 (2006): 270–92.

Lake, Peter, and Michael C. Questier. "Puritans, Papists, and the 'Public Sphere' in Early Modern England." *JMH* 72, no. 3 (2000): 587–627.

Lambert, Sheila. "The Printers and the Government, 1604–1637." In *Aspects of Printing from 1600*, edited by Robin Myers and Michael Harris, 1–29. Oxford: Oxford Polytechnic Press, 1987.

Lamont, William. *Marginal Prynne, 1600–1669*. Toronto: University of Toronto Press, 1963.

Langelüddecke, Henrick. "'I finde all men & my officers all soe unwilling': The Collection of Ship Money, 1635–1640." *JBS* 46, no. 3 (2007): 509–42.

Latour, Bruno. *Science in Action: How to Follow Scientists and Engineers through Society*. Cambridge, MA: Harvard University Press, 1987.

Latour, Bruno, and Steve Woolgar. *Laboratory Life: The Construction of Scientific Facts*. Princeton, NJ: Princeton University Press, 1986.

Laud, William. *The Works of the Most Reverend Father in God, William Laud*. 7 vols. New York: AMS Press, 1975.

[Laud, William]. *The Autobiography of Dr William Laud: Archbishop of Canterbury, and Martyr*. Oxford: J. H. Parker, 1839.

Lecky, Katarzyna. "Archiving Ordinary Experience: Small-Format Cartography in the English Renaissance." *Journal of Medieval and Early Modern Studies* 47, no. 2 (2017): 359–90.

Lecky, Katarzyna. *Pocket Maps and Public Poetry in the English Renaissance*. Oxford: Oxford University Press, 2019.

Leonard, H. H. "Distraint of Knighthood: The Last Phase, 1625–41." *History* 63, no. 207 (1978): 23–37.

Letters Addressed from London To Sir Joseph Williamson While Plenipotentiary at the Congress of Cologne in the Years 1673 and 1674. 2 vols. Edited by W. D. Christie. London: Camden Society, 1874.

Levy, F. J. "How Information Spread amongst the Gentry, 1550–1640." *JBS* 21, no. 2 (1982): 11–34.

Levy Peck, Linda. *Court Patronage and Corruption in Early Stuart England*. London: Unwin Hyman, 1990.

Levy Peck, Linda. *Northampton: Patronage and Politics at the Court of James I*. London: Unwin Hyman, 1990.

Little, Patrick. "John Thurloe and the Offer of the Crown to Oliver Cromwell." In *Oliver Cromwell: New Perspectives*, edited by Patrick Little, 216–40. Basingstoke, UK: Palgrave Macmillan, 2009.

Love, Harold. "The Look of News: Popish Plot Narratives, 1678–1680." In *The Cambridge History of the Book in Britain*, vol. 4, *1557–1695*, edited by John Barnard and D. F. McKenzie, 652–56. Cambridge, Cambridge University Press, 2002.

Love, Harold. *Scribal Publication in Seventeenth-Century England*. Oxford: Clarendon, 1993.

Lyall, R. J. "Materials: The Paper Revolution." In *Book Production and Publishing in Britain, 1375–1475*, edited by Jeremy Griffiths and Derek Pearsall, 11–29. Cambridge: Cambridge University Press, 1989.

Lyon, Gregory. "Baudouin, Flacius, and the Plan for the Magdeburg Centuries." *JHI* 64, no. 2 (2003): 253–72.

MacMillan, Margaret. *Dangerous Games: The Uses and Abuses of History*. New York: Modern Library, 2009.

Maginn, Christopher, and Steven Ellis. *The Tudor Discovery of Ireland*. Dublin: Four Courts Press, 2015.

Malcolm, Noel. "Thomas Harrison and his 'Ark of Studies': An Episode in the History of the Organization of Knowledge." *Seventeenth Century* 19, no. 2 (2004): 196–232.

Manning, Roger. "Antiquarianism and the Seigneurial Reaction: Sir Robert and Sir Thomas Cotton and Their Tenants." *HR* 63 (1990): 277–88.

Marshall, Alan. *Intelligence and Espionage in the Reign of Charles II, 1660–1685*. Cambridge: Cambridge University Press, 1994.

Marshall, Alan. "Sindercombe, Miles (d. 1657)." In *Oxford Dictionary of National Biography*. Oxford University Press, 2004. Online ed., 2004. https://doi.org/10.1093/ref:odnb/25637.

Marshall, Alan. "Sir Joseph Williamson and the Conduct of Administration in Restoration England." *HR* 69, no. 168 (1996): 18–41.

McCormick, Ted. *William Petty and the Ambitions of Political Arithmetic*. Oxford: Oxford University Press, 2012.

McElligott, Jason. *Royalism, Print, and Censorship in Revolutionary England*. Woodbridge, UK: Boydell & Brewer, 2007.

McGee, J. Sears. *An Industrious Mind: The Worlds of Sir Simonds D'Ewes*. Stanford, CA: Stanford University Press, 2015.

McKisack, May. *Medieval History in the Tudor Age*. Oxford: Clarendon Press, 1971.

McMahon, Madeline. "Matthew Parker and the Practice of Church History." In *Scholarship and Confessionalism*, edited by Nick Hardy and Dmitri Levitin, 116–53. Oxford: Oxford University Press, 2019. Published for the British Academy.

McRae, Andrew. "Reading Libels: An Introduction." *HLQ* 69, no. 1 (2006): 1–13.

McRae, Andrew. "Stigmatizing Prynne: Seditious Libel, Political Satire, and the Construction of Opposition." In *The 1630s: Interdisciplinary Essays on Culture and Politics in the Caroline Era*, edited by Ian Atherton and Julie Sanders, 171–88. Manchester: Manchester University Press, 2006.

Mears, Natalie. *Queenship and Political Discourse in the Elizabethan Realms*. Cambridge: Cambridge University Press, 2005.

Mendelson, Sara, and Patricia Crawford. *Women in Early Modern England*. Oxford: Oxford University Press, 1998.

Mendle, Michael. "De Facto Freedom, De Facto Authority: Press and Parliament, 1640–1643." *HJ* 38, no. 2 (1995): 307–32.

Merritt, J. F. "Power and Communication: Thomas Wentworth and Government at a Distance during the Personal Rule, 1629–1635." In *The Political World of Thomas Wentworth, Earl of Strafford, 1621–1641*, edited by J. F. Merritt, 109–32. Cambridge: Cambridge University Press, 1996.

Messick, Brinkley. *The Calligraphic State: Textual Domination and History in a Muslim Society*. Berkeley: University of California Press, 1993.

Miller, John. "Public Opinion in Charles II's England." *History* 80, no. 260 (1995): 361–67.

Miller, Peter N. *Peiresc's Mediterranean World*. Cambridge, MA: Harvard University Press, 2017.

Millstone, Noah. "Designed for Collection: Early Modern News and the Production of History." *Media History* 23, no. 2 (2017): 177–98.

Millstone, Noah. "Evil Counsel: The *Propositions to Bridle the Impertinency of Parliament* and the Critique of Caroline Government in the Late 1620s." *JBS* 50, no. 4 (2011): 813–39.

Millstone, Noah. *Manuscript Circulation and the Invention of Politics in Early Stuart England*. Cambridge: Cambridge University Press, 2016.

Millstone, Noah. "Seeing Like a Statesman in Early Stuart England." *P&P* 223 (2014): 77–127.

Millstone, Noah. "Sir Robert Cotton, Manuscript Pamphleteering, and the Making of Jacobean Kingship during the Short Peace, c1609–1613." *JBS* 62, no. 1 (2023): 134–60.

Milton, Anthony. *Catholic and Reformed: The Roman and Protestant Churches in English Protestant Thought, 1600–1640*. Cambridge: Cambridge University Press, 1995.

Milton, Anthony. "The Creation of Laudianism: A New Approach." In Cogswell,

Cust, and Lake, *Politics, Religion and Popularity in Early Stuart Britain*, 162–84.

Milton, Anthony. "Laud, William (1573–1645)." In *Oxford Dictionary of National Biography*. Oxford University Press, 2004. Online ed., 2004, modified May 21, 2009. https://doi.org/10.1093/ref:odnb/16112.

Mishra, Rupali. "In the Company of Merchants: Edward Sherburne, the East India Company's Secretary." In Bulman and Dominguez, *Political and Religious Practice in the Early Modern World*, 77–96.

Morgan, Jennifer. *Reckoning with Slavery: Gender, Kinship, and Capitalism in the Early Black Atlantic*. Durham, NC: Duke University Press, 2021.

Morton, Adam. "Intensive Ephemera: *The Catholick Gamesters* and the Visual Culture of News in Restoration London." In *News in Early Modern Europe: Currents and Connections*, edited by Simon Davies and Puck Fletcher, 115–40. Leiden, Neth.: Brill, 2014.

Morton, Adam. "Popery, Politics, and Play: Visual Culture in Succession Crisis England." *Seventeenth Century* 31, no. 4 (2016): 411–49.

Moss, Ann. *Printed Common-Place Books and the Structuring of Renaissance Thought*. Oxford: Clarendon, 1996.

Mueller, Lothar. *White Magic: The Age of Paper*. Translated by Jessica Spengler. Cambridge: Polity, 2014.

Müller-Wille, Staffan, and Isabelle Charmantier. "Carl Linnaeus's Botanical Paper Slips (1767–1773)." *Intellectual History Review* 24, no. 2 (2014): 215–38.

Mullett, Charles F. "The 'Better Reception, Preservation, and More Convenient Use' of Public Records in Eighteenth-Century England." *American Archivist* 27, no. 2 (1964): 195–217.

Munda, Brandon. "The Spyglass and the Mirror: The Intelligence State in Conflict and Crisis during the War of Spanish Succession." PhD diss., College of William & Mary, 2023.

Murison, Barbara. "The Talented Mr Blathwayt: His Empire Revisited." In *English Atlantic Revisited: Essays Honouring Professor Ian K. Steele*, edited by Nancy L. Rhoden, 33–58. Montreal: McGill-Queen's University Press, 2007.

Nelles, Paul. "The Library as an Instrument of Discovery: Gabriel Naudé and the Uses of History." In *History and the Disciplines: The Reclassification of Knowledge in Early Modern Europe*, edited by Donald R. Kelley, 41–57. Rochester, NY: Rochester University Press, 1997.

Newman, Jane. "The World Made Print: Luther's New Testament in an Age of Mechanical Reproduction." *Representations* 11 (1985): 95–124.

Nummedal, Tara. *Alchemy and Authority in the Holy Roman Empire*. Chicago: University of Chicago Press, 2007.

Ogborn, Miles. "The Capacities of the State: Charles Davenant and the Management of the Excise, 1683–1698." *Journal of Historical Geography* 24, no. 3 (1998): 289–312.

Ogborn, Miles. *Indian Ink: Script and Print in the Making of the English East India Company*. Chicago: University of Chicago Press, 2007.

O'Neill, Lindsay. *The Opened Letter: Networking in the Early Modern British World*. Philadelphia: University of Pennsylvania, 2015.

Orders of the High Court of Chancery and Statutes of the Realm Relating to Chancery, From the Earliest Period to the Present Time. 2 vols. Edited by George William Sanders. London: A. Maxwell & Son, 1845.

Ovenden, Richard. *Burning the Books: A History of the Deliberate Destruction of Knowledge*. Cambridge, MA: Harvard University Press, 2020.

Ovenden, Richard. "Scipio le Squyer and the Fate of Monastic Cartularies in the Early Seventeenth Century." *Library*, ser. 6, 13, no. 4 (1991): 323–37.

Parliament Rolls of Medieval England. 16 vols. Edited by Chris Given-Wilson, Paul Brand, Seymour Phillips, Mark Ormrod, Geoffrey Martin, Anne Curry, and Rosemary Horrox. Woodbridge, UK: Boydell & Brewer, 2005. Available via British History Online, https://www.british-history.ac.uk/no-series/parliament-rolls-medieval.

Parry, Graham. *The Trophies of Time: English Antiquaries of the Seventeenth Century*. Oxford: Oxford University Press, 1995.

Parker, Geoffrey. *The Grand Strategy of Philip II*. New Haven, CT: Yale University Press, 1998.

Partington, Gil, and Adam Smyth, eds. *Book Destruction from the Medieval to the Contemporary*. Basingstoke, UK: Palgrave Macmillan, 2014.

Paterson, Samuel. *A Catalogue of the Manuscripts of the Right Honourable and Right Worshipful Sir Julius Caesar*. London, 1757.

Patterson, Annabel. *Censorship and Interpretation: The Conditions of Writing and Reading in Early Modern England*. Madison: University of Wisconsin Press, 1984.

Peacey, Jason. "Cromwellian England: A Propaganda State?" *History* 91, no. 302 (2006): 176–99.

Peacey, Jason. "'A Knowing but a Discrete Man': Scribal News and Information Management in Restoration England." *PH* 41, no. 1 (2022): 19–36.

Peacey, Jason. *The Madman and the Churchrobber: Law and Conflict in Early Modern England*. Oxford: Oxford University Press, 2022.

Peacey, Jason. "Managing Dutch Advices: Abraham Casteleyn and the English Government, 1660–1681." Special issue, *Media History* 22, no. 3–4 (2016): 421–37.

Peacey, Jason. "'My Friend the Gazetier': Diplomacy and News in Seventeenth-Century Europe." In Raymond and Moxham, *News Networks in Early Modern Europe*, 420–42.

Peacey, Jason. "Print Culture and Political Lobbying during the English Civil Wars." *PH* 26, no. 1 (2007): 30–48.

Peacey, Jason. *Print and Public Politics in the English Revolution*. Cambridge: Cambridge University Press, 2013.

Peacey, Jason. "'Written According to My Usual Way': Political Communication and the Rise of the Agent in Seventeenth-Century England." In Kyle and Peacey, *Connecting Centre and Locality*, 94–115.

Peacock, Timothy. "Cromwell's 'Spymaster'? John Thurloe and Rethinking Early Modern Intelligence." *Seventeenth Century* 35, no. 1 (2020): 3–30.

Peck, Imogen. "'Of no sort of use?': Manuscripts, Memory, and the Family Archive in Eighteenth Century England." *Cultural and Social History* 20, no. 2 (2023): 183–204.

Peltonen, Markku. *Classical Humanism and Republicanism in English Political Thought, 1570–1640*. Cambridge: Cambridge University Press, 1995.

Peter, Hugh. *Good Work for a Magistrate, or A Short Cut to Great Quiet*. London, 1651.

Peters, Kate, Alexandra Walsham, and Liesbeth Corens. *Archives and Information in the Early Modern World*. Oxford: Oxford University Press, 2018.

Pettegree, Andrew. *The Invention of News: How the World Came to Know about Itself*. New Haven, CT: Yale University Press, 2015.

Petyt, William. *The Ancient Right of the Commons Asserted*. London, 1680.

Philipot, John, and William Ryley. *The Visitation of the Country of Buckingham*. Edited by W. Harry Rylands. London: Mitchell, Hughes, & Clark, 1909.

Platt, F. Jeffrey. "The Elizabethan 'Foreign Office.'" *Historian* 56, no. 4 (1994): 725–40.

Pincus, Steven. "'Coffee Politicians Does Create': Coffeehouses and Restoration Political Culture." *JMH* 67, no. 4 (1995): 807–34.

Pincus, Steven, Tiraana Bains, and A. Zuercher Reichardt. "Thinking the Empire Whole." *History Australia* 16, no. 4 (2019): 610–37.

Pocock, J. G. A. *The Ancient Constitution and the Feudal Law: A Study of English Historical Thought in the Seventeenth Century*. Cambridge: Cambridge University Press, 1957.

Pollard, A. F. "Wilson, Sir Thomas (d. 1629)." Revised by Sean Kelsey. In *Oxford Dictionary of National Biography*. Oxford University Press, 2004. Online ed., 2004, modified January 3, 2008. https://doi.org/10.1093/ref:odnb/29690.

Pomata, Gianna. "Observation Rising: Birth of an Epistemic Genre, ca. 1500–1650." In *Histories of Scientific Observation*, edited by Lorraine Daston and Elizabeth Lunbeck, 45–80. Chicago: University of Chicago Press, 2011.

Pomata, Gianna, and Nancy Siraisi, eds. *Historia: Empiricism and Erudition in Early Modern Europe*. Cambridge, MA: Harvard University Press, 2005.

Popkin, Jeremy. *Revolutionary News: The Press in France, 1789–1799*. Durham, NC: Duke University Press, 1990.

Popofsky, Linda. "The Crisis over Tonnage and Poundage in Parliament in 1629." *P&P* 126 (1990): 44–75.

Popper, Nicholas. "Archives and the Boundaries of Early Modern Science." *Isis* 107, no. 1 (2016): 86–94.

Popper, Nicholas. "From Abbey to Archive: Managing Texts and Records in Early Modern England." *Archival Science* 10, no. 3 (2010): 249–66.

Popper, Nicholas. "An Information State for Early Modern England." *JMH* 90, no. 3 (2018): 505–35.

Popper, Nicholas. "Inscription and Political Exclusion in Early Modern England."

In *Negotiating Exclusion in Early Modern England, 1550–1800*, edited by Naomi Pullin and Kathryn Woods, 221–39. London: Routledge, 2021.

Popper, Nicholas. "Joseph Williamson and the Information Order of the Early English Empire." In *Far from the Truth: Distance and the Problem of Credibility in the Early Modern World*, edited by Michiel van Groesen and Johannes Muller. Forthcoming.

Popper, Nicholas. *Walter Ralegh's "History of the World" and the Historical Culture of the Late Renaissance*. Chicago: University of Chicago Press, 2012.

Potter, David, ed. *Foreign Intelligence and Information in Elizabethan England: Two English Treatises on the State of France*. Cambridge: Cambridge University Press, 2004.

Powell, Thomas. *Direction for Search of Records Remaining in the Chancerie. Tower. Exchequer*. London, 1622.

Powell, Thomas. *The Repertorie of Records*. London, 1631.

Premo, Bianca. *Enlightenment on Trial: Ordinary Litigants and Colonialism in the Spanish Empire*. Oxford: Oxford University Press, 2017.

Prynne, William. *Antiquae Constitutiones Regni Angliae*. London, 1672.

Prynne, William. *Aurum Reginae*. London, 1668.

Prynne, William. *Brevia Parliamentaria Rediviva*. London, 1662.

Prynne, William. *A Breviate of the Life of William Laud, Archbishop of Canterbury*. London, 1644.

Prynne, William. *Canterburies Doom*. London, 1646.

Prynne, William. *Exact Abridgement of Parliamentary Records in the Tower of London*. London, 1657.

Prynne, William. *The First [Third] Tome of an Exact Chronological Vindication, and Historical Demonstration of our British, Roman, Saxon, Danish, Norman, English Kings and Supreme Ecclesiastical Jurisdiction in, and over all Religious or Ecclesiastical Matters*. London, 1668.

Prynne, William. *The First Part of a Brief Register, Kalendar and Survey of the Several Kinds, Forms of all Parliamentary Writs*. London, 1659.

Prynne, William. *The First Part of an Historicall Collection of Parliaments of England*. London, 1649.

Prynne, William. *The Fourth Part of a Brief Register, Kalender and Survey . . . of Parliamentary Writs*. London, 1664.

Prynne, William. *Hidden Workes of Darkenes Brought to Publike Light, or A Necessary Introduction to the history of the Archbishop of Canterburie's Triall*. London, 1645.

Prynne, William. *Irenarches redivivus*. London, 1648.

Prynne, William. *A Plea for the Lords*. London, 1648.

Prynne, William. *The Second Part of a Brief Register and Survey . . . of Parliamentary Writs*. London, 1660.

Prynne, William. *The Soveraigne Powers of Parliament and Kingdomes*. London, 1643.

Pulton, Fernando. *A Collection of Sundrie Statutes*. London, 1618.

Queller, Donald. "The Development of Venetian *Relazioni*." In *Renaissance Venice*, edited by J. R. Hale, 174–96. London: Faber and Faber, 1973.

Questier, Michael. "Sir Henry Spiller, Recusancy, and the Efficiency of the Jacobean Exchequer." *HR* 66, no. 161 (1993): 251–66.

Rama, Angel. *The Lettered City*. Edited and translated by John Charles Chasteen. Durham, NC: Duke University Press, 1996.

Raman, Bhavani. *Document Raj: Writing and Scribes in Early Colonial South India*. Chicago: University of Chicago Press, 2012.

Ramsay, Nigel, ed. *Heralds and Heraldry in Shakespeare's England*. Donington, UK: Shaun Tyas, 2014.

Raphael, Renee. "In Pursuit of 'Useful' Knowledge: Documenting Technical Innovation in Sixteenth-Century Potosí." *Journal for the History of Knowledge* 1, no. 1 (2021): 1–14.

Rawcliffe, Carole. "A Tudor Nobleman as Archivist: The Papers of Edward, Third Duke of Buckingham." *JSA* 5, no. 5 (1976): 294–300.

Raymond, Joad. *The Invention of the Newspaper: English Newsbooks, 1641–1649*. Oxford: Oxford University Press, 1996.

Raymond, Joad. *Pamphlets and Pamphleteering in Early Modern Britain*. Cambridge: Cambridge University Press, 2003.

Raymond, Joad, and Noah Moxham, eds. *News Networks in Early Modern Europe*. Leiden: Brill, 2016.

Raymond, Thomas. *The Autobiography of Thomas Raymond and Memoirs of the Family of Guise of Elmore, Gloucestershire*. Edited by G. Davies. London: Royal Historical Society, 1917.

Read, Conyers. *Mr. Secretary Walsingham and the Policy of Queen Elizabeth*. 3 vols. Cambridge, MA: Harvard University Press, 1925.

Read Foster, Elizabeth. "The Painful Labour of Mr. Elsyng." *Transactions of the American Philosophical Society* 62, no. 8 (1972): 1–69.

Riordan, Michael. "'The King's Library of Manuscripts': The State Paper Office as Archive and Library." *Information & Culture: A Journal of History* 48, no. 2 (2013): 181–93.

Riordan, Michael. "Materials for History? Publishing Records as a Historical Practice in Eighteenth- and Nineteenth-Century England." *History of the Humanities* 2, no. 1 (2017): 51–77.

Rockett, William. "*Britannia*, Ralph Brooke, and the Representation of Privilege in Elizabethan England." *Renaissance Quarterly* 53, no. 2 (2000): 474–99.

Rose, Jacqueline. "Robert Brady's Intellectual History and Royalist Antipopery in Restoration England." *EHR* 122, no. 499 (2007): 1287–1317.

Roseveare, Henry. *The Treasury 1660–1870*. London: Allen & Unwin, 1973.

Ross, Richard. "The Memorial Culture of Early Modern English Lawyers: Memory as Keyword, Shelter, and Identity, 1560–1640." *Yale Law School Journal of Law and the Humanities* 10, no. 2 (1998): 229–326.

Rubies, Joan-Pau. "Instructions for Travellers: Teaching the Eye to See." *History and Anthropology* 9, no. 2–3 (1996): 139–90.

Rule, John, and Ben Trotter. *A World of Paper: Louis XIV, Colbert de Torcy, and the Rise of the Information State*. Montreal: McGill-Queen's University Press, 2014.

Rushworth, John. *Historical Collections of Private Passages of State*. 6 vols. London, 1721.

Russell, Conrad. *The Fall of the British Monarchies, 1637–1642*. Oxford: Clarendon, 1991.

Russell, Conrad. *Parliaments and English Politics, 1621–1629*. Oxford: Clarendon, 1979.

Russell, Conrad. *Unrevolutionary England, 1603–1642*. London: Hambledon, 1990.

Ryley, William. *Placita Parliamentaria*. London, 1661.

Sandall, Simon. "Custom, Common Right and Commercialisation in the Forest of Dean, c. 1605–1640." In *Custom and Commercialisation in English Rural Society: Revisiting Tawney and Postan*, edited by James P. Bowen and A. T. Brown, 161–78. Hatfield, UK: University of Hertfordshire Press, 2016.

Scarborough King, Rachael. "The Manuscript Newsletter and the Rise of the Newspaper, 1665–1715." *HLQ* 79, no. 3 (2016): 411–37.

Schobesberger, Nikolaus. "Mapping the *Fuggerzeitungen*: The Geographical Issues of an Information Network." In Raymond and Moxham, *News Networks in Early Modern Europe*, 216–40.

Scott, Jonathan. "England's Troubles: Exhuming the Popish Plot." In *The Politics of Religion in Restoration London*, edited by Tim Harris, Paul Seaward, and Mark Goldie, 107–31. Oxford: Basil Blackwell, 1990.

Scott-Warren, Jason. "Reconstructing Manuscript Networks: The Textual Transactions of Sir Stephen Powle." In *Communities in Early Modern England: Networks, Place, Rhetoric*, ed. Alexandra Shepard and Phil Withington, 18–37. Manchester: Manchester University Press, 2000.

Scribner, Robert. *For the Sake of Simple Folk: Popular Propaganda for the German Reformation*. Oxford: Clarendon, 1994.

Sellers-Garcia, Sylvia. *Distance and Documents at the Spanish Empire's Periphery*. Stanford, CA: Stanford University Press, 2014.

Shapin, Steven. "The Invisible Technician." *American Scientist* 77, no. 6 (1989): 554–63.

Shapin, Steven. *The Social History of Truth: Civility and Science in Seventeenth-Century England*. Chicago: University of Chicago Press, 1994.

Shapin, Steven, and Simon Schaffer. *Leviathan and the Air-pump: Hobbes, Boyle, and the Experimental Life*. Princeton, NJ: Princeton University Press, 1985.

Shapiro, Barbara. *Political Communication and Political Culture in England, 1558–1688*. Stanford, CA: Stanford University Press, 2012.

Sharpe, Kevin. *The Personal Rule of Charles I*. New Haven, CT: Yale University Press, 1991.

Sharpe, Kevin. *Rebranding Rule: The Restoration and Revolution Monarchy, 1660–1714*. New Haven, CT: Yale University Press, 2013.

Sharpe, Kevin. *Selling the Tudor Monarchy: Authority and Image in Sixteenth-Century England*. New Haven, CT: Yale University Press, 2009.

Sharpe, Kevin. *Sir Robert Cotton, 1586–1631: History and Politics in Early Modern England*. Oxford: Oxford University Press, 1979.

Shepard, Alexandra. "Worthless Witnesses? Marginal Voices and Women's Legal Agency in Early Modern England." *JBS* 58, no. 4 (2019): 717–34.

Sherman, William. *John Dee: The Politics of Reading and Writing in the English Renaissance*. Amherst: University of Massachusetts Press, 1995.

Sherman, William. *Used Books: Marking Readers in Renaissance England*. Philadelphia: University of Pennsylvania Press, 2008.

Siddique, Asheesh. "The Archival Epistemology of Political Economy in the Early Modern British Atlantic World." *WMQ*, 3rd ser., 77, no. 4 (2020): 641–74.

Siddique, Asheesh. "Governance through Documents: The Board of Trade, Its Archive, and the Imperial Constitution of the Eighteenth-Century British Atlantic World." *JBS* 59, no. 2 (2020): 264–90.

Siddique, Asheesh. "Mobilizing the 'State Papers' of Empire: John Bruce, Early Modernity and the Bureaucratic Archives of Britain." *JEMH* 22, no. 5 (2019): 392–410.

Siddique, Asheesh. "Paperwork, Governance, and the Archive in the British Empire during the Age of Revolutions." PhD diss., Columbia University, 2016.

Slack, Paul. "Government and Information in Seventeenth Century England." *P&P* 184 (2004): 33–68.

Slauter, Will. "The Paragraph as Information Technology: How News Traveled in the Eighteenth-Century Atlantic World." *Annales: H.S.S.* 67, no. 2 (2012): 253–78.

Slauter, Will. "Write Up Your Dead: The Bills of Mortality and the London Plague of 1665." *Media History* 17, no. 1 (2011): 1–15.

Smith, Alan G. R. "The Secretariats of the Cecils, c. 1580–1612." *EHR* 83, no. 328 (1968): 481–504.

Smith, Alan G. R. *Servant of the Cecils: The Life of Sir Michael Hickes, 1543–1612*. London: J. Cape, 1977.

Smith, David Chan. *Sir Edward Coke and the Reformation of the Laws: Religion, Politics and Jurisprudence, 1578–1616*. Cambridge: Cambridge University Press, 2014.

Smuts, Malcolm. "Force, Love, and Authority in Caroline Political Culture." In *The 1630s: Interdisciplinary Essays on Culture and Politics in the Caroline Era*, illustrated ed., edited by Ian Atherton and Julie Sanders, 28–49. Manchester: Manchester University Press, 2013.

Smyth, Adam. *Material Texts in Early Modern England*. Cambridge: Cambridge University Press, 2018.

Sobecki, Sebastian. "John Peyton's 'A Relation of the State of Polonia' and the Accession of King James I, 1598–1603." *EHR* 129, no. 540 (2014): 1079–97.

Sobecki, Sebastian. "'A Man of Curious Enquiry': John Peyton's Grand Tour to

Central Europe and Robert Cecil's Intelligence Network, 1596–1601." *Renaissance Studies* 29, no. 3 (2015): 394–410.

Soll, Jacob. *The Information Master: Jean-Baptiste Colbert's Secret State Intelligence System*. Ann Arbor: University of Michigan Press, 2011.

Somerville, Johann. "King James VI and I and John Selden: Two Voices on History and the Constitution." In *Royal Subjects: Essays on the Writings of James VI and I*, edited by Daniel Fischlin and Mark Fortier, 290–322. Detroit: Wayne State University Press, 2002.

Somerville, Johann. "Selden, Grotius, and the Seventeenth-Century Intellectual Revolution in Moral and Political Theory." In *Rhetoric and Law in Early Modern Europe*, edited by Victoria Kahn and Lorna Hutson, 318–44. New Haven, CT: Yale University Press, 2001.

Sommerville, C. John. *The News Revolution in England: Cultural Dynamics of Daily Information*. New York: Oxford University Press, 1996.

Stagl, Justin. "The Methodising of Travel in the 16th Century: A Tale of Three Cities." *History and Anthropology* 4, no. 2 (1990): 303–38.

Stallybrass, Peter. "'Little Jobs': Broadsides and the Printing Revolution." In *Agent of Change: Print Culture Studies after Elizabeth L. Eisenstein*, edited by Sabrina Alcorn Baron, Eric N. Lindquist, and Eleanor F. Shevlin, 315–42. Amherst: University of Massachusetts Press, 2007.

Stallybrass, Peter, and Heather Wolfe. "The Material Culture of Record-Keeping in Early Modern Archives." In Peters, Walsham, and Corens, *Archives and Information in the Early Modern World*, 179–208.

Starza Smith, Daniel. *John Donne and the Conway Papers: Patronage and Manuscript Circulation in the Early Seventeenth Century*. Oxford: Oxford University Press, 2014.

Steele, Ian K. *The English Atlantic, 1675–1740: An Exploration of Communication and Community*. New York: Oxford University Press, 1986.

Stern, Virginia F. *Sir Stephen Powle of Court and Country: Memorabilia of a Government Agent for Queen Elizabeth I, Chancery Official, and English Country Gentleman*. Selinsgrove, PA: Susquehanna University Press, 1992.

Sternberg, Giora. "Manipulating Information in the Ancien Régime: Ceremonial Records, Aristocratic Strategies, and the Limits of the State Perspective." *JMH* 85, no. 2 (2013): 239–79.

Stewart, Alan. "Familiar Letters and State Papers: The Afterlives of Early Modern Correspondence." In Daybell and Gordon, *Cultures of Correspondence in Early Modern Britain*, 237–52.

Stewart, Richard. *The English Ordnance Office, 1585–1625: A Case Study in Bureaucracy*. London: Royal Historical Society, 1996.

Stoler, Ann Laura. *Along the Archival Grain: Epistemic Anxieties and Colonial Common Sense*. Princeton, NJ: Princeton University Press, 2009.

Stretton, Tim. "Women, Legal Records, and the Problem of the Lawyer's Hand." *JBS* 58, no. 4 (2019): 684–700.

Stretton, Tim. *Women Waging Law in Early Modern England*. Cambridge: Cambridge University Press, 1998.

Summit, Jennifer. *Memory's Library: Medieval Books in Early Modern England*. Chicago: University of Chicago Press, 2008.

Swann, Marjorie. *Curiosities and Texts: The Culture of Collecting in Early Modern England*. Philadelphia: University of Pennsylvania Press, 2001.

Sweet, Rosemary. *Antiquaries: The Discovery of the Past in Eighteenth-Century Britain*. London: Hambledon, 2004.

Tadmor, Naomi. "The Settlement of the Poor and the Rise of the Form in England, c. 1662–1780." *P&P* 236 (2017): 43–97.

Taviner, Mark. "Robert Beale and the Elizabethan Polity." PhD diss., University of St. Andrews, 2000.

Taylor, Frank. "The Books and Manuscripts of Scipio le Squyer, Deputy Chamberlain of the Exchequer, 1620–59." *Bulletin of the John Rylands Library* 25, no. 1 (1941): 137–64.

te Heesen, Anke. "The Notebook: A Paper-Technology." In *Making Things Public: Atmospheres of Democracy*, edited by Bruno Latour and Peter Weibel, 582–89. Cambridge: MIT Press, 2005.

Tessier, Alexandre. *Réseaux diplomatiques et République des Lettres: Les correspondants de Sir Joseph Williamson (1660–1680)*. Paris: Honoré Champion, 2015.

Tessier, Alexandre. "Un apprentissage diplomatique: La correspondance entre Sir Joseph Williamson et William Blathwayt, secrétaire d'ambassade à La Haye (1668–1672)." *Revue d'histoire diplomatique* 127, no. 3 (2013): 239–58.

Teuscher, Simon. *Lords' Rights and Peasant Stories: Writing and the Formation of Tradition in the Later Middle Ages*. Translated by Philip Grace. Philadelphia: University of Pennsylvania Press, 2012.

Thirtieth Annual Report of the Deputy Keeper of the Public Records. London: H. M. Stationery Office, 1869.

Thornton, Helen. "John Selden's Response to Hugo Grotius: The Argument for Closed Seas." *International Journal of Maritime History* 18, no. 2 (2006): 105–27.

Thrush, Andrew. "The House of Lords' Record Repository and the Clerk of the Parliament House: A Tudor Achievement." *PH* 21, no. 3 (2002): 367–73.

Thrush, Andrew, and John Ferris, eds. *The House of Commons 1604–1629*. 6 vols. Cambridge: Cambridge University Press, 2010. Published for the History of Parliament Trust.

Tite, Colin G. C. *The Early Records of Sir Robert Cotton's Library: Formation, Cataloguing, Use*. London: British Library, 2003.

Tite, Colin G. C. *Impeachment and Parliamentary Judicature in Early Stuart England*. London: Athlone Press, 1974.

Toomer, Gerald J. *John Selden: A Life in Scholarship*. 2 vols. Oxford: Oxford University Press, 2009.

Tortorici, Zeb. *Sins against Nature: Sex and Archives in Colonial Spain*. Durham, NC: Duke University Press, 2018.

Trevelyan Papers, Part III. Edited by Sir Walter Calverley Trevelyan & Sir Charles Edward Trevelyan. London: Camden Society, 1872.

Trivellato, Francesca. *The Familiarity of Strangers: The Sephardic Diaspora, Livorno, and Cross-Cultural Trade in the Early Modern Period.* New Haven, CT: Yale University Press, 2009.

Trouillot, Michel-Rolphe. *Silencing the Past: Power and the Production of History.* 2nd ed. Boston: Beacon Press, 2015.

A True Transcription and Publication of his Maiesties Letters Pattent For an Office to be Erected, and Called the Publicke Register for Generall Commerce. London, 1611.

Tu, Hsuan-Ying. "The Dispersal of Francis Walsingham's Papers." *Sixteenth Century Journal* 50, no. 2 (2019): 471–92.

Tuck, Richard. *Philosophy and Government, 1572–1651.* Cambridge: Cambridge University Press, 1993.

Underdown, David. *Royalist Conspiracy in England, 1649–1660.* New Haven, CT: Yale University Press, 1960.

Underwood, Matthew Carl. "Ordering Knowledge, Re-Ordering Empire: Science and State Formation in the English Atlantic World, 1650–1688." PhD diss., Harvard University, 2010.

Van Norden, Linda. "The Elizabethan College of Antiquaries." PhD diss., University of California–Los Angeles, 1949.

Venning, Timothy. "Thurloe, John (*bap.* 1616, *d.* 1688)." In *Oxford Dictionary of National Biography.* Oxford University Press, 2004. Online ed., 2004, modified January 3, 2008. https://doi.org/10.1093/ref:odnb/27405.

Vernier, Veronika. "Maps for Intelligence Gathering? Rediscovered Seventeenth-Century Manuscript Maps from the Queen's College, Oxford." *Imago Mundi* 63, no. 1 (2011): 76–87.

Vernon, Christopher. *Considerations for Regulating the Exchequer.* London, 1642.

Vincent, Augustine. *A Discoverie of Errours in the First Edition of the Catalogue of Nobility Published by Raphe Brooke, Yorke Herald, 1619.* London, 1621.

Vine, Angus. "Commercial Commonplacing: Francis Bacon, The Waste-Book, and the Ledger." *English Manuscript Studies, 1100–1700* 16 (2011): 197–218.

Vine, Angus. *In Defiance of Time: Antiquarian Writing in Early Modern England.* Oxford: Oxford University Press, 2010.

Vine, Angus. *Miscellaneous Order: Manuscript Culture and the Early Modern Organization of Knowledge.* Oxford: Oxford University Press, 2019.

Vismann, Cornelia. *Files: Law and Media Technology.* Translated by Geoffrey Winthrop-Young. Stanford, CA: Stanford University Press, 2008.

Waddell, Brodie. "Writing History from Below: Chronicling and Record-Keeping in Early Modern England." *History Workshop Journal* 85 (2018): 239–64.

Walsham, Alexandra. Introduction to "The Social History of the Archive: Record Keeping in Early Modern Europe," edited by Liesbeth Corens, Kate Peters, and Alexandra Walsham. Supplement, *P&P* 11 (2016): 8–48.

Warneke, Sara. *Images of the Educational Traveller in Early Modern England.* Leiden, Neth.: Brill, 1995.
Warner, Michael. *The Letters of the Republic: Publication and the Public Sphere in Eighteen-Century America.* Cambridge, MA: Harvard University Press, 1991.
Watson, Andrew G. "The Manuscript Collection of Sir Walter Cope (d. 1614)." *Bodleian Library Record* 12 (1985–88): 262–97.
Watt, Tessa. *Cheap Print and Popular Piety, 1550–1640.* Cambridge: Cambridge University Press, 1995.
Webb, Stephen Saunders. "William Blathwayt, Imperial Fixer, 2 pts: Part 1. From Popish Plot to Glorious Revolution." *WMQ*, 3rd ser., 25, no. 1 (1968): 3–21.
Webb, Stephen Saunders. "William Blathwayt, Imperial Fixer, Part 2: Muddling Through Empire." *WMQ*, 3rd ser., 26, no. 3 (1969): 373–415.
Weber, Max. *The Theory of Social and Economic Organization.* Edited by Talcott Parsons. Translated by A. M. Henderson. New York: Oxford University Press, 1947.
Weil, Rachel. *A Plague of Informers: Conspiracy and Political Trust in William III's England.* New Haven, CT: Yale University Press, 2013.
Weil, Rachel. "Thinking about Allegiance in the English Civil War." *History Workshop Journal* 61, no. 1 (2006): 183–91.
Weld, Kristen. *Paper Cadavers: The Archives of Dictatorship in Guatemala.* Durham, NC: Duke University Press, 2014.
Wernham, R. B. "The Public Records in the 16th and 17th Centuries." In *English Historical Scholarship in the 16th and 17th Centuries,* edited by Levi Fox, 11–30. London: Oxford University Press, 1956. Published for the Dugdale Society.
Weston, Corinne. "Legal Sovereignty in the Brady Controversy." *HJ* 15, no. 3 (1972): 409–31.
Weston, Corinne, and Janelle Greenberg. *Subjects and Sovereigns: The Grand Controversy over Legal Sovereignty in Stuart England.* Cambridge: Cambridge University Press, 1971.
White, Sophie. *Voices of the Enslaved: Love, Labor, and Longing in French Louisiana.* Chapel Hill: University of North Carolina Press, 2019. Published for the Omohundro Institute of Early American History and Culture.
White, William. "Parliament, Print, and the Politics of Disinformation, 1642–3." *HR* 92, no. 258 (2019): 720–36.
The Whole Business of Sindercombe, from first to last. London, 1657.
Whyman, Susan. *The Pen and the People: English Letter Writers, 1660–1800.* Oxford: Oxford University Press, 2009.
"William Lambarde's Reading, Revision and Reception: The Life Cycle of the *Perambulation of Kent.*" Special issue, *Journal of the Warburg and Courtauld Institute* 81, no. 1 (2019): 129–210.
Williams, Meghan K. "Unfolding Diplomatic Paper and Paper Practices in Early Modern Chancellery Archives." In Brendecke, *Praktiken der Frühen Neuzeit: Akteure, Handlungen, Artefakte,* 496–508.

Williamson, Elizabeth. "Archival Practice and the Production of Knowledge in the office of Sir Francis Walsingham." In Brendecke, *Praktiken der Frühen Neuzeit: Akteure, Handlungen, Artefakte*, 473–84.

Williamson, Elizabeth. "'Fishing after News' and the *Ars Apodemica*: The Intelligencing Role of the Educational Traveller in the Late Sixteenth Century." In Raymond and Moxham, *News Networks in Early Modern Europe*, 542–62.

Williamson, Elizabeth. "A Letter of Travel Advice? Literary Rhetoric, Scholarly Counsel, and Practical Instruction in the Ars Apodemica." *Lives and Letters* 3, no. 1 (2011): 1–22.

Wilson, Thomas. "The State of England (1600)." *Camden Miscellany*, 3rd ser., 52 (July 1936): 1–47.

Wood, Andy. *The Memory of the People: Custom and Popular Senses of the Past in Early Modern England*. Cambridge: Cambridge University Press, 2013.

Wood, Andy. *Riot, Rebellion, and Popular Politics in Early Modern England*. Houndmills, UK: Palgrave, 2002.

Wood, Andy. "Tales from the 'Yarmouth Hutch': Civic Identities and Hidden Histories in an Urban Archive." In "The Social History of the Archive: Record Keeping in Early Modern Europe," edited by Liesbeth Corens, Kate Peters, and Alexandra Walsham. Supplement, *P&P* 11 (2016): 213–30.

Woolf, Daniel R. *The Idea of History in Early Stuart England: Erudition, Ideology, and the "Light of Truth" from the Accession of James I to the Civil War*. Toronto: University of Toronto Press, 1990.

Woolf, Daniel R. "John Selden, John Borough, and Francis Bacon's 'History of Henry VII,' 1621." *HLQ* 47, no. 1 (1984): 47–53.

Woolf, Daniel R. *Reading History in Early Modern England*. Cambridge: Cambridge University Press, 2000.

Woolf, Daniel R. *The Social Circulation of the Past: English Historical Culture, 1500–1730*. Oxford: Oxford University Press, 2003.

Worthen, Hannah. "Supplicants and Guardians: The Petitions of Royalist Widows during the Civil Wars and Interregnum, 1642–1660." *Women's History Review* 26, no. 4 (2016): 528–40.

Woudhuysen, H. R. *Sir Philip Sidney and the Circulation of Manuscripts, 1558–1640*. New York: Clarendon, 1996.

Wright, C. J, ed. *Sir Robert Cotton as Collector: Essays on an Early Stuart Courtier and His Legacy*. London: British Library, 1997.

Wright, Kirsty. "The Exchequer of Receipt in the Palace of Westminster, 1548–1662." PhD diss., University of York, 2023.

Wynne, William. *The Life of Leoline Jenkins*. 2 vols. London, 1724.

Yale, Elizabeth. "The History of Archives: The State of the Discipline." *Book History* 17 (2015): 332–59.

Yale, Elizabeth. *Sociable Knowledge: National History and the Nation in Early Modern Britain*. Philadelphia: University of Pennsylvania Press, 2016.

Yale, Elizabeth. "With Slips and Scraps: How Early Modern Naturalists Invented the Archive." *Book History* 12 (2009): 1–36.

Yamamoto, Koji. *Taming Capitalism Before Its Triumph: Public Service, Distrust, and 'Projecting' in Early Modern England*. Oxford: Oxford University Press, 2018.

Yax, Maggie. "Arthur Agarde, Elizabethan Archivist: His Contributions to the Evolution of Archival Practice." *American Archivist* 61, no. 1 (1998): 56–69.

Yeo, Geoffrey. "'Let Us See What Is Meant by the Word *Recorde*': Concepts of Record from the Middle Ages to the Early Twentieth Century." *Archivaria* 93 (2022): 6–41.

Yeo, Richard. *Notebooks, Virtuosi, and Early Modern Science*. Chicago: University of Chicago Press, 2014.

Yeo, Richard. "Thinking with Excerpts: John Locke (1632–1704) and His Notebooks." *Berichte zur Wissenschaftsgeschichte* 43, no. 2 (2020): 180–202.

Young, Michael B. "The Origins of the Petition of Right Reconsidered Further." *HJ* 27, no. 2 (1984): 449–52.

Youngs, Deborah, ed. *The Letter-Book of Henry, Lord Stafford (1501–1563)*. Bristol, UK: Staffordshire Record Society, 2012.

Zakim, Michael. *Accounting for Capitalism: The World the Clerk Made*. Chicago: University of Chicago Press, 2018.

Zaret, David. *The Origins of Democratic Culture*. Princeton, NJ: Princeton University Press, 2000.

Zook, Melinda. *Radical Whigs and Conspiratorial Politics in Late Stuart England*. University Park: Pennsylvania State University Press, 1999.

Zuercher Reichardt, Al. "War for the Interior: Imperial Conflict and Formation of North American and Transatlantic Communications Infrastructure, 1727–1774." PhD diss., Yale University, 2017.

Index

Page numbers in italics refer to figures.

access to records, mediation of, 54–56, 79–80

Agarde, Arthur: Bowyer's methods compared with, 75; consolidation of sources and, 67, *68*; copies of indexes by, 259–60n58; on Dissolution of the Monasteries, 74; Domesday Book reinterpretation of, 91–93; Exchequer records and, 73–76, 78–79, 80, 259n46, 260n62; methods of, 66–81, *71*, *72*, 260n60; notes on register of the Abbey of Osney, 67; production of texts by, 67–79; on record storage, 74–75; register of Treaties of, *78*; on skills for Deputy Chamberlain of the Exchequer, 79, 261n77; Treasury Chart of, *77*

Ancient State, Authoritie, and Proceedings of the Court of Requests (Caesar), 94–95, 98, 265n25

Anglo-Dutch War, Third, 189, 217

Archeion (Lambarde), 94

archives: accumulation of materials in, 9–10; Britain's legacy of, 228; circulation and, 57, 80; as conditioned, 155; considerations for contemporary, 19, 239; disjuncture between world and, 50–51; dispersed, 64, 73; knowledge production and, 4, 17, 39; oversight of institutional, 22; role of paper technologies in, 33; role of women in, 3–4; searchability of, 29; space and structure of, 5; study of British, 16–17; Wilson's compact, 114, 117. *See also* State Paper Office; Tower of London Record Office

archives/collections, personal: bundles and, 82; Caesar's, 83–89, 261–62n98; Coke's, 24, 54, 64–65, 195; consequences of, 49–51; as dispersed archives, 73; Lake's, 81–82; letters in, 59; as proxies, 64–66; Ralegh's, 106; Starkey's, 79; Williamson's, 204–5, 210–19

archivists, 4, 7

archivization, 155; administration and, 233, 295n25; Arthur Agarde and, 71–72, 74–76, *77*; appropriation and concealment in, 175, 177–78; attempts at early, 24; authority of knowledge and, 51, 185; Blathwayt in Plantation Office and, 231; William Bowyer and, 25–30, 33, 37–39; Caesar and, 85–88; Chancery records and, 40; codex information and, 27, 29; considerations for contemporary, 19, 239; consolidation and, 214–16; coordination of state and, 120; definition of, 7; disorder of English records and, 74–75;

INDEX

archivization (*continued*)
  disorder of personal collections and, 83–86; of experience, 52; finding aids and, 40; fragmentation, 215; Heneages and, 32–33, 36; information overload and, 90; information warfare and, 155, 186; inscription and, 229; knowledge formation and, 23, 49–52; Lambarde's "Pandect" and, 33; mediating access and, 53–56; motivations for record use and, 35–39; organization technologies and, 33; Powell and, 79; public good and, 178, 183–84; Raymond and, 194; recombination and, 225–26; record bundles and, 82; during reign of Elizabeth, 23; replication and portability in, 217–18; "Rough Coat Books" and, 33; Squyer and, 123; statecraft and, 41–46; storage and, 23; survival of documents and, 157; Thynne and, 37–39; Tower of London Record Office and, 1, 25, 27, 33; travel reports and, 42–46, 49; Tucker and, 204–5, *206*, 293–94n11; Williamson and, 194–95, 204–9, *207*, 209–16, 226–27; Wilson and, 103–4, 110–19; Wilson's compact archives and, 117–18. *See also* Agarde, Arthur; State Paper Office; Tower of London Record Office; Williamson, Joseph; Wilson, Thomas
Arlington, 1st Earl of (Henry Bennet), 189, 194, 196–200, 216–18, 230
artes apodemicae, 43, 46, 103, 201, 232
Arundel, 4th Earl of (Thomas Howard), 65, 97, 124, 140–41, 146
Ashmole, Elias, 188–89
Astle, Thomas, *78*, 235, 237
Augustus, emperor of Rome, 118, 208
Aylmer, G. E., 120

Bacon, Francis, 43–44, 54, 58, 65, 126, 140

Bacon, Nicholas, 40
Bales, Peter, 13–14
Ball, Henry, 196, 222
Bancroft, Richard, 54
Beale, Robert, 21, 44–45, 49–51
Beauchesne, Jean de, 30
Bennet, Henry (1st Earl of Arlington), 189, 194, 196–200, 230
binding of records, 85–89, 204, 289n80
Black Book of the Exchequer, 92–93
Blathwayt, William, 230–34, 238
"Book of Occurrences," 231
"Book of Offices": Queen Mary's, *11*; role of handwriting in, *14*, 14–15, 250n43; trajectory of, 10–15; Williamson's notebooks and, 215; Thomas Wilson's, 103, 114
"Book of Plots and Discourses," 41, 50
"Book of Statutes," 20
Borough, John, 27, 139–46, 151–53, 162–63
Boswell, William, 143, 286n18
Bowyer, Robert, 27, 51–56, 62, 80, 96–97
Bowyer, William: book production of, 26–30, *28*, 51–52; contributions to Tower records by, 33; "Heroica Eulogia," 30, *31*; as Keeper of the Tower Records, 25–27, 258n25; methods of, 51; organizational methods of, 26–27, 29; political motivations for manuscripts of, 32; profiting in role as keeper, 63; relationship with Lawrence Nowell, 25, 251n13; "Repertorium," 27, *28*; volumes borrowed from Robert Cotton by, 65–66; volumes of, 30–32, 51–52
Braddick, Michael, 229
Bradshaw, John, 194
Brady, Robert, 228
Brevia Parliamentaria Rediviva (Prynne), 183, 284n125

Breviate of the Life of William Laud (Prynne), 159–60, 161, *162*
Britannia (Camden), 20, 126
Brooke, Ralph, 125–26
Browne, Robert, 164–66
Brydall, John, 208–9
Buckingham, 1st Duke of (George Villiers), 114, 118
bundles/bags of records, 24, 41, 81–82, 86, 208
bureaucracy, emergence of, 120–21, 227
Burghley, 1st Baron (William Cecil): Caesar volume to, 95; communication with Stephen Powle, 47–48; manuscripts, use of by, 20, 22, 25; on record keeping and problems in Ireland, 251n5; travel instructions by, 42–44, 255n78; treaty interpretation and, 37; Wilson's use of tract by, 116

Caesar, Sir Julius: *Ancient State, Authoritie, and Proceedings of the Court of Requests*, 94–95, 98, 265n25; binding practice of, 85–88; collection catalogs of, 85, 88; commissioning of Agarde, 69; commissioning of John Borough, 140–41; on Court of Requests, 94–96; on extraparliamentary taxation, 153; information management of, 84; innovations in government, 121, 265n48; letter to Proby, 63; on Lord President of the Council, 96–97, 264n32; organizational instruments used by, 87–89, 262n106; personal archive of, 83–86, 261–62n98; on projects for new offices, 100; reinterpretations of offices of English government by, 94–98; traveling library of, 84
Calendar of State Papers Domestic, 7
Camden, William, 125–26

Carleton, Dudley (1st Viscount Dorchester), 143–44
Carr, Robert, 106–7
Casteleyn, Abraham, 221
catalogs: Agarde's production of, 73, 75–76, 79–80; archivization and role of, 33; Bowyer's "repertorium" and, 27; Caesar's production of, 83–88; inconsistency of, 1; Lambarde's "Pandect" and, 33, *34*; Tucker's production of, 205, *206*, 229; Wilson's production of, 112–14. *See also* archivization; codices
Catalogue of Nobility (Brooke), 126
Cavill, Paul, 263n17
Cecil, Robert, 20, 43, 69, 73, 103, 266n63
Cecil, William. *See* Burghley, 1st Baron (William Cecil)
Chancery Records: reforms to, 40; to Tower of London, 1, 5, 26–27, 29, 32
Chapter House of Westminster Abbey, 24, *68*, 70, 73
Charles I, King of England: destruction of records by, 156–57; William Laud and, 158–59; Personal Rule and, 152; regime of inscription and reign of, 122, 130–32, 136–38, 145; Tower Record Office and, 146
Charles II, King of England: freeing of Williamson, 190; orders to William Ryley, 174; praise of Prynne, 158; Scottish state papers and, 173–74
Church Settlement, 22
circulation, economy of: Agarde and, *78*, 79, 89–90; archives and signification of, 17; bundles of records and, 82; Sir Julius Caesar and, 83–84; Caesar's archives and, 89; celebrity and, 58–59; as constituent of political life, 229; constraints on information in, 234–35; inventories in, 80–81; *London Gazette* and, 220–22; manuscripts versus

circulation, economy of (*continued*) print in, 58; media sphere and, 66; mediation of record access in, 56–57; profits for keepers in, 63; replication of personal archives in, 64–65; role of paper in, 5; role of replication and collection in, 59–60; scholarship on print in, 57–58; social function of, 62; Williamson and, 219; Williamson's newsletters in, 221–24; Wilson's packets in, 114

citation: by Agarde, 70, *71*, *72*; Bowyer's volume and, 29–30; Williamson's notes and lack of, 214

Clanchy, Michael, 5

clerkships, proliferation of, 98

codices: Agarde's, 76, 79, 92; archivization and paper, 33; Caesar's, 85, 87–88; for Chancery records, 40; Ryley's "Vetus Codex" and, 147; use in Tower records, 27, 29, 52; Williamson's "Generall Calendar" and, 217, 289n80

Coke, Edward: collection of, 24, 54, 64–65, 195; *Institutes*, 130; Prynne's criticism of, 181–83, 228; use of records, 129–30, 134, 182

Colbert, Jean-Baptiste, 187–88

collecting: Agarde and, 93; bundles of records and, 82; "collectomania" and, 9; knowledge formation and, 16–17; scale of, 18; Williamson and, 193, 215; Wilson and, 81–82

"Committee about Records," 197

commonplace books, 6, 84, 193

Confederate Catholics, 156

Congress of Cologne and Williamson's "Generall Calendar," 218

Cope, Walter, 101, 265n51

copying/replication: Agarde's register of Treaties and, *78*; perpetuation of materials through, 50, 52, 89–90, 119, 121, 234; role of paper in, 5, 63; seeding of new archives, 57–59,

64; significance of, 9–10, 57, 100; State Paper Office fees for, 104; Tower Record fees for, 60–61; of Tower records, 64; as translation of archives, 9; by Wilson, 114–15

Cordell, William, 26, 27, 30

"Cornetts and Coullors" (Ryley), 164, 166

correspondence and letter writing: Blathwayt and, 230–33; circulation of, 58–59; conventions of, 201–2; credibility of, 203; productive redundancies in, 231–32; Williamson's, 197–203, 227

Cotton, Robert: brief on House of Commons, 129; collection of, 52, 124; network of, 64–66; Prynne correcting texts of, 182; relationship with Wilson, 268–69n103; role in circulation of Tower records, 55–56, 64–65; use of records by, 132–33

counselors: *artes apodemicae* and, 42–43, 46, 201; authority of records and, 20–23, 49, 53, 121, 139, 151; copying of documents for, 60; use of paper, 6, 8, 13

Court of Chancery, 98–100

Court of Chivalry, 141–42

Court of Receipt, 76

Court of Requests, 94–96

Cromwell, Oliver: assassination plots against, 170–72; suppression of newsletters by, 220; Thurloe and, 168–71

Cromwell, Thomas, 6, 21, 58, 68

Crowne, William, 164–66

custodes rotulorum, 61

Danegeld, 93

De bello Gallico (Caesar), 144

Declaration of Causes, 37, 138

Denmark, John Rogers's embassy to, 36

"Descriptio Italiae Modernae" (Powle), 47, 48

INDEX

Description of Hertfordshire (Norden), 20
"Descriptio of Italy" (Powle), 46
de Vere, Aubrey, 176–78
Devereux, Robert (2nd Earl of Essex), 58
Dewey, Melville, 229
diplomacy: Tower records and, 36–37, 114–16; Williamson and, 196, 217, 220
Direction for Search of Records Remaining (Powell), 80
Discourse touchinge the Office of principall Secretarie of Estate (Faunt), 45
Discoverie of Errours (Vincent), 125–26
Dissolution of the Monasteries, 22, 67, 74, 107
Domesday Book, 67, 75, 91–94, 124
"Dominium Maris Britannici" (Borough), 144–45
Dorchester, 1st Viscount (Dudley Carleton), 143–44
Dudley, Robert (1st Earl of Leicester), 29–32

ecclesiastical history, use of, 22
Egerton, Thomas: innovations to Chancery by, 99; personal archive of, 98–99, 264n37; record searches of, 264n39; Thynne and, 37–38
Elizabeth I, Queen of England: conferral of positions by, 31, 47; on Lambarde's "Pandect," 253n45; Low Countries and, 36–37; ordering transfer of records, 27, 40
Elsynge, Henry, 51, 55
Elton, G. R., 120
Essex, 2nd Earl of (Robert Devereux), 58
Exact Abridgement of Parliamentary Records in the Tower of London (Prynne), 182, 184
Exact Chronological Vindication, An (Prynne), 184

Exchequer catalog (Agarde), 79, 80
Exchequer records: Agarde's role in circulation of, 66; Agarde's storage recommendations for, 74–75; disorder of, 74–75; inventory of, 69–70, 73; use in Parliament of 1628, 137; to Westminster, 5

Faunt, Nicholas, 45
Filmer, Robert, 179–81, 183
finding aids, 40, 69–73, 84. *See also* codices; commonplace books
First Part of a Brief Register (Prynne), 182–83
First Part of an Historicall Collection of Parliaments (Prynne), 181
Five Knights Case, 134
Flacius Illyricus, Matthias, 22
Fleetwood, William, 12
Floyd, Edward, 128–29
Foedera (Rymer), 237
"Forme of Proceeding" (Borough), 141–42
formwork, 6, 8. *See also* paperwork
Fourth Part of a Brief Register (Prynne), 184
Frampton, Richard, 99–100
Freeholders Grand Inquest (Filmer), 179, 180

Gajda, Alexandra, 263n17
genealogical inquiry, 123–24
"Generall Calendar of Treatyes" (Williamson), 217–18, 291n115
Gerard, John, 170
Glamorgan treaty, 156, 278n3
Goddard, John, 232
Godwin, Francis, 61
Gorges, Arthur, 101
government, English: administrative practices during Interregnum, 169; authority, records, and, 130–33, 180–84; bureaucracy and, 120–21; consequences of records for, 228;

government, English (*continued*)
continuity with past of, 151; creating rival visions of, 132–33, 138–39, 151–53 (*see also* Parliament of 1628); disarray of documentary record and, 155; influence of Caesar's *Ancient State* on, 95; as information state, 229; information warfare and, 154–55; institutional innovation and, 98, 102, 146; news as critical of, 220–21; paperwork and imperial administration in, 232–33, 295n25, 296n35; proliferation of clerkships in, 98, 100–102; recalibration by inscription of, 228–29; regime of inscription and, 42–46, 91, 120; reinterpreting offices of, 97–98; routinization of practices in, 227; sovereignty of the seas and, 142–44; texts and institutionalization of, 93–94; volume of offices in, 11, *11*; Williamson's influence on, 187–88, 215, 217; Williamson's newssheets and, 223–24; Wilson's miniature archives and, 117–18; Wilson's political use of archives and, 115–16, 119; Wilson's State Paper Office and, 110, 119
Grand Remonstrance, 151
Grenville, George, 236–37
Greville, Fulke, 129
Grimbald, Reyner, 143–44

Haarlem Courant, 220, 221, 223
Halsted, Laurence, 228
handwriting, inscription and role of, 14, 14–15
Hatton, Christopher, 36–37, 49
Haward, Lazarus, 15
Hay, James, 116
Heath, Robert, 135
Helmers, Helmer, 220
Heneage, Michael, 32–33, 36–38, 79–80
Heneage, Thomas, 32–33, 36–38, 79–80

Herbert, Edward, 114
"Heroica Eulogia" (Bowyer), 30
Heveningham, John, 134–35
Hilliard, Christopher, 10
histories: critiques of, 126–27; of offices, 67, 94–98, 123–24, 137, 152, 225; record use in, 37–39, 42, 97, 137
Histories (Tacitus), 20
History of Henry VII (Bacon), 140
History of the Exchequer (Madox), 237
Histriomastix (Prynne), 179
Holinshed's Chronicles (1587), 37
Holles, Denzil, 184
Holmes, George, 235, 237
House of Commons, 128–29, 135–37, 228
Howard, Henry (1st Earl of Northampton), 54, 124–25
Howard, Thomas (4th Earl of Arundel), 65, 97, 124, 140, 146
hybrid texts, 12, 95, 144, 201, 215–19, 224–27

imperial administration, 232–34, 295n25
indexes: Agarde's production of, 69, 72, 92; Bowyer and, 29, 52; Caesar and, 85, 88–89; of Chancery records, 40, 99; Heneages and, 33; Lambarde and, 33; of Petty Bag office, 40; Ryley and, 147; Squyer and, 123; Williamson and, 211–12
information management: accessibility and, 18; Agarde's Treasury Chart and, *77*; Blathwayt and, 230–33; Caesar's methods of, 84–85; caution with, 239; conventions of correspondence as, 203; destruction of records as, 157; disorder and copying in, 89–90; as foundation for information state, 188; increase of paperwork and, 81; innovations to Chancery and, 99; motivations

for, 91; registers to centralize commerce and, 101–2; surveillance as, 168–72; techniques for, 54; travel reports and, 42–46; Williamson's notebooks and, 193, 205–6, *207*, 212–16, *213*; Williamson's organization methods and, 204–9, *207*, 211–16; Thomas Wilson and, 102–3, 111–14, *113*, 119
information overload, 57, 80–81
information state: England's government as, 17–18; foundation of, 4, 121, 188; limitation of perspectives in, 234–35; modalities, state formation, and, 229; public sphere and, 224; Williamson and, 226
information warfare: appropriation as, 172–78; definitions of, 277–78n1; intended use of, 185–86, 279n14; modes of, 154–55; Prynne's techniques of, 158–61; renewed House of Commons debate and, 228; role of print in, 178, 185; scholarly concerns about, 186; spycraft as, 162, 165, 167, 170; surveillance and, 168–69
inscription, regime of. *See* regime of inscription
Institutes (Coke), 130
interpretation of records, 124–29, 133–34, 137–39
inventories: Agarde production of, 67, 69, 73; information management and, 81; of Tower records, 27, 33, 51–52
Ireland as archival object, 49–51, 61, 251n5, 264n9
Irenarches Redivivus (Prynne), 181
Italy, travel reports on, 46–48

James I, King of England, 105, 106, 110, 111
Jenkins, Leoline, 218, 228
Jennings, Ralph, 1–2, 27, 184

Keeling, John, 135
Keepership of Tower of London Record Office, 26–32, 35, 63
Kelsey, Sean, 169
Kishlansky, Mark, 135, 274n60
knowledge formation: archivization and, 17, 23, 49–52; concentrated circulation networks and, 234–35; concerns with, 239; destruction of records and, 157; disruption in contemporary, 19; in English government, 151–52; inscriptions as instruments of, 123; methods of, 22; paperwork and, 187; power and, 19; reconstruction and, 22; records as tools in, 4–5, 53; role of letters in, 200–202; volume of texts and, 18; Williamson and, 190; world as mediated by texts and, 52
Knox, William, 235–37
Knyveton, St. Loe, 123–27, 272n21

Lake, Thomas, 61, 81–82, 116
Lambarde, William: *Archeion*, 94; death of, 51; "Pandect of the Records in the Tower," 33, *34*, 253n45; presentation of "Pandect" to Queen Elizabeth, 253n45
Laud, William, 147–51, 157–62, *162*, 276n113
"Laws and Privileges Granted to English Clerics" (Ryley), 147–49, *148*
Laws of Oleron, 143–44
Leicester, 1st Earl of (Robert Dudley), 29–32
Lenthall, William, 164
L'Estrange, Roger, 221
letters. *See* correspondence and letter writing
Letters and Papers of the Reign of Henry VIII (L&P), 7
Ley, James, 115
Licensing Act of 1679, 221
Loci Communes (Vermigli), 20

INDEX

London Gazette, 221–23
Lord Chancellor, rights and duties of, 38–39
Lord President of the Council, 96

Madox, Thomas, 237
Magdeburg Centuries, 22
Manner of Holding Parliaments (Elsynge), 130
Manners, Edward, 3rd Earl of Rutland, 42–44
manuscripts: "Book of Offices" and, 10–12, 15; Bowyer's volumes and, 26–32; Burghley's collection of, 20–21; Caesar's binding practices and, 85–88; circulation of, 58–59, 65, 146, 178; as gifts, 10; replication of, 12–13; role of, 10, 12, 14; survival of, 7
Mare Clausum (Selden), 145
Mare Liberum (Grotius), 143
Martin, Lucy, 266–67n77
May, Algernon, 1, 227
media revolutions, 19, 239
media sphere, 51–53, 66, 89, 94, 153, 219–23
Memoires (de Comines), 20
Milton, John, 169
Modus Tenendi Parliamentum, 130
Montagu, Edward, 129
Moore, George, 76
Morland, Samuel, 169
Mortimer, Roger, 131
Muddiman, Henry, 221

Nani Mirabelli, Domenico, 20
National Archives at Kew, UK, 7, 16, 40, 204
Neville de Latimer, Edmund, 36
Newcombe, Thomas, 172
news: power of, 219–21; use of, 198, 201–3, 223, 229
newsletters, 42, 47, 58, 219–23
Nicholas, Edward, 156, 175, 189, 194

Nicholson, Otho, 61–62
Nightingale, Thomas, 167
Nijmegen and "Generall Calendar" (Williamson), 218
Nineteen Propositions, 151
Northampton, 1st Earl of (Henry Howard), 54, 124–25
Nowell, Alexander, 25
Nowell, Lawrence, 22, 50

Oates, Titus, 225
"Order of the Paper Office" (Williamson), 209
Overton Plot, 170
Oxford Gazette, 221. See also London Gazette

Pandectae Locorum Communium (Foxe), 84
"Pandect of the Records in the Tower" (Lambarde), 33, 34, 253n45
paper, technology of: "Books of Offices" and, 16; circulation and, 57–59; consolidation of information through, 101–2; coordination of communication and, 8–9; definitions in, 249n19; emerging political dependence on, 5–6, 8, 10, 21, 237–38; finding aids and, 40; importation of, 6–7, 227; increase in writing and, 9; maintenance of power and, 8; organization and, 33; significance of proliferation of, 18
paperwork: as imperial constitution, 232; information overload and, 81; information warfare and, 186–87; role of, 6, 21, 227, 238; statecraft and, 39, 41–46, 98, 138, 169, 187
parchment, 5–6
Parker, Matthew, 21–22
Parliament, institutionalization of, 263n17
Parliament of 1628: Petition of Rights and, 134–35; record use in, 128,

133–38; tonnage and poundage and, 136–37
Parliament rolls, transcriptions of, 51
Parry, Thomas, 25
"particulars," 9
Paulet, William (1st Marquis of Winchester), 29–30
Peacey, Jason, 220
Peers, John, 14–15
Personal Rule, 139, 146–47, 152, 277n128
Perwich, William, 198, 201–2
Peter, Hugh, 182
petitioning, 8–9
Petition of Rights, 134, 274n51
Petty Bag Office, 40
Petyt, William, 228–29, 238
Placita Parliamentaria (Ryley and Ryley Jr.), 147, 178
Plantation Office, 230–33
Player, Thomas, 220
Plea for the Lords (Filmer), 181
political knowledge: Bowyer's volumes creating, 30–32; circulation and, 219; correspondence and, 203; paper technologies and, 10; role of print in, 57–58
Popish Plot, 190, 225, 228
Pory, John, 108
Powell, Thomas, 79
power, 19, 89, 102, 178, 185
Powle, Stephen, 46–49
Pownall, John, 235–37
"Prerogative of Parliaments" (Ralegh), 65
preservation: archivization and, 16, 89, 103, 175; political practice and, 52, 66, 157, 237; practices of, 7; regime of inscription and, 18; storage and, 23, 74–75
Primrose, Archibald, 173
print: "explosion" of, 6, 57; information warfare and, 178–81, 185–86; scholarly focus on, 57–59

Privileges of the Baronage (Selden), 129–30
Privy Council, 94–96, 97, 228–29
property rights, 92–93
property rights and records, 60–63
Prynne, William: *Brevia Parliamentaria Rediviva*, 183, 284n125; *Breviate of the Life of William Laud*, 159–60, 161, *162*; campaign against Laud, 157–62; debate with Coke, 228; on disorder of Tower records, 184–85; *Exact Abridgement*, 184; *Exact Abridgement of Parliamentary Records in the Tower of London*, 182; *An Exact Chronological Vindication*, 150, 184; *First Part of a Brief Register*, 182–83; *First Part of an Historicall Collection of Parliaments*, 181; *Fourth Part of a Brief Register*, 184; *Histriomastix*, 179; information warfare and, 154, 160–61; *Irenarches Redivivus*, 181; as Keeper of the Tower Records, 158, 284n127; on printing Tower records, 179–83, 185; *Soveraigne Powers of Parliament and Kingdomes*, 179; use of print, 179–86; weaponizing archives and, 157–59; works of (see *individual works*)
public sphere, 58–59, 66, 152, 219, 224
Pulton, Ferdinando, 55–56

Ralegh, Walter, 58, 105–6
Ramism, 43
Ramus, Petrus, 43
Randolph, Ambrose, 158, 193–94, 286n18, 286n20
Randolph, Edward, 232–33
Raymond, Thomas, 193–94, 286nn19–20, 287n25
records: appropriation of, 172–78; authority of, 5, 62–63, 67–68, 73, 130–33, 228; bundles of, 82; circulation of, 4; coordination and

records (*continued*)
  proliferation of, 6–10; destruction/survival of, 156–57; diversity of, 8–10; as forms of exclusion, 3–4; as instruments of profitability, 63, 131–33; interpretation of, 124–29, 133–34, 137–39; knowledge formation and, 4–5; as legal instruments, 32, 180–81; maintenance of, 2–3; political use of, 128–29, 138–39; powers of church and, 147–49; visibility of, 186; as weapons of division, 152; Williamson's Restoration recovery of, 194–97. *See also* archivization; preservation

regime of inscription: access to texts and, 22–23; adoption in England, 18; Agarde's catalog and, 79; archivization, knowledge production, and, 39; authority of records in, 53, 62–63; "Books of Offices" and, 10–16; Bowyer and Thynne's manuscripts and, 37–39; bureaucracy and, 120–21; as causal force, 17; circulation and, 57–59; competition in, 124–27; consequences of, 16, 50, 61; correspondence and, 203; creation of new offices through, 100, 102; definition of, 4–5; development of personal archives and, 21; empire and, 229–30; entrenchment and limitations of, 237–39; in Europe, 18; "explosion of print" and, 6; fleeting moments and, 10; as foundation of political practice, 21; impacts on contemporary Britain of, 227–28; imperial administration and, 232–34, 295n25; information overload in, 80–81; information state and, 17; information warfare and, 154–55, 185–86; inhibiting consensus in, 134, 150–51; innovation proposed by Wilson and, 108, 109, 113, 119; institutional innovation and, 94–95, 98, 102; internalization of, 228–29; interpretation conflicts and, 128, 138–39; knowledge formation and, 16, 18, 50, 187, 234–35; methodological restructuring and, 16; methods of legitimization and, 122; overview of development of, 17–18; personal advancement and, 120, 124–25; personal collections and, 23; powers of church and, 147–50; preservation of materials and, 7; records as weapons of division in, 152–53; reflection versus reconstitution in, 19; reinterpretation of political offices in, 98, 102; replication and, 57; revenue extraction and, 115, 119; scale of Elizabethan materials and, 42; state as project in, 41–42, 91; technology of paper and, 5; travel reports and, 42–46, 49; uses or records in, 89; Williamson and, 194–99, 209–10, 226; Wilson's miniature archives and, 117–18; Wilson's political use of records in, 116

registers, 35–37, 101–2
relazioni, 43–45, 47, 82
Repertorie of Records (Powell), 79
"Repertorium" (Bowyer), 27, *28*
"Repertory Rolls," 40
replication. *See* copying/replication
Richard II, King of England, 131
Richier, Isaac, 232
Rodwey, Stephen, 47
Rogers, John, 36
rolls, 24, 26–29, 40
"Rough Coat Books," 33
Royal Society, 188
rubrication, 70, *72*, 76, 80
Ryley, William: accusations of espionage against, 163–68; appropriation and, 172–78; information warfare and, 154; as Deputy Keeper of the Tower Records, 139, 142–51, 184,

281–82n78, 285n133; "Laws and Privileges Granted to English Clerics," 147–49, *148*; *Placita Parliamentaria*, 147, 178–79; "Soveraigntie of the English Seas," 144; spycraft and, 162–68; "Vetus Codex," 147; Joseph Williamson commissioning of, 195; work during reign of Charles II, 176

Ryley, William, Jr.: appropriation and, 172–78; information warfare and, 154; as Deputy Keeper of the Tower Records, 1–2; management of Tower records, 184, 285n133; petitions of, 163–68; *Placita Parliamentaria*, 147, 178–79; work for Charles II, 176

Rymer, Thomas, 237

Scottish state papers, 173–75
"secret histories," 158
Secret Treaty of Dover (1670), 217
Selden, John, 65, 129–30, 134–35, 145, 146, 276n103
Sexby, Edward, 170
Shelton, Richard, 134–35
Ship Money, 145–46
Shute, William, 48
Siddique, Asheesh, 233
Sidney, Robert, 46
Sindercombe, Miles, 170–71
Snelling, Thomas, 87
Society of Antiquaries, 37, 67, 92
Solemn League and Covenant, 174
Soveraigne Powers of Parliament and Kingdomes (Prynne), 179
"Soveraigntie of the English Seas" (Ryley), 144
"Soveraignty of the British Seas" (Borough), 142–43, 275n94
Spain: "Book of Offices" for, 103; Wilson's use of archives concerning match with, 116–17
"Speculum Chartophylacii Regii" (Brydall), 208

spycraft: as information warfare, 162, 165, 167, 170; reports and, 47; Wilson and, 103, 105

Squyer, Scipio Le, 123
Stafford, Edward, 46
Starkey, Ralph, 58, 79, 261n77
"State of England. c. 1600" (Wilson), 103
"State of Germany" (Beale), 44–45
State Paper Office: decline of, 235–37; focus on, 16–17; organization of, 110–14, 208–10, *210*, *211*; prioritization of, 250n47; Prynne and, 158; Robert Yard at, 200; transfer of papers to, 40; as treaty depository, 196, 216–17; weaponization of, 158; Williamson and, 193–94, 197, 199–200, 222; Wilson and, 104, 110–14, *113*, 119
storage procedures for records, 74–75. *See also* preservation
Stouppe, Jean-Baptiste, 171
Strafford, 1st Earl of (Thomas Wentworth), 25–26, 61, 63
surveillance: generation of paperwork and, 228; as information warfare, 168–72; Williamson's correspondents and, 198
Swaddell, John, 199

"Table Book" of Walsingham's books, 41
Tessier, Alexandre, 199
Test Act, 190, 225
textual instruments, 23–24, 30, 80, 100, 187, 229
Theatrum Orbis Terrarum (Ortelius), 20
Thompson, William, 1–2
Thurloe, John: information work of, 169–72, 178; State Paper Office requests of, 194; threat management of, 156–57, 168–70
Thynne, Francis, 37–39, 51, 254n58

Tower of London Record Office: in 1670s, 1; accounting at, 3; Borough and Ryley keepership of, 139–43, 146; Bowyer's organization method for, 27, *28*, 29; Bowyer's political use of, 32; calls to systematize, 23, 26, 33; changes in access and use of, 2, 24–25; continued relevance of, 227–28; cost of visit to, 35, 253n47, 282–283n94; disorganization of rolls in, 24; focus on, 16–17; identity and motivations of users of, 35–39; image of, *236*; information warfare and, 154; keepership of, 26–32, 35, 63; Knyveton's use of, 124; as model of organization, 235, 237; as neutral territory, 163, 280n37; Personal Rule and use of, 139, 146; prioritization of, 250n47; property rights and, 60–63; Prynne's keepership of, 158; Prynne's use, 179–83, 185; register in, 35–39, 59–61; replication and changing reliance on, 64; role of clerks in, 2; Ryley's defense of, 177–78; searchability of, 29; as storage facility, 23; Thynne's use of, 37–39; toxicity of records in, 51; transfer of Chancery records to, 26–27; use in Parliament of 1628, 137; visits by term at, 35; wages for employees of, 2–3; Williamson and, 197; women and, 2–4, 238, 248n10

travel reports: in 1580s, 44–45; archivization and, 42–49; newsletters versus overviews as, 47; of Stephen Powle, 46–49

treaties, use of, 36–37, 75–76, *77*, *78*, 114–17, 196, 216–18

Treaty of Breda (1667), 174–75, 218

Tucker, John, 204–6, *206*, 210, 229, 293–94n11

"Vetus Codex" (Ryley), 147

Villiers, George (1st Duke of Buckingham), 114, 118

Vincent, Augustine, 125–27, 272n17

Wallis, Abraham, 10

Walsh, Goody, 3–4

Walsingham, Francis, 8, 21, 41, 43

Watts, Richard, 201, 203

Weber, Max, 120–21

Wentworth, Thomas (1st Earl of Strafford), 25–26, 61, 63

Westminster archives, 75, 123, 177

Williams, John, 115

Williamson, Joseph: archive of, 204–5, 210–19, 285n4; assessment of records by, 155–56; attention to entry books, 196; background of, 188–90; to Cologne, 217–18; control of diplomatic materials, 216–17, 291n104; correspondence of, 197–203, 221–23, 230–31, 233, 289n68; epistemic infrastructure of, 188, 190, 210–11, 224, 227, 285n1; epistolary corpus of, 199; fall of, 225, 227; "Generall Calendar of Treatyes," 217–18, 291n115; as information hub, 224; instructions to Robert Yard, 199–200; as Keeper of State Papers, 193–94, 196, 200, 208–9; knowledge formation and, 190; *London Gazette* and, 221–23; manuscript newsletters of, 221–26; method as empirical epistemology, 225; notebooks of, 191–93, 205–7, 212–16, *213*, 226, 290n100; "Order of the Paper Office," 209; organization methods of, 204–16, *207*, 224–26, 287n25, 289n80; Popish Plot and, 190; record recovery and preservation by, 194–99, 204; records as instruments of diplomacy and, 196, 216–19, 223–24; regime of inscription and, 187–88; role of news and, 220–21; scribbling and note-taking of, 190–91, 291n113; on space of archive as ideal, 226; text collecting of, 193–99, 213–16

Wilson, Thomas: attempts to create offices, 107–9, 119; Caesar's consultation of, 96–97; career of, 103–9, 119, 266–67n77; cataloging innovations of, 111–14, *113*, 119, 269n111; catalog of Thomas Lake's papers, 81–82, 261n84; communication with King Charles, 118; compact archives of, 117–18; engagement with King James, 106, 110, 114, 116; information management of, 103–7, 119, 266n66; innovation in government, 102, 121; interrogation of Walter Ralegh, 105–6; proposed newsletter of, 108–9, 268n97; "Register of Knighthood" by, 108, 267n94, 268n95; relationship with Robert Cotton, 268–69n103, 270n130; reshaping of State Paper Office by, 110–14, 119, 268nn101–2, 269n104, 269n106; services for Carr, 106–7; "State of England. c. 1600," 103; texts of, 116–18; Williamson's adoption of methods of, 208–9; work for Robert Cecil, 103, 266n63–64

Winchester, 1st Marquis of (William Paulet), 29–30

Wiseman, Samuel, 1

women at Tower of London Record Office, 2–4, 238, 248n10

Yard, Robert, 199–200